Understanding Biblical Israel

A Reexamination
of the Origins of Monotheism

Understanding Biblical Israel

A Reexamination
of the Origins of Monotheism

by Stanley Ned Rosenbaum

Mercer University Press 2002

ISBN 0-86554-702-5 MUP/H519

Understanding Biblical Israel:
A Reexamination of the Origins of Monotheism.

Library of Congress Cataloging-in-Publication Data

Rosenbaum, Stanley Ned, 1939–
    Understanding Israelite history : a reexamination of the origins of
monotheism / by Stanley Ned Rosenbaum.— 1st Edition.
    p. cm.
Includes bibliographical references and index.
    ISBN 0-86554-702-5
    1. Bible. O.T.—History of Biblical events. 2. Jews—History—To 70
A.D. 3. Judaism—History—To 70 A.D. 4. Monotheism. I. Title.
    BS1197 .R585 2000
    296'.09'01—dc21
                                                        2001006493

Contents

Maps, Charts, Figures, and Diagrams

[†]The black-and-white Teleilāt-Ghassūl "rosette" follows the full-color frontispiece reproduction in *Teleilat Ghassul, I: compte rendu des fouilles de l'Institut biblique pontifical, 1929–1932*, ed. Alexis Mallon, Robert Köppel, and René Neuville (Rome, 1934) and appears here by permission of Editrice Pontificio Istituto Biblico, Piazza della Pilotta 35, 00187 Roma, Italia.

Acknowledgments

I wanted this book to have the unity of vision that an individual can impart, as opposed to the multiplex perspective of history-by-committee, so I chose to write it alone. Of course, no one writes alone. I am indebted to teachers and colleagues, students, and the scholars whose works I have used. I hope I have represented them adequately.

Teachers I wish particularly to acknowledge are Raymond Bowman, Gösta Ahlström, and Coert Rylaarsdam of the University of Chicago; Michael Astour, Nahum Glatzer, Cyrus Gordon, and Nahum Sarna of Brandeis; and Chaim Rabin and Haim Tadmor of Hebrew University. Prof. Thomas L. Thompson of Copenhagen was a prompt and helpful e-mail correspondent. Prof. Thomas Drucker, now of the University of Wisconsin–Whitewater, provided the Arthur Conan Doyle quote; his friendship over the past fifteen years, even more than his enormous erudition, has contributed much to my intellectual growth.

Dr. Silvine Farnell, formerly of Dickinson College, offered important stylistic criticisms in the book's early stages, while Assistant Director Marc Jolley and former Marketing Director Maggy Shannon of Mercer University Press were more than helpful in the latter stages. Two of my Dickinson students, David Chauvin and Daniel Green, read and commented on some of the material. Bro. Paul Quenon secured my admission into the library at Gethsemani Monastery.

I should have had a lot more people to thank, but at some point you have to decide it is time to stop consulting and begin writing, knowing as you do so that your work will be partly obsolete even before it sees the light of day. I apologize to those scholars whose ideas I have either overlooked or inadvertantly seem to have credited as my own when it was not so.

Mercer's senior editor, Edmon L. Rowell, Jr., shepherded the manuscript in all its aspects and phases as one would guide a wayward child, saving me from many errors and offering many constructive suggestions; the result rather reminds me of seeing a poem by T. S. Eliot after Ezra Pound had been at it, but that hardly does Edd justice—none of Eliot's poems were 300 pages long.

The choice of Bible translations is somewhat eclectic; in some places I have felt compelled to offer my own. In any case, the book's shortcomings are uniquely, gloriously, and embarrassingly my own.

Dedication

There is one person for whom no amount of recognition is adequate. During all of my forty years of wandering in the wilderness we call Biblical Studies, my wife Mary Heléne has been behind me, beside me, or ahead of me as the situation warranted. Her love and trust, to say nothing of her talents and patience as in-house editor, critic, and writer of her own biblical novels, cannot be captured in words, mine or anyone else's.

To Mary, then, this book is affectionately dedicated.

Chapter 1

Introduction

§1. "What Is Truth?" —Pilate (John 18:38 NRSV)

Every historian will have his or her own answer to Pontius Pilate's question, because as someone once said, "History [hence, historical truth] is what historians tells us it is." And not only historians. Fourteen hundred years ago, Muslims accepted Jews and Christians because Islam acknowledged the truth of these older "people of the book."

Until the late nineteenth century, the people whose book it was thought their Bible was not merely the oldest book in the world, but the Word of God himself. Having this "Word of God" in written form has had a significance through most of history that we, battling a Noah's flood of computer-generated babble, can scarcely imagine. The Bible is considered Sacred History, so many people consider it immune from the questions and revisions that, like fleas, dog secular history.

The written text itself has been invested with an almost magical property, a fact which, as we shall see (chap. 5), tells against modern theories that the text is both late and fabricated. What exactly "the text" is, however, has been legitimately subject to different opinions. Hebrew Scripture is not and never was uniform. Writing and spelling were not standardized[1] and generations of copyists, despite painstaking attention to detail, still introduced "scribal errors," only some of which later generations corrected. And some of the corrections are themselves suspect for various reasons.

The case with Greek manuscripts is more difficult. For example, the Jewish community of Alexandria, which authorized the first Greek translation in the third pre-Christian century, wanted to present something that would not unduly shock or offend Gentile neighbors. They therefore introduced textual changes to make it both more accessible and acceptable.

In Christian circles, discussion of Greek and Hebrew text variants long remained academic. Before the invention of moveable type around 1450 CE, the Roman Catholic Church authorized only Latin bibles. They needn't have bothered to be so exclusionary. Most Europeans could not read any language, and early bibles were rare and expensive, costing as

---

[1]See, e.g., James Barr, *The Variable Spellings of the Hebrew Bible* (London: Oxford University Press, 1989).

much as a family farm. Nonetheless, Christians who did read Scripture in any of its Greek versions—which often differ significantly from the Hebrew and from each other—were anathematized by the Church.

Until the seventeenth century, few questioned the Bible's divine provenance, its divine authorship, or—in the case of the Authorized (King James) Version of 1611—the divine inspiration of its translators. The few people such as Galileo who questioned official church teaching were refuted, censored, or, in extreme cases, imprisoned and killed. Most early commentators were not historians, in any case, but rather theologians bent upon interpreting the Bible for their own denominational purposes.

Giovanni Garbini points out that some Christians still persist in reading the "Old Testament" in the light of the "New" and can point to at least fifty places in which, they say, Jesus' life is foreshadowed.[2] Nietzsche observed, "To have glued this New Testament, a kind of rococo of taste in every respect, to the Old Testament, to make one book . . . that is, perhaps, the greatest audacity and 'sin against the spirit' that literary Europe has on its conscience."[3] What, I wonder, would Nietzsche have thought of Friedrich Delitzsch's (1922) claim that Jesus was an Aryan and not at all Jewish?[4]

Tendentious theologizing, however, is the monopoly of no one religion. Haim J. Yerushalmi notes that early Jewish scholars wrote "lachrymose [crybaby] histories of Judaism."[5] These were mainly apologies for what struck them—or, they thought, might strike the Gentile neighbors— as questionable, even abominable, behavior on the part of the patriarchs and some kings of Israel itself, or complaints about unjustified treatment of Jews by surrounding peoples and attacks on Jewish sectarians such as the Karaites.[6]

---

[2]Giovanni Garbini, *History and Ideology in Ancient Israel* (London: SCM, 1988) 1-20.

[3]Friedrich Nietzsche, *Beyond Good and Evil* (New York: Vintage, 1966) 52.

[4]Quoted by Mogens T. Larsen, "The 'Babel/Bible' Controversy and Its Aftermath," in *Civilizations of the Ancient Near East*, 4 vols., ed. Jack S. Sasson et al. (New York: Scribner, 1995) 1:95-106.

[5]Haim J. Yerushalmi, *Zakhor* (New York: Schocken, 1989). We must bear in mind that Jewish history is pockmarked with "diasporas," periods when Jews fled or were involuntarily exiled from their land.

[6]Karaites (Heb. *karaim*) or "Scripturalists"—the name comes from the Hebrew verb *qr'*, "to read"—accepted only what was read, namely, Scripture, not the "oral Torah" of the rabbis. The sect began in Baghdad in the mid-eighth century CE and has attracted adherents into modern times. One might say that modern Reform Judaism began as a

Since Muslims consider Ishmael, Isaac's older brother, to be their progenitor, Islamic histories are not immune from bias, either. Jews, then, have to defend their history and themselves against supererogation by Muslims claiming to be their older brothers as well as against supersession by Christian "heirs after the spirit." So Christians, Muslims, and Jews, having all claimed Israel's history as their own, have vested, if conflicting, interests in how they have interpreted it.[7] It is no wonder histories of Israel written by adherents of any of the three great monotheisms are far from evenhanded.

Modern scholars entered this triangular battlefield only about 170 years ago, after centuries of traditional tramplings of it. But the problems they began to discover were not only the denominational partisanships of previous generations. As we shall see, the major repository of Israelite history, the Hebrew Bible, is itself a patchwork of partisanships.

§2. Choosing What to Pack

"Wouldn't this be a good time for the Messiah to come?" (*Fiddler on the Roof*)

In the 1996 film *Independence Day*, the United States (along with the rest of the world) is attacked by implacable aliens bent upon its destruction. Let us imagine for a moment that the attack succeeds, but that some of us manage to escape and establish settlements in out-of-the-way places in Canada or Mexico. When we have children or grandchildren, what will we tell them? How will we explain why God let America be destroyed?

Americans have a wealth of information upon which to draw; any one-volume history of the United States would be enough to keep memories of the past alive, and most of us can read. Even so, we would still not have a single, satisfactory answer for "Why?" Judeans in a similar situation faced a cognitive overload with fewer resources. There were no books, only scrolls that not everyone could read, and conflicting stories of the past. For Judeans, *their* Temple was *the* place where God had caused His name to dwell; it had stood for nearly 400 years, almost twice the length of time the U.S. has been a nation. They, too, would have to ask "Why?"

---

spiritual descendant of this school.

[7]Some Muslim histories refer to the land west of the Jordan River as Cisjordan or just Cis ("on this side," as opposed to Transjordan) because they do not recognize the modern State of Israel.

Judeans would have had little difficulty in explaining the destruction of their sister kingdom, Israel, in 722 BCE. The North, which rejected Davidic dynastic kingship and retained bull-bovine religious objects, had clearly been punished for its apostasy. This conclusion was buttressed by Jerusalem's own miraculous escape from an Assyrian siege some twenty years later. Now, the unthinkable had happened: their own kingdom was destroyed and its temple demolished. How might this catastrophe be explained?

§3. Constructing a History

History is not as important as it used to be. —Hans Barstad[8]

Writing any history is a difficult enterprise. As Arnaldo Momigliano laments:

> [The historian] must know about statistics, technical developments, the subconscious and unconscious, savages and apes, mystical experiences and middle town facts of life; besides that he must make up his mind about progress, liberty, moral conscience, . . . [and earlier]. It makes the life of a historian a hard one.[9]

He might have added that any one "thing" we study invariably leads to many others, much like James Burke's delightful excursions through history in *The Knowledge Web*.[10] Choosing which connections to make is harder than following Ariadne's thread. She, after all, was trying to find her way out of the Labyrinth. We are trying to find our way in.

Momigliano is referring to armchair historians with great libraries at their disposal. The collectors/writers of what we call Hebrew Scripture hadn't the leisure to amass the background information he speaks of. Moreover, biblical historians would not be greatly interested in persons, processes, or events except as these directly affected their small world.

---

[8]Hans Barstad, "History and the Hebrew Bible," in *Can a "History of Israel" be Written?*, European Seminar in Historical Methodology 1, ed. Lester L. Grabbe (Sheffield UK: Sheffield Academic Press, 1997) 44 = JSOTSup 245, 1:997.

[9]Arnaldo Momigliano, "A Hundred Years after Ranke," in *Studies in Historiography* (New York: Harper, 1966) 109. Robert K. Merton, *On the Shoulders of Giants* (New York: Harcourt, Brace, Jovanovich, 1985) 164, quotes Lawrence Sterne's Tristram Shandy to much the same effect.

[10]James Burke, *The Knowledge Web* (New York: Simon and Schuster, 1999).

Biblical history was collected, edited, and reedited, and some of it was composed in the wake of catastrophe.

What was ultimately produced—Hebrew Scripture—is akin to what a family might retrieve after a tornado ripped through its trailer park—only some of their own possessions, broken and mixed with those of others, overlapping, contradictory, and not necessarily in order. For example, the books of the "minor prophets" are not in their proper chronological order, and some are quite fragmentary: Obadiah has only twenty-one verses; Ezra and Nehemiah should properly follow Chronicles, not precede it; and so forth. Moreover, the Bible itself mentions nineteen or twenty other books, about half the number it contains, that are no longer in existence but, presumably, would be included if they were, or that have been drawn on to produce the present text.

One mystery surrounding the Bible's compilation is why, after the dust of destruction had safely settled, did those in charge of passing on the story not update and homogenize their traditions, eliminate contradictions and duplications, and suppress those aspects that put Israel's founders and monarchs in a bad light? That they did not do so is an indication of some truth in their accounts, though far from proving its total accuracy.

Contemplating this situation now, almost two millennia after the text achieved its present form, modern biblical historians have even more complex problems than the original text collectors had. For one thing, we now know that Israel was not "one man's family," however dysfunctional. It emerged from a welter of civilizations and was composed of many peoples, all of which exerted continuing influence.

This requires us to know all we can of the languages and cultures of the ancient Near East—more of which are continually being discovered—from their barest beginnings to the start of what was once presumed to be a Patriarchal Age.[11] And that would merely get us to the beginning of Israelite history. No wonder that a recent seminar was convened under the

---

[11] Only the most committed conservatives continue to uphold the idea of a "Patriarchal Period." A lively discussion is ongoing in the pages of *Biblical Archaeology Review*, e.g., William Dever's "Save Us from Post-Modern Malarkey," *Biblical Archaeology Review* 26/2 (March/April 2000): 28-35 and 68-69.

title "Can a 'History of Israel' Be Written?"[12] Though the answer was affirmative, it was hedged about with many qualifications.

Since there is an ever-increasing amount of data available, it is next to impossible to keep up with the literature in all the other relevant fields such as anthropology, sociology, history and archaeology, and linguistics. Most of us become specialists in one of the many subdisciplines that make up the field and, like Fenimore Cooper's Indians jumping out of trees at a flatboat that has already slipped downstream, fall farther and farther behind the many streams of scholarship that pass by our perch. Of necessity, then, we read selectively, taking each other's word for things we haven't the time or expertise to verify, stringing these words like the glass beads in Herman Hesse's *Magister Ludi* (*The Glass Bead Game*) to form our own narratives.

Traditionalist or modern, each of us necessarily employs only a selection of facts, many of which are disputed, supplemented by hypotheses and guesses to support our often partisan positions. This is because Scripture can be approached on at least four levels: (1) as a record of what actually happened—what we call "history"; (2) as an account of what the collectors of Scripture honestly thought had happened, a thing scholars call "holy history" or the "history of salvation" (*Heilsgeschichte*); (3) as a story that the collectors wished to perpetrate on their readers, in other words, a pious fraud; or (4) as a "duffle bag" of undifferentiated accounts, fables, legends, and myths containing among them a number of events that *may* have happened.

Traditionalists of all denominations are naturally most at home in the first level; they are what Garbini airily dismisses as *Alttestamentler*, which I would loosely translate as "Sunday school teachers." These are people usually trained by members of their own faith, even their own denomination, and they aim to produce works by which faithful may profit. This may have a useful social value, but it often does not serve the ends of scholarship.[13]

---

[12]Grabbe, ed., *Can a 'History of Israel' Be Written?* (n. 8, above).

[13]Thomas Thompson, in *The Historicity of the Patriarchal Narratives: The Quest for the Historical Abraham*, BZAW 133 (Berlin: Walter de Gruyter, 1974), offers telling criticisms of G. Ernest Wright and Roland de Vaux by quoting them to the effect that their faith as Christians requires them to accept the essential historicity of the Bible. Some Christian Bible translations, such as the 1952 Revised Standard Version's Gen. 49:10, read with the Syriac, making of the place name "Shiloh" a messianic allusion (see RSV

Conversely, Garbini himself and some of the most recent commentators—sometimes referred to as "minimalists"—are especially fond of the third level for reasons that may include the desire to startle readers, or may even reflect post-1948 anti-Jewish feeling. Their claim that the entirety of Hebrew Scripture is a late product, even a forgery, surely throws out the baby with the bathwater.

In the recent film The Patriot, *British soldiers are shown committing Nazi-style atrocities, no doubt to make the story of the American Revolution more emotionally gripping for modern audiences. Yet the film makers' introduction of these anachronisms does not mean that the Revolution itself never took place.*

The task is grown so great that multivolume histories written by single scholars such as Heinrich Graetz in the nineteenth century are superseded by single volume works written by many scholars, such as editor Haim Hillel Ben-Sasson's *A History of the Jewish People*.[14] It is a daunting task for any one person to attempt to paint Israel's history in words, whether many or few. One can appreciate Walter Prescott Webb's response to a questioner who asked him how he wrote such and so many good books. "Just get a theory," the American Historical Association president said, "and find the facts to fit it."[15] As we will see, this advice seems to have been heeded willy-nilly by many scholars.

Starting "before the beginning," I hope to work my way through to the fourth level and produce, not the "right story" of Israel's emergence,

---

note and contrast KJV and NRSV). Psalm 2:7's *bar*, read as Aramaic "son" (KJV, RSV, NRSV, NJPS); or Isaiah 7:14's *ha'almah* as "virgin" (*b'tulah*)—where the actual word means "young woman"—are, similarly, tendentiously translated.

Even such an impeccably mainstream scholar such as Harold H. Rowley, *Worship in Ancient Israel* (Philadelphia: Fortress, 1967) 2n.3, suggests that early Protestant interpreters saw the prophets as "antiritual" because they themselves were.

[14]Essays by Abraham Malamat et al. (Cambridge MA: Harvard, 1976). Similarly, Michael D. Coogan, ed., *The Oxford History of the Biblical World* (New York: Oxford University Press, 1998). Some more recent works are less constrained by denominational theologies than others, but few histories written by Roman Catholic scholars before, say, 1964 when the Vatican began to allow Catholic scholars freer rein, have much merit.

[15]Walter P. Webb, "History as High Adventure," *American Historical Review* 64/2 (January 1959): 265-81.The converse is also true, as some scholars find ways of denying facts that upset their theories. Some scholars have been compelled to argue against such things as the age of the Siloam Tunnel Inscription or the historicity of King David by suggesting that supporting materials are faked or forged, e.g., Garbini, *History and Ideology in Ancient Israel*, 38-47. Their cries of "foul" sound increasingly forced.

but what Hans Barstad terms *"the most likely story"*[16]—not what necessarily was, but what might have been. It requires imaginative forays cantilevered like Frank Lloyd Wright roofs beyond the standing walls of evidence but, I hope, sufficiently supported by them to sustain my structuring of things past.

§4. It Gains a Lot in Translation[17]

The process of textual transmission itself produces a kind of historical compression; it distorts what it preserves. If the Bible were our only resource, we would not know that Omri and his son Ahab, kings of the North (885–853 BCE), were more important to their contemporaries than David and his son Solomon.

Scholars have determined that much North Kingdom (Israelite) material is included in our Bible. It was probably brought south by refugees from the Assyrian destruction of Israel in 722 BCE[18] and later adapted to serve Southern concerns and prejudices. In addition to putting their own "spin" on it, the Judeans were responsible for the collection, selection, and transmission of the documents.

The Bible's treatment of the Judean monarchy becomes less impartial through time. To realize this, one need only compare the rather evenhanded treatment of Solomon in Kings with the virtual whitewash given him by the later Chronicles. The end result of this process is an *ex parte* (partisan) statement which centuries of tradition have caused many modern Jews, Christians, and Muslims to accept uncritically.

> *O.J. Simpson's denial of guilt in the murder of his wife and Ron Goldman is an* ex parte *statement; even if true it is no proof of what is claimed.*

Crediting the Bible with the best of intentions, still, Scripture was not cast in its present shape until hundreds of years after some of the events

---

[16]Barstad, "History and the Hebrew Bible," 61; emphasis his. I thought of this as "metahistory" before learning of Hayden White's *Metahistory* (1973), cited in Momigliano, *Essays*, 5-6.

[17]See Stanley N. Rosenbaum, "It Gains a Lot in Translation," in *Approaches to Teaching the Hebrew Bible as Literature in Translation*, ed. Barry N. Olshen and Yael S. Feldman (New York: Modern Language Association, 1989) 40-44.

[18]Just as Samarian refugees fled Alexander's invasion in the fourth century, so we may assume that some Northerners fled south to escape the advancing Assyrians. See n. 26, below.

it purports to describe. Descriptions of some events are all too often breathtakingly brief, indicating that much has been forgotten, was not deemed worthy of remembering, or was recorded in documents no longer extant. Moreover, things that happened centuries apart might be conflated and then remembered as though they were contemporaneous.

That this kind of conflation did indeed happen may be inferred from the more modern tale of the Pied Piper of Hamlin that we learned as children. Very briefly, a pipe player hired by city elders around 1550 to rid the city of rats was not paid as he had been promised, so he lured their children away. This story is not mere fable, nor is it just a moral tale, but one must go to Hamlin to find the historical kernel hidden within it.

It seems there are two stories here. The first concerns someone who indeed attempted to rid the city of rats. How well he succeeded is no longer remembered, but he was apparently dissatisfied with the city's remuneration for his efforts. Shortly after that, a representative from a nobleman in Bohemia appeared with promises of cheap farmland. Since Hamlin had the same land-tenancy problems that much of Europe still has, namely, the impossibility of infinite subdivision of family property, children, especially younger sons, were attracted by the offer and left. (There may also be an element of memory of the Black Plague and its connection both to rats and to child mortality.)

What we know as "The Pied Piper," then, is a conflation of at least two roughly contemporary stories. If this can happen so quickly and so close to modern times, how much more are we entitled to believe that it has also happened in the case of the Bible? Furthermore, the Bible's oral origins probably predate our written text by 200 to 800 years, a period during which no one would have objected to some changes in the telling.[19]

Written biblical texts themselves cover a period of more than a thousand years. Texts including the Song of Moses (Exod. 11:1-15); the Song of Deborah (Jdgs. 5); Balaam (Num. 22–24); and Moses' farewell (Deut. 33) are generally thought to come from the twelfth century BCE. Scholars place the composition of the Book of Daniel in the second pre-Christian century. Over such a long period as this, purposive changes or

---

[19]Raymond F. Person, "The Ancient Israelite Scribe as Performer," *Journal of Biblical Literature* 117/4 (1998): 601-609, esp. 609. And see below, chap. 11, §3 for an example of compression.

simply differing understandings of various words would be likely. Of course, conservatives of all faiths argue that the Bible's writers and collectors, sometimes even its translators, were inspired by God and so none of the usual story-drift-and-compression would have taken place. But this is a partisan position. It rests on the prior assumption that what the Bible (via our religious traditions) tells us is infallible, inerrant, true. That is not the position taken here.

§5. "Convergence of the Twain"   —Thomas Hardy

Whether one identifies the beginnings of modern scholarship with Renaissance Humanists or with Baruch Spinoza[20] in the late seventeenth century, if we take the scholarly path we quickly find that it divides like that in Robert Frost's woods. The traditional and more travelled path maintains that the biblical record is substantially correct, that persons mentioned in it were real, historical figures, and that events concerning them happened more or less the way the text reports despite apparent exaggerations and contradictions.

A less-travelled, because more recent, path holds that the entire record is a pious fiction made up during the Judean monarchy, or possibly not until the Persian occupation of Judea. One proponent of the latter, Thomas Thompson, says that we cannot use the biblical record even to reconstruct its history, because the verb "reconstruct" implies that there are enough pieces lying around to make a coherent picture if only we could arrange them properly.[21] In Thompson's view, there are not enough such pieces.

The present "reexamination" steers a middle course. It assumes our text has endured considerable drift over the course of centuries, like a ship slipping its anchor over time and tide. But, like that ship, I propose it began its journey at or near a recognizable coastline. Thus, even seemingly fabulous biblical accounts such as the Flood may be the confused echo of events that happened thousands of years before—for example, the Mediterranean incursion into the Black Sea (see below, chap. 2). This is not to say that all of the Bible's accounts have factual

---

[20]Richard E. Friedman, *The Disappearance of God* (Boston: Little, Brown) 1995; or Baruch Halpren, *The First Historians: The Hebrew Bible and History"* (University Park PA: Pennsylvania State University Press, 1988).

[21]Thompson, *The Historicity of the Patriarchal Narratives*, 13-16.

bases. In picking my course through much biblical flotsam, I hope I can steer into the open sea of "inspired conjecture" and avoid the shoals of "scholarly wishful thinking."[22]

One aid in plotting my course is to throw classical Greek navigational tools overboard. In thinking about the Bible, we moderns unconsciously use a framework provided by Greek thought, such as Aristotle's axiom, "A is *not* not-A." If we force the Hebrew stories onto a bed of Aristotelian logic, we are making a king-sized mistake. Assuming that what calls itself history must either *be* history or be false is like trying to measure temperature with a yardstick. Furthermore, it is a mistake the biblical storytellers themselves would not have comprehended. "History" was not their only—nor, I think, their most important—purpose, so we need to be aware of the purposes that do underlie their stories.

Many biblical stories have ends in mind that are clearly etiological, that is, explaining why a present situation has come to be: Why is there death? How did we discover clothing, metal, music? Other stories, such as that of Esther and Daniel, are hortatory fictions, telling us to "keep the faith" in the face of adversity and hold community interests above personal desires or fears.

Jonah, who supposedly made a remarkable sea voyage, is a fiction—and not merely because the tale smells fishy. The original author, I think, had a different and far higher purpose in mind than simply recording events, a purpose we can discern from the use made of the story by later Jewish tradition.

Jonah's story is presently read in synagogues on Yom Kippur, the last of the ten days of repentance. It makes a *misgeret* (framework) with the story of the binding of Isaac, which is read on the first day. How are these two texts connected? Abraham agrees unquestioningly to do an almost inhuman and certainly unreasonable thing, while Jonah refuses to perform a task that was hardly more than an inconvenience. Taken together, as they should be, they compel the conclusion that though God prefers pure trust unalloyed with reason, he will, in the end, cause us to do what is right and thus save ourselves. A comforting scenario!

Clearly, the Jewish tradition has recognized that the two stories represent extreme ends of human response to the divine call. I would maintain that this high moral purpose is not vitiated if either or even both

---

[22]The first phrase is Henri Frankfort's, the second Donald Redford's.

of the main characters are fictional. Stories, especially those from Israel's premonarchic past, thus had somewhat the same function as Teutonic myths in Germany: they enabled originally diverse groups of people to identify a common past, to cooperate in their mutual present, and to anticipate a common future. Creating such a "national history" is by no means unique to Israel.

The Bible's storytellers, however, often wrote better than they knew. Centuries of repetition obscured much of the deeper meaning in their stories, so that the average believer, whether Jew, Christian, or Muslim, came to accept the Word—all the printed words, which, as we have already indicated, many could not read—at face value. For example, Thorlief Boman correctly identifies Isaiah 14:12-13 as a "satire upon the king of Babel [Nineveh],"[23] but some Christians use it as a "proof" of the existence of Satan (Lucifer).[24] In our day, when most people approach the text only through translations, the problem of determining what the Bible actually says has increased enormously.

§6. Awakening Sleeping Beauty

Our long, enchanted sleep began to end when scientific, archaeological, and linguistic discoveries systematically eroded some major presuppositions of traditional biblicists. The Kepler/Galileo rediscovery that the sun did not revolve around the earth, but rather the other way round, was suppressed by the Roman Catholic Church. Galileo was made to recant upon pain of death, but the tide of change was flowing. Later, through William Smith's early nineteenth century fossil studies,[25] we discovered that the world was far older than the Bible knew, that there had been no universal flood, and that many civilizations had flourished and disappeared before biblical times. Still later in the nineteenth century, the decipherment of Akkadian, the grandfather of Semitic languages, showed us that Hebrew was not the language God spoke to Adam.

Similarly, since the early nineteenth century our knowledge has been augmented, or supplemented by archaeological finds—especially texts from places such as Amarna, Mari, Nuzi, Ugarit, Ebla—leading to the

---

[23]Thorlief Boman, *Hebrew Thought Compared with Greek*, trans. Jules L. Moreau (New York: W. W. Norton; Philadelphia: Westminister, 1960) 178.

[24]Contrast KJV ("O Lucifer") with NJPS, NRSV, and even NIV.

[25]William Smith, *The World according to Organized Fossils* (1815).

(premature) conclusion that Israel was anything but unique. In the late nineteenth century, theories of extensive borrowing in and multiple authorship of the Pentateuch gained a wide following. Scholars found, or thought they found, at least four "documents" or sources that were combined to make up the Bible.

Julius Wellhausen's version of this Documentary Hypothesis[26] divided the Pentateuch into four "documents" stemming, he said, from four different sources: J (Yahwist [with a J in Wellhausen's German], Judean); E (Elohist, Israelite); P (Priestly—but which priests?); and D (Deuteronomist, "historical"). I'll return to this subject in chapter 3, but for now note that the J source presents most things Judean in a favorable light, most things Samarian[27] negatively. E, a Northern source, sees things the other way round. And, if Richard Friedman's engaging hypothesis is correct, the P source says "A pox on both your kingdoms!" because P comes from a circle of doubly disenfranchised Northern priests.[28]

(All this polemicizing reflects the bad blood that followed the North's "secession" from the united monarchy, a subject I will examine in chapter 9. For now, let me say that the term "united monarchy" is something of a misnomer. The kingdom of Israel was united briefly under Saul in response to outside pressures and held together largely by David's charisma and Solomon's efficient but repressive bureaucracy.)

This documentary division was called by its proponents the "Higher Criticism" as opposed to earlier expositions, the "lower criticism" that began with textual unity as a given. Here, however, we have to note a disturbing political-religious subtext. Solomon Schecter, speaking at the turn

---

[26]The Documentary Hypothesis grew from the work of Georg H. A. von Ewald, Abraham Kuenen, and Wilhelm M. L. de Wette, earlier in the nineteenth century. Julius Wellhausen's *Prolegomena to the History of [Ancient] Israel* (New York: Meridian, 1957; orig. 1878, ET 1883) was the first exposition to capture a wide audience.

[27]I use Samarian, not Samaritan, to identify the old Northern Kingdom because of the modern connotations of Samaritan. Harold L. Ginsberg, similarly uncomfortable, coined his own term. See H. L. Ginsberg, *The Israelian Heritage of Judaism* (New York: Jewish Theological Seminary, 1982).

[28]In his *Theological-Political Treatise* (New York: Dover, 1951) 1:120-31, Baruch de Spinoza had the temerity to suggest that the first five books of the Bible could not have been written by Moses and were probably written by Ezra. For this he was "excommunicated" by the Jewish community, in part because they feared collective punishment from their Gentile neighbors, for whom this view was also heresy. Halpren, *The First Historians*, chap. 2, has a good account of the handful of men who preceded Spinoza.

of the century for many in the Jewish community,[29] termed Wellhausen's hypothesis "the Higher Anti-Semitism." Jews saw this hypothesis of inauthenticity and partisanship in Hebrew Scripture as a "continuation of policy by other means," as the German chancellor, Prince Bismarck, had recently said of war. The attack was disturbing because it was done by scholars, not uneducated bigots and demagogues.

Conversely, modern Jewish scholars such as Ada Feyerick,[30] sensitive to Arnold Toynbee's Hitler-era characterization of Judaism as a "fossil-ized relic of Syriac civilization,"[31] emphasize Israel's originality. Others are at pains to explain or justify actions of the patriarchs that seem dis-tasteful or incomprehensible to the modern mind.

That there are different sources for the Bible is, however, well-nigh indisputable, but if that were the worst of it, serious religious people could make the necessary adjustments, as they indeed have. Now, scarce-ly a hundred years later, other scholars, among them Garbini, Thompson, Niels Peter Lemche, Philip Davies, Keith Whitelam, and John van Seters, are proposing that the Bible is an entirely late development, removed from the history it purports to describe by as much as a thousand years, and consequently that nothing in it may be taken at face value. The newest (Copenhagen) school of scholars, mainly Gentiles whom Baruch

---

[29]See Jon D. Levenson, *The Hebrew Bible, the Old Testament, and Historical Criticism* (Louisville: Westminster/John Knox Press, 1993) 43. Similarly, Eugene Merrill in *A Historical Survey of the Old Testament*, 2nd ed. (Grand Rapids MI: Baker Book House, 1991) 28-30, writes that if the Documentary Hypothesis (DH) were true, Jesus would certainly have known about it and consequently would have had something to say about it. His silence, therefore, means that the hypothesis is false!

Two major Israeli scholars, Umberto Moshe David Cassuto, *The Documentary Hypothesis* (Jerusalem: Magnes, 1953) and Moses Hirsch Segal, *The Pentateuch, Its composition and Authorship and Other Biblical Studies* (Jerusalem: Magnes, 1967), mounted what they hoped were serious refutations of the DH. Another major scholar of that era, Yehezkel Kaufmann, in *The Religion of Israel: From Its Beginnings to the Babylonian Exile* (Chicago: University of Chicago Press, 1960), an abridged translation of his *Toledot haEmunah HaYisraelit: Mimei Qedem ad Sof Bayit Sheni*, which began appearing in 1937, took a more tolerant view. Levenson's work ranges him alongside the stronger opponents.

[30]Ada Feyerick, with Cyrus H. Gordon and Nahum M. Sarna, *Genesis: World of Myths and Patriarchs* (New York and London: New York University Press, 1996). The book is a series of alternating essays by Cyrus Gordon and Nahum Sarna, both of whom were my teachers at Brandeis.

[31]A. J. Toynbee, *A Study of History* (New York and London: Oxford University Press, 1957) 2:8. See the reply by Maurice Samuel, *The Professor and the Fossil* (New York: Knopf, 1965).

Halpren calls "negative fundamentalists," holds that there is not any significant evidence for the existence of David, Solomon, or a kingdom of Judah before the mid-eighth century BCE, let alone that the patriarchs existed.[32]

Whatever one's view, there is in all this a disturbing tendency to divide along religious lines, with Gentiles (Davies, Whitelam, Lemche, Thompson, R. P. Carroll; Israel Finkelstein is a notable exception) deconstructing, and Jews (Halpren, William Dever, Nahum Sarna, Cyrus Gordon, Benjamin Mazar, and especially Martin Buber) defending the tradition. Despite all the scholarly reverence for "objectivity," there seems to be considerable bias operating in all quarters.[33]

Some progress has been made toward bridging this considerable "appreciation gap" as even conservative religious scholars back away from literalism. John H. Hayes and J. Maxwell Miller's *A History of Ancient Israel and Judah* (1986)[34] struggled to find an effective compromise position. The authors admitted that much of what they proposed was "intuitive speculation," but even this honest approach did not protect them from ridicule.

How do we balance such and so many opposing views? First, if we are to attempt to do a biblical history at all, perhaps it is well to remember Franz Rosenzweig's words:

> Our eyes, it is true, are only our own eyes, but it would be folly to imagine that we have to pluck them out in order to see straight.[35]

---

[32]See "Face to Face: Biblical Minimalists Meet Their Challengers," *Biblical Archaeology Review* 23/4 (July/August 1997): 26-42. Halpren, *The First Historians*, 16, quotes J. Huizinga's opinion: "It is precisely the hypercritical historian, the skeptic extraordinaire, who is most often compelled for his own dissenting presentation of the facts, to adopt such fantastic constructions that he himself is propelled from critical doubt to bottomless credulity."

[33]C. H. J. de Geus, *The Tribes of Israel: An Investigation into Some of the Presuppositions of Martin Noth's Amphictyony Hypothesis* (Assen: Van Gorcum, 1976) 81, notes that all Israeli scholars except Yohanan Aharoni hotly contest attempts to read Dan (and Judah) out of tribal lists, e.g., in Ps. 108. John Emerton, in a review of Niels P. Lemche's *Ancient Israel in Vetus Testamentum* (1990), criticizes E. R. Leach for imputing motive to scholars in general, but partiality is an all-too-common feature of biblical histories.

[34](London: SCM Press) 1986.

[35]Nahum Glatzer, *Franz Rosenzweig: His Life and Thought* (New York: Shocken, 1953) 179.

That is to say, not only is beauty in the eye of the beholder, but also his or her historical judgments. And when he or she has a personal stake in it, such judgments are bound to be subjective.

Second, archaeological discoveries increasingly seem to confirm, if not the general outline of history as the Bible tells it (especially in the early period), a kernel of particular truths. We have only recently discovered an ever-increasing number of details about Bronze Age people, places, and customs that biblical-era Jews could not have remembered and would be ideologically predisposed not to invent.

By the same token, we should not repeat the error of trying to understand Israelite history as a completely novel intrusion into the history of the ancient world. However differently the history of Israel has tracked from that of surrounding peoples, it grew organically from its ancient Near Eastern context. Israel was a hybrid of various peoples who carried with them a small galaxy of beliefs and practices derived from various places of origin.

§7. A Unified Field Theory of Religion?

In the nineteenth century, the infant science of anthropology sought a linear progression for religious development. The search for a "unified field theory" of religion, or at least some central concept that serves as an organizing principle, has been as attractive as it is elusive. Attempts by Edward B. Tylor, James G. Frazer, Karl Marx, Sigmund Freud, Emil Durckheim, and others were first embraced and then superseded.[36]

Influenced by Hegelian[37] and Darwinian notions of "progress," authors who did most of their research in libraries proposed that Christianity was the acme of religious development. Toynbee recognized twenty-one societies—of which Israel was emphatically not one—that had paved the way to this crowning achievement. While Toynbee's particular piece of fatuousness is now thoroughly discredited, no combination of previous theories or insights allows us to propose a new attempt at a "unified field" based upon the ancient Israelites. They coalesced only relatively late in the history of their area of settlement, so they do not

---

[36]Ably discussed in Daniel Pals, *Seven Theories of Religion* (New York: Oxford University Press, 1996).

[37]Georg W. F. Hegel was no Christian, but many think his "trinitarian" dialectic of Thesis, Antithesis, Synthesis is influenced by Christianity.

give us the more or less uncontaminated "laboratory" conditions for study that, for example, the Azande, Dinka, Nuer, or Australian aborigines do. Recent scholars such as Fernand Braudel have concluded that the early goal of a "Right School" was a chimera, a false goal, perhaps because they recognize how complex even supposedly "homogeneous" societies are. Instead their efforts are concentrated on "thick descriptions"[38] of individual societies or even subsets of the same. Students or adherents of all these schools will recognize the use I have made of their insights. Based upon them, let me hazard the following propositions for understanding biblical Israelite religion.

(1) Like all religion, Israelite religion is largely the outgrowth of natural human anthropomorphism (as recently argued by Stewart Guthrie[39]). That is to say, we invest religious phenomena with the characteristics of human beings: our gods not only look like us, they can even assume human shapes and characteristics.

(2) It is anthropocentric and ethnocentric. Israel, like any group of humans, tended to see itself as the center of the universe.

(3) It explains natural events in religious terms using a flawed, cause-and-effect linear logic: What comes after is necessarily caused by what comes before.

(4) Israelite religiosity was unconsciously framed by the very language in which it was thought and, consequently, written.[40]

As Philo of Alexandria observed, "the Bible speaks the language of man" and must therefore use simile, metaphor, and, above all, allegory in trying to fathom the unfathomable. But Philo lived in Jesus' time; his sophistication—the use of this Greek word indicates what influenced him most—is a development that comes after long millennia of religious evolution. Biblical Israel is the product of a period that, I will argue, stretches back 40,000 years. The cumulative effect of all this is to produce ideas such as that God is Israel's "king" and "father" who punishes his "children" for their sins and rewards them for proper behavior—but we are getting ahead of ourselves (more below).

---

[38]Clifford Geertz in Pals, *Seven Theories of Religion*, 233-67.

[39]Stewart Guthrie, *Faces in the Clouds* (New York: Oxford, 1995).

[40]I am indebted to the theories of Benjamin Lee Whorf, *Language, Thought, and Reality* (Cambridge MA: MIT Press, 1956) and Edward Sapir, *Culture, Language, and Personality* (Berkeley: University of California Press, 1964).

In saying this I acknowledge a debt to Braudel and the French *Annales* school of historians who see human development as taking place in long "cycles." But while their *longue duree* is counted in centuries, mine must be measured in millennia. I suggest that traces of ancient beliefs decisively influenced by natural events and technological discoveries may still be discerned as substructure for Israelite religion (see chart, chap. 2, p. 33). Some of these features may be found by a judicious sifting of the biblical record itself, some by appeal to archaeological discoveries and the insights of sociology and anthropology. In trying to encompass all of the above, and with profound apologies to Momigliano, I attempt here to retrace the path by which Israel emerged from the mists of history. Following are some of my suppositions.

1. *What moves, lives.* Monotheism is even today professed by less than half the world's population because it is not a self-evident proposition. Israel's own monotheism emerged like a lazy butterfly, taking 800 years or more to leave its cocoon behind. This is understandable because in prescientific times—a period that embraces most of human history—we would explain the movement not only of humans, animals, and plants but also of such things as the sun, moon, stars, and sea as due to some animating force within or controlling the things themselves.

Even if this "animistic < animatistic" view of the universe did not evolve in the linear fashion suggested by Tylor, when we come to study the period with which this book begins, the Near East would have been fully polytheistic for a very long time.

2. *Humans see the universe anthropomorphically and anthropocentrically.* We see "faces in the clouds," as Stewart Guthrie's title aptly puts it, because we use ourselves and our experiences as a kind of matrix within which to place what comes through our senses. We see events in nature, especially the momentous ones, as happening *to* us or *because of* our actions. The Bible claims that God made humans in his image; it is equally just to suggest that some of us have been returning the favor ever since.

Understandably, the picture of God that we arrive at is far from static. Thorkild Jacobsen[41] traces a millennial evolution of gods from providers to rulers to parents as the human societies that worship them evolved.

---

[41]Thorkild Jacobsen, *The Treasures of Darkness* (New Haven: Yale University Press, 1976).

That Jews refer to God as "father," and Christians uphold a doctrine of Incarnation, shows that the evolutionary process has not ceased.

3. *Semitic languages both reflect and reinforce the idea that the universe is essentially dualistic.* Max Müller[42] said that religion was a "disease of language," an unfortunate phrase that deflects people from seeing the truth that it stumbles toward. He probably was unaware of the Jewish philosopher Saadia Gaon (eighth to ninth century CE), who had already pointed to deficiencies in language's ability to express certain thoughts such as describing God. What Müller meant, I'm sure, was that language in fact shapes thought, sometimes in ways of which even its speakers are unaware. As Julian Jaynes observes, "Language is an organ of perception, not merely a means of communication."[43]

Hebrew provides a number of examples of perceptual conditioning, the most obvious being its lack of a neuter gender. Along with all animal species, we observe that humans are divided into males and females. This perception may also be reflected in the biblical roster of gods and goddesses (see below, chap. 4).

That animals also physically "mirror" humans so closely is, already, a great reinforcement for seeing a duality in the universe. (Herbert Spencer,[44] who first saw this universal duality, was right—if not for the right reasons.) Further, looking at ourselves in a mirror, we see that humans, like other animals, are bilaterally symmetric: that is, all our parts are duplicated, right and left. This conduces to seeing the universe in sets of polar opposites, a dualistic perception that should not surprise us.

Hebrew has a well-developed dual number for indicating things that come in pairs. Curiously, in Hebrew all paired body parts—with the notable exception of testicles—are feminine. Why? It could be an extrapolation from the observation of female secondary sexual characteristics,[45] that is, female breasts as both a vital and a noticeable pair;

---

[42]Friedrich Max Müller, "Semitic Monotheism," in *Chips from a German Workshop* (Chico CA: Scholars Press, 1985) 337-74.

[43]Julian Jaynes, *The Origin of Consciousness in the Breakdown of the Bicameral Mind* (Boston: Houghton Mifflin, 1976) 50.

[44]Herbert Spencer, *Descriptive Sociology* (New York: D. Appleton, 1873–1881).

[45]The Hebrew word for "breasts" is *shaddaim*, a dual. This has led some scholars to posit that the enigmatic appellation for God, *El Shaddai*, masks a deity with a pronounced fertility function, presumably a female deity.

therefore, all pairs are feminine unless exclusively masculine (more below, in the excursus to chap. 4, "Numbers and Numerology").

4. *The "Farming Revolution," that phase of human development that began about 10,000 years ago, remains critical to our view of ourselves.* Just past the last Ice Age, farming became possible in the ancient Near East, but deliberate agriculture requires accuracy in predicting seasons. (The frivolous American observance of Groundhog Day rests upon this serious idea, as do many other religious and secular holidays that we will discuss.) Farming also entails a need for some sort of record keeping, and that leads to writing. Note that the earliest extant Israelite/Canaanite writing is the "Gezer Calendar," dating perhaps to the tenth pre-Christian century. It seems to be a schoolboy exercise tablet that records the eight crop seasons of the area.

Once human beings adopt anything like a sedentary or even dimorphic[46] mode of life, we develop a lively interest in the stability of our settlements and the fertility of animals and humans. Deities that ensure fertility and protect the newborn become prominent, then dominant. For the most part, these are female.

5. *Technological developments influence societies, either directly or indirectly at all levels.* Elisha G. Otis (1811–1861) did not intend to invent modern cities, but it was his elevator that made skyscrapers possible. The discovery of metal smelting techniques about 6,500 years ago was another revolution with far-reaching consequences. Metal tools allow us to clear forests, build ships, dig wells, canals, and cisterns, and even shape stones for building cities (but not for Solomon's altar—Exod. 20–22). Also, metal weapons help us kill, conquer, and enslave each other. This leads to a replacement of what Robert Redfield[47] calls the pre-civilized "moral order" by a "technical order" in which high status shifts from elders to specialists.

Also, it may be argued that because mining, forging, and using such early weapons as the spear and sword required upper body strength, men and the male gods whom they supposedly reflect came to overshadow,

---

[46]"Dimorphic" is a term borrowed from crystallography. Applied to human societies, it denotes a society in which the inhabitants regularly transit between two more or less fixed points, say, summer pastures at higher altitudes and winter quarters at lower ones.

[47]Robert Redfield, *The Primitive World and Its Transformations* (Ithaca NY: Cornell University Press, 1953) 32-37.

though they did not displace, the earlier female fertility goddesses. (Assyrians and Cretans deified their weapons,[48] making Isaiah's famous plea to "beat . . . swords into plowshares" [Isa. 2:4] particularly poignant.)

Writing itself represents a revolution, too. Growing from simple accounting, writing was originally pictographic, and this source was not completely lost even when it became alphabetic. Hebrew's first letter, א *'aleph*, is named for the word *'aleph*, both the domestic ox and Taurus, the Bull of Heaven that once marked the Shavuot harvest season.

6. *Cities + weapons = social stratification. Weaker, lower, or dissident elements, if not killed or enslaved, were cast out.* Examples of tribes or nations forming from collections of outcasts can be found, from America's Apaches to Australia and Georgia (both used by Britain as places of exile for convicts). I contend that the Hebrews who became Israel began their history as, preponderantly, just such a status group (including but not limited to the *habiru* of the Amarna Letters),[49] and that their dislike and distrust of "civilization" and its trappings reflect this origin. It is no accident that the first murderer, Cain, was also said to be the first city builder.[50]

Certainly it is no coincidence that the first ancient Near Eastern countries with recognizable dynastic rulers arose around 3000 BCE, shortly after the start of what we call the Bronze Age. It's not that human society wasn't hierarchical before that time, but that cities, weapons, and writing accelerated the process.

---

[48]A similar situation occurred when Great Britain transported convicted criminals to the colonies of Georgia and Australia, but the same thing can be seen even in nonindustrialized societies. The Apaches of North America were, in origin, not a tribe but a collection of outcasts from other tribes. Richard Wyatt Hutchinson, *Prehistoric Crete* (Harmondsworth: Penguin, 1962) 224-25; Morton [Mordecai] Cogan, *Imperialism and Religion: Assyria, Israel, and Judah in the 8th and 7th Centuries BCE*, SBLMS 19 (Missoula MT: Scholars Press, 1974) 53, 63.

[49]The "Amarna Letters" were correspondence to Egypt from Egyptian vassals in 14th century BCE (pre-Christian) Palestine. Many were requests for military assistance against a group called *habiru*. For an identification of this group, see James B. Pritchard, *Ancient Near Eastern Texts Relating to the Old Testament*, 2nd ed. (Princeton: Princeton University Press, 1955) 483-90; hereafter cited as ANET².

[50]Isaac Kikawada, *Before Abraham Was: The Unity of Genesis 1–11* (Nashville: Abingdon, 1985). Retribalization theories are not new.

7. *The original impetus for the collection and editing of Hebrew lore and its canonization was the national trauma of conquest and exile in 586 and the consequent need for a paradigm capable of explaining it.* Though it had been predicted, for example by Jeremiah, the fall of Jerusalem and its temple was a near-fatal shock to the people whom we may now call "Jews" (Judeans). They responded by canonizing the Torah, what Heinrich Heine later called a "portable Fatherland." Why the Jews didn't simply give up and disappear out of history is a mystery that this study does not attempt to answer.

8. *Though collected, edited, and partly written only after 586, the remainder of Hebrew Scripture may be used, must be used, along with the Pentateuch, if any history of the period is to be written at all.* Hebrew Scriptures are an amalgam, at once artful and clumsy, of constituent tribal stories and lore which may be mined for actual historical events. I hold with Braudel (more in chap. 2) that the text contains echoes or survivals from events or from civilizations that went into decline before biblical Israel was born, including some things that could not have been known and others that would surely not have been invented by people who lived a thousand years later.[51]

Why would Scripture credit patriarchs with actions that contravened later Israelite law, or remember the foul deeds of so many legendary heroes such as Judah or of such national leaders as David and Solomon? Though collected much later than some of the events described, the biblical text, supported by evidence from outside sources, allows us to attempt an imagining of Israel's history.

§8. Returning to Eden: A Provisional Road Map

The Bible reports (Gen. 2:10ff.) that a river issued from Eden and then divided into four branches. In the first part of this work I also trace four "paths": (1) the physical geography of the land; (2) the concomitant "mental landscape" of its inhabitants; (3) the effect of Semitic language (Hebrew) upon the thought of those inhabitants; and (4) the religious background of the second pre-Christian millennium in which the proto-Israelites shared.

---

[51]John Bright, *A History of Israel*, 4th ed. (Philadelphia: Westminster, 2000) 77-83.

These paths will not lead us back to Eden. Just as the Garden is guarded by cherubs with flaming swords, so the way back into Jewish history is guarded, littered, and twisted by the Judeans who first preserved and edited it for their own purposes, and by modern Jews, Christians, and Muslims, each with their own theological agendas. However, a careful scrutiny of what we have may get us close enough to peer through Eden's gate and to imagine what might have been.

Reading the first two sections of the Hebrew canon, Torah and Prophets, the Documentary Hypothesists had been struck by the many duplications, doublets, and outright contradictions they contained, for example, the account of the Israelite "conquest" under Joshua in Deuteronomy is gainsaid by the account in Judges. There are two versions of the Ten Commandments, one in Exodus 20 and the other in Deuteronomy 5, plus two other sections of similar legal statements (Exod. 21–23 and 33–34). Furthermore, while the Ten Commandments can be read to imply that great-grandchildren can be punished for the sins of their great-grandparents, Deuteronomy 24:14 (backed up by Ezekiel, the prophet some think authored the Deuteronomical passage) holds that people die (only) for their own sins.

The modern scholars concluded from this that the Torah was a late product cleverly engineered to give divine authority to the Establishment that promulgated it. In fact, the "engineering" had another purpose. If the collectors wished to command any loyalty from all the disparate groups of survivors, retention of double accounts (doublets), even if they contain contradictions, is explicable. Also, under the circumstances of destruction and diaspora, it would be best to preserve anything that spoke of God's will. Thus they retained Kings' accounts of David's adultery and Solomon's ruthlessness in dealing with potential political enemies.

Using a flawed, linear logic, they further reasoned that if God had punished them, then they must have done something to deserve it. The collectors of Scripture were not simply trying to rescue personal belongings, like people in the aftermath of a tornado or an earthquake. They also had to make sense of what had turned their world upside down.

Jews—for now we may so label the remnant of Israel—would not have arrived at a coherent theology all at once, especially since, like an earthquake, the shock of 586 would have produced numerous aftershocks. A major aftershock was the assassination of Gedaliah in 582 BCE, which ended Jewish autonomy—forever, for all they then knew. Subsequent collectors of biblical traditions had the job of trying to hold together the survivors of two (or more)[52] Israelite "kingdoms" now scattered from Elephantine in Egypt to which many had fled, to Babylon in the east to which even more had been exiled.

Job asks, "Shall we accept good of the LORD and not also accept evil?" (2:10, my translation). Jews concluded that the One God proclaimed by men like Amos and Hosea—who had prophesied the destruction of the North—and Jeremiah and Isaiah, who had said the same of the South, were *nebi'im,* "prophets," that is, they were now regarded as YHVH's spokesmen. For them YHVH was in fact the only extant God, hence both universal and responsible for the evil as well as the good. But even apparent evil might mask the good. Isaiah 45:1, written after the fact, names as Israel's savior that Cyrus of Persia who was born more than a century after (First) Isaiah died. Job take note. . . .

We do not know who all the transmitters of tradition were, especially because some later writers, such as Second Isaiah, wrote in the names of earlier figures. Ezra, a fourth-century scribe who claimed a descent of fourteen generations from Aaron—the first Levitical priest and Moses' older brother—may indeed have been a transmitter. If so, his job would have been more to propagate than to collect and edit Scripture: for most of this century scholars have thought that the first two sections of the Jewish Bible, "the Law and the Prophets" (to which Jesus refers in Matt. 5:17), were canonized even before Ezra returned from Babylon. But Ezra also had a political mission, namely, to wrest control of Jerusalem from those Samarians and Ammonites who controlled it.

If all the stories and lore could be sorted out, it would not happen all at once or in a vacuum. The "final edition" of the received text seems to date only from approximately 100 CE. Consequently, some scholars believe the Bible also reflects Israel's mixed reaction to exposure not only to the Persian but also to the following Hellenistic culture that increased dramatically in the wake of Alexander's conquest of the area (333 BCE). Greek art, architecture, drama, athletics, and philosophy became very attractive on the popular level, the more so since one did not necessarily have to change religions in order to enjoy them.[53]

---

[52]Undue attention to the secession of the North diverts us from understanding that there were, at times, more than two "kingdoms" within greater Israel.

[53]Isocrates (436–338 BCE) said that persons who shared Greek culture were entitled

The biblical organizers' task was not wholly inductive; they had already arrived at an ideological conclusion, an agenda. On the official level, nothing Greek, not even the language,[54] was worth a fig. In this light the Book of Proverbs, canonized in the third section of the Hebrew Bible or TaNaKh (TNK, acronym for *torah*, teaching; *nebi'im*, prophets; *k'tuvim*, writings), may be read as a thinly veiled attack upon Greek wisdom, "Sophia," personified as a harlot who leads young men astray.[55]

Trying to compensate for biblical bias is a bit like allowing for windage on an archery range: one needs to determine which way and how strongly the wind is blowing. Because Tanakh is the statement of a Judean faith community trying desperately to keep itself together, we cannot simply take as historical truth whatever the Bible says. For the biblical period, roughly 1250 BCE to 100 CE, Israelite history is the story of survivors who consciously imparted their own spin upon—some would say invented—the history they told.

My purpose in writing this book is nothing less than to discern how Israelite religion managed to disentangle itself from the welter of powers and principalities that populated the world of its birth. To understand "Jewish" history we have to read it diachronically,[56] as though we were contemporaries of all the generations of people who caused it to assume the shape in which we have it.

I have no intention of rehearsing at face value what is essentially the Bible's own record, which is both incomplete and partisan. Filling in the too-many gaps in the biblical record is something else again. It wants the skill of nineteenth-century historians who lived before history was declared a science and divorced from poetry, philosophy, and the art of the novel.

---

to call themselves "Hellenes."

[54]Saul Lieberman, *Greek in Jewish Palestine* (New York: Feldheim, 1965) 16, quotes R. Joshua (early 2nd century CE) as saying, "Greek education is forbidden inasmuch as it interferes with the study of the Law." However, it should be noted that R. Joshua himself spoke Greek. Of all aspects of Greek culture, philosophy (*philo-sophia*) was the most seductive and the most dangerous because it asks questions. For pious Jews, the study of Torah should preclude such questions.

[55]A star-studded collection of essays on Wisdom is found in Martin Noth and D. Winton Thomas, eds., *Wisdom in Israel and in the Ancient Near East*, Festschrift H. H. Rowley, VTSup 3 (Leiden: E. J. Brill, 1969).

[56]For more on diachronic reading of the text, see chap. 13.

Keeping Thompson's caution in mind, I will not try to reconstruct the history of premonarchic Israel, but rather to "reimagine" it. To borrow a title from Joseph Heller, I think "something happened" toward the end of the Bronze Age that precipitated the creation of the people/state of Israel.

I often write with more confidence than I feel, in contrast with more cautious tomes, for example that written by my own teacher, the late Gösta Ahlström.[57] Such books often pick their way slowly through minefields of scholarly conjecture; they are valuable to other scholars, but they make for slow reading. I hope my version of Israel's history makes for a better "read," and if my tale receives equal criticism from both historians and novelists, that will be some measure of its success.

---

[57]Gösta Ahlström, *The History of Ancient Palestine* (Minneapolis: Fortress, 1993).

Chapter 2

Physical Geography, Mental Landscape

§1. The Face of the Land

Tradition, as brought down to us by Jewish tradents and their Christian and Muslim followers, tells us that Abraham's planet was less than 2,000 years old. All of the world's "pre-Israelite history" is covered in Genesis's first eleven chapters. Little is said there about the land the Israelites were to inhabit, and the text reflects no reliable trace of previous people. We now know that the reality is much more complex; the land is far older and its peoples considerably more varied than Genesis represents. If we are to understand Israelite history at all, we should begin with a bird's-eye view at the land and its earliest inhabitants.

Israel is part of what we call the ancient Near East, an area running from modern Ethiopia to Turkey and the borders of India. The area is roughly bounded by four great bodies of water: the Black Sea (north), the Persian[1] Gulf (east), the Red Sea (south) and the Mediterranean (west). It comprises nearly 4,000,000 square miles. None of the early inhabitants could have had any notion of its extent.

In addition to its seas, the area's most outstanding features, those most likely to influence the thought and behavior of the inhabitants are the mountain ranges of Taurus, Amanus, Zagros, Caucasus, and Lebanon, and the individual peaks represented in Israel itself by Carmel, Ebal, Gerizim, Hermon, Tabor, and Gilboa—but not Mt. Zion until rather later.[2]

---

[1]Whether one calls this body of water the Arabian Gulf or Persian Gulf is a matter of no small moment in the area in question. "Persian" is preferred by Iraq, "Arabian" by Saudi Arabia and other Arab states. The Caspian Sea (NE) could be a fifth "boundary water," but it is farther from Israel than any of the others and considerably harder to get to. A Babylonian tablet from ca. 600 BCE that shows a "map" of the world surrounded by water may be found in Feyerick et al., *Genesis: World of Myths and Patriarchs*, 41.

[2]"Zion" is not one place but a theological concept. See Helmer Ringgren and Johannes Botterweck, eds., *Theological Dictionary of the Old Testament* 7:395. By way of contrast, Sinai/Horeb, lying somewhere outside Israel, was probably sacred to area residents long before Israel took shape, but we don't know which mountain or mountains the names represent. The present tourist spot in southern Sinai was established by Greek Christians only in the 5th century CE. Interestingly, neither Mt. Zion nor this Mt. Sinai is the highest peak in its own immediate vicinity.

Map 1. *Satellite View of Sinai Peninsula and Southern Levant*

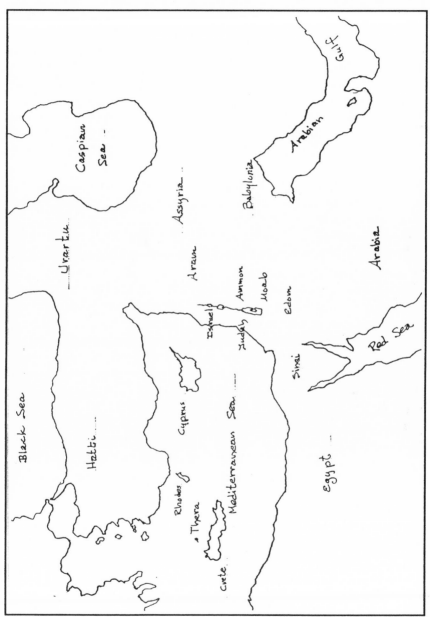

Map 2. *Ancient Near East*

That part of the ancient Near East we are most interested in is a New Jersey-sized piece of real estate at the eastern end of the Mediterranean. Less than 10,000 square miles in extent, it is but a minuscule percentage of the whole area. We can get a clear, contextual picture of the area from satellites (see map 1); our late-coming Israelite ancestors, however, usually saw it from no greater height than donkey- or, eventually, camel-back.

I say "late-coming" because the Eastern Mediterranean area that includes Israel was inhabited as early as the Lower Paleolithic era 700,000 years ago. For these anthropoids the "ends of the earth" were scarcely beyond their own boundaries; most of them probably lived and died within a short distance from where they were born. Their isolation was increased by the nature of the land, mostly hilly and arid, which discouraged travel.

Early settlements depended on water. Therefore, springs, rivers, intermittent wadis, and the seacoast provided the earliest hominid habitats, but in between their time and ours the very face of the land will have changed many times. To cite a comparatively recent example, after the last Ice Age, about 12,000 years ago, retreating glaciers poured so much melt water over the northern hemisphere that sea levels rose all over the world. The entire Jordan Valley filled with water, while elsewhere in the Near East large freshwater lakes appeared where none had been before. This process was temporarily reversed during the Younger Dryas period (10500 to 9400 BCE) and again from 6200 to 5800 during a prolonged "cold snap"[3] that does not have an official name.

This book will refer to the general area lying between the Jordan River and the Mediterranean north of the Wadi El-Arish and south of the Litani River as "Canaan" before 1250 BCE, as "Israel" in the period from circa 1250 to 922 BCE, and "Israel" and "Judah" for the succeeding period. By any name, the land is divided by a deep north-south-running valley that takes its biblical name, Jordan, from the Hebrew root *y-r-d*, "go down," because it in fact does so. Rising from several sources in the north, the river finds its way through the Huleh marsh and into Kinneret (the Sea of Galilee), where it is already 650 feet below sea level.

At various times in its history the area has been called *Retenu* by the Egyptians; *Amurru* by the Assyrians; *Lu Ki-nah-ah-hum meš* at Mari,

---

[3]See William Ryan and Walter Pitman, *Noah's Flood* (New York: Simon and Schuster, 1998) 184-85.

giving us "Cana'an" in the Bible that Jews and Christians use. The Roman Empire called it Palestine, a name derived from the Egyptian word *Pilishtim*. These were among the "Sea Peoples," seaborne enemies who settled there in the thirteenth pre-Christian century after Egypt forestalled their invasion.

Ancient Israel claimed or occupied lands east as well as west of the Jordan River. The Jordan valley is part of a 6,000-mile geologic fault that extends deep into Africa. In Israel the valley is flanked on both sides by mountain ranges rising almost to 3,500 feet above sea level, broken by occasional steep ravines that debouch into the Jordan.

East of the river, the mountains subside onto the high tableland of King Abdullah's Jordan. On the west they fall to foothills and thence to flat, marshy plains, wider in the south than in the north, which shelve the Mediterranean. The land's uneven texture lends itself to the creation of small, independent settlements, in other words, tribalism. As we shall see later, this resulted in Israel's being well "behind the curve" of political development elsewhere.

It is noteworthy that Elijah, Israel's first national prophet, is a ninth-century figure. Elijah was from Tishbe in Gilead, a fertile and therefore coveted area on the east bank of the Jordan. Gilead extended from somewhere south of the Sea of Galilee to somewhere north of the Dead Sea.

The Dead Sea is a mineral-rich saltwater sea at the southern end of the Jordan (see map 2, p. 29). Lying 1,300 feet below sea level, it has no outlet and is the most prominent feature in Israel proper. Other important features are such individual mountains as Carmel on the Mediterranean coast, Tabor in the Jezreel Valley, and Hermon in the north; springs such as En Gedi and Banyas; the great depression, the Makhtesh of the northern Negev; and the Huleh marsh north of the Sea of Galilee.

The Huleh marsh was drained by Israel after 1948 to make more farmland, but the Israelis now find they need to restore it because of its ecological importance.

§2. Before the Beginning: the Human Mental Landscape

There is no society, however primitive, that does not bear the "scars of events,"
nor any society in which history has sunk completely without a trace.

—Fernand Braudel[4]

It is appropriate that the Book of Genesis begins with the world in darkness. Our knowledge of what really happened "before the beginning" is
a bit dim, also. Hominid occupation of Canaan is at least 100,000 years
old, but we cannot connect even Neolithic with biblical peoples with any
certainty because the Bible is not much interested in pre-Israelite
inhabitants. Only in Genesis 6:4 is it noted that once there were *rephaim*,
"giants," in the land. These "giants" were said to be the offspring of
divine male beings cohabiting with human females (never the converse).
The story may be pure fable, or invented simply to supply credibility to
the later account of Joshua and the other spies whom Moses sent to
reconnoiter the land, or to hold up these earlier inhabitants as a kind of
bad example whose behavior justified their expulsion.[5]

One purpose of this chapter is to explore the human history of the
eastern Mediterranean with an eye toward shedding light on how much
early thought may still be reflected in Israelite tradition. I contend that
influences from remote times are visible in "Israelite" thought. What we
call the "dawn of civilization," especially in that part of the world that
includes Israel, comes relatively late; by any calculation it is at least
1,000 years before Abraham, that is, before Israel's traditional beginning.

Frank Frick gives three dates for Abraham, all of them too early. I
think he is deferring to biblical life-span numbers—or to readers who take
them seriously. Cyrus Gordon, for whom genealogy is more important
than putative life spans, puts Abraham around 1450 BCE.[6] I examine the

---

[4]Fernand Braudel, "Histoire et science sociales: la longue duree," *Annales. Economies,
Societe, Civilizations* 13 (1958).

[5]People familiar with African basketball players like Hakeem Olajawon and Dikembe
Mutombo might suggest that tribes of exceptionally tall people did live in Palestine at one
time. Another compelling speculation is that the notion derived from findings of fossilized
remains of large prehistoric animals.

[6]Frank Frick, *A Journey through the Hebrew Scriptures* (Fort Worth TX: Harcourt
Brace College Publishers, 1995) 156. Both Cyrus Gordon and Nahum Sarna in Feyerick
et al., *Genesis: World of Myths and Patriarchs*, put Abraham in the 15th century on the
basis of material found at Nuzi that seems to reflect customs and practices similar to

historicity of the patriarchs in chapter 6; meanwhile, my feeling is that Abraham's time is toward the end of the Bronze Ages, about 1500 BCE, or 1,500 years after the "dawn of civilization."

Dealing with such vast stretches of time requires a theoretical framework that is best provided by the French *Annales* school of history with its idea of short-, medium-, and long-term processes, especially the last named. However, I'm not sure even Braudel, its best-known exponent, would approve of my multiplying his long periods tenfold. But some such framework is necessary when we consider that the Lower Paleolithic period, a time during which little change in hominid culture in the eastern Mediterranean basin can be observed, alone covers about 100,000 years—from 200,000 to 100,000 years ago.

This is a time when the inhabitants of the area may not be human, but are already "racially mixed," something that will be important to us later on. Few points of "history" are discernible during this early time, but a dozen of more-or-less datable events of the past 50,000 years would include the following.

1. 40,000—recognizable speech, careful burial;
2. 30,000—mother goddess figurines; and, closer to our own time:
3. 12,000—end of last Ice Age, domestication of animals;
4. 10,500—fishing, salting and smoking for preservation;
5. 10,500–9,400—Younger Dryas "mini Ice Age";
6. 8,500—cemeteries;
7. 7,500—walled cities, earliest metal technology;
8. 6,500—agriculture < accounting < writing, and viticulture < deliberate fermentation as a preservation process; earliest pottery;
9. 6,200–5,800—"cold snap";
10. 5,500—Mediterranean incursion into Black Sea;
11. "Metal ages" (subdivided as follows)
    Chalcolithic—5600–3500
    Early Bronze—3500–2000
    Middle Bronze—2000–1500
    Late Bronze—1500–1200
    Early Iron—1200–900
12. 4,000?—wheel-made pottery, early urban complexes;
13. 3,500—first writing; and
14. 3,000—rise of cities < kingships in Egypt and Sumer.

---

those of the Patriarchal Period.

All of these events and later innovations such as movable sails, irrigation, terracing, plastered cisterns, deep-well technology, and camel domestication led to profound changes in social and economic organization. If we may extrapolate from later times, as well as from the practices of modern totemic tribes, these "technical developments" will have had profound effects on the religion of the inhabitants (more in chap. 4, below).

We should take special note here of two outstanding datable natural events. These will have produced long-lasting psychological as well as physical aftershocks, especially the ones that happened closer to biblical times. The most important such event, without doubt, was the sudden incursion of the Mediterranean Sea into the Black Sea, which happened about 5500 BCE.

William Ryan and Walter Pitman, whose twenty years of research have recovered evidence of this catastrophe, suggest that various peoples had sought refuge from the "cold snap" of 6200–5800, leaving higher altitude habitations and settling around what was then a freshwater lake, the Black Sea. At that time it was 400 feet lower than the Aegean branch of the Mediterranean and separated from it by a thin arm of earth. When this was breached, the new falls roared down at fifty miles an hour, causing the water level to rise as much as a foot a day, and forcing those inhabitants who survived to higher ground.[7] This meant they had to retreat at the astounding rate of a quarter to half a mile a day—for an entire year.

The volume of salt water that cascaded into the Black Sea was, the authors estimate, 1,000 times the volume of Niagara Falls, and produced a roar that could be heard in the Crimea—soon to become the Crimean Peninsula. By the time equilibrium with the Mediterranean was reached, the Black Sea was nearly 500 feet deeper. Sixty thousand square miles of surrounding land, an area greater than Iowa, had disappeared forever under the sea.

There have been and continue to be other catastrophic floods in the area; Henri Frankfort[8] points to one in 1831 that destroyed 7,000

---

[7]Tablet 11:108-112 of the Gilgamesh Epic seems to allude to this event. Recent discoveries beneath the Black Sea have brought to light structures that apparently stood on the ancient shoreline. (Robert Ballard writes about this in the May 2001 issue of *National Geographic*.)

[8]Henri Frankfort, *The Birth of Civilization in the Near East* (Garden City NY: Doubleday, 1956) 53.

houses in a single night, but the Black Sea disaster must certainly be at least part of the basis for the Bible's world flood story. It was remembered—How could it be forgotten?—for two millennia until finding written form in the epics of Ziusudra, Gilgamesh, and Atrahasis—and in the story of Noah.

It is directly after the flood story that the Bible informs us that humans began viticulture, the cultivation of wine grapes. Colin Renfrew[9] proposes that sedentary agriculture seems to have begun in eastern Anatolia about 8,000 years ago. If so, refugees from the Black Sea disaster could have carried it southward, into Israel—which might account for one of the sudden and dramatic increases in population found there.

If this flood was a unique event, there were others equally disastrous that were comparable. The whole area is an earthquake zone and dotted with volcanos. One of these, Thera (Santorini), exploded with cataclysmic force sometime in the late seventeenth or mid-sixteenth pre-Christian century. It is worth taking a moment to examine the incident.

Located eighty-seven miles north of Crete, Thera was a volcanic island of approximately thirty square miles that blew up in 1628 or 1550 BCE. The explosion threw molten rock and pumice for miles, making the seas impassable for an entire year. It sent tidal waves crashing all around the eastern Mediterranean, severely damaging the north coast of Crete and mangling the Minoan civilization's home base, a blow from which Minoan civilization never recovered.

We can estimate the force of Thera's blast because we have a modern example of it, Krakatau, a volcano between Java and Sumatra that blew up in 1883. Contemporary eyewitness accounts tell of utter darkness at 9:00 a.m., and colossal tidal waves. Its sonic boom reverberated around the world seven times; its column of smoke and aerosols reached fifty kilometers into the sky and turned sunsets red for years afterward. And yet this blast is estimated to have been only a third to a tenth as violent as Thera's.

Accepting the lower dating, there seems to be some contemporary notice of the event in the Egyptian records of Ahmose I:

---

[9]Colin Renfrew, *Archaeology and Language: The Puzzle of Indo-European Origins* (London: Penguin, 1987) 171.

The sky came on with a torrent of rain, and [dark]ness covered the western heavens while the storm raged without cessation . . . [the rain thundered(?)] on the mountains, (louder) than the noise at the 'Cavern' that is in Abydos. . . . and for a period of [x] days no light shone in the two Lands.[10]

It is too much to suggest that Thera produced the very wave that drowned the Egyptian army in Exodus, but there is no need to make such an extravagant claim. Given the number of times foreigners fled or were expelled from Egypt, it is perfectly possible that the explosion was roughly contemporary with one such flight. Memories of this volcanic event and its unprecedented consequences, such as the plague of darkness and the "pillar of cloud by night and fire by day," might very well have been incorporated by subsequent refugees/escapees as part of their stories, too. We will see more in chapter 7. For the present, remember that events that happen over a long period of time may be and are compressed, both accidentally and deliberately, by people looking back at them through a long haze of history.

Nonvolcanic mountains are important, too. The well-beloved Psalm 121 begins with an explicit denial of mountains' divinity. It reads, "I will raise my eyes to the hills; from whence will my help come?" (my translation). Unfortunately, the 1611 King James or Authorized Version, by omitting the question mark implied at the end of verse 1, manages to say just the opposite. Still, many peoples hold certain mountains to be the abode of gods. And for good reason.

Mountains may seem to keep the sky from falling upon us, and it is from mountains that rainstorms come. Storm rain or melting snows provide needed water, but anyone who has experienced a mountain storm, as I did on the traditional Mt. Sinai in April 1969, knows why fierce gods/goddesses were thought to dwell there. These gods need to be propitiated. Conversely, if the mountain doesn't "send" enough water, those depending upon it likewise will have to do something about that.

---

[10]Donald B. Redford, *Egypt, Canaan, and Israel in Ancient Times* (Princeton NJ: Princeton University Press, 1992) 420. In support of the higher dating see Hendrik J. Bruins and Johannes van der Plicht, "The Exodus Enigma," *Nature* 5/382 (18 July 1996): 213-14, but the evidence from Crete itself suggests otherwise. See J. D. S. Pendlebury, *The Archaeology of Crete* (New York: W. W. Norton, 1965) 224.

Unusual recent melting on Nevado de Ampato in Peru revealed that the local inhabitants sacrificed teenaged girls on it as late as the 15th century CE, apparently because of a water shortage. Remarkably, the bodies were found at the 19,000 foot level. The effort involved in getting to such an altitude indicates that considerable importance was attached to this act.[11]

§3. A Place Called Home

We don't know what the earliest Canaanites called their land. As noted above, *Cana'an* is derived from a later Akkadian name for the area. Early inhabitants lived in small groups; settlements capable of sustaining as many as a hundred people are not found until the Natufian period (see below). For another thing, groups were already racially mixed, not homogeneous. Each group probably thought of its immediate area—generally centered on some such salient feature as a mountain, river, or spring—as a "topocosm," a term coined by Theodor Gaster[12] but reflecting an internal reality of the inhabitants.

The world's topocosmic mountains would include Mt. Ida (Crete), Ararat, of course, Fuji (Japan), Kilimanjaro and Ol Doinyo Lengai (Tanzania), Olympus (Greece), Azurki (Morocco), Ampato and Llullaillaco (Peru), and Ayer's Rock (Alice Springs, Australia). In prebiblical Canaan the list would include Tabor and Gilboa, Hermon and Carmel.

The thirty-foot Neolithic tower at Jericho might also have served a topocosmic purpose.[13] Jericho, with its good spring, temperate climate,

---

[11]Johann Reinhard, "New Inca Mummies," *National Geographic* (May 1998). Since then, additional sacrifices have been found at even higher elevations on Cerro Lullaillaco.

[12]Theodor Gaster, *Thespis: Ritual, Myth, and Drama in the Ancient Near East* (Garden City NY: Doubleday, 1961) 24. The term indicates the immediate area in which one lives, an area that usually has a significant topographical feature. Note that European names are often toponymics, e.g., anything ending in *hurst = horst*, "meadow."

[13]There seem to be no Israelite parallels to Silbury Hill near Avebury in Wiltshire, England, but it is worth a brief discussion here. Silbury is a man-made hill of 130 feet, making it by far the tallest thing in the area. It contains 463,000 cubic yards of earth, meaning that a lot of human effort went into its construction. No one knows why it was built, but neither defense nor burial seem to be its chief function. It could be a lookout tower, but that seems unnecessary as nearby Kennet Long Barrow, a grave that once contained fifty-three skeletons, stands on a hill nearly as high.

Barrows are found on hills so that the dead might have easier access to their sky home and the people living in their environs would have a communal center of gravity.

and command of a major north-south trade route was a major center millennia before biblical history began. (Note that the circle of stones, a kind of cromlech, that Joshua is said to have engineered at Gilgal, is adjacent to Jericho.)

On the other hand, Mt. Zion, understood to denote Jerusalem by Judeans and their monotheistic descendants, may very well be a late appropriation of this concept rather than a particular mountain (more on this below).

Even in secular America there is a reflection of the "holy mountain" in the massive sculptures of four U.S. Presidents on Mt. Rushmore.

Anthropoid remains dating to 600,000 years ago have been found in Canaan. For Yabrudians,[14] our name for Canaan's earliest hominid inhabitants (ca. 100,000 BCE), the locus of their topocosm would have meant primarily caves by the then-seashore or the thousand-foot-deep lake that filled the Jordan Valley or one of the above-named mountains. One Natufian burial was placed in a half-sitting position facing Mt. Hermon, no doubt the center of that area's topocosm.[15] Other burials have been discovered in foothill caves such as Mughara or El-Wad, facing the Mediterranean and probably a lot closer to it than the present shoreline indicates, or near springs or water courses.

Water was essential for drinking, nonsystematic irrigation, and especially for fishing. Why "especially"? Already by Mesolithic times, around 14000, there is evidence that fishing was an important source of food. With the end of the Ice Age, increased moisture in the air would have contributed to greater, denser forest growth, making habitation in forested areas more difficult—remember, this is long before people had effective forest-clearing tools—so coastal areas would become the locus for much human habitation. The beginning of serious ocean or rivermouth fishing must have begun in cases where the fish came to the fisherfolk on a

---

Could Silbury have been a rallying point and a place for spiritual orientation, like the steeple of a church?

Gilgal, in the hills near Jericho, may have a parallel in the cromlechs of Europe, or in the Big Horn Medicine Wheel in Montana.

[14]Even these hominids are relative latecomers to the area. Remains of *homo erectus* dating to 700,000 BCE have been found near modern Pella. Emanuel Anati, *Palestine before the Hebrews* (New York: Alfred Knopf, 1962) 72-76.

[15]James Mellaart, *Earliest Civilizations of the Near East* (London: Thames and Hudson, 1965) 27 has pictures of the burial.

regular schedule. Chinook Indians of the American Northwest take their name from the Chinook salmon. Lox, the Yiddish name for salmon, is remarkably close to the fish's proto-European name, suggesting the length of time that this fish has been an important food source there.

Reaching further afield for a moment, we may posit that the stone rows at Carnac in France could represent votives erected by tribes who gathered yearly for the salmon run.[16]

We don't normally think of salmon, herring, or smelt as Near Eastern fish, but in the postpluvial period it's likely that their runs were driven farther south than is the case today.[17] Developments in fish-catching tools, such as barbed hooks and net sinkers, and advanced techniques "induced some groups to settle down in permanent hamlets,"[18] of which Einan, near the Sea of Galilee, is one and Kebara another.

These Natufian people, named for one of their settlements at Wadi en-Natuf, were a fully human group that practiced agriculture—whether deliberate or opportunistic we don't know, but wild cereals that grow near permanent water sources provided food beyond any immediate needs. Natufians had settlements all over the area and left artifacts including decorations of their dead. We cannot accurately place these folk on the hominid/human continuum, but one of their burials clutched the jawbone of a boar in his skeletal fingers.[19]

They had a 4,000–5,000 year "run," before disappearing around 10,000 years ago. The cause of this disappearance seems to have been the Younger Dryas "mini Ice Age," a sort of glacial burp emitted by the

---

[16]In "The Astronomical Significance of the Large Carnac Menhirs," *Journal for the History of Astronomy* 2/3/5 (October 1971): 147-60, Alexander and Archibald Stevenson Thom make a sound case for Carnac having the function of tracking and predicting eclipses. But this may not have been their only function. The Akkadians knew that "Nanna, the moon, causes carp floods." They weren't alone in making this sort of connection. Samoans can harvest a species of *Palaeacanthocephala*, a parasitic marine worm, only during the waxing of the moon in October. See chap. 4.

[17]Karl W. Butzer, "Environmental Change in the Near East and Human Impact on the Land," in Sasson et al., *Civilizations of the Ancient Near East* 1:123-51.

[18]Anati, *Palestine*, 142.

[19]Why a jawbone? Is it too much to suggest that this represents the Hyades—that astral jawbone with which Orion slew Taurus, according to Hertha von Deshend and Giorgio di Santillana, in *Hamlet's Mill* (Boston: David R. Godine, 1977) 165-78—transposed into the jawbone of an ass in the Samson story? The possibility of continuity even from so remote a time is appealing.

retreating ice. This period of well over a millennium of renewed glacier growth forced people to come down from high altitude settlements in search of warmer habitations such as are found around the shores of the Black Sea.

We may posit that after the advent of fishing and systematic agriculture some 12,000 years ago, most people died within sight of the place they had been born and, if you asked them, they would have said they much preferred it that way. Egyptian society and culture, for example, were based on the premise that everything should remain as it had always been.

Farming in the area may go back to 10,000 years ago, which is probably 6,500 years before Abraham (see chap. 6). At this time Natufians harvested grain with sickles outfitted with small stone teeth called "lunates" because they are shaped like crescent moons. When we consider that hunting-and-gathering cultures had successfully subsisted for 100,000 years, the introduction of deliberate farming around 8000 would have produced a revolution[20] comparable to the domestication of fire and the development of human speech. Subsequent improvements such as terracing led to more permanent settlements, especially in hilly areas where farming had previously been unknown.

§4. Tendrils of Trade

Under the spreading chestnut tree
the village smithy stands. —Henry Wadsworth Longfellow

Driven by the common human need for implements of war, agriculture, and building; food and clothing for the living and the dead; marriageable

---

[20]Not all revolutions are immediately successful. Some Far Asians resisted the introduction of cereals because cultivation would mean an end to their nomadic way of life. No one, I think, realized that eating cereal could end life itself. People who grind cereal in stone bowls introduce a lot of stone dust into their food and this dust grinds down their teeth, making them subject to abscesses. Pharaoh Raamses II apparently died of an infected abscess, albeit at the ripe old age of ninety.

Another consequence of the cereal revolution was the invention or discovery of beer—and its effects. Grain ferments naturally on its way to spoiling, but controlled fermentation is an effective way of "storing' it in a form that remains stable for long periods.

Not surprisingly, women were most often entrusted with brewing as well as with running the "ale houses" in which beer was sold, because they tended to stay closer to home.

partners; and even such luxury items as jewelry and cosmetics, the history of the ancient Near East has long been a history of trade.

Early human settlements were not self-sufficient[21] or at least engaged in trade for luxury items. Jarmo (5000 BCE) imported obsidian from Lake Van. Prepottery Neolithic B (6500 BCE; the term is Kathleen Kenyon's) Jericho's thirty-foot stone tower is often cited as evidence for trade at a very early period. (Renfrew disputes this.) In Prepottery Neolithic B levels elsewhere, marine shells, minerals for jewelry, and obsidian from Anatolia were found in interior settlements.[22] Equally old faience from Egypt has been found as far away as Denmark, leading my teacher Cyrus Gordon to say that since the Neolithic period no civilizations have grown up independently. He also pointed out that one can sail from Israel to Denmark without losing sight of land; shipwrecks such as the famous one off Uluburun in southern Turkey indicate that "coasting" routes were preferred down to the Late Bronze Age.

In the Bible, "Canaanite" means "trader," so some scholars have concluded that Canaanites were traders while Israelites were not. This is a specious distinction because, as we shall see (chap. 6), a goodly part of the Israelite confederation were autochthonous peoples, and all lived in Canaan, making them ipso facto *Canaanites by geography.*

The Bible's relative silence on this era drastically foreshortens the period between the Neolithic Farming Revolution and the next revolution represented by the Copper and Bronze Ages (4500–900 BCE). New evidence suggests that experiments with metals started much earlier than was previously known, but exploitation of them grew slowly. (The Mediterranean incursion into the Black Sea sent some of the residents who survived to higher ground in the Balkans, where they would fortuitously stumble onto significant deposits of metals.)

Getting and forging metals from the womb of Mother Earth was more than a revolution; it represented a sort of magic, as Celtic, Old English, Norse, and German myths of "Wayland the Smith" amply demonstrate. Shaped metal could conquer both wood and stone. People could now clear forests, build ships, dig deep wells. Rock-hewn cisterns represented

---

[21]Wolfram von Soden, *The Ancient Orient* (Grand Rapids MI: Eerdmans, 1994) 12.
[22]Ahlström, *History of Ancient Palestine*, 93.

a considerable advance in the storage and safeguarding of crop surpluses or of water, as seen later in the cavernous cisterns at Masada.

Systematic metallurgy would soon have given rise to a warrior class, as first copper, then bronze, then iron initiated quantum leaps in weapons technology. (In the Near East, a high degree of skill in metalworking was achieved by 3200 BCE, as can be seen by the hoard of 429 objects found in the "Cave of the Treasure" at Nahal Mishmar.) Because the new weapons required upper body strength to wield, it would ordinarily be men who went to war.

James G. Frazer reports that Thompson Indian women of British Columbia prayed to their menfolk's weapons to bring them back from war. (Similarly, perhaps, Cretans and later Assyrians deified the weapons that brought them victory.) [23] *Because of their prowess, Cretan (Cherethite) mercenaries formed David's personal bodyguard, as they no doubt did for many other monarchs.*

In the same vein, metalworking made miners—and even more than they, smiths—important. Ezra/Nehemiah take note of "the son of Barzillai who had married a daughter of Barzillai (the Gileadite) and had taken his [lit. their] name" (Ezra 2:61 = Neh. 7:63 NJPS; cf. 1 Esdras 5:38). (The borrowed Akkadian *barzillu/parzillu* becomes *barzillai*, "smith.") Why? Because for his strength and skill a smith would be his village's most important person. This held well into modern times, as Longfellow's poem, "The Village Blacksmith" (1840, and a popular poem well into the twentieth century), attests.

Another contemporary technological advance is represented by the introduction of wheel-made pottery in which dry or fermented grain could be kept. "Tournette" pottery replaced the centuries-old hand-thrown stuff. Whether this development led to or, with Colin Renfrew, was caused by, population growth, there was a greater need for vessels for eating and storage and for transport of commodities.

Because of these technological advances, the Bronze Ages witnessed the rise of powerful trading empires. Note that an oval 2,000 miles long

---

[23]James George Frazer, *The Golden Bough* (New York: Macmillan, 1951) 31. See F. Willesen, "The Philistine Corps of the Scimitar from Gath," *Journal of Semitic Studies* 3 (1958): 327-35. See also Morton Cogan, *Imperialism and Religion: Assyria, Judah, and Israel in the Eighth and Seventh Centuries B.C.E.*, SBLMS 19 (Missoula MT: Scholars Press) 53.

and 1,000 miles broad, drawn with Phoenician Palestine (named later for incoming Philistines) at its center, would reach from Athens to Isfahan in Persia and from Aswan to the Black Sea. At various times, Sumer, Egypt, Crete, Hatti, Urartu, Akkad, and Assyria maintained dominant positions in this area. Sumer and Egypt, the two earliest land-based civilizations in the ancient Near East, both arose only about 5,000 years ago; at various times, both Crete and Greece were home to major sea powers.

International trade controlled by major players began by the mid-third millennium, some by sea and some by donkey caravan.[24] Pharaoh Sahure (ca. 2600) reported bringing forty shiploads of cedar from Lebanon (Seti I relief), as did Gudea of Lagash (ca. 2000) from the Amanus mountains. Pharaoh Pepi I (ca. 2350) imported grapes and figs from Retenu (Canaan). Many smaller players were hardly less important: Mari, Mitanni, and Ebla were established on inland trade routes, and Ugarit, Sidon, and Byblos on the seacoast. Interior Canaanite city-states such as Hazor, Shechem, and Megiddo were also part of the international system of trade. Cities, however, are by nature not self-sufficient; they needed exchange with the hinterland for foodstuffs, but not merely that.

All the players wanted base metals for weapons and tools; precious metals and stones for ornamentation; gum and spices for embalming and cosmetics; obsidian for arrowheads; cedar and cyprus for building ships or houses; and all sorts of foodstuffs, but especially wine and olive oil.

Olive oil is the major ancient Near Eastern commodity. Olive oil was to the ancient Near East what petroleum is to us: it was used in lamps, for cooking and cleaning, and even in cosmetics. Interestingly, the commercial value of olive oil has recently been rediscovered in Israel.

Though a relative backwater, biblical Israel was much less isolated from its usually more powerful neighbors than, say, Switzerland is from its neighbors. Israel straddled good north-south trade and military routes and usually lacked the means to keep the neighbors from transiting or occupying its territory, so it was subject to both peaceful and warlike incursions.

There are several places in the Bible where "Canaanite" actually means "trader": Isaiah 23:8; Zechariah 14:21; Proverbs 31:24; Job 40:30

---

[24]Michael Astour, "Overland Trade Routes in Ancient Western Asia," in Sasson et al., *Civilizations* 3:1401-20.

[41:6].[25] Even if these texts are late, that is to say, postexilic, it is likely
the designation is much older. Israel's central location on the eastern
shore of the Mediterranean made it a natural marketplace not only for
goods, but also for the ideas carried by soldiers, travellers, and traders—
religion from Egypt, philosophy from Greece, law from Mesopotamia.
(This, of course, is a far too simplistic division of international influences
upon Israel, but a fuller discussion must wait for chap. 13, below.)

Israel itself grows things other peoples would want and might not
have in sufficient quantity, for example, cedar and other woods, minerals
and salts from or near the Dead Sea—where ancient Jericho stood—and,
when urban areas became too crowded for agriculture, wine and olive oil.
The famous Samaria Ostraca include items indicating that in monarchic
times these commodities were sent to Israelite kings from crown estates.
Some were consumed, but surpluses could be used in trade (see below,
chap. 9).

Chart 2. *What's on Offer in the ANE*

This list indicates what was, at various times, on offer and where.

Afghanistan — lapis lazuli
Arabia — spices, gums, camel's hair (?)
Arabian Gulf — shells
Aram/Lebanon — cedar wood
Armenia — obsidian, antimony
Canaan — wine, oil, ivories, foodstuffs
Crete — bronze
Cyprus — copper
Egypt — gold, ebony
Greece — fine pottery
Hatti — tin, woolens
Oman — copper
Phoenicia — purple dye
Various places in the Caucasus — silver

---

[25]Variously translated as "trader" or "merchant," even "trafficker" (KJV). See, e.g.,
D. Redford, *Egypt, Canaan, and Israel in Ancient Times*, 195-96; and Edmon L. Rowell,
Jr., "Canaan, Inhabitants of," *Mercer Dictionary of the Bible* (Macon GA: Mercer
University Press, 1990ff.) 130.

§5. The Social Consequences of Trade

In [those] days . . . caravans ceased. (Judges 5:6)

A recent discovery at Tell Hamoukar indicates that urban clusters date from as early as 4000 BCE. We don't yet know much about their society, but Egypt developed a pyramidal organizing scheme that we may refer to as "kingship" around 3000 BCE. The first kingship established in Mesopotamia some 700 years later was that of Sargon I, a Semitic ruler whose birth narrative contains elements suspiciously like those of Moses. Kingship was at first perhaps *ad hoc*, opportunistic, situational. Dynastic kingship was a later, logical development, but once it was established the beneficiaries of dynasticism would not wish to remember a time when that system was not. The Sumerian King List maintains that kingship descended directly from heaven—a claim later repeated by European monarchs—putting their claims beyond dispute and entitling them to the fruits and profits of international trade.

It is no mere coincidence that circa 3000 also marks the time when societies became more hierarchical. The need for metalworkers, potters, sky readers and other diviners, accountants, and scribes further promoted a nondemocratic caste system in which the requisite specialists enjoyed high places. The lowest people on the totem pole were the "teamsters" who hauled goods between cities or countries.[26]

Later we will take a close look at who these teamsters were, but for now note that Giorgio Buccellati points out that developing deep-well technology enabled those people who had previously been confined to river valleys to open up the steppes.[27] If some of these people were outcasts at first, they ultimately began to look for their own ethnic unity, and to reject the urban heritage that they quickly forgot to recognize as historically their own.[28]

Deep-well technology also allowed the donkeys that carried the goods greater range. The well-known traverse from Asshur on the Euphrates to Kanesh in Anatolia is 450 miles one way, *by air*. The land route was con-

---

[26]See again Redford, *Egypt, Canaan, and Israel in Ancient Times.*

[27]Giorgio Buccellati, *Cities and Nations of Ancient Syria: An Essay on Political Institutions with Special Reference to the Israelite Kingdoms*, Studi Semitici 26 (Rome: Instituto di Studi del Vicino Oriente, Università di Roma, 1967) 26.

[28]Von Soden, *The Ancient Orient*, 29-31.

siderably longer; some other routes were as much as four times as long[29] and, I estimate, took six months on the road in each direction.

The royal trading "partners' " success, sometimes established by treaty, was underwritten by their mutual interest in obtaining needed goods and luxury items with profit to the trading parties; it was guaranteed only by their ability to protect caravans or punish molesters who lived out of reach of central governments, such as *bene yaminu* and various *'apiru* groups (see below). This wasn't always easy.

As early as the end of the reign of Pepi II of Egypt (twenty-third century BCE), caravans were subject to the depredations of neighboring tribes; an Egyptian ass train from the South was set upon by Red Sea Asiatics, another by Nubians who held the body of its leader for ransom. (Jews ransom bodies also, so we will return to this subject in chap. 6.) If this was the case then, on Egypt's very borders, think about how difficult trade was to sustain later when its tendrils stretched far and wide.

The kingdoms tried every available means to keep the trade routes open.[30] They were ultimately unsuccessful. Cracks were apparent in the Amarna age (14th century BCE), as we know from such letters sent by Egyptian vassals as Abdu-Heba's in Palestine to Pharaoh Akhenaton. This situation was echoed later in Judges, quoted above. Judges doesn't say why the caravans ceased, but we can posit a combination of factors that would cause the fabric of civilization to unravel.

Trade, migration, or conquest provide especially potent disease vectors. In modern times, the spread of such previously regional diseases as the Ebola virus and possibly AIDS has been linked to unprecedented tourism. In coastal lowlands like prebiblical Canaan's, disease was already endemic because the natural basalt dikes that parallel the coast blocked drainage of west-flowing streamlets, causing swamps to form. Elsewhere man-made dams and canals would increase the salinization of delta regions—as modern Egypt is again finding out—rendering them unfit for agriculture.

In Egypt there was weakness in dominant dynasties caused by inbreeding or disputes concerning succession; in Mesopotamia, Ann

---

[29]Astour, "Overland Trade Routes," 1419.
[30]Victor J. Kean, *The Disk from Phaistos* (Athens: Efstathiatis Group, 1985), interprets it as part of a series carried by Cretans to Libya in an attempt to dissuade North African raiders from disrupting trade.

Gibbons claims that a disastrous period of 300 years of drought "hung the Akkadian Empire out to dry."[31] Drought-induced famine would accelerate the spread of disease, especially if it caused affected people to migrate in search of better land. War, trade, and migration opened up previously isolated populations to penetration by germs, viruses, and bacteria for which they had little or no immune protection.

Americans are all too familiar with movies depicting soldiers and cowboys violently wiping out Native Americans, but even more damage was done to native peoples by the importation of smallpox and measles.

The Bible's *herem*, a quarantining of sick people "outside the camp," is, in some respect, a medical measure; nonetheless it's another reason for some people to be cast out. Where would they go? S. Streuver suggests that

The areas just beyond [these] villages would have received "excess" population and would therefore have been areas of disequilibrium in which adaptive change would have been favored.[32]

As we will see in chapter 7, some proto-Israelites might have been broken loose from their previous habitations for medical reasons. In any event, near the cusp of the Bronze-Iron Ages, about 1200, some such combination of things occurred, plunging the "ancient Near Eastern economic community" into the black hole of anarchy.[33] It was about this time, too, that Egypt was attacked and Hatti overrun by groups from the northwest, the "Sea Peoples," as Egyptians called them. These included Sardinians and Sicilians, to judge by the transliterated names given them by the Egyptians, who managed, barely, to turn them aside. Here too were the Philistines. Coincidentally, it is at this time that tradition tells us

---

[31]Ann Gibbons, "How the Akkadian Empire was Hung Out to Dry," *Science* 5/261 (20 August 1993): 985. A similar period of desiccation occurred between 1000 and 1900 of our era, making much of the land useless for agriculture.

[32]*Prehistoric Agriculture*, ed. S. Streuver (Garden City NY: Natural History Press, 1971) 49.

[33]See *The Crisis Years: The 12th Century B.C.: From beyond the Danube to the Tigris*, ed. William A. Ward and Martha Sharp Joukowsky (Dubuque: Kendall/Hunt, 1992). George Mendenhall makes a good case for bubonic plague having been the cause and subject of "The Incident at Beth Baal Peor" (Num. 25), in *The Tenth Generation* (Baltimore: Johns Hopkins, 1973) 105-22.

significant elements of what would shortly become Israel made their way to Canaan.

The decline of the ancient Near East was so precipitous that it produced a power vacuum in which smaller political entities, Israel among them, might flourish. Before going on to explore the emergence of Israel, however, we need to examine the development of what is arguably the most far-reaching of all technological changes: writing.

Chapter 3

Semitic Language, Hebrew Thought

§1. "On earth as it is in heaven. . . . "   (Matthew 6:10)

At that time, the earth had one language and few words.
(Gen. 11:1; my translation)

Horses dream. So do dogs and cats, though what they make of their dreams is hard to fathom. There is no doubt that even before acquiring language we humans also "spoke" to ourselves, as we still do, in our dreams. After we acquired spoken language, dreams could be seen as a medium of communication that gods use in speaking to some individuals.[1] Hence, they were important to biblical Joseph—as well as to his latter-day descendant Sigmund Freud.[2] Deuteronomy (13:2) and Jeremiah (23:32) warn against the uncritical acceptance of such communications, but "dreamers of dreams" as well as dream-interpreters dot the biblical landscape.

Julian Jaynes takes this a giant step further. He suggests that until about 5,000 years ago one side of the brain "spoke" to the other without being recognized as internal speech.[3] According to Jaynes, the "voices" heard by people like Abraham would have come from inside their own heads. No one, however, seems to have accepted this hypothesis and it still doesn't tell us much about the origin of language per se. The development of language was a process of very long duration indeed.

In this chapter we will attempt to assess what influence the Hebrew language had on the people who thought, wrote, and lived the Bible. We can say that Hebrew was hardly the language in which God spoke to

---

[1]We may contrast the prescientific appreciation of dreams with Carl Sagan's *The Dragons of Eden* (New York: Ballantine, 1977) 177.

[2]Sigmund Freud, *Interpretation of Dreams* (London: Oxford University Press, 1999 [1913]). We now recognize the very attractive possibility that the left hemisphere of the neocortex is suppressed in the dream state, while the right hemisphere—which has an extensive familiarlity with signs but only a halting verbal literacy—is functioning well. Nor was Freud the last to explore this area. See Rami M. Shapiro, *Minyan: Ten Principles for Living a Life of Integrity* (New York: Bell Tower/Harmony, 1997) 138-45.

[3]Julian Jaynes, *The Origin of Consciousness in the Breakdown of the Bicameral Mind* (Boston: Houghton Mifflin, 1976). Richard Leakey and Roger Lewin, *Origins Reconsidered* (New York: Macmillan, 1992) 241, add "[T]here will be an underlying structure common to all language."

Adam; rather it is the product of a long period of evolutionary development even within its own family.

Humans apparently developed the physiological ability to produce
"modern" language sounds only about 40,000 years ago. What words the
cave paintings from Altamira, Lascaux, or elsewhere and dating to
20,000–30,000 years ago may represent can hardly be guessed. Marija
Gimbutas,[4] however, sees signs of linguistic intentionality in the doubling
marks on representations of pregnant mares from Lascaux caves. These
marks, she says, indicate the wish that twins be foaled. It may be so.

Our earliest spoken language was probably composed of single
"open" or "closed" syllables. Scholars represent these syllables by the
patterns Cv (Consonant-vowel) and CvC. English examples would be our
words "Hi" and "Mom" respectively. (Note the inherent "dualism" here;
more below.) In Morris Swadesh's list of 100 "basic core vocabulary"[5]
words, twenty-five percent are single syllables,[6] but this number was
probably higher in earlier stages of linguistic development.

It would be fanciful to suggest that a subsequent stage simply com-
bines these into the triconsonantal "Himom." However, note that the
largest group of Hebrew words shares that same pattern, for instance *shalom*, s-l-m. Hebrew shows traces of evolutionary development from
mono- to bisyllabic words in some nouns, the so-called "segolates" of
CvCC (Consonant-vowel-Consonant-Consonant) pattern. For example
malk (king) changes to the dominant CvCvC *melek* (king). But this does
not get us terribly far.

The earliest writing that we know to be "language" is picture writing
(pictographic) from Sumer and Egypt, about 3500 BCE. As the name
suggests, words were represented by increasingly stylized pictures such
as the following.[7]

---

[4]Gimbutas, Marija Alseikaité, *The Language of the Goddess* (San Francisco: Harper
Collins, 1989) 161-73.

[5]Cited in Renfrew, *Archaeology and Language*, 114.

[6]John Huehnergard, "Semitic Languages," in Sasson et al., *Civilizations* 4:2128,
writes, "There is evidence of an earlier pre-Semitic system in which some verbal roots
had two consonants."

[7]Derived from Arno Poebel and widely reprinted, e.g., in Ignatz J. Gelb, *A Study of
Writing*, 2nd ed. (Chicago: University of Chicago Press, 1963) 70.

N.B.: All such "charts," here and on following pages, read from left to right and are
designed to show something of a sign's evolution/development.

ᚴ ᚨ Ҡ ᚷ ᚪ א (a)   bull

ᚱ ᚺ ᚱ ∕ᐱ נ (n)   snake

Writing eventually developed into logographic—a system in which each sign stands for a word—then syllabic, then alphabetic, but the development was not neat. Even in a strictly syllabic system such as Akkadian, the 800 syllabic signs have, among them, 36,000 different meanings. Hieroglyphic Egyptian contains all three of the above elements, as though one had photographed a solid as it sublimated through liquid to gaseous form.

> *Although "real" writing is not apparent until well into the Bronze Age (about 3500 in Sumer), its antecedents in the farming period can be inferred. Writing derives from accounting. Bullae, clay balls containing pellets indicating numbers of small animals, were used as a trade tool.*[8] *When John Donne wrote "Do not send to know for whom the bell tolls," the word "tolls" refers to counting (the number of years the deceased had lived); a linguistic survival of this usage is the "teller" at your local bank.*

An attractive theory of origin is that the alphabet is not the independent creation of some Neolithic Newton who then revolutionized writing, but a crude, popular form of the centuries-old scribal craft. It seems, in fact, to have been invented by Semites working in the Sinai for Egyptian overlords, and dates to the early second millennium.[9] This is not to suggest that "Israelites" invented the *aleph-bet*; indeed, its invention probably predates the formation of any recognizable Israelite entity by several centuries. As has been pointed out above, early forms of the *'aleph*, probably borrowed from Egyptian, resembled the horned head of a bull: that *'aleph* is the first letter of the Hebrew *aleph-bet* is no accident, as we shall shortly see.

Alphabetic writing was simple to learn and required no government subvention or scribal schools, as did Akkadian or Egyptian. An Egyptian fable recognizes and laments this turn of events: Thoth, the god of

---

[8]Denise Schmandt-Besserat, "Record Keeping before Writing," in Sasson et al., *Civilizations*, 4:2097-2106.

[9]Cited in *Biblical Archaeology Review* 26/1 (January/February 2000): 12.

Wisdom, comes to Ptah, chief of Gods, with a new invention, the alphabet. This, he says, will make writing much easier. But Ptah is not pleased. He complains that the new writing will cause everyone to abandon the Egyptians' wonderful artistic system of hieroglyphics—a consequence which ultimately in fact occurred.

For us, however, the "moral" of this tale is that technological advances and discoveries have unlooked-for sociological and religious ramifications, as Karl Marx later recognized. The learning of writing had been a profession that only a trained elite could practice. Perhaps only as few as one percent of (mostly) males could write, and not all of them were able to read what they transcribed.[10] Because of its relative simplicity, alphabetic writing was able to survive the civilizational collapse at the end of the Bronze Age. Some observers think its increasing use democratized societies that employed it.[11] Of these societies, the Hebrew-speaking Israelites interest us most.

§2. The Emergence of Hebrew

" . . . the tongue of Canaan." (Isaiah 19:18)

Hebrew is classified as a "northwest Semitic" language, which means it is one of a group of languages (the northwest group) which in turn is part of a larger group of about seventy. Akkadian, the language of Mesopotamia from around 3000, is the oldest of the Semitic language family. (Semitic languages were so named in the eighteenth century, by the Austrian philologist A. L. Schloezer, for Noah's son Shem.) Egyptian is classified as "Hamito-Semitic," meaning that it's something of a hybrid between Asian and North African tongues.

We don't know what Hebrew would have looked like if it had grown up in isolation from other languages, Semitic and non-Semitic, as Basque has, but this did not happen. Scholars have long postulated what they call proto-Semitic, the language from which Hebrew eventually developed. Speakers of proto-Semitic could have interacted with the speakers of other tongues when both inhabited the western shores of the Black Sea, assuming that they all did not then speak the same language. In fact,

---

[10]Richard Parkinson, *Cracking Codes: the Rosetta Stone and Decipherment* (Berkeley: University of California Press, 1999).

[11]Renfrew, *Archaelogy and Language*, however, argues that the alphabet was not, in fact, a democratizing element in society.

biblical Hebrew, like English, owes its vigor to the many language streams that fed it, not surprising when you consider that its speakers ultimately settled at a crossroads of the ancient Near East.

The texture of an alphabetic language such as Hebrew is very different from Egyptian or Akkadian because each word that one hears also carries the overtones of words built from the same root. As Cynthia Ozick's Ruth Puttermesser exclaims,

> "[A] stunning mechanism: three letters, whichever fated three, could command all possibility simply by a change in their pronunciation or the addition of a wing letter fore and aft."[12]

As the triconsonantal word became normative, many formerly biconsonantal roots were expanded by the use of so-called prosthetic letters such as 'aleph and *yod* as first letters. Thus *dam*, "blood," yields *'adam*, "man," and *'adamah*, "earth/ground"; *sof*, "end," yields *'asaf*, "gather" and *yoseph* (Joseph), "addition."

Did nouns or verbs come first? Jaynes thinks neither.[13] Such qualifiers as "here" or "there," he says, accompanying a pointing finger will have come first, followed by commands and then nouns. Again, we don't know, but names of nouns later lent themselves to creation of an alphabet on the acrophonic principle.

This principle—possibly the greatest human discovery since the domestication of fire—uses the first (*acro-*) sound (*-phone*) of a word as the pronunciation of its first letter, as in *'aleph* = "A" from *'aleph*, ox. (Compare NATO's and the United States Army's use of Alpha, Bravo, Charlie, Delta, and so forth, for the letters of the alphabet.) The alphabet or, as we should more properly say, *aleph-bet*, is the result.

§3. Why Is "A" the First Letter?

You shall not muzzle an ox while it is threshing. (Deut. 25:4 NJPS)

These days, even those of us who grew up with Sesame Street may not fully appreciate the magic of our letters; we do not ask such questions of

---

[12]Cynthia Ozick, *The Puttermesser Papers* (New York: Knopf, 1997) 5.

[13]Jaynes, *Origin of Consciousness in the Breakdown of the Bicameral Mind*, 129-33, thinks "qualifiers" came first. This is like the "pooh-pooh theory" mentioned in Otto Jespersen, *Language: Its Nature, Development, and Origin* (New York: W. W. Norton, 1964).

them as, Why is "A" the first letter? To our ancestors, however, the letters themselves must have had enormous potency.

> *This does not, however, justify recent "practitioners" who have reprised the ancient practice of "laying on" of Hebrew letters as therapy, as if the letters themselves had independent power. An almost idolatrous level of respect for the text has not ceased. On the other hand, anyone who has handled even the facsimile edition of the Leningrad Codex (ca. 1000 CE), the oldest complete manuscript of the Bible, feels a certain power and majesty emanating from it.*

Each letter designates something important in the life of the society, pride of place being given the most important letter. *'Aleph* is the name of the first Hebrew letter, but the word *'aleph*, from the triliteral root *'-l-p*, means "domestic cattle": that is, what can be tamed, *bos primigenius*, a descendant of the now extinct aurochs.

I think it also refers to Taurus, the Bull of Heaven (name from *s-v-r*, steer), with its first magnitude star, Aldebaran. Taurus is the second of the twelve zodiacal constellations counting Aries the Ram first. Taurus's spring rising in May/June (or perhaps the sun entering Taurus) signalled the time for harvesting barley.

In Hebrew the name for barley, *s'orah*, means "bearded grain," a word-picture that reeks of antiquity. Even before einkorn and emmer wheat, I think, barley (L. *hordeum*) was the first grain to be harvested, a conclusion I came to before finding out that the Greeks also thought so.[14] Judges 7:13 identifies barley as symbolizing Gideon, and I note that in the Gezer Calendar, roughly contemporary with Gideon's judgeship, barley is mentioned while wheat is not.

Wild barley is still found in Israel, where it long remained the staple of poor people's (Jews') diets; it was replaced by wheat only in Mishnaic times. Barley has a shorter growing season than wheat and can grow in poor soils with scant rainfall, conditions that mark much of biblical Israel's land and account for barley's being so widely sown there. So ubiquitous was barley, in fact, that the size and value of a field (Lev. 27:16) was calculated on the amount of barley required to sow it.

Earthly oxen were instrumental in milling the grain that Taurus's rising showed was ready for harvest. Although other animals can be and

---

[14]*Encyclopedia Judaica* 4:241.

were used for this task, the ox was most often used because of its strength and endurance. A western ox, of course, is a castrated bull. A bull's sheer physical strength is matched by his sexual potency, something that animal husbandmen would have long observed.

In some societies, wearing or eating bull's horns or consuming bull genitalia was thought to convey this latter trait to the consumer, a notion from which even Israelites were not immune (more on this in chap. 9).

Putting these things together, the choice of 'aleph as first letter of the Hebrew *aleph-bet* seems deliberate.

Most likely the same kind of pedigree could be uncovered for each letter of the alphabet,[15] but we'll restrict ourselves to just a few here. The second Hebrew letter is *bet*, house (courtyard, really); the third letter, *gimel*, was formerly thought to mean "camel" because of the phonic similarity of the two, but is more likely "throw stick";[16] *dalet*, the fourth letter, was mistakenly seen to come from *delet*, "door," but probably derives from *dag*, fish, as can be seen from the following progression.

 ד (dalet)

The earliest example of the fifth letter, *heh*, dating from about 1900 BCE, shows a stick figure with arms raised as if in supplication. The sound of the letter is its name "heh," like a breath or, perhaps, a sigh. G. R. Driver derives it from the Egyptian determinative for man.[17] The raised arms seem to indicate prayer to the gods that live on high.

Other picture-letters include:

י *yod*—arm

מ, ם *mem*—water (in Hebrew *mayim*)[18]

---

[15]*Encyclopedia Judaica* 2:675. This can still be seen, e.g., in Mordecai Kamrat and Edwin Samuel's *Roots* (Jerusalem: Kiryat Sefer, 1969) though the meanings of some letters have drifted from the originals.

[16]*Encyclopedia Judaica* 2:675. Godfrey Rolles Driver, *Semitic Writing*, Schweich Lectures 44 (London: Oxford University Press, 1948) 163.

[17]Alan Gardiner, *Egyptian Grammar* (London: Oxford University Press, 1964) 442 (A4) and 444 (A30). Godfrey Rolles Driver, *Semitic Writing*, 162.

[18]According to Gimbutas, *Language of the Goddess*, 18, the symbol for water is recognizably 40,000 years old.

נ, ן *nun*—fish or serpent[19] (In Hebrew, *nahash* is a kind of snake. A *nahash* was the tempter of Eve and Adam.)

פ, ף *peh*—mouth

ק *qof*—palm (of hand).[20]

Colin Renfrew complains that no one pays attention to verbs.[21] Some seem to be derived from nouns, while for other noun-verb pairs the opposite seems to be the case. Either way, we observe that some verbs also seem to have begun life as single, closed syllables. These are the "geminates," so called because the second letter (or both initial letters) duplicates itself to form a three letter root, for example, $\sqrt{g\text{-}l} < \sqrt{g\text{-}l\text{-}l}$, "to revolve."

> *Gilgal, the circle of twelve stones set up by Joshua, was the first Israelite shrine west of the Jordan. The* LXX *(or* Septuaginta, *the Greek translation of Scripture by the Jewish community of Alexandria in Egypt) dissimilates the name to Golgotha, "place of the skull," where Jesus was executed.*

Many geminates are onomotopoeia, that is, they imitate the sounds of the actions they denote, as in our "crunch," "buzz," and "swish." Thus: $\sqrt{n\text{-}tz\text{-}tz}$, "crunch," $\sqrt{k\text{-}tz\text{-}tz}$, "chop" and $\sqrt{r\text{-}tz\text{-}tz}$, "smash" (compare the dialect variant $\sqrt{r\text{-}s\text{-}s}$ in Amos). But those sounds, like so much else in Scripture, are lost in translation.

§4. Language and Speech

"I call it like I see it." —Howard Cosell

Previous histories of Israel generally omit serious consideration of the influence of the Hebrew language upon Israelite thought. This is an important omission. Languages are not merely transparent membranes through which we all see, more or less, the same universe. As Jaynes says, language is an "organ of perception."[22] When the late football

---

[19]With *Encyclopedia Judaica* 12:1272, G. R. Driver, *Semitic Writing*, 183, lists Ethiopic *nahas* (serpent); cf. p. 170, the Egyptian sign for serpent or "cobra." Aramaic *nun* = fish. The confusion may be due to a knowledge of seagoing snakes.

[20]For a chart, see William D. Whitt, "The Story of the Semitic Alphabet," in Sasson et al., *Civilizations* 4:2379-97.

[21]Renfrew, *Archaeology and Language*, 111.

[22]Jaynes, *Origin of Consciousness in the Breakdown of the Bicameral Mind*, 50. Thorleif Boman's *Hebrew Thought Compared with Greek* (New York: W. W. Norton,

sportscaster Howard Cosell magisterially opined, "I call it like I see it," he failed to recognize that the very language he was using shaped and colored the universe he saw.

What he and we initially see is a system of binary oppositions, that of each human body and between human genders. That is, normally humans are divisible into two genders and each person is bilaterally symmetric. Every appendage or visible organ on the right side is paralleled by a virtually identical counterpart on the left. As John Rogerson says, "[T]he binary system . . . derives from the nature of the human mind."[23] We might add that it mirrors the construction of the human brain, too, but we will have more to say about this in our next chapter.

The observation of human duality is not simply objective; various value judgments attach to it. This is most apparent in *sinistrum*, Latin for "left-handed" which also means "dark, sinister" or, if you will, "sneaky," because most of us are right-handed. In Judges, left-handed Ehud craftily concealed a weapon on his right side and used his offhandedness to kill King Eglon of Moab.[24]

Hebrew has singular and plural nouns, as English does, but Hebrew also has a fairly extensive "dual" ending for nouns that occur in pairs.

French still retains seconde *for the second of only two things, but English has come to prefer "two" as an adjective over words like "brace" for a pair. We use "second" in the French sense only for one who accompanies a friend to a duel.*

As we noted, with the exception of "testicles," Hebrew identifies all paired body parts as feminine. Why? The labelling of paired body parts is an extension of the observation that the most uniquely noticeable and vital of the body's paired parts are female breasts. Since breasts are feminine *par excellence*, the "twoness" of all paired body parts except testicles became a "feminine" trait. This may also explain why Pythagoras held that even numbers are feminine, odd ones masculine.[25]

1960) posits that Hebrew conduces to concrete thought, Greek to abstract.

[23]John R. Rogerson, *Anthropology and the Old Testament* (Oxford: Basil Blackwell, 1978) 106-107.

[24]Halpren, *The First Historians*, 39-75. Only with the publication of Saul M. Olyan's *Rites and Rank: Hierarchy in Biblical Representations of Cult* (Princeton NJ: Princeton University Press, 2000) do we see a study that takes any account of binarism.

[25]Alternatively, Gimbutas, *Language of the Goddess*, 163, thinks buttocks are first and foremost and has many illustrations, all of females, to bolster her view. Here again the

A "gendered" universe is a natural consequence of experiencing a world filled with *living* things. Hebrew, unlike English or German, has no neuter gender and therefore invites its speakers to think in starkly contrasting terms such as right/left, day/night, good/evil. Nouns have to be either masculine or feminine—occasionally both—but the gender designations of Hebrew are not arbitrary. They reflect the perceived "maleness" or "femaleness" of the things so identified, such as *yeled* "male child" and *yaldah* "female child," which are both from the verb *walad*, "to give birth."

Note that English identifies gender only in some things: for example, ships, cities, or colleges, all of which can be seen as carrying or nurturing, are feminine. There is a similar judgment in Hebrew.

Not all cultures assign exactly the same gender to everything,[26] but that they assign gender at all is a reflection of seeing the universe in anthropomorphic terms. In the case of Hebrew, this view is part of a thoroughgoing dualism and may have far-reaching implications. I think Max Weber hits close to home when he notes "the dualistic nature of its [Jewry's] in-group out-group morality."[27] Of course, any ethnocentric group will have such a worldview, but this mentality is precisely what one would expect an essentially dualistic language to facilitate.

Here, briefly, are some other examples that also reflect the dualism of both Hebrew language and Hebrew-speaking society.

1. As noted above, even the syllables of Hebrew are of only two kinds: Consonant-vowel (Cv, "open") and Consonant-vowel-Consonant (CvC or "closed").

2. Hebrew lacks a partitive (the word "a"), so nouns are definite or indefinite depending on the presence or absence of the definite article (*ha-*). This distinction would seem a small matter, but in fact it has had enormous theological significance. For example, in Isaiah

---

principle would be doubling as abundance. On the development of buttocks, see Elaine Morgan, *The Descent of Woman*, 4th ed. (London: Souvenir Press, 1997; [1]1972). One theory does not exclude others.

Dualism, often represented as the fight between Light and Darkness / Life and Death is reflected or projected upon the screen of the cosmos all over the world in divine combats: Balder-Hother (blind dupe of Loki); Two Brothers (Cain and Abel, Horus and Set, Marduk and Tia'mat).

[26]Mesopotamian "moon" is both masculine and feminine.

[27]Max Weber, *Ancient Judaism* (Glencoe IL: Free Press, 1952) 343-55.

7:14, Christian tradition sees the prophecy of *a* Virgin Birth, even though the Hebrew text (*ha-almah*) indicates that a known and presumeably present female, the wife of King Ahaz perhaps, is being referred to.[28]

3. The actions of "active" verbs are said to be complete (Latin *perfectus*) or incomplete (*imperfectus*); contrast the "trinity" of past/present/future that our verb system exhibits. Further, there are two kinds of stative verbs in Hebrew: one denotes such temporary conditions as hunger; the other, permanent states such as death.

4. In Hebrew there are basically two kinds of enemy,[29] a fact that Weber might find surprising, since one is foreign (*'oyeb*) and the other domestic (*reša'*). Americans will note that this is the same division that is found in their presidents' oath of office.

5. Early Israelite priests decided important questions of state using a sort of primitve binary "computer" called Urim and Thummim (1 Sam. 10:19-21; 14:40-42; Josh. 7:16-18) that could provide only either/or answers.

A dualistic view of the universe has extensive ramifications, especially when and as Israel moved toward monotheism. Perhaps too-simply stated, it is this: in societies that were already hierarchical and male-dominated, it was natural to assume that the One God must be male also—this despite the evident theological contradiction that an Infinite Being could not be thus limited.

In fact, there is an increasing amount of evidence to suggest that the God of Israel was not quite as Alone as we now hold him to be. However, further discussion of the evidence for a divine consort must be left for next chapter.

---

[28]The meaning of Isaiah 7:14 continues to be a topic of lively discussion, with Jews and Christians each having reasons for interpreting it the way they respectively do. Christians necessarily see "Old Testament prophecies" as sometimes going unfulfilled for centuries and do not seem to mind that the definite article "the" rather than an indefinite "a" accompanies the noun.

[29]Stanley N. Rosenbaum, "The Concept 'antagonist' in Hebrew Psalmography: A Semantic Field Study" (diss., Brandeis Univ., 1974). Also see Othmar Keel, *Feinde und Gottesleugner: Studien zum Image der Widersacher in den Individuelen Psalmen*, Stuttgarter Biblische Monographien 7 (Stuttgart: Verlag Katholisches Bibelwerk, 1969).

§5. Hebrew Dialect

Il n'y a que dialect. —Ferdinand de Saussure[30]

Note that the apocryphal book Wisdom of Jesus ben Sirach (Ecclesiasticus) is the first to refer to the language of the Bible as "Hebrew" (prologue). In Isaiah 19:18, probably written 600 years earlier, what is spoken in Israel—presumably Isaiah's own language—is called *sfat Cana'an*, the "tongue of Canaan" (see Isa. 19:18—lit. "lip of Canaan"). This is a bit misleading, because even if all the residents of Canaan/Israel spoke "the same language," their varying dialects would have made them, in many cases, mutually unintelligible.[31]

> *Genesis 11's identification of a single ur-language, however, is perhaps not simply a theoretical postulate based on the notion that we all necessarily come from a single human pair, Mr. and Mrs. Noah. It might also be an echo of the then-not-too-distant time when the many peoples who lived around the Black Sea spoke languages that were, at least, mutually intelligible.*

That Hebrew has dialects should not surprise us; it would be a surprise if it did not. Every language has dialects: the United States has hundreds. Even Great Britain,[32] small as it is, is the home of twelve major dialects which are not all mutually comprehensible. If this is so despite the U.K.'s standardized education and the presence of radio and television, how much more so Israel at the beginning of the Iron Age?

That Hebrew itself always had dialects we know from putting Judges's *Sibboleth* incident (12:5-6) next to the story of Peter's denying Jesus. Peter's Galilean accent makes his origins audible: "Certainly you are also one of them, for your accent betrays you" (Matt. 26:73 NRSV). It is true that "accent" does not equal dialect, but these two incidents act as linguistic "book ends" for the entire first pre-Christian millennium. They

---

[30]Ferdinand de Saussure, *Course in General Linguistics*, 3rd ed. (New York: Philosophical Library, 1916).

[31]In Chinese this is still the case, according to Prof. Barbara Goldstein, University of Kentucky (private communication).

[32]On sabbatical in Oxford in 1992–1993 I had occasion to experience the many dialects that still persist in England, Wales, and Cornwall—to say nothing of Scotland and Ireland.

indicate considerable variation in accent and dialect throughout Israel"s history.

Different languages, even different dialects of the same language, are often tribal "markers." About 400 BCE, Nehemiah complains (13:23-24) that half of Judah's children speak Ashdodite, Ammonite, or Moabite,[33] languages of their non-Jewish mothers. Earlier, the linguistic situation was probably one of even greater diversity—though one could argue the converse.

How comprehensible were these Israelite/Semitic dialects to the speakers of each? We do not have a lot of information on this. Joseph's Egyptian was not comprehensible to his brothers, but that Aramaic (="the Syrian language," Isaiah 36:11 KJV) was all too understandable we learn from the story of the Assyrian seige of Jerusalem in Kings.

More important than all of the above, however, is the realization that the scriptures reflect, as in a murky pool, the various dialects of Hebrew in which they were perhaps first cast. Moreover, biblical spelling is not standardized. The Bible spells words variously, even—maybe especially— proper names. Examples are Huldah's father-in-law in Kings and Chronicles; Dothan/Dothain in the same Genesis passage; even "Isaac," usually spelled *Yitzhaq*, is spelled *Yishaq* four times (twice in Amos, once in Jeremiah, once in a Northern psalm).[34] There were probably at least as many dialects in biblical Israel as there are today in the U.K.—and trying to identify them is fraught with peril.

One apparently dialectal difference is the use of *'ani* and *'anokhi* for the first-person pronoun "I." That this reflects a difference in dialects is, however, not the only theory offered by scholars. Some say the longer form is older, the shorter one newer, or that they represent the difference between poetic and prosaic usage. Gary Rendsburg suggests a difference between spoken and literary Hebrew, and Randall Garr that it represents class differences.[35]

---

[33]There are few inscriptions in Moabite, but its closeness to Hebrew, like the closeness of Danish, Swedish, and Norwegian, was immediately noted. However, as Edward Sapir reminds us, "Closely related languages—even a single language—[may] belong to distinct cultural spheres." *Language* (New York: Harcourt Brace, 1921) 213.

[34]Surprisingly, this is not noted by James Barr, *The Variable Spellings of the Hebrew Bible* (London: Oxford University Press, 1989) 20-21.

[35]Gary A. Rendsburg, "Evidence for a Spoken Hebrew in Biblical Times" (diss., New York University, 1980).

That they are simply synonyms is probably the weakest explanation. The book of Amos uses *'anokhi* ("I") eleven times, but *'ani* ("I") only once and that in a verse many scholars think is added (6:1). If they were synonymous, one would think the distribution would be more even. Alexander Sperber accounts for the two forms of "I" as a dialectal difference based upon geography.[36] That makes the most sense to me.

Such North-South differences exist in French, Italian, German, and Norwegian, to name a few. Robert Pennock's *Tower of Babel* discusses the well-known American regional variations such as "youse" and "y'all" on the second person pronoun "you."[37]

§6. Words and "the Word"

> [T]he fact is that there is no equivalent for things originally written in Hebrew.
> (Sirach [Ecclesiasticus] "Translator's Foreword" v. 22, NJB)

Ben Sirach's "editor's" observation, of course, could be made about any language. Each language has its own *Weltanschauung* ("worldview")—there is no other word for it: our paraphrase "particular perspective on the world" is about the closest we can come. But translating Hebrew is complicated because many key Hebrew words have multiple meanings: *ruach*—what "brooded over the face of the the the deep" in Genesis 1:2—can mean "wind," breath," or "spirit." The multiple meanings allow for wordplays and resonances that are unique to Hebrew. But if we put a capital S on Spirit, for example, in the phrase Your Holy Spirit, we have decisively altered its meaning. (Hebrew has no capital letters.)

Naturally, translations that insist on single English words for single Hebrew words will make a lot of outright mistakes, such as the traditional insistence that *nephesh* means "soul." Leaving aside, for the moment, whether or not the Hebrews ever had a clear conception of "soul" in the Greek sense, as separate from the body, there are many places where it clearly means "appetite" or "desire."[38]

Even where the translation is undertaken with the best of intentions, far-reaching errors can result from the inability of Indo-European

---

[36]Alexander Sperber, *A Historical Grammar of Biblical Hebrew* (Leiden: E. J. Brill, 1966).
[37]Robert Pennock, *Tower of Babel* (Cambridge MA: Massachusetts Institute of Technology Press, 2000) 127-28.
[38]Already in Francis Brown, Samuel R. Driver, and Charles A. Briggs, *Hebrew and English Lexicon of the Old Testament* (Oxford: Clarendon, 1907) 660.

languages effectively to capture the meaning of some Hebrew words. For example, Hebrew *lachen* is given in LXX as *ergo* and comes into English as "therefore" as in: "You offended God, therefore evil will come upon you." (Implied: "He has decided to punish you.") Hebrew *lachen*, however, means natural consequence. For example, when Nadab and Abihu, with the best of intentions, rush up to save the Holy Ark from falling over (Lev. 10:1-2; Num. 3:4; 26:61) they are "holied" to death by its power. This seems a rather harsh thing to have happen in response to what is, essentially, a good deed. But the Ark does not "choose" to kill them any more than a hot stove chooses to burn the person who touches it.[39] A better English translation of *lachen* than "therefore" might be the simpler, less academic "so."

Greeks disdained other tongues, calling their speakers *barbaroi* (< our "barbarians") because the other languages sound to them like a babbling of "bar-bar-bar." By way of contrast, Hebrews do not seem to have been disdainful of other languages. In a crossroads—and sometimes in a crossfire—culture, Hebrew, at least in the more cosmopolitan North, was open to foreign linguistic influence. We note the presence of such loan words as pharaoh (Egyptian *per aa*, "great house"), or of the Egyptian foreign names Hophni and Pinchas of sons of the Shilonite priest, Eli. Amos shows a number of foreign words or forms.[40]

Babylonian, probably Hurrian, Ugaritic, Eblaite, and some Phoenician words are also found in Scripture. In addition, linguistic borrowing may be seen in the later use of the Greek *symphonia* (Daniel) and Persian *pardes*, "garden" (which comes into English as "paradise"); even, perhaps, there are traces of Dravidian, a language of south India.[41] Most biblical borrowing—about 400 words—is from Akkadian, the grandfather of Semitic languages and the area's *lingua franca* already by the time Israel arose. Examples include *barzillu/parzillu* which becomes *barzillai*, "smith," and *abarraku*, "out of the way," which was aparently used even as far afield as Egypt.

---

[39]Prof. Chaim Rabin lecture, Hebrew University, Jerusalem, 1968, as reported by Mary Rosenbaum.
[40]Rosenbaum, *Amos*, chap. 7.
[41]Prof. Chaim Rabin lecture, Brandeis University, Waltham MA, 1966.

With a certain amount of pride, the Bible reports that when Joseph rode through Egyptian cities people ran before him shouting this word— "Abrek!" > abarraku—to clear the streets (Gen. 41:43).

Curiously, the Bible contains only about three dozen Egyptian words. This is far fewer than one would think if all Israel had lived there for the traditional 400 (or 430) years just before returning to Canaan, but not so surprising if the proto-Israelites who went down to Egypt were few, largely isolated and remained for only four generations.

What we need to remember is that for Hebrews, the Bible is "the Word" of God. Hebrew *dabar*, "word," also means "thing." Proof of this is that Hebrew for "nothing" is *lo-dabar*[42]—upon which Amos puns in 6:13. So the spoken Word is a palpable Thing. This still leaves us with the question: How to read it?

§7. Resolving the Chord: How to Read the Bible

"An Orc would never say 'Elbereth.' "
—Sam Gamgee (in J. R. R. Tolkien, *Lord of the Rings*, III)

Any language is an instrument upon which speakers play the harmonies they find in nature. Our tune, even our key signature, will vary with the instrument we use. Western music, for example, is based on the octave— eight notes, a number that reminds us of Earth plus the seven major celestial objects that the ancients who spoke of "the music of the spheres" knew. I don't think this is coincidental.

In any case, Hebrew language goes back to and in part reflects a Middle Bronze Age patriarchal society. Consequently, Hebrew sees a dualistic world from a male-dominated perspective, if not exclusively then at least to the point that female sources and contributions to the nation have been masked—though not necessarily as extensively as Harold Bloom would have us believe.[43] The Bible is a collection of different documents from different times and places within history and it contains several dialects, however difficult these may be to discern.

---

[42]Thorleif Boman, *Hebrew Thought Compared with Greek*, 56.

[43]That feminine sources and influences have been extensively masked—particularly in scripture—is one of Bloom's main theses, most notably in David Rosenberg and Harold Bloom, *The Book of J* [Translation by Rosenberg of those portions of the Pentateuch that derive from the so-called J document, with introduction and commentary by Bloom.] (New York: Grove Weidenfeld, 1990).

Even the most conservative of commentators would admit to at least a 700-year gap between the "giving of the Torah to Moses on Sinai" around, say, 1250 BCE and the last verses in 2 Chronicles which we may confidently date after 539 BCE. The language of Jewish scripture, like all languages, changed along the way. The problem is more complicated because subsequent writers didn't simply add layer upon layer to what they had, like people continually repapering old walls, but consciously edited and reedited what they were passing down until it became illicit to do so (more on this in chap. 13).

True, Hebrew was or became a "holy tongue" and therefore its words changed more slowly, but some change is visible. The same word in two different books can have different meanings. A textual example of this may be the obvious difference in meaning between *hokmah* as it is used in Job as opposed to the same term in Proverbs. Job may be seen as an essay in epistemology, that branch of philosophy which asks the question: How do we know? and answering that true knowledge (= *hokmah*, usually translated "wisdom") is only with God.[44] In Proverbs, on the other hand, *hokmah* seems so readily available that it is almost a commodity. As I read it, Proverbs seems to be edited late enough that it may be said to contain a thinly veiled attack on Hellenistic wisdom. The constant references warning young men to keep away from loose women refers not only to common prostitutes, but also, perhaps, to that most dangerous of Greek girls, *sophia*, whom we met in chapter 1, above.

> *Conversely, Plato thought that "wisdom" had begun in the East,[45] but there, alas, is where we shall have to leave it. The subject of ancient Near Eastern and/or biblical "Wisdom" is its own subdiscipline replete, as usual, with many competing theories.*

What we have inherited is a set of documents in which faith is foremost, complicated by the realization that the transmitters sometimes misconstrued what they were handing along. Some words must have changed meaning in the intervening centuries, so that it is perilous to use

---

[44]Such is the burden of Job 28, a sort of internal precis for the whole book, whether or not by the same hand.

[45]This accords with the thesis of Michael Astour's *Hellenosemitica* (Leiden: E. J. Brill, 1965). See also James Kugel and Rowan Greer, *Early Biblical Interpretation* (Philadelphia: Westminster, 1986) 25, who report that Plato (in the *Timaeus*, 21-25) supports such a contention.

the meaning of terms found in late texts to illustrate the meaning of the "same" words found in earlier ones.

One positive side effect of all this is that it provides yet another argument against those who claim the entire Bible is a Persian-era creation. The parts that the Bible signifies as old are marked by words and forms that became obsolete long before the Persian period. Hence, they could hardly have been recalled even by conscious archaizers bent on deception.

Given all of this, the short answer to the question of how to read the Bible is, "Carefully!" Needless to add, in order to avoid some of the pitfalls inherent in translating between Semitic and Indo-European languages, it should be read in Hebrew if at all possible.[46] A more developed response concludes this book.

---

[46]Stanley N. Rosenbaum, "It Gains a Lot in Translation," in Barry N. Olshen and Yael S. Feldman, eds., *Approaches to Teaching the Hebrew Bible as Literature in Translation* (New York: Modern Language Association, 1989) 40-44. This is not my opinion alone: in his prologue to his translation of his grandfather's writings (*Ecclesiasticus* or the *Wisdom of Jesus Son of Sirach*), ben Sirach's grandson notes that translating Hebrew Scripture into Greek is a hazardous proposition. (Ironically, ben Sirach was only available to us in Greek until pieces of it in Hebrew began to surface after 1896.)

Chapter 4

Pre-Israelite Religion: Pieces of Eight

§1. "I met a traveller from an antique land . . . "
—Percy Bysshe Shelley ("Ozymandias," 1819)

We may be fairly certain that when our Stone Age ancestors got up of a morning and stumbled to the mouth of their cave they probably did not see a world ordered and run by a single god, but by many.[1] These ancestors might not have been sophisticated enough to have organized their gods into anything like the Ogdoad of Hermopolis (Upper Egyptian eight-god/goddess pantheon) or the similar four initial pairs of Mesopotamia, but, as we shall see in the excursus at the end of this chapter, eight is a number that acquires nearly universal importance. There are, in any case, enough seemingly independent forces at work in the world that monotheism is a decidedly counterintuitive, hence a late-blooming, proposition. As Giorgio Buccellati puts it,

> What religion describes is ultimately a form of entropy. In this regard, polytheistic religion appears more rational than its Israelite counterpart [monotheism].[2]

In this chapter we will examine the beginning of Israel's continuing attempt to extrude monotheism from the matrix of powers and principalities that populated the ancient Near East before its birth. To do this requires a long look back into human prehistory.

Stewart Guthrie, in *Faces in the Clouds*, stoutly maintains that all religion is, at base, human projection of our own sense perceptions upon the screen of the cosmos: in a word, anthropomorphism.[3] Genesis tells us that God created Humankind in His own image—and some of us have, so to speak, been returning the favor ever since. Guthrie cites the oft-

---

[1] Contra such nineteenth-century "anthro-apologists" as Wilhelm Schmidt and Andrew Lang of *The Blue Fairy Book*. I am not convinced that Neolithic peoples were, in any sense, monist, but Leakey and Lewin, *Origins*, 349, estimate that humanity has at 100,000 religions, so perhaps any and all varieties of religious experience are possible.

[2] Giorgio Buccellati, "Ethics and Piety in the Ancient Near East," in Sasson et al., *Civilizations* 3:1687.

[3] Guthrie, *Faces in the Clouds*. Leakey and Lewin, *Origins Reconsidered*, 349-50, quote Edward O. Wilson: "The predisposition to religious belief is the most complex and profound force in the human mind and in all probability an ineradicable part of human nature."

paraphrased words of Xenophanes: "If horses had gods, they would look like horses."[4] Our religion, then, is anthropocentric as well as anthropomorphic. It mirrors us and, until astronomers proved otherwise, it literally revolved around us.

That people should think they have personal lucky and unlucky stars is, of course, a staggering piece of anthropocentrism. And yet, such chutzpah is not to be wondered at. In a recent television *Dateline* poll seventy-five percent of the respondents believed they had, personally, been visited or assisted by an angel. Imagining astral influences is but a logical extension of the very real influences people felt from the sun and moon[5] and that animals seem to feel from various celestial objects, objects which I will consider shortly (§10, below).

§2. *Ars gratia artis?*

[D]ecoration for decoration's sake did not exist in the Neolithic era.

—Dorothy Cameron[6]

The cave paintings in northern Spain and southern France of 20,000–30,000 years ago are probably mankind's earliest religious "texts," but unlike the pedestal in Shelley's "Ozymandias," quoted at the head of this chapter, they have no written accompaniment. So we cannot be certain what or even whether deities are being appealed to. However, I note that this is the same period in which we first see Mother Goddess figurines. Appeals to goddesses and gods would certainly include entreaties for fertility and nurture of humans and, later, of their domesticated stock. As we saw in the previous chapter, Gimbutas thinks that the "doubling" marks inscribed on some figures express the wish for twin foals.[7] As we said, it may be so.

---

[4]"If cattle and horses, or lions, had hands, or were able to draw with their feet and produce the works which men do, horses would draw the forms of gods like horses, and cattle like cattle, and they would make the gods' bodies the same shape as their own." Xenophanes (ca. 570–ca. 475 BCE) *Fragment* 15. Montesquieu (1689–1755) paraphrased geometrically: "If triangles had a god, he would have three sides."

[5]It is no accident that one name for aberrant behavior is "lunacy" ("moonstruck"). Lupus, the condition that probably gives rise to the notion of werewolves, is affected by light.

[6]See Dorothy Cameron, *Symbols of Birth and Death in the Neolithic Era* (London: Kenyon-Deane, 1981). Also, E. O. James, *Origins of Sacrifice* (Port Washington NY: Kennikat Press, 1971 [1933]) 24.

[7]Gimbutas, *Language of the Goddess*, 161-74.

It could not have taken long for our Mesolithic ancestors to make some connection between intercourse and pregnancy, though false theories of how women might become pregnant were not immediately put to flight. Humans 12,000 years ago had domestic dogs—mammals with short gestation periods to observe—and egg-laying birds.

Other appeals would have been for rain, or, in the case of later Egypt, the Nile flood, and for such things as success in the hunt, or the regular return of seasonal game or fish. As we know from totemic societies, the chief item of diet is often either itself deified or has a deity connected with it.[8]

Religion, however, is a process. As civilizations evolved, so did our religions.[9] It is likely that early religion was animist. Simply stated: what moves, lives. How else explain the motion of sun and moon, wind, sea, and stars? In a polytheistic society, although not only there, deities might wax and wane in importance. This would largely depend upon their "performance" of our requests. The musical *Camelot* contains an amusing example of a divine patron falling out of favor. Guinevere, distraught at being sent from France to England to marry King Arthur, runs away and sings this complaint to her patron saint:

St. Genevieve, I've run away, / Eluded them and fled;
And from now on I intend to pray / To someone else instead.[10]

For prescientific humans, though, effective religion was scarcely a source of amusement; they had no certainty that tomorrow would resemble today, and life itself too often hung in the balance. As Erich Neumann says, "Exposed to the dark forces of the world and the unconscious, early man's life feeling is necessarily one of constant endangerment."[11]

---

[8]Freud, *Totem and Taboo* (New York: Vintage, 1918). Durckheim, in Pals, *Seven Theories of Religion*, 103-108.

[9]Edward B. Tylor's progression: animism < animatism < polytheism < henotheism < monotheism is doubtlessly too simple, but many peoples have believed that even so-called inanimate objects have indwelling spirits: how much more so things that move? The totemism of hunting clans might have evolved into a polytheism that will have included a rain god, a fertility goddess/earth mother, the sun, moon, Venus, and, at some point, constellations.

[10]Alan Jay Lerner (music by Frederick Loewe), "Where Are the Simple Joys of Maidenhood?" *Camelot* (1960).

[11]Erich Neumann, *The Origins and History of Consciousness*, trans. R. F. C. Hull, Bollingen series 42 (repr.: Princeton NJ: Princeton University Press, 1970) 40.

Thus, disastrous natural events, which ancient humans could not explain, might also produce changes in belief. For example, on Easter Island the religion represented by the famous megalithic heads was replaced by another, equally unsuccessful, one as the inhabitants' civilization failed.

Conversely, Blenkinsopp regards the Book of Jonah as a sapiential (from the Wisdom tradition), antiprophetic work that speaks to situations in which predicted disasters don't happen.[12]

What the people fleeing the Black Sea flood thought was the cause of their flight may be backread from the various flood stories it seems to have spawned: divine caprice or, alternatively, righteous anger at human sinfulness. In the Gilgamesh epic (tablet XI), the lesser gods themselves, cowering, flee to heaven to escape, while those responsible for the deluge regret their decision. Just such a disaster, I think, is behind the dawning of a belief in One God. I will return to this idea in chapter 7, but note here that the monotheism for which Israel is often credited—perhaps the first revolution in human thought—is at least the seventh great human revolution. It comes after those caused by the development of speech (40,000 years ago), domestication of animals (12,000), deliberate farming (8,000) metallurgy (4,500), writing (3,500), and urbanization (3,000).

§3. Sensory Data

Nothing is in the mind that has not been in the senses. . . .

—Locke, as paraphrased by Leibniz[13]

Modern psychology has shown the deficiency of Locke's statement, but most people do organize and relate to their universe mainly through sensory data. According to Steven Toulmin, Empedocles' Greeks divided their world into four basic elements—Earth, Air, Fire, and Water—

---

[12]Joseph Blenkinsopp, *A History of Prophecy in Israel* (Philadelphia: Westminster, 1983) 268-73. Michael A. Fishbane, *Biblical Interpretation in Ancient Israel* (Oxford: Clarendon, 1986) 285-86.

[13]John Locke (1632–1704), arguing for empiricism over reason or rationalism—following Aquinas who followed Aristotle—said that "Nothing exists in the mind not first presented to the senses. Our knowledge, in other words, is always limited to the natural world" (*Essay concerning Human Understanding*, 1690). In his refutation of Locke, Gottfried Wilhelm Leibniz (1646–1716) paraphrased Locke, "Nothing is in the mind that has not been in the senses," but added "*except the mind itself*" (*New Essays on Human Understanding* [1703, pub. 1765] bk. 2, chap. 1).

because, in their steep-sided, volcanic homeland that's simply what they saw.[14]

In the *Phaedo*, Plato identifies sight and hearing as superior senses.[15] As Leonardo da Vinci observed, sight has the furthest range. (In descending order of "range," the senses are [1] sight; [2] hearing; [3] smell; [4] touch; [5] taste.) The Bible agrees, at least in regard to the first two: Job says, "I had heard of you with the hearing of the ear, but now I see you with the seeing of the eye . . . and repent in dust and ashes" (Job 42:5-6). We still say that "seeing is believing."

Our own sense of smell no doubt encouraged us to burn animal sacrifices in order to carry prayers "up" to the gods. The Gilgamesh epic speaks of gods, unfed for seven days, hungrily scarfing up the odor of tardy sacrifices, and 2 Kings 18:5 claims that Israelites were still offering incense to the Bronze Serpent Moses had allegedly made, five hundred years later.[16]

Sacrifices, even of humans, have been widely used to propitiate deities. A trenchant example of this may be inferred from Flag Fen, on England's low-lying east coast. Around 1400 BCE, the Fenians seem to have sacrificed a fine imported quern, then a roe deer, and finally a teenaged human male, in a vain attempt to appease the deity who was flooding them out as the climate changed over a period of years. As mentioned previously, mummified children sacrificed only 500 years ago have recently been found high in the mountains of Peru. Their deaths were meant to ensure that the mountains would provide life-giving rain.

The practice was abhorrent to later Israel, but was this always the case? Two Israelite Kings, Ahaz in the eighth century and Manasseh in the seventh, engaged in such human sacrifice. In Exodus 13:2 God demands that that which "opens the womb" of man and beast be dedicated to him. The planet Saturn was often seen as the god that demanded this sort of sacrifice, not as a "thank offering," but because it

---

[14]Steven Toulmin, *Night Sky At Rhodes* (New York: Harcourt, Brace & World, 1964) 33-38.

[15]Plato says that seeing and hearing are the superior senses, no doubt because they have the furthest range. We see the stars, hear the roar of a distant ocean. Odors can also be detected at some distance, but touch and taste require contact.

[16]Abraham's third wife's name, Keturah, means "incense," which, I think, represents what he and other traders brought from Saudi Arabia. Of Keturah's six "children," four bear recognizable Saudi place names.

was believed that the god himself had engendered the first offspring and that it was proper to return the firstborn to its male parent. Beneath the plain reading of the Exodus text, I think, lurks the idea that the offspring is God's because he physically put it there.

Jewish tradition comes closest to this idea when it reports that *nephilim* (Gen. 6:4) were the offspring of divine beings cohabiting with human women. Divine paternity would not be at all foreign to Greeks, and in the case of Jesus' parentage it is a matter of faith for Christians.

Perhaps the most widely practiced, because various, forms of religious discerning or influencing the will of the gods can be gathered under the rubric "divination." Even today the Yoruba of Nigeria practice it on a daily basis. We may be certain that it was also a feature of daily life in the ancient Near East. Various means of divination were used, of which the best known is hepatoscopy, the reading of sheep livers. Other forms of divination include: libanomancy, "reading" the pattern of smoke from burning incense; lecanomancy, the pouring of oil on water or the reverse, a practice engaged in by Mesopotamian "doctors"; belomancy, a random act such as shooting an arrow into the air and "reading" its flight and landing place;[17] cledonomancy, giving weight to a chance remark heard or elicited from a stranger because he/she might be a god; psephomancy, interpreting the fall of pebbles or bones from a container—as Queequeg does in Melville's *Moby-Dick*. These are popular, perhaps because they are inexpensive, methods of induction, eliciting the divine response.[18]

> *Urim and Thummim are a kind of lot used by Israelite priests. In a kind of psephomancy, they can decide between two alternatives. They were used, for example, to determine that the family of one Achan had violated the herem—a ban against looting imposed on Israel at the conquest of Ai—and to choose Saul as Israel's first king.*

Divination has echoes in the Bible. Joseph famously used his wine cup for divination, probably by reading its lees, the patterns of sediment left at the bottom, in much the same way that modern psychics "read" tea leaves. Here Joseph was probably following an Egyptian practice, as he did in interpreting dreams. Joseph's dream interpretation is too well

---

[17]Some people do this without going outside, by opening their Bibles at random and reading the first verse their eyes fall upon.

[18]See William Hallo and William K. Simpson, *The Ancient Near East: A History* (New York: Harcourt, Brace, Jovanovich, 1971).

known to need rehearsing here, but we may note that there are Egyptian texts that tell their readers what various things seen in dreams portend. (Luckily for us, Joseph's pharaoh doesn't seem to have had a copy.)

Taste may be represented by the psalmist's "taste and see that the LORD is good" (Psa. 34:8) and by Ezekiel's scroll that "tasted as sweet as honey" (3:3). That this last use is metaphoric matters not to European Orthodox Jews, who use the practice of putting honey on leaves of the Talmud to make Ezekiel's words more than a figure of speech. Note also Isaiah's Temple vision (chap. 6), which begins with a messenger from God touching a glowing coal to the prophet's lips, fitting him to speak the Word.

It's not a "sixth sense," but we also need to note, even if we cannot puzzle out, what the dreams of human beings meant to them before and after they had speech. Sagan is right when he observes that "by and large we invest the dream content with reality."[19] The Bible certainly does, stating that God communicates with prophets in dreams—and not only with prophets.

All of these divinatory methods necessarily depend upon the senses, but lumping all sense data together would be too simple. More to the point, no sensory impressions cross the threshold of religion, I think, until we have speech. What may be inferred from the earliest, datable human expressions of the time after humans began to speak?

§4. What Ties Us Together

[T]he forms of the earth correspond to the forms of the heavens; the stains on the skin are a mark of incorruptible constellations. —Jorge Borges[20]

Note that the word "religion" comes from the Latin *res ligare*, "things that tie us together." This can be best appreciated when one stands inside one of the great cathedrals of Europe, such as Chartres or Erfurt or St. Mark's in Venice, and realizes how many generations of people were occupied in building such edifices. Society, then, is a whole that is greater than the sum of its parts, but it cannot remain that way unless something keeps the parts from grinding upon each other.

Freud says that religion performs this function by dictating norms to individuals, keeping us from acting on our natural impulses toward

---

[19]Sagan, *Dragons of Eden*, 154.
[20]Jorge Borges, *Ficciones* (New York: Grove Press, 1962) 153.

murder, incest, and cannibalism.[21] Such activities are antithetical to the construction of great civilizations. In repeating this, however, I don't wish to neglect a component that we usually omit from consideration: ancient Near Eastern societies also included the dead.

A Sumerian hymn castigates the Amorite (="Westerner") "who does not bury his dead companion,"[22] as though to be human meant to practice inhumation. Burial, however, meant more than simple disposal of corpses, just as the grave goods from nearly 10,000 years before the rise of Sumer are more than decoration of the corpse. A Natufian chief who was buried facing Mt. Hermon had a skull decorated with cowrie shells and dentalia.[23] Since cowrie shells resemble female genitalia and are often colored red when used in this way, what we witness here could also reflect a belief in rebirth.[24]

Later, ossuaries—stone sarcophagi containing the bones of dead ancestors—were sometimes brought into the houses of the living, and plastered skulls have been found under thresholds, for example, at Neolithic Jericho. In both cases the ancestors thus represented could presumably be appealed to for guidance and guarding. This strongly implies a belief in the continued existence of the spirits of the dead; what once had life might live again.

That being so, graves of whatever sort were portals between this world and the next It also mattered where one's bones were laid, because proper burial effected where and even whether one entered the next world. The tombs of Egyptian pharaohs provide the most elaborate evidence for this belief, but it may also be inferred from elaborate European shaft graves such as Gavrinis in Normandy, which according to Gimbutas represent a return to the womb of earth from whence one is reborn.[25]

The Egyptian official, Sinuhe,[26] left a comfortable life in Lebanon for an uncertain reception in Egypt in order to be buried in his native land.

---

[21]Freud, *The Future of an Illusion* (Garden City NY: Doubleday, 1964).

[22]Feyerick et al., *Genesis: World of Myths and Patriarchs*, 96.

[23]Mellaart, *Earliest Civilizations of the Near East*, 27, illus. 8.

[24]It is possible that, despite Dorothy Cameron's assertion (see above, 68), these were intended for decoration, but I do not think so. Often the shells were found far from their place of origin and, in addition, many skulls were painted with red ocher, supporting the idea that some continued life or rebirth was expected.

[25]Gimbutas on rebirth: *Language of the Goddess*, 207, 215, 219, etc.

[26]"The Tale of Sinuhe" dates from ca. 1960 BCE, ANET[2] 18-22.

Similar beliefs may be inferred from the Bible's stories. For example, Abraham could not bury his wife without buying the property in which she was to be interred. Great-grandson Joseph, despite his success in Egypt, opined that his bones would not be comfortable resting there, so he made his family promise to carry his remains back to Canaan (Gen. 50:25-26), which his great-grandnephew Moses duly did (Exod. 13:19).

Belief in a netherworld is apparent in early monarchic Israel, too. Saul called up the shade of Samuel who, though greatly angered at being disturbed, appeared. Where was he coming from? The Bible's word for this place of the dead is *sheol*, not a place of punishment or reward, but merely the total of all graves and the abode of their spirit-residents. Punishment and reward seem to belong in the domain of the living and to be the province of sky deities, the Sun and the Moon.

§5. "You Are My Sunshine"   —Louisiana Governor Jimmy Davis

Long before the French King Louis XIV named himself the "Roi de Soleil," the Mesopotamian kings Azitawadda and Hammurabi[27] called themselves the Sun. Like a king, the sun is the dispenser of judgment, but for most ancient Near Eastern people the sun (Sumerian *UTU*; Heb. *shemesh)* is worthy of reverence because of its sheer power. It gives the "reward" of crop growth and the "punishment" of drought.

From his name, Samson (Heb. *Shimshon,* from *shemesh)* was long thought to be derived from a sun myth, but this is no longer held (see below). Such an identification did not wash, or should not have, in Israelite circles. Prof. Nahum Sarna taught me that Psalm 19:6 carefully says the sun is only *"like* a bridegroom."

God asks Job: "Where were you when I laid the earth's foundations? . . . When the morning stars sang together . . . ?" (Job 38:4a, 7a NJPS). As a God-fearing Hebrew should, Job denied worshipping any celestial bodies:

> If I have looked at the sun [Heb. light] when it shone,
>   or the moon moving in splendor,
> and my heart has been secretly enticed,
>   and *my mouth has kissed my hand* [emphasis added: see below];

---

[27]Hammurabi's dates are 1792–1750 BCE according to Saggs, *Greatness That Was Babylon,* 503. His name means "the sun [god] is my healer."

this also would be an iniquity to be punished by the judges,
for I should have been false to God above. (Job 31:26-28 NRSV)

Note that the Akkadian syllables *KA* ⊨⊣ "mouth" + *ŠU* ⊨ "hand" = "pray." This indicates that, had Job *kissed his hand*—that is, had he *prayed*—to these celestial objects, he would have been deserving of the punishments that had come upon him. After all, in 1 Kings 19:18 God spared only 7,000 in Israel: "every knee that has not knelt to Baal and *every mouth that has not kissed him*" (NJPS; emphasis added).[28] Is kissing an image of the deity, then, or your hand to it, a standard expression of devotion? It would certainly seem so. In the ancient Near East kissing even a representation of the deity was more than a pious gesture. The deity was immanent, in some sense residing in his icon.[29]

Even today, the line between icon and "object of veneration" may be hard to draw; the stone statue of St. Peter at St. Peter's in Rome has had its right great toe actually kissed off by generations of pilgrims, while of course the practices of kissing the house mezuzah and the passing Torah scroll are well known in Jewish circles.

Similarly, the Egyptian determinatives for "adore" and "praise" are both men with raised hands/arms.[30] As we saw in chapter 3, the earliest alphabet, from around 1900 BCE, features as its fifth letter a human stick figure with arms raised. Among the well-known fourteenth/thirteenth-century basalt group found at Hazor is one featuring a pair of hands raised to the moon.

Later Jews, of course, would deny that the sun or moon were ever objects of veneration because veneration of such gods became apostasy (see chap. 13). But it was not always so. We may infer from the Bible itself that far into recorded history Israelites continued to regard planets either as sources of life to be worshipped or as dangerous powers to be propitiated. Even into modern times Jewish stones on graves of *cohanim*

---

[28]But see the problematic Psalm 2:11b-12a.

[29]Thorkild Jacobsen, "The Graven Image," in *Ancient Israelite Religion*, ed. Patrick Miller, Paul Hanson, and S. Dean McBride (Philadelphia: Fortress, 1987) 15-32. This is similar, perhaps, to the "holy people" of the Navajo. See Amanda Porter, *Power of Religion* (New York: Oxford, 1998).

[30]Gardiner, *Egyptian Grammar*, 442, 445.

(descendants of the priestly line) feature two hands—giving the Priestly Benediction.[31]

Our problem isn't simply trying to shed light on the patriarchal period, though, but also to penetrate the "cultural coulisses" (the phrase comes from Thomas Mann's *Joseph and His Brothers*) of the preceding millennia. To guide us, Braudel's *Annaliste* idea of *la longue duree* applied to pre-Israelite history suggests that "patriarchal religion" was close enough in time to the Neolithic (farming) revolution, and even more so to the Bronze Ages, that practices and beliefs from those remote periods might still be reflected in the second millennium, the time of Abram.

Can we, may we, look heavenward for religious beliefs that Israel ultimately inherited? Can we or should we try to see archaic ideas at work in, under, or behind premonarchic, even prepatriarchal practices? Helmer Ringgren suggests, "It is not worth the effort to isolate those religious concepts and practices of later Israel. . . . and read them back into the patriarchal period."[32] The caution is well taken, but to turn our backs on an even remoter past is to concede that monotheism owes nothing to what preceded it.

Tradition presents Abram's spiritual departure as, if not self-generating, then springing full-blown from God's forehead. Even if this were so, we want to know the religion of the parents from whom Abraham allegedly broke. Genesis doesn't say anything about the religion of his parents, a deficiency addressed by later *midrashim*, but the biblical text does give us some hints.

Ur and Haran, the cities Abram is associated with, were centers of moon worship.[33] The names of Terah, Abram's father, and Jericho, the city of his nephew, Lot, are both from the root $\sqrt{y\text{-}r\text{-}h}$ (moon). His wife Sarah's name is cognate with Akkadian *šarratu* (= Ningal, wife of Sin, the moon). The evidence seems to suggest that Abram/Abraham's ancestors were moon worshippers, something that should come as no

---

[31]Arnold Schwartzman, *Graven Images* (New York: H. Abrams, 1993) 12.

[32]Helmer Ringgren, *Israelite Religion*, 2nd ed. (London: SPCK, 1969) 26-27.

[33]In Hebrew "moon" is masculine, and in Ur III (Sumer, ca. 2100–2000) the moon is represented as a young bull with crescent horns—as is Ugaritic El—and a beard(!) of lapis lazuli. There is a similar representation of Nabonidus, king of Babylon from the seventh century, just before the Hebrews cast up in Babylon. Moon worship remains very important (see Stephanie Dalley's map).

surprise so deep into the era that began with the "farming revolution" (more on this in chap. 12).

§6. Once in a Blue Moon

You plant roots in the old moon.
If you plant in the full moon you get only tops.   —Lodovico Somenzi
Bread is something more than carnal fodder.
                                                —A. De St. Exupery (*Flight to Oran*)

When people began to practice deliberate agriculture some 8,000 to 10,000 years ago, the sun was important for growing crops, but the moon even more so. Not only does the moon mark months—as the etymologies of both words tell us[34]—but its phases also signal useful information, as the above quote of my wife's grandfather tells us. Farmers needed to know times and seasons for planting and harvesting. For example, the heliacal rising of the constellation Pleiades (May 1st) marks the spring planting season. If Pleiades is bright, farmers plant early; if dull, later. This is because Pleiades' brightness is a function of atmospheric water vapor, which is a growth factor for young plants. Did our early farming ancestors know this? Well, they had a long stretch of time in which to puzzle it out.

It's not accidental that the earliest piece of Canaanite writing we have is what seems to be the schoolchild's exercise tablet we have mentioned above, the Gezer Calendar, recording the twelve months of the agricultural year.

Two months of ingathering.
Two months of sowing.
Two months of late sowing
Month of pulling flax.
Month of barley harvest.
Month when everything [else] is harvested.
Two months of pruning [vines].
Month of summer fruit.[35]

---

[34]Alexander Marshack, *The Roots of Civilization: The Cognitive Beginnings of Man's First Art, Symbol and Notation* (London: Weidenfeld & Nicolson, 1972), thinks markings found on bones in the Dordogne indicate moon phases, reflecting a practice of the Bay of Bengal Nicobar Islanders today.

[35]D. Winton Thomas, *Documents from Old Testament Times* (DOTT) (New York: Harper, 1958) 201.

Note that although there are twelve months, there are only eight "seasons," a fact that will be important later in this discussion.

Long before agriculture, however, another human connection with the moon was apparent. The congruence of moon months and the menstrual cycle in women is arguably the most important single sense datum in human consciousness.[36] Why? Menstruation—note that our word for it comes from Latin *mensis*, "month"—is mysterious: women bleed but do not die.[37] It is universal, happening to all women at puberty. Furthermore, when women live together, for example in college dormitories, they quickly get on a congruent menstrual cycle. If that's so today, how much more so 10,000 years ago, and how much more powerful would this be in the consciousness of tribespeople?

> *The sequestering of menstrual women is still practiced in many societies, for instance among Samaritans in modern Israel; practices of* niddui, *family purity, among observant Jews famously continues to reflect the sense of awe and fear regarding the phenomenon of bleeding without dying—as well as providing overworked women with a religiously mandated respite from domestic duties.*

It is possible that in the Bronze Age, lifelong poor diet or other factors made the menstrual cycle slightly longer than it is today. Christopher Knight asserts that the cycle used to last twenty-nine and a half days.[38] If so, then menstruation would always take place at the same time in the lunar month. When? Grahn asserts that ovulation took place in the full moon, so menstruation would coincide with the dark of the moon.[39] It would be singularly appropriate for women to perform the dark

---

[36]Judy Grahn, *Blood, Bread, and Roses: How Menstruation Created the World* (Boston: Beacon, 1993).

[37]Menstruation involves the issue of blood, in which is the "life force" (Hebrew *nephesh hayyah*), that Leviticus forbids Israelites to consume. This ultimately leads to the Jewish Orthodox practice of abstaining from intercourse both during the menstrual period and for a week thereafter. H. Sigerist, *A History of Medicine* (London: Oxford University Press, 1951) 280, reports that the Egyptians had a charm against menstrual flow—which, no doubt, worked.

[38]Christopher Knight, "Menstrual Revolution," *Tikkun* 7:3 (May/June 1992): 45-48, 88-94.

[39]Grahn, *Blood, Bread, and Roses*, 14. Katherine H. Baker, Penn State University, confirms this (personal communication).

and mysterious act of menstruating during the period of no moon (whence our "New Moon" and its attendant rituals).

Because of this connection, it would seem that the moon should be seen as feminine, like the Romans' Diana, but this is not always the case. Whether the moon is seen as male or female, however, its perceived connection with child bearing is the same. The moon "controls" pregnancy, as it were, by informing women whether or not they are carrying. Deuteronomy 21:10-14 rules that captive women be given a month to "mourn their mothers and fathers," but the word used is *yareah*, "moon," not *hodesh*, "month," and obviously means a period sufficient to determine whether or not they are pregnant.

It would be natural for childless women such as biblical Hannah to petition the moon for a conception. We do not know to whom Hannah (1 Sam. 1:12; ca. 1050) was praying, but in Canaan, Astarte and Anath were known as "goddesses who conceive but bear not," an identification that may underlie the Greeks' virgin moon goddess, Artemis. Alternatively, she might invoke protection from Lamashtu, the she-demon who affects pregnant women and nursing mothers.

That some sort of moon-goddess worship was going on for a very long time we can infer from the fertility figurines that dot the archaeological landscape even in Israel at all periods. They didn't all belong to the Canaanite "hired help," as later Judaism clumsily asserts.

> *Centuries later European Judaism was still forbidding Jews to marry on Monday because it was "governed" by the moon. How far back this prohibition goes I cannot determine. Judaism finally dealt with lunar phenomena by co-opting the period of the New Moon as a time for women's prayer. Modern Judaism retains Rosh Hodesh (the New Moon) as a female holiday, though much paled in importance from what presumably was once the case.*

Goddess worship was largely suppressed in the biblical text, so its place and persistence in Israel is only beginning to be understood. Tikvah Frymer-Kensky considers the Israelite use of female figurines to be non-divine, a "tolerated nonconformist worship" and no threat to Israel's god in the way that, say, Ba'al was. She says, "[T]hey are a kind of tangible prayer for fertility and nourishment."[40] As we shall see in chapter 8, this may be too mild a judgment.

One clue to the importance of female deities, or deities for females, is the biblical history remembering that King Asa deposed his own mother from the "office" of queen mother (1 Kings 15:13) because she made an *asherah*, that is, an iconic green tree or pole. Why was it erected? To insure female fertility. The same or other asherahs were removed twice more by reforming kings (Josiah, 2 Kings 23:4; Hezekiah, 2 Chron. 29:16); obviously the first two "asherah-ectomies" weren't successful.

I discuss this more fully in chapter 8. For the present, I would simply say that, given that women's status in Middle Eastern communities was (and remains) so heavily dependent upon producing (male) children, it would be hard to fault Hannah or anyone else for "hedging her bets."

§7. Who Was That Lady?

"Hail to thee, Alma Mater" —college song

We know that goddess worship has a respectably ancient pedigree, going back as much as 30,000 years. Even if we no longer worship goddesses overtly, we still refer to Mother Nature and Mother Earth—it is the earth, of course, from which crops spring. The use of capital letters indicates our usual tendency to assign nature and the earth a personality and gender (typically female).[41]

In Hebrew the female earth (*adamah*) provides the material from which God makes *'adam*, "man." If the relationship between these two quickly becomes disharmonious, it is in a sense the paradigm for a struggle for supremacy between "female" and "male" principles. Such contests are hardly unique to the Hebrews.

Enuma elish, the Babylonian creation epic, is usually read as the triumph of Marduk, the city-god of Babylon, over Ti'amat, the unruly saltwater ocean who constantly threatens to engulf the dry land.[42] But on another level, *Enuma elish* could also bear the meaning of patriarchal

---

[40]Tikvah Frymer-Kensky, *In the Wake of the Goddesses* (New York: Free Press, 1992) 159.

[41]Gimbutas, *Language of the Goddess*, 141-59 and elsewhere.

[42]The *Enuma elish* can be found in Alexander Heidel, *Babylonian Genesis* or in ANET[2] 60-98.

religion, backed and made necessary by the development of metal tools and weapons, supplanting the earlier matriarchalism sometime in or after the mid-fourth millennium. If not, why should Marduk be male and his major adversary, Ti'amat, female?[43]

It is from *tehom* "the deep" of Genesis 1:2, cognate with Ti'amat, that we backread our theologically inspired order-out-of-watery-chaos. The Bible also identifies *tehom* as feminine in the majority of cases, but not in all—for reasons I cannot confidently explain.[44]

However, I propose that the common identification of the sea with chaos is not merely a theoretical observation or some external manifestation of the infantile human psyche. If, indeed, it is to be connected with these things, is it not also the dim echo of actual events? How often was there significant flooding such as we noted in chapter 2, namely, the massive eruption into the Black Sea of the Mediterranean about 5500 BCE? This happened close enough to historical times to have left its imprint in our memory, and it could not have been explained by those who survived it in any way except as a conflict among gods. What moves, lives. But not all of our deities move.

§8. "Rocky Mountain High" —John Denver

Has the rain a father . . . ? (Job 38:28a NRSV)

As we observed in chapter 2, many societies have sacred mountains. In the ancient Near East names construed with *-hr* "mountain," such as Jacob-har and 'Anat-har have been found, for example, borne by Hyksos rulers in Egypt in the mid-second millennium. Obviously, the second element has a theophoric meaning; the mountain is a deity. In that case, we may ask, What is its gender?

Mountains are often seen as explicitly feminine and so named, from the Paps of Jura in Scotland to the Grand Teton of Wyoming. Why? Like Gerizim and Ebal, the two close-set mountains at biblical Shechem (modern Nablus), high hills not only resemble women's breasts, but also like breasts they "give" life-sustaining rain.

---

[43]If water is usually female, this will be because oceans, lakes, and rivers give forth fish, like women giving birth to human offspring. Moreover, the human birth process is accompanied by release of a salty "water," the amniotic fluid.

[44]Similarly, at Ugarit, Ba'al's enemies are Prince Sea and Judge River, both identified as male.

With our bloodless scientism, we explain rainfall as due to condensation
of water vapor as it rises over mountains and cools to the point where
it precipitates. But I have stood on the eastern ridge of Jerusalem and
watched menacing rain clouds roll up, then disappear as they pass over
the deep Jordan valley, only to reappear over the Jordanian plateau;
mountains give rain.

Paradoxically, rain, the fructifying fluid that causes plants to grow,
is exclusively masculine (eighty-seven times) in Scripture. The association
seems rather with sperm than breast milk.

The name Shaddai has been identified as cognate with Akk. *sedu*,
"demons," but this makes no sense to me. Some scholars think El
Shaddai, the name that God tells Moses was the one used in patriarchal
times, is connected with the root √*š-d* "breast." If so, the Tetragrammaton, the name of the masculine god revealed to Moses, represents a
step away from the "female principle" of creation/nourishment/guidance
and toward the male. Another may be Israel's use of the epithet "my
Rock" for its God.

The point here is that there are many beliefs and practices from pre-
Israelite times that have been incorporated with appropriate modifications
into Israel's scheme. Nor does the appropriation of previous sancta stop
with Israel.

§9. Fish Story

"I will make you fishers of men." —Jesus (Matthew 4:19 RSV)

Christianity's choice of the fish as a symbol is neither coincidental nor
merely dependent upon the fact that the early disciples were fishermen.
The traditional explanation that *ichthus* (Gk. "fish") is an acronym for the
Greek title meaning "Jesus Christ, Son of God, Savior," does not explain
the mystical power the symbol was thought to have in the early Christian
era. Rather, it is probably an example of taking over symbols that were
used in earlier worship. Far earlier.

Catching migratory fish, which seems to date from about 14,000 BCE,
is an early and relatively easy form of hunting. Peoples who lived on
coasts where they already harvested shellfish could observe eagles, bears,
or whatever other land-based fish-catchers they lived near, catching
returning salmon. Salmon do not now run so far south as to be fished
from rivers flowing into the eastern Mediterranean, but was this always

the case? The last Ice Age must have pushed salmon (or similar fish runs such as shad, smelt, or herring) far to the south of where they are now. People wouldn't have known—any more than bears or eagles did—why these fish returned every year, or even if they would continue to do so. Consequently, fisherfolk would seek to insure the return by appropriate rituals before and/or after the catch. North American Chinook Indians, named after the Chinook salmon, throw their fish bones back into the sea thinking that they re-form there to return the following year. And by the logic of *post hoc ergo propter hoc*, they do, or at least they did until dams on the rivers made this impossible.

We have seen a similar logic in the ancient Near East. That Nanna, the moon, "causes carp-flood in the rivers"[45] is a primitive way Akkadians recognized the coincidence of fish runs with a certain moon phase. Though they would be unable to explain daily and monthly tidal fluctuations in the terms of modern science, they would note that these regularly recurring phenomena were connected with the moon.

It has been suggested that Jonah's adventure with a "great fish" (*dag gadol* is *not* a whale) masks a Philistine or other fish cult such as that of Athirat-yam on the Mediterranean coast.[46] The Philistine god Dagon, known to the Bible as a cereal god, probably began life as a fish god, especially if the Philistines were originally Mediterranean islanders. A shift from fish to cereals as their main dietary staple would explain the change.[47] That the fourth letter of the Hebrew alphabet, *dalet*, stands for *dag*, fish, is further evidence for the importance of fish. So is Deuteronomy 4:18's specific prohibition of fish worship.

---

[45]Athirat-yammi is goddess/patroness of fisherfolk. (See Frymer-Kensky, *Wake of the Goddesses*, 156.) Note the later story of Atargatis and her son Ichthys being thrown into the sea (or a lake) at Ascalon, one of five Philistine cities, where they were swallowed by fish and rescued by Poseidon. Robert Graves, *The Greek Myths*, 2 vols. (Baltimore: Penguin, 1955) 2:253, cites one Xanthus of Lydia as claiming that Ascalon was founded by Greeks.

[46]Frymer-Kensky, *Wake of the Goddesses*, 156.

[47]This view is supported by Cyrus H. Gordon, *Ugarit and Minoan Crete* (New York: W. W. Norton, 1966) 24. In Hebrew, "bread" also means "food," while in Arabic *basr* means both "flesh" and "food." (A similar synecdoche survives in the English use of "meat" meaning food, for instance in the phrase "meat and drink"; a parallel cultural trope similarly uses "bread," as in "to put bread on the table.")

§10. Disasters and Lucky Stars

"The fault, dear Brutus, is not in our stars,
But in ourselves. . . . "
—Cassius (Shakespeare, *Julius Caesar* 1.2.140-41)

For most of us nowadays, the stars are simply things of beauty to admire on cloudless nights, but for the ancients, they had both practical and metaphysical significance. One *can* sail from Egypt to Denmark without losing sight of land, but the Minoans of Crete, to name one seafaring people, must have to be able to read the stars or they would never have come home from the sea. Until the invention of the magnetic compass in modern times, such stars as Thuban in Draco and the Big Dipper's Polaris, and constellations such as Orion were invaluable aids in navigation or land travel—for example, to Christianity's Magi.

If there is any truth to the tradition, what the Wise Men saw was not a supernova, but a triple conjunction of Mars, Saturn, and Jupiter that occurred about 8/7 BCE in that part of the sky which the Babylonians called "the House of the Hebrews."

Planets owe their reputation for strange, wandering behavior to the fact that they ride on the line of the earth's equator; that is, all are in the same plane and not on the ecliptic as the stars are, so, seen from the earth, they sometimes appear to go backwards like distant objects seen through a moving train's window. (How old is knowledge of this sort?)

The five "wandering stars" (planets) were seen lined up as early as the twenty-fifth pre-Christian century by Chinese observers,[48] and Job 38:33 knows that stars have regular routes. Ptolemy, the second-century Greek astronomer, held that the earth is overarched by seven heavens—hence, our expression "I'm in seventh heaven"—ruled by the sun, the moon, and the five planets visible to the naked eye, namely, Mars, Mercury, Jupiter, Venus, and Saturn (to give them the order they retain in latinate day names). Ptolemy's system is much later, but it's worth noting that he also counted forty-eight constellations.

Actually, the skies abound with 6,000 fixed stars, 2,500 of which are visible in a hemisphere, singly or in constellations.

---

[48]With von Dechend and de Santillana, *Hamlet's Mill*, I think the knowledge of constellations and their precession is very old.

With all this, we still cannot be sure that Neolithic peoples had a thoroughgoing knowledge of astronomy, but some celestial objects would have been known from earliest times.

Venus, the third brightest object in our sky, is often symbolized by an eight-pointed star and represented as part of a triad with the sun and moon.[49] It reaches its highest point above the horizon in spring and hence marks the spring mating season. Jewish Purim, the festival that begins with a king of Persia choosing a Jewish "mate," covers and co-opts this (see below). Our acknowledgement of Venus as the Goddess of Love is a vestige of this earlier identification.[50]

Sirius, the Dog Star, is the brightest star in the sky and hence its fourth-brightest object. Its heliacal rising after a seventy-day absence marks the start of the Nile flood and the beginning of their civil year. The Egyptians certainly knew this by 2773 BCE, and by inference perhaps as early as 4233. *We* know that Sirius does not cause the Nile flood, but to the Egyptians the star was Sothis, a goddess, who made the Nile rise. By following the logic of "what comes before causes what comes after," as with the crowing rooster seemingly causing the sun to rise, it was natural for people to connect astral events, conjunctions, and configurations with events in the natural or human sphere. The question is, again, how early in human history did this happen?

Certainly, one of the first star groups to have attracted our attention would have been Orion, which "may lay claim to being the most glorious of all the constellations." Often known as "The Hunter of the Sky," Orion is "prominent during winter nights."[51] In Greek mythology Orion uses the net of the Pleiades to catch Taurus the Bull. Elsewhere, Orion is identi-fied with legendary heroes (Samson) or newly dead rulers (Pharaoh). A

---

[49]Venus has universal importance, but its influence is not always benign. The Mayans kept elaborate track of Venus to avert its evil. See Anthony F. Aveni, "Astronomy in Ancient Mesoamerica," in *In Search of Ancient Astronomies*, ed. Edwin C. Krupp (Garden City NY: Doubleday, 1977, 1978) 156-57.

[50]In the Esarhaddon Vassal Treaty—James B. Pritchard, ed., *The Ancient Near East*, vol. 2, *A New Anthology of Texts and Pictures* (Princeton: Princeton University Press, 1975) 63: ¶42 (428)—Venus is invoked against treaty breakers: "let your wives lie in the embrace of your enemy before your very eyes." See also Cyrus Gordon, *Ugaritic Texts*, Acta Orientalia 38 (Rome: Pontifical Biblical Institute, 1965) nos. 137 and 68.

[51]Patrick Moore, *The Amateur Astronomer*, 11th ed. (Cambridge: Cambridge University Press, 1990) 289.

recently discovered shaft in the Great Pyramid points to Orion's two first-magnitude stars, Rigel and Betelgeuse. Along with Thuban in Draco, which in early times was the North Star, Orion was important in guiding the ascent of the dead pharaoh to his merging with Osiris the god.

There may be a reflection of this in biblical tradition, also. In *Hamlet's Mill*, Giorgio de Santillana and Hertha von Dechend point out that Samson shares an unusual characteristic with Orion: both are blind.[52] But the coincidences don't end there. The Book of Judges gives much more space to Samson's rather bizarre exploits than to any of the other twelve (counting Deborah and Barak separately) personages it contains. Samson kills "thousands" of Philistines with the "jawbone of an ass," after which he is thirsty so God provides water from that selfsame jaw-bone. This seems to make little sense until we note that in *Enuma elish*, the Babylonian creation epic, Marduk snares Ti'amat with the net of the Pleiades and kills her with the (watery) Hyades, the jawbone of Taurus. Since Orion does likewise, what is the connection between these myths?

Samson's exploits, and his quick temper, are reminiscent of Hercules's, and, significantly, Samson is a Danite. We will see in chapter 6 that his tale might have come from the Mediterranean world. Is Samson the "Hebrew Hercules"? Perhaps. But it is also possible that for Israelites this connection represents an attempt to denigrate the belief in the importance of constellations while, at the same time, making Samson himself "kosher" by including him in Judges. Such a thing would also serve to give the tribe of Dan some pride of place in Israel's national history.

The Hebrew root $\sqrt{\text{k-s-l}}$ seems to give us both cesil, Orion and cesil, "stupid person," a label that might easily attach to Samson after he lets Delilah's Philistine cohorts shear, bind, and blind him.

If denigration of astral worship was the main message of the Samson story, it often fell on deaf ears. Israel was still a long way from heeding Cassius's observation quoted above. Perhaps Job didn't pray to the sun, moon, or stars, but we may be confident that some Israelites did. Ordinary people felt that their lives were influenced by what went on "up there," and consequently worshipped stars as well as God.

The Hebrew word for "constellations" (*mazzalot*) is unique, found only in 2 Kings 23:5. The otherwise total absence of this word may be

---

[52]Deshend and Santillana, *Hamlet's*, 178. For these authors, this detail is "clinching."

a silent argument indicating later Jewish suppression of the concept it originally represented. Here *mazzalot* seems to have escaped later censorship precisely because it's in the list of newly prohibited sacred sites that Josiah ordered destroyed.

> *The word* mazal *survives in the modern Hebrew expression* mazal tov. *The connotation of this phrase is "congratulations," but its ancient meaning is "(may you have a) lucky star." Each month, each week, has lucky and unlucky days—as Caesar's wife feared when she told him to "beware the ides of March"—signalled by various stars and combinations.*

§11. Pieces of Eight

asterisk . . . *n.* 1. the figure of a star (*) (*Random House Collegiate Dictionary*)

The asterisk is a star, but it is far older than the Greek derivation ("little star") in the dictionary. As a glyph, we saw that the eight-pointed star goes back as far as the Akkadian *An* sign,[53] often used as a symbol for Venus. To attempt to trace its history before the time of writing, we need to go back to the great Neolithic revolution that produced agriculture.

The Teleilat el-Ghassul rosette[54] (see below) that dates from the Chalcolithic period is six feet in diameter. What was its purpose? Congruent with Cameron's observation quoted at the beginning of this chapter, Jirku also opines this star was "not profane."[55]

When we became dependent upon cereals (1) we "promoted" their yearly growth as we did the return of fish through sympathetic magic practices and fertility rites; (2) since we knew what "vindictive" Nature could do to our crops we prophylactically offered sacrifices to this ever-

---

[53]René Labat, *Manuel d'Epigraphie Akkadienne*, 4th ed. (Paris: Imprimerie Nationale, 1963).

[54]Teleilat el-Ghassul, just northeast of the Dead Sea, is the largest known Chalcolithic site in the Jordan Valley. The 50-acre site of the town, merely a series of low mounds, would be unimpressive were it not for the remarkable paintings on some of the plaster walls of the densely packed, multiroom houses. The most famous wall painting is the so-called *Star of Ghassul*, an eight-pointed star, almost six feet across, painted with red, black, and white mineral paints, and surrounded by various mythological creatures. The function of this painting—and in fact of most of the paintings at Ghassul—is unknown. At one time, scholars thought the buildings containing the paintings might be religious shrines, but this is far from certain. (N.B.: The Chalcolithic [Copper-Stone] Period or era was ca. 4500–3200 BCE.)

[55]Anton Jirku, *The World of the Bible* (Cleveland: World, 1957) 8.

Figure 1. *The Star of Ghassul*

present, ever-hungry maw on a regular schedule, so that it would not take more later. In the case of the Bible's "first fruitings," the sacrifice was also an expression of confidence that God would supply more. How did we ascertain the right schedule?

It probably didn't take ancient Near Eastern humans long to recognize the four solstitial and equinoctial points of the year.[56] Krupp adds, "For convenience, additional sunrises, midway between each solstice and the subsequent equinox, might be noted." This would give us a calendar with eight significant points on it, which is what the rosette at el-Ghassul has. (In the Gezer Calendar, as noted above, there are twelve months, but eight, admittedly unequal, "seasons.")

Each of these periods is about ninety-one days long, but they do not in themselves mark growing seasons. Moreover, seasons vary with a society's distance from the equator, which, in turn changes the times for plant-

---

[56]Krupp, *In Search of Ancient Astronomies*, 14.

ing and harvesting. A three-harvest cycle in Canaan is evident from Ugaritic mythology. In Israel, too, there are also three, the pilgrimage festivals of Passover (wheat), Shavuot (barley), and Sukkot (tree fruits, vines). These three major harvests of Israel might have been celebrated closer to one of the eight cardinal points of the rosette, but their times have been fixed into a calendar that is keyed to the moon rather than the sun.

There are sometimes twelve, sometimes thirteen new moons in a solar year, so the festivals now shift by up to a month. In any nineteen-year period there will be seven years in which there will be a thirteenth lunation. Keeping track of the moon was so important that, as we know from megalithic alignments such as Stonehenge[57] and the Cheyenne, Wyoming, Medicine Wheel, people went to great lengths to build "machines" for this purpose.

The rather odd succession of twelve and thirteen moon-months is reflected in the twelve/thirteen tribes of Israel and the twelve/thirteen disciples of Jesus. The thirteenth moon before the new solar year will be seen as a time of peril, hence anxiety. This danger motif may be seen also in the twelve-plus-one fairies of Sleeping Beauty when number thirteen comes in, as it were, before number twelve. (See excursus, below.)

In Israel the thirteenth month, Adar II, is inserted in the spring right before the equinox. Purim (and Mardi Gras) fall at this season. And in both holidays celebrants don costumes (and masks) to confuse evil demons. European Mardi Gras celebrations included a reversal of social roles (as occurs in the Purim story) and an opportunity for mating.

§12. The Bull from Everywhere; the Serpent from Nowhere

A black bull of Poseidon, a bull from the sea. —Mary Renault[58]

The Golden Calf of Exodus is justly infamous, but we have to ask why Aaron made a calf rather than something else, say, a golden armadillo? Aaron's own explanation (Exod. 32:24 NJPS)—"They gave it [their gold] to me and I hurled it into the fire[59] and out came this calf!"—is highly

---

[57]Gerald Hawkins, *Stonehenge Decoded* (New York: Dell, 1965).

[58]Mary Renault, *The Bull from the Sea* (repr.: New York: Vintage Books, 2001; orig.: New York: Pantheon, 1962).

[59]Rabbi Solomon ben Isaac, 'Rashi,' French, eleventh century CE, glosses: "without knowing what would emerge. . . . "

suspicious.[60] A golden calf with crescent-(moon-)shaped horns is known from Ur III (2113–2006 BCE), in Mesopotamia. This is well before the time even of Abraham. Alternatively, Israelites would have encountered bull/cow worship during their Egyptian stay. Two Hathor heads top the First Dynasty Narmer Palette; the Serapeum in Memphis, resting place of the Apis bull, existed well into Christian times; Amenophis II (mid-late fifteenth century) is called "The Mighty Bull"; and the Twelfth Nome was symbolized by Zabnuti, "the divine calf." All this undermines Aaron's feigned surprise at what emerged from the fire.

Later Jewish tradition found it convenient to blame Jeroboam ben Nebat (931–909 BCE), the secessionist king of Israel, for inventing the calf. By calling Jeroboam an "innovator," traditionalists such as Samson Raphael Hirsch attempted to discredit both him and the German Reform Jews whose then-new movement was an affront to their orthodoxy. Of course, Hirsch was not the first such critic.

The charge against Jeroboam, however, is patently untrue. Bull figurines have been found in Israel in premonarchic strata at Khirbet Raddana—including, oddly enough, the *bos indicus* or Indian hump-backed bull. The bull or calf was, then, an object of worship of long standing for many Israelites. Accreditation to Aaron is likely an attempt at justification, just as Moses is credited with making the bronze serpent, *Nehushtan*. Both bull and serpent have long histories.

To the Greeks, Poseidon, Earth-Shaker, was the Bull from the Sea, and Cretan propitiation of Poseidon featured bull jumping, as Mary Renault so compellingly conjectured and Cyrus Gordon[61] proved. The modern-day running of the bulls in Pamplona, Spain, I submit, is a provincial survival of the bull dancing on Crete. But Greeks were hardly the first peoples to worship bovine deities.

---

[60]"Aaron's excuse: It just happened, I had little to do with it." *The Torah. A Modern Commentary*, 4th ed., ed. W. Gunther Plaut (New York: Union of American Hebrew Congregations, 1985; [1]1981) 648n.

[61]Cyrus Gordon, *Before the Bible. The Common Background of Greek and Hebrew Civilizations*, 2nd ed. (New York: W. W. Norton, 1965) 51-52, 70, 275-76. See also A. H. W. Curtis, "Some Observations on 'Bull' Terminology in the Ugaritic Texts and the Old Testament," *Old Testament Studies* 26 (1990): 17-31. Curtis (31) thinks YHVH, as El in the Old Testament, survived by "taking over the attributes of the storm-god."

At Çatal Hüyük in Anatolia, James Mellaart found representations of bulls, and actual heads dating to more than 8,000 years ago.[62] Even so, the appeal to a bull deity may be far older, perhaps as old as the cave paintings in northern Spain and southern France of 20,000–30,000 years ago. Why? Earthly bulls are avatars of the "Bull of Heaven," whom we know as Taurus.

In the previous chapter we saw how Taurus might have given its name to the first letter of the Hebrew *aleph-bet*; its religious significance is greater, and far older. Of the twelve zodiacal signs, perhaps the most important is Taurus, the Bull of Heaven. When the sun is in Taurus, it marks the harvest of barley, man's first grain. As we have noted, while the Gezer Calendar mentions barley, it does not mention wheat.

The constellations of the zodiac (= circle of small animals), of which Taurus is one, are found in a band running eight degrees at a twenty-three to twenty-five degree angle on both sides of the equator—called the ecliptic because they seem to rise and set. That is, they are periodically eclipsed.

If the bull needed to be accounted for by Israelite religion, so did the ancient serpent. But while the bull is beneficial, hence good, the serpent is pure evil. Why? Already in the Gilgamesh Epic (ca. 1800 BCE) the serpent is guilty of stealing the Tablets of Destiny, conferring the immortality that Gilgamesh worked so hard to acquire for humanity upon serpent-kind instead. This theft is reflected in the biblical story of Eden. As I demonstrate elsewhere,[63] there is permanent "death-hostility" between humans and serpentkind because, in robbing us of our intended immortality, they have, in effect, "murdered" every human being who dies.

Despite this fatal deception, snake worship was so deeply imbedded in pre-Israelite cultures, including among people who became part of Israel, that it could not be extirpated by even so strong a fiat as that contained in the Ten Commandments. Quite the contrary. Moses himself, at God's direction (Num. 21:8-9), constructed a Bronze Serpent so soon

---

[62]Mellaart, *Earliest*, 93. Closer to our time, Larissa Bonfante, *Etruscan Life and Afterlife* (Detroit: Wayne State Press, 1986), shows that bulls were prominent in the Etruscan belief structure.

[63]Stanley N. Rosenbaum, "Israelite Homicide Law and the Term 'eyvah in Gen. 3:15," *The Journal of Law and Religion* 2/1 (Winter 1984): 145-51.

after Sinai that one might think there was still rock dust in the grooves of the two tablets.[64]

Interestingly, despite the serpent in the Garden of Eden's identification as masculine, there is a strong feminine association with the serpent, from the pythia at Delphi and the Cretan Snake Goddess to various goddesses of Mesopotamia. Heinrich Greseman suggested that the serpent who tempted Eve was female, and connected her name with serpentkind. Medieval Christian illustrations of the Garden scene sometimes pictured the snake as female, indicating that this identification has a long, if checkered history. In *Faust* (part 1) Mephistopheles cheerfully identified the serpent as his aunt! (For more on this see below, chap. 7.)

§13. Religious Evolution

Time and chance happeneth to them all. (Ecclesiastes 9:11 KJV)

The Greeks were right about one thing: even the gods are subject to the Fates. Gods of ancient Near Eastern peoples were not immutable either, just the opposite. In Mesopotamia gods changed gender, shifted names, and waxed and waned in importance. No doubt the emphasis shifted from time to time, either amongst the gods, as with the ascendancy of Marduk, or between aspects of the same god, as with the short-lived reform of Akhenaton in Egypt.

That worship should evolve is hardly surprising. As we saw above, mutely eloquent testimony to a real succession of gods appears on Easter Island where the giant heads were supplanted by birds whose likenesses were carved in cliffs, often in places so difficult of access that more than one religious artist must have fallen to his/her death trying to achieve it. Changes, however slow, might also reflect the paradigm shifts in human societies, partly as a result of syncretism or appropriation by one society of another's gods.

It may be hazardous to look back to eras where intelligible written evidence is absent, but the "Farming Revolution" must necessarily have produced sweeping religious changes. For one thing, dependence upon crops could not help but focus attention on the parallels between "Mother" Earth and earthly mothers. Religion would have had a primary interest in promoting the fertility of the former and the fecundity of the

---

[64]Astour, *Hellenosemitica*, 90-91, connects the name Levi with the mythical serpent Leviathan.

latter. Consequently, the time between, say, 6000 and 4500 BCE would have been a period of ascendancy for female deities.

Farming kept people closer to one spot for longer periods of time than they had been in hunting and gathering societies; this would have given rise to what Lewis Mumford calls "the first cities," that is, necropolises.[65] In turn, the presence of burial grounds would itself be a powerful pull, keeping people physically closer to their ancestors.

Beginning with the advent of copper smelting, around 4500 BCE in the ancient Near East, male gods associated with tools and weapons and the strength needed to manufacture as well as to wield them tended to eclipse female goddesses. Frymer-Kensky reports that a "marginalization" of female deities is apparent from the first few centuries of Akkadian literature.[66]

> *Of course the time periods in question would vary by locale, because their ends are marked not by fixed dates, but by the times at which various societies began serious agriculture and the time that metallurgy sparked the next great revolution. For places on the periphery of civilization such as Britain, similar changes may be looked for closer to our own time.*

We might ask, what is the evidence for this religious evolution? A general answer is that all religions evolve, but we can do better than that. Transition to a straight agriculture/trade-based economy and away from dimorphic pastoralism and hunting entailed a paradigmatic shift away from the moon, too. In earlier societies, the moon had been more important than the sun; now the masculine sun began to eclipse the feminine moon because it is the sun, *UTU*, that is identified with the king.[67] Jacobsen[68] identifies Mesopotamian gods in the fourth pre-Christian millennium as "providers," because by this time ancient Near Eastern peoples were well into the agricultural revolution.

Jacobsen characterizes the gods of the next millennium, the third, as "rulers" mirroring the development of city-state empires. These in turn

---

[65]Lewis Mumford, *The City in History* (Harmondsworth: Penguin, 1961) 15.
[66]Frymer-Kensky, *Wake of the Goddesses*, 70-80.
[67]Note the prominence of the sun and crescent moon in the Ur-Nammu Stele. See Ada Feyerick, Cyrus H. Gordon, and Nahum M. Sarna, *Genesis, World of Myths and Patriarchs* (New York and London: New York University Press, 1996) 82.
[68]Jacobsen, *Treasures of Darkness*, 23-73.

are gradually superseded by second-millennium gods, whom Jacobsen says are worshiped as "parents." It's hardly surprising, therefore, to see the Hebrew Bible take the next logical half-step and refer to God as "Father."

> *Though Jacobsen's work stops at the second millennium, we needn't. Extrapolating from the line that his development suggests, we can see that the gods are ever more immanent, coming closer and closer to their human worshipers. The penultimate step on this road is found in Christianity, in which God allegedly incarnates, but this entails something that I would like to call "Friedman's Paradox." I take the idea from Richard E. Friedman's* The Disappearance of God.
>
> *Friedman argues that by entering history, God in fact becomes more distant and ultimately disappears. Jesus' death is an outstanding example of this, but Friedman traces increasing distances between God and his people through the course of Hebrew Scriptures—a trend that the Jewish tradition acknowledges but blames on our increasing unworthiness for more direct contact.*

We also owe to the Hebrews the notion of a God who is no longer simply seen in and through nature, but directing human history as well.[69] Friedrich Nietzsche's proclamation that because "God is dead" we must perforce become gods and rule our own history is an intriguing and tragic bit of human arrogance; however, it takes us far beyond the scope of the present discussion. We can say that the "problem" with a historically active God is the problem of theodicy: the rain falls on the just and the unjust alike, evildoers live comfortably long lives, and too often history seems not to reflect any divine concern for the suffering of innocent people. For Jews, if not also for Christians, the Holocaust offers dramatic proof.

---

[69]George Ernest Wright, *God Who Acts: Biblical Theology as Recital*, Studies in Biblical Theology 8 (London: SCM, 1952).

§14. A Twilight of the Gods

Every miracle can be explained—after the event. —Franz Rosenzweig[70]

Pre-Aristotelian societies could regard the same god in conflicting, complementary, or hypostatic ways, as Egyptians manifested by their multiplex treatment of Re. Egypt entertained competing cosmologies with no problems as long as society coped with its circumstances. But in the fourteenth century Egyptians and Hittites fought each other to exhaustion. This made the Hittites easy prey to migrating Sea Peoples, invaders whom the Egyptians had barely enough strength to fight off. But the failure of the ancient Near Eastern economic community at the end of the thirteenth century only added momentum to a paradigm shift that had begun much earlier. If I am correct, a shift toward patriarchal deities followed upon the development of metal technology.

New religious forms emerged and while some, such as Akhenaton's henotheism, don't seem to have succeeded, there were others that ultimately did. It is here at the cusp between the Late Bronze and Early Iron ages that we should look for the birth of Israelite monotheism.

Having said that, it is not really possible to examine the "state of 'Israelite' religion" in the last half of the second millennium because the very phrase begs the question. There was no "Israelite religion" as such then, but rather a number of religious elements that seem to have come together with centripetal force. Israel's religion seems to have come from various sources: "wandering Arameans," refugees from Egypt, Moses' Midianite fathers-in-law, "native" Canaanite sources, and migrants from Mesopotamia as well as from the Mediterranean.

Such multiple origins are consistent with and reflected by the three dozen or so divine names in Scripture, including many construed with El, such as El Shaddai, El Elyon. Many of the names are unique to the Book of Job, but El himself is now known as the father of Ba'al and 'Anat of Ugarit. Further proof of this divine plethora may be inferred from Moses' victory song, conceded to be almost contemporary with the events it describes, asking, "Who is like you among the *gods*, O Adonai?" (Exod. 15:11; emphasis added).

---

[70]Glatzer, *Franz Rosenzweig*, 290. Jon Levenson, "Is There a Counterpart in the Hebrew Bible to New Testament Anti-Semitism?" *Journal of Ecumenical Studies* 22 (1985): 247-60.

For all that, the Ten Commandments' "You shall have no other gods before me" implies that there are or then were many to choose among: prohibition presupposes previous practice. Whose gods were these? The seventy nations of the world each had their own god (Deut. 32:8, as emended by BH³).

Tradition insists it was gods of the Canaanites who too often lured Israelites into apostasy. But the picture has an entirely different cast if we acknowledge that these deities were ones that were worshipped by some of proto-Israel's own constituent elements, a fact made clear enough by Joshua's challenge to the people on the eve of the "Conquest." (See below, chap. 7.)

Early Israelite acknowledgement of the "gods of other peoples" changes over the centuries to derision and outright denial. There are, finally, no other gods. But dictating them out of existence and actually causing them to cease are two different things. It is probably 600 years after Moses' career that monotheism becomes anything like firmly established in Israel. This is the time of Josiah, and it is his well-documented reign that we will examine in the next chapter. First, however, let me invite you to enjoy the excursus on "Numbers and Numerology" that follows.

Excursus to Chapter 4

Numbers and Numerology

§1. Numerology

Things are numbers. —attributed to Pythagoras

"Ehad Mi Yodea?" ("Who Knows One?") —Passover song

Today few numbers retain any deep or symbolic meaning: Three, for the Trinity; Seven, the well-nigh universal "lucky number"—though as we shall see, Eight is more significant—and Thirteen, the principal "unlucky one" are notable exceptions. But how did all this get started?

In the world of trade and agriculture, numbers may have been invented to keep track of flocks or commodities, or the days of the month,[1] but to the ancients numbers were more than an accounting tool. Using a logic that we would reject,[2] they reasoned as follows.

The universe has order. (major premise)
Numbers describe order. (minor premise)
Therefore, numbers describe the universe.
Conclusion: numbers as such are important
    for understanding the universe.

Like most beginnings, the origin of symbolic numbers is obscure, but we can trace number symbolism back to Hammurabi, well before any Israelites could be called by that name. In the course of their history, ancient Near Easterners, like seventeenth-century Mechanists, came to see numbers as key to understanding the plan and purpose of the universe.[3]

---

[1] Schmidt-Besserandt, "Record Keeping," in Sasson et al., *Civilizations.* The Ugaritic alphabet has thirty letters, with #30 identical to #19. The megalopolitan city-state of Ugarit disappeared out of history from before Moses was born until 1929 CE, but in the Late Bronze Age it was commercially important and technically advanced. That is to say, inventors of its alphabet could not simply have run out of ideas for symbols and so duplicated one.

I think the thirty characters are chosen with a thirty-day(?) lunar month in mind, and the duplication is a built-in facility for keeping track of the nineteen-year great moon cycle.

[2] This is the fallacy of Excluded Middle. In tandem with the fallacy of *post hoc ergo propter hoc* ("what comes after is caused by what comes before"), we can see why our ancestors came to vastly different conclusions about the universe than do we.

[3] John J. Davis, *Biblical Numerology* (Grand Rapids MI: Baker Book House, 1968) 106. In a 1992 lecture at the Yarnton, England, Post-Graduate Centre for Hebrew Studies, Prof. Jacob Bazak said that medieval commentators were so captivated by numerological

They would doubtless have agreed with Pico della Mirandola who wrote, "By number, a way may be had for the investigation and understanding of everything possible to be known."[4]

But the ancients also saw potency in the numbers themselves. In Israel each number came to have deep symbolic meaning, and some had magical potency as well.

Kugel and Greer write that "pursuit of *hokmah* [wisdom] in Israel implied the existence of an underlying plan to all reality."[5] Put another way, to some people the universe may be seen as a giant paint-by-numbers scheme. Since, however, the paint has already been applied, it is the task of the adept to look beneath the painted surface in order to discern the numerical substructure upon which the universe rests.

Such a belief could lead to apostasy, so later Jews developed or invented a series of historical, even mundane, associations that substituted elements of their national ideology for mystical potency. Somewhat like a modern recording artist "covering" another's song, the Passover song cited above is a cover, but with an important difference: the song seeks to disguise what it is covering so that original associations may be safely forgotten. This particular form of covering is probably part of the reaction that set in with the Enlightenment and Rationalism. Our song is a rather late composition, but many societies have counting songs, so it is possible that it rests on a far older base.

In "Who Knows One?" used as our epigraph, most numbers from one to thirteen (!) are connected with some one aspect of Israelite history/ belief. Actually, many more connections, both biblical and Talmudic, might be adduced for each number, and are so by Ronald H. Isaacs in *The Jewish Book of Numbers*.[6] Judaism would want a schedule of "kosher" identifications for the numbers. Here is an antiphonal list of some numerical things that the Passover song might be covering. The song's own referents are those prefaced by italicization of the numbers.

---

manipulation that it produced a reaction in the Enlightenment period.
[4]Burke, *Knowledge Web*, 200.
[5]Kugel and Greer, *Early Biblical Interpretation*, 25. This could be reflected in the substructure of Hebrew poetry. See Alisdair Fowler, *Silent Poetry: Essays in Numerological Analysis* (London: Routledge & Kegan Paul, 1970).
[6]Ronald H. Isaacs, *The Jewish Book of Numbers* (Northvale NJ: Jason Aronson, 1993).

•One: God

1–As we have seen, Venus is often called simply "star" and represented by an eight-pointed rosette,[7] the ancestor of our asterisk. Alternatively, *Kocab* (="star") in the Little Dipper was used by the earliest Egyptians to help determine true north, the direction toward which their pyramids are oriented.[8]

•Two: Tablets of the Law

2–Sun and moon, or the two snakes of the Greek caduceus, that Hebrew calls *Nehustan.*

•Three: Patriarchs

3–There are three days of moon-darkness/menstruation. Our figure of 3 derives from this and might go back to a pictographic representation of the female pubis: [⊳⊲] V, ⇗, 3, 3

•Four: Matriarchs (compare the rivers of Eden, the metal kingdoms of Daniel)

4–Seasons, winds, or quarters of earth; the major Mesopotamian gods An, Enki, Ninlil, and Ninhursaga (older daughter and two sons). (Compare the four canonical Gospels; there are many gospels that are not canonical.)

Note: 3+4=7: The "seven heavens" may be "covered" by the seven patriarchs and matriarchs of Hebrew tradition. We might also note the Three Virtues and Four Submissions of the Confucian woman.

•Five: Books of the Torah (and divisions in Psalms)

5–Planets visible to the naked eye.

•Six: Orders of the Mishnah (or work days, or Rachel and Leah tribes)

6–Number of visible stars in the constellation Pleiades, which marks the spring planting season.

•Seven: Days of creation

7–Days in each phase of the moon, or stars in the Big Dipper, or the number of major celestial objects, or the Seven Evil Gods of Mesopotamian mythology.

•Eight: Days to circumcision

8–The "eight" seasons of planting and harvesting of barley, flax, wheat, olives, grapes, and so forth on the Gezer Calendar, which has eight segments of 2, 2, 2, 1, 1, 2, 1, and 1 months. Most often, eight arms mark the early cuneiform sign for "star."

---

[7]Labat, *Manuel d'Epigraphie Akkadienne,* #13.

[8]See von Dechend and de Santillana, *Hamlet's Mill,* 137.

•Thirteen: Divine attributes identified by R. Moses Maimonides (also the years to *bar mitzvah*).

13–Lunations in a year in seven out of nineteen years. This is "covered" in both Judaism and Christianity. Tradition teaches that Jesus had twelve disciples, corresponding with the twelve tribes of Israel, but in fact there are thirteen of each, used twelve at a time. Judas is replaced by Matthias (Acts 1:26), and the landholding tribe of Joseph splits into Ephraim and Manasseh while Levi inherits no land.

The unluckiness of thirteen is thought to stem from the Last Supper with its thirteen attendees, or that the next day, Good Friday, was the thirteenth. These are late, Christian overlays. Thirteen was unlucky a long time before. It represents the uncertainty caused by the thirteenth new moon in seven of nineteen solar years mentioned above. (The fifty-six Aubrey Holes that ring Stonehenge may be a device to keep track of this phenomenon.)

In Sleeping Beauty, a secular overlay on this theme, the thirteenth, uninvited, fairy shows up before the twelfth. Her evil is partly undone by the twelfth fairy, who comes last.[9]

A pale reflection of this is our American reference to the second full moon in a calendar month as a "blue moon." The color is a matter of happenstance; the meaning is simply that of an indeterminate, but long, time.

§2: Numerical Ruminations

Two, four, six, eight! Who do we appreciate? —traditional cheer

Robert Graves suggests that eight is the most important number of all.[10] It certainly figures prominently in many religions: Mesopotamian creation myths featuring eight gods in four pairs; the Taoist immortals; the Buddhist Eightfold Path—Right Views, Aspiration, Speech, Conduct, Vocation, Effort, Mindfulness, Rapture; and the eight Islamic spheres.

---

[9]Private communication from Prof. Mara Donaldson, Dickinson College.

[10]Robert Graves, *The White Goddess: A Historical Grammar of Poetic Myth*, enl. ed. (New York: Noonday Press, 1966) 284, says, "Eight was sacred to the Sun in Babylonia, Egypt, and Arabia, because 8 is the symbol of reduplication—2x2x2. Hence the widely distributed royal sun disc with an eight-armed cross on it."

Judaism seems to have gone to great lengths to "cover" eight with layers of Jewish significance. In addition to the days before circumcision there are also

—the eight-day agricultural festivals of Passover-Matzot and Succoth-Shemini Atzeret;

—the eight days between Rosh Hashanah and Yom Kippur;

—the fully historical, if embellished, eight days of Hanukkah;

—eight kinds of *trefe* (nonkosher foods);

—eight days to the consecration of priests;

—"Solomon's Seal," an eight-pointed figure made by superimposing one square at a forty-five degree angle to a second;

—David, an eighth son; and

—Psalm 119, composed of twenty-two eight-verse stanzas, or eight separate alphabetic acrostics.[11]

This concern may also be found in Christianity. Ordinary crosses have eight "points," two on each of their four "arms," a fact that is abundantly apparent in the Maltese Cross which, by the way, is far older than Christianity. Note, too, the Celtic crosses that are imposed on circles. Surely this may represent the overlay of Christianity upon the religion of pagan worshippers of a cyclical Nature.

Of course all discrete things may be expressed or represented by number and, with a limited number of numbers, coincidences are bound to occur.[12] How can we be sure that any of this is more than coincidence? I suggest that for Israelites eight is an especially significant number because it may be said to represent a "perfect" week: that is, one with two Sabbaths, a sort of Jewish parallel to the octave in the Christian liturgical calendar.

Seven is a "good" number because it represents the completion of the first week of Creation, so six is not so good because it represents incompleteness. Further, multiples of both numbers share in their complete or

---

[11]Stanley N. Rosenbaum, "Warp and Woof in Ps. 119," paper delivered at AAR/SBL Annual Meeting, San Francisco, 1997. The literature on Psalm 119 is voluminous.

[12]For example, there were forty-two Nomes (administrative districts) in Egypt. This must be sheer happenstance, mustn't it? (See n. 14, below.) Similarly, in the Passover song, ten is for the Ten Commandments, but it is also the number of males needed for a quorum (minyan), and the *sefirot* of Kabbalism. Obviously, ten will play a major role in most counting systems.

incompleteness. Six hundred sixty-six, 6x111, is an obvious example from the dark side, hence the "number of the beast" in Revelation 13:18 is 666. Forty-nine, the number of years before the Jubilee, is an example from the good side, as is seventy, the number of years of a normal, complete life.[13] Ezra cites a fourteen-generation genealogy that connects him with Aaron to reinforce his claim as the valid interpreter/transmitter of Jewish law in Jerusalem.

The number forty-two is of particular interest because it is a multiple of both six and seven. Occurrences of this number in Scripture include precisely forty-two "boys" killed by two she-bears that Elisha called out of a wood—Who stopped to count the bodies?—and the forty-two Judean princes killed by Jehu when they came north to try to persuade their king, Ahaziah, to withdraw from the war against Aram. I am convinced that the former story, the Elisha fragment, refers in some way to the latter, but the connection is obscure. Still, why precisely forty-two?[14]

The "time, two times, and half a time" of Daniel refers to the forty-two month desecration of the Temple by Antiochus Epiphanes between 168 and 164 BCE. This period is also noted by Revelation 13:5, where the beast is allowed to reign for forty-two months.

Finally, Jesus' genealogy in Matthew 1 is divided into three sections of fourteen generations each, the total, of course, being forty-two. Since the periods involved, from Abraham to David, David to the Exile, and the Exile to Jesus, are widely varying in length (if they can be accurately known), one wonders why this scheme is used. The answer seems to be that Matthew, a Jew writing to and for other Jews, wanted to show that Jesus was the "seventh seven," the Jubilee, the completion of what began with Abraham, the resolution of a situation that was then "at sixes and sevens" to use a modern expression indicating a mixed-up situation.

But six plus seven is thirteen. . . .

---

[13]Psalm 90:3. Note that the minimum age qualification to become president of the United States is thirty-five, half of one's biblically ordained span and, presumably, sufficient years to confer wisdom.

[14]Graves, *White Goddess*, 287n.2, gives a complicated and unconvincing "Libyo-Thraco-Pelasgian" origin for this choice of number. But at least he notices it. Elsewhere (336) he writes, "Seven is Jehovah's mystical number; so was 42, the number of letters in his enlarged Name." Forty-two also fascinated Charles Lutwidge Dodson; see Ellis Hillman "Why 42?" in *Jabberwocky. The Journal of the Lewis Carroll Society* 22/2 (Spring 1993): 39-41, who gives many references based on numbers in the Book of Revelation.

§3. Wait! . . . It Gets Worse

"Things mean what I want them to mean."

—the Red Queen (in *Alice in Wonderland*)

Thirteen is not only the sum of six and seven, but also what remains when you subtract the square of six from that of seven (49 − 36 = 13). That would seem to identify thirteen as particularly potent for evil until one notices that the same relationship holds between any two adjacent integers for any x ($[x+1]^2-x^2=2x+1$). It is hardly a wonder that Rationalism dismisses playing with numbers as foolishness. And yet thirteen is so fraught that many American hotels don't have a thirteenth floor and most American athletes won't wear the number on their uniforms.

There is one other aspect of numerology that needs to be discussed, *gematriyah* ("Gematria"). The word is derived from the Greek word for "geometry," but in Hebrew parlance it refers to the practice of assigning numerical value to letters. Thus one could arrive at a numerical value for any word: the four-letter name of God (YHVH), for example, has a numerical value of 26. It might therefore be represented by any other combination of letters with the same numerical equivalent.

We know that both Greeks and Babylonians as far back as the eighth pre-Christian century used *gematriyah*. Jewish interpreters of the Bible have found it, for example, in the story of Abraham's pursuit of the kings who had kidnapped his nephew, Lot. The story says that Abraham's household consisted of 318 men, a figure that Cyrus Gordon and many others take at face value.[15] *Gematriyah*, however, observes that 318 is the numerical value of the name Eleazar, Abraham's servant, and so claim that Abraham accomplished Lot's rescue with only Eleazar alongside him.

This kind of thing is called *aggadah* ("Haggadah"), "story" or "lore" and so is not credited with probative value. But why, when so many biblical numbers are rounded off, is this seemingly unimportant one kept in what we may assume is its original state? The situation becomes even more curious when we discover the number 318 is also found as constituting the retinue accompanying one Giluhepa, princess of Hatti, on her

---

[15]Cyrus Gordon, *The Ancient Near East* (New York: W. W. Norton, 1965) 87n.1, terms the number "conventional," but his explanation stops there.

way to marry a son of pharaoh and thus cement the Egyptian-Hittite peace treaty.[16]

Now, if ever there were a case that could be dismissed as coincidence, this would seem to be it. But one more fact needs to be adduced here. In a lunar year of 354 days, the moon is visible on 318. Another coincidence? I don't think so, because on the flip side, the remainder, thirty-six, corresponds with the days in a lunar year when the moon is not visible, the days of female menstruation, as we noted earlier in this chapter.

Thirty-six also happens to correspond with the number of Just Men (*Lamed-Vavnikim*) of later Jewish legend. These men, unknown to each other and even to themselves, are necessary to exist for God to continue to preserve the world despite its evil. Their demise would mean the end of the world, as Andre Schwarz-Bart effectively chronicled in his 1960 novel, *The Last of the Just*.[17] Again, why thirty-six?

Scholars have apparently not got beyond the suggestion that thirty-six is related to decans (L. *decanus*, "chief of ten," star groups that Egyptians used to signal or rule over their ten-day weeks, whence our word "dean," as in dean of students). I cannot trace the "negative potency" of thirty-six back to biblical times, but already in the Talmud the notion of thirty-six righteous (along with many other symbolic numbers) can be found.[18]

What we seem to have here is the suggestion of a numerical substructure of reality with potentials for good and for evil. I propose that the "hidden" thirty-six stand against the thirty-six days of moondark. It is the hidden light of divine righteousness that, when the moon's light is absent, keeps the world from going completely dark. Numbers themselves not only represent "good" and "evil," but, because they are themselves complete (seven) or incomplete (six) participate in it.

---

[16]The so-called Treaty of Kadesh of the early 13th century BCE—the year depends on which archaeological records one refers to—between the Hittites and Egyptians, like the Treaty of Tortesillas in 1494 CE between Spain and Portugal, divided the world they competed for into spheres of influence. The Treaty of Kadesh, incidentally, signed by the newly crowned Hittite King Hattusilis III and Egyptian Pharaoh Ramses II, was the earliest-known (written) parity peace treaty in history.

[17]André Schwarz-Bart, *The Last of the Just*, trans. Stephen Becker (New York: Atheneum, 1960).

[18]Compare Talmud's thirty-six transgressions, *Keritot* 1:1, for which one is *karet*, "cut off" from the people of Israel. *Encyclopedia Judaica* 10:1367.

Multiples of six somehow partake of its incompleteness. Hence, even the familiar *hai*, "life," which many modern Jews wear as necklaces, is a sign of our finitude, our incompleteness. Its numerical value is . . . eighteen.

This brief discussion should suffice to show that the possibility of using numbers as a tool for understanding the workings of the universe may go back a long way, indeed, to the time when humans first learned to count. It certainly is a feature of the Israelite understanding of the cosmos. As we will see below, in chapter 13, the calendar is really an elaborate scheme for keeping count of "times and seasons."

Chapter 5

Posttraumatic Hebrew Historiography

§1. Decline and Fall

A people without history, is not redeemed from time.

—T. S. Eliot (*Little Gidding*)

Kingship arose in Egypt about 3000 BCE. Nearly 2,000 years later, when the nascent Israelite state asked Samuel the prophet to "appoint a king for us, to govern us like all other nations" (1 Sam. 8:5b NJPS), he counselled in the negative, pointing out the impositions a monarchy would make on the very people who clamored for it. A thing Samuel didn't mention was that creating a nation would lead to the formation, the reconstruction, even the invention of a national history.

Israel finally created just such a history after 586 BCE, that is to say, after the catastrophic sack of Jerusalem and the destruction of its temple, but before we get to that we need briefly to set the historical stage.

From the time of Jehu's revolt in 841, Israel and Judah had been allied with—really vassals of—Assyria; the famous Black Obelisk[1] shows Jehu accepting Assyrian vassalage. An even more important extrabiblical source is the Assyrian Eponym List.[2] This is a capsule summary of events involving Assyria from 892 to 648 BCE. Though the list is fragmentary on both ends, it contains the critically important information that in a certain year, in the month of *Simanu*, an eclipse of the sun took place. We can confidently identify this as having happened in June 763 BCE. Thirty-nine years later the Eponym List records the three-year siege of Samaria that the Bible also records. We know, then, that Samaria fell in 722 BCE. At this point we have solid extrabiblical evidence to support the Bible's own story, and once having established this base, we can extrapolate back into the dimmer reaches of the past—but that is a matter for succeeding chapters.

It took thirty-six years for the pro-Assyrian policy to become fully effective and, in the meantime, Israel suffered greatly at the hands of the

---

[1]A reproduction of the Black Obelisk of Shalmaneser III may be found in Thomas, *Documents from Old Testament Times* (DOTT), 54. The two sides of the obelisk are also reproduced in James B. Pritchard, *The Ancient Near East*, vol. 1, *An Anthology of Texts and Pictures* (Princeton NJ: Princeton University Press, 1958) nos. 100A, 100B.

[2]See Assyrian Eponym List in Thiele, Edwin Richard, *The Mysterious Numbers of the Hebrew Kings* (Grand Rapids MI: Zondervan, 1983) 221-26.

Arameans. Ultimately, however, the Assyrians proved an effective counterweight to the threat to Israel posed by Aram/Damascus. Having a friend at the rear of your enemy was just as desirable then as it later was to nineteenth-century France, which allied itself with czarist Russia when confronted with a growing German menace.

> *The German Chancellor Prince Otto von Bismarck said something to the effect that, "You forget the importance of being in a party of three on the European chessboard."*[3] *Germany's attack on France in 1940 was preceded and made possible by the German-Soviet Mutual Non-Aggression pact of 1939, which separated Russia from France.*

When Assyria was weakened by internal struggles or occupied elsewhere, Israel and Judah continued the fratricidal struggle that had begun when the monarchy split in 931 BCE. Using a foreign policy that Bismarck would have approved of, Judah enlisted Aram/Damascus against Israel, and Israel sought alliance with Egypt at Judah's rear. After 735, however, Israel made common cause with Aram and both attacked Judah. The purpose of the attack seems to have been to compel Judah to join the north-Syrian coalition against Assyria, now grown mighty under the ruthlessly capable leadership of Tiglath-Pileser III (745–727).

The confederates doubtlessly remembered that a similar coalition had been able to withstand Assyria several times in the mid-ninth century, and it is hard to blame them for wanting, in effect, to "fight the First World War over again." Judah, however, responded by seeking help from Assyria, which attacked and took Damascus, killing its king. Samaria was itself destroyed in a three-year campaign that began in 724, after the Assyrians learned that its king, Hoshea, was making traitorous overtures to Egypt. The siege, destruction, and subsequent annexation of Samaria in 720 BCE are corroborated from Assyrian records.[4]

By the last half of the seventh century, Josiah's time, Judah was precariously perched between three "world powers." Assyria, which was literally camped on his doorstep; perennially empire-minded Egypt; and, after 627 BCE, upstart Babylonia were competing for regional hegemony. A fourth power, Urartu in eastern Anatolia, had been strong enough to

---

[3]I owe this allusion to the late Prof. K. Robert Nilsson of Dickinson College's Political Science department. All politics, Bismarck concluded, reduce to this formula: "Try to be a *trois* in a world governed by five powers."

[4]The Assyrian records of annexation may be found in ANET[2] 284-85.

influence affairs for centuries by challenging Assyria for supremacy in northern Mesopotamia, but it had faded from the scene by Josiah's reign.[5]

With the northern threat removed, the Egyptians and Assyrians became serious economic rivals and political enemies. Assyria invaded Egypt several times in the seventh century, the last in 663 BCE, but that was forgotten when Babylon, a kingdom founded by an Assyrian prince who failed to succeed to his father's throne, began to put on strength in the south.

If Judah was too weak to be a major player on the stage of world politics, neither could it become simply a spectator. The main land routes over which the powers in Mesopotamia and Africa traded with or assailed each other ran through Israel's entire length from north to south. Judah had the choice of opposing or allowing invading armies a right of passage, but either choice would make enemies.

Using familiar Middle Eastern logic, Jesus later put it this way: "Whoever is not with me is against me" (Matt. 12:30; Luke 11:23 NRSV). Real neutrality was impossible for Israel in any case, in much the same way that America's declared "neutrality" during the Spanish Civil War was a calculated aid to Franco's Fascists.

§2. Theological Triumphalism

By Judean reckoning, the Northern Kingdom's destruction was richly deserved, but not merely because of its international political treachery. All kingdoms engaged in double-dealing. Religiously, however, the Samarians were a "sinful kingdom." The North had never repudiated such ancient bovine images as the golden calf as symbols for the divine. Worse, they had rejected the Davidic dynasty. When Solomon died, eight (not ten)[6] Northern tribes "seceded from the union" and set up their own capital, first at Tirzah and finally at Samaria.

While refurbishing the Temple in 622 BCE——exactly a century after the destruction of its rival—Judean officials found the "Book of the Law," as 2 Kings 22 reports.[7] Most scholars agree this contained at least

---

[5]Boris B. Piotrovsky, *The Ancient Civilization of Urartu* (New York: Cowles, 1969).

[6]The North had—I think—eight tribes. Simeon had long since been absorbed into Judah, and Reuben's adherence to the coalition is questionable.

[7]Verses 8 and 11 NRSV. It is called the "Book of the Covenant" in 2 Kings 23:2 (which report continues the same episode). NJPS has "scroll of the Teaching" and "covenant

the core of our Deuteronomy, most likely chapters 12–26. In this book, probably in little need of editing, Judeans would have proof out of its own mouth that the North stood convicted and that its punishment was just. Deuteronomy 11:13 and following, which is presently used as the response to the *Sh'ma* (Deut. 6:4) in Jewish services, lays out a deterministic scheme of reward and punishment for good and bad behavior. Using the common, if fallacious, logic that what happens after is caused by what happens before, Israel's destruction was proof enough of its crimes. Besides, had not Amos warned Israel of God's wrath only about forty years[8] before it happened?

> *As I read it, Amos's prediction of Israel's eclipse and Judah's revival,*
> *"On that day I will restore the 'booth of David' that is fallen" (9:12;*
> *my translation), meant that he, and his words, would be welcomed in*
> *Judah, to which he was promptly exiled (7:14). (See below, chap. 9.)*

European scholars such as Julius Wellhausen[9] suggested that Josiah found this book in the Temple because he had planted it there. Wellhausen alleged that it was a forgery designed to help push religious reforms and support Josiah's political agenda, namely, reunification with the estranged Northern kingdom (Israel), centralization of worship at Jerusalem, and a pro-Babylonian (as opposed to a pro-Egyptian/Assyrian) policy. That these scholars assumed Josiah's constituents would automatically accept such manipulation may tell us more about anti-Semitism in Wellhausen's Germany than it does about Judah in the seventh century BCE, though variations on his theory continue to be held.[10]

There is another explanation for what Josiah's priest, Hilkiah, found. Along with many other scholars, I believe what was uncovered were some elements of Samarian (Northern) Torah. Inspired by Northern prophets such as Amos[11] and Hosea, these Northern accounts would have

---

scroll," respectively.

[8]Using my date of ca. 760 BCE for Amos's activities. Those scholars who would reduce the date by twenty years can make an even stronger case for the prophet's words being remembered in 724 BCE.

[9]Wellhausen, *Prolegomena*, 76-82.

[10]Friedman, Richard Elliott, *Who Wrote the Bible?* 2nd ed. (San Francisco: Harper Collins, 1997) 170-77. See below, chap. 13, n. 15.

[11]I was surprised but delighted to see that Frymer-Kensky in *In the Wake of the Goddesses*, 154, *assumes* Amos is a Northern prophet, with no apparent knowledge of my *Amos of Israel: A New Interpretation* (Macon GA: Mercer University Press, 1990).

been carried south and deposited in the Jerusalem Temple by refugees fleeing the Assyrian invasion.

Why deposited and not destroyed? Because although the two kingdoms had long been estranged, the "Word of God" was more than letters on parchment; as we saw in chapter 3, the word *dabar* means both "word" and "thing." It shared power with God himself. If we may read back from Talmudic regulations, written material with God's name on it could not be destroyed, but must be laid by (in a *genizah*[12]), as is still the case. So the Northern documents would have been at hand later. When these materials were suitably adapted for Josiah's expansionist purposes, they could be incorporated into what was taking form as the Bible.

The same identification of the "word" with God is reflected in the opening of the Gospel of John, "In the beginning was the Word, and the Word was with God and the Word was God." (John 1:1 NRSV; and see above, in chap. 3, "§6. Words and 'the Word'," 62ff.).

Perhaps Josiah was particularly influenced by what has since become the central and only credal statement in Judaism, Deuteronomy 6:4's

---

[12]*Genizah*: from √גנז √*gnz*, "to cover (up)," "hide"; thus a "hiding place" or "storeroom," even "treasure room"; or in modern parlance, a "lumber room." A *genizah* is that place in a synagogue where old or worn Torah scrolls and prayer books are set aside since, bearing the name of God, they cannot be destroyed.

Ezra 6:1 is instructive: Darius ordered a search for the decree of Cyrus, so "they searched in the house of the rolls/scrolls/books where the treasures (*gnz*) were deposited there in Babylon" (cf. Ezra 5:17: the "royal archives," lit. "house of treasure(s)" [*gnz*]). Such official *archives* or *storerooms* were set up much later in Israel (probably because of the proliferation of scriptures and the need for some system for managing their disposition). "During the Middle Ages, a room was set aside in almost every synagogue as a *genizah* for old or imperfect books or ritual objects. Such synagogue hiding places for sacred works have often provided later generations with precious pages of books considered lost" (*Oxford Dictionary of the Jewish Religion* [1997] 269).

The most famous such *genizah* is the so-called Cairo Genizah, discovered at the Ezra Synagogue in Fostat (Old Cairo). The Cairo Genizah has so far produced more than 200,000 (!) manuscripts (mostly fragments). The research and manuscript-acquisition work of Solomon Schecter in late 1896 brought the Cairo Genizah to scholarly attention. Yet the work of cataloging and publishing all the manuscripts found there is still far from complete.

In 1947 and following, a different kind of *genizah*—a real "hiding place," hidden for centuries—was discovered in the caves among the cliffs above the Dead Sea. This *genizah* probably dates to some time before 68 CE, and of course produced the Dead Sea Scrolls (almost 850 ancient Jewish documents) which have opened a new chapter in the study of Judaism.

"Hearken O Israel, YHVH is our God, YHVH alone."[13] However one stands on Josiah's deviousness, or lack thereof, the policy aims that Wellhausen saw were clear enough. Josiah had two wives, one from the South and one from the North, holding out hope to Northerners that their "blood" might sit on David's throne—as indeed did happen for a short time after his death (see chap. 12, below). Another way of gaining Northern support for Josiah's visions of a new empire would be to incorporate their lore or some of it, into the *torah* (teaching) that Judeans would come to revere.

There was no lack of material to chose from. Most originally Northern texts could not be used by Southerners until some changes were made, for example, in psalms written by the Northern psalmists Korah and Asaph. In Deuteronomy itself specific references to Northern holy sites had to be edited out.[14] Conversely, the oracle against Judah in Amos seems to have been added—but subsequently eviscerated—to make the prophet's words more pertinent in the South.

Most tellingly, the modern Samaritan Torah still reads Deuteronomy 12:5 as identifying mounts Gerizim and Ebal, near Shechem, their religious capital, as Zion, "the place where God causes His name to dwell." For Southerners, of course, that place was Jerusalem, but how that got to be is worth investigating. One of the most enduring distortions produced by Southern stewardship of Torah has been the complete identification of "Zion" with Jerusalem.

How not? For nearly three millennia, Jerusalem has been *the* Zion of the South, just as Salt Lake City is for Mormons and Boston for Christian Scientists. Yet it was not always so. First, Gilgal, where Joshua set up the ring of stones as a sort of Israelite "Plymouth Rock," then Shiloh, both north of the border, were previous central worship sites. Tradition equates the word *zion* with the word Jerusalem, but there is no etymological support for this position. The best we can say is that *a* "zion" is *a* place where God causes his name to dwell.

Following Botterweck and Ringgren,[15] I would like to propose that *zion* is a variant spelling of *sion*, identified in Deuteronomy 4:48 with Mt.

---

[13]I prefer "hearken" to "hear" and, with NJPS and NRSV, "alone" to "is One." See NJPS note and NRSV note at Deut. 6:4.

[14]From our perspective as heirs of Judah we suspect the Samarians of inserting references to their holy places into the text, but is it not we, rather, who have edited them *out*?

[15]TDOT 7:395.

Hermon, or with *siryon*, the Sidonian name for Hermon found in Deuteronomy 3:9 and Psalm 29:6. At 9,000 feet, Mt. Hermon is the only snowcap in Israel's immediate vicinity. Recall the Natufian chief buried in a sitting position facing it. Anyone who has turned a corner in Safed, some thirty miles south, and suddenly seen the mountain with snow standing far down its shoulders, immediately understands why it was an object of veneration.

Emerging Israelite theology might use such mountains as Hermon, Tabor, or Carmel as places where God appeared, but the mountains themselves ought not to be venerated on that account. As we have seen, Psalm 121 begins with an implicit denial of the holiness of mountains per se:

> I look to the mountains;
>   from whence shall my strength come?
> My strength comes from the LORD. (Psalm 121:1, my translation)

Note again that one of the appellatives of Israel's God is "my Rock," perhaps another way of appropriating the regard previously directed toward mountains.

In later Jewish theology, the understanding of "zion" shifts from a generic connotation to a specific denotation that, in the hands of Southerners, leads to the identification of capital-Z Zion with Jerusalem, a city on a hill. Paradoxically, this prominence is lower than the hills that flank it both to the east and to the west. (Remember that in this regard Jerusalem resembles the best-known Mt. Sinai, the mountain in southern Sinai, which is not the tallest peak in its immediate vicinity, either.)

§3. What Goes Around, Comes Around

"Judge not, that you be not judged." —Jesus (Matthew 7:1 RSV)

Scripture remembers Josiah as Israel's greatest king except for David. Second Kings 23:25 rhapsodizes, "There was no king like him before . . . nor did any like him arise after him" (NJPS). Chronicles is even more detailed, crediting him with major religious reforms beginning in the eighth year of his reign, "while he was still young" (2 Chron. 34:3). But there is so much more that we should like to know about the young king and the circumstances that brought him to the throne.

Josiah was only six years old when his father Amon became king. Were there other sons, older or younger, children of other wives who were even theoretically in contention for the throne? If so, how certain could the assassins of Amon have been that the next regime would change the policies and practices that they apparently objected to? If not, what could they hope to gain? And who were these assassins, anyway?

Both Kings and Chronicles identify the killers only as Amon's "courtiers" who, we are told, were subsequently all put to death by the "people of the land," who then put Josiah on the throne (2 Kings 21:23-24). But were the executions mandated by members of the priesthood, or by Amon's wife and Josiah's mother, Jedidah (mentioned only in 2 Kings 22:1), in the period after the assassination? Chronicles does not even mention her. Did queen mothers have a voice in choosing their husbands' successors? If Amon was too young to have had many, perhaps any, children older than Josiah, choosing such a young boy to rule necessarily meant a de facto regency. So, who were Josiah's principal advisors?

Firm answers to these questions are impossible given the terseness of the biblical record, but the following scenario is at least plausible.

A pro-Babylonian faction at court will have dated from the time of Hezekiah's near-disastrous dalliance with Merodach-baladan or (with NJPS) Berodach-baladan (2 Kings 20:12 ‖ Isa. 39:1). Despite the failure of their policy, they saw how desperate was the need to have a friend in the rear of their principal enemy—even though they were still on officially friendly terms with Assyria.

The repressive regime of Manasseh must have offered them no scope for political maneuvering. Besides, Babylon had not yet emerged as a serious contender for Mesopotamian hegemony. When Manasseh died, the pro-Babylonians looked for a change, something like the Northerners hoping for relief from Solomon's son. As this did not materialize during Amon's first two years, they decided on more drastic action.

It is possible some of Amon's couriers were already agents of the pro-Babylonian faction. Having spies in rivals' camps was a tried-and-true method of influencing policy; it had saved David's life when Absalom listened to his "counsellor" and David's secret agent, Hushai, and did not pursue the king after an initial victory. Alternatively, the courtiers might have been bribed to do the deed and then killed before they could expose the people who had paid them.

The precipitate murder of the assassin of Alexander's father King Philip of Macedon, that of Lee Harvey Oswald, (an?) assassin of President John F. Kennedy, and that of the killer of Benigno Aquino of the Philipines immediately come to mind.

The pro-Babylonian faction must have been involved in the assassination, because Josiah subsequently pursued a pro-Babylonian policy and religious reforms that as an eight-year-old he could hardly have been expected to understand. Even Chronicles, fulsome in its praises, does not have Josiah doing anything until the eighth year of his reign. Kings knows of nothing before the finding of the "Book of the Law" in Josiah's eighteenth year.

Josiah did not proclaim this newfound book of the law to be "torah" on his own authority; there is no reason to suppose he could have done so. It had been a long time since the king was *ipso facto* head of the state religion. Besides, the book *was* "Northern torah" and therefore suspect. It might be given an *imprimatur*, that is, cleared for use by Judean religious authorities, but which ones?

Being perhaps extra careful, or politically astute, Josiah did not send the scroll for evaluation to his friend Jeremiah. Probably the leading prophetic voice in Judah at the time, Jeremiah was nonetheless the descendant of *Northern* priests. One might argue that after generations in the South, he would have lost track of his roots, but his book abounds with Ephraimite speech forms[16] showing again, I think, how much regional loyalties counted for throughout Israel.

What is more important, Jeremiah shared Josiah's pro-Babylonian political views, so the prophet's "testimony" would likely not convince other political factions. Josiah therefore sent the scroll to one Huldah. We now[17] know her(!) to have been a respected prophet of presumably neutral politics who apparently stationed herself at the south wall of the Temple.

Even more revealingly, Josiah sent the scroll in the hands of a delegation of five: two known pro-Babylonians; two known pro-Assyrians; and one of his own officers acting, no doubt, as a kind of referee.[18] This "bipartisan commission" was carefully constructed, apparently to ensure that Huldah's decision as to the book's legal/religious acceptability

---

[16]Robert R. Wilson, *Prophecy and Society in Ancient Israel* (Philadelphia: Fortress, 1980) 135-46.

[17]The Huldah Gates known from Talmudic times have been recently uncovered, adding additional credence to this biblical account, unless one posits that she, too, was part of the "conspiracy."

[18]I owe this observation to a private communication from Nahum M. Sarna. Exponents of a Wellhausian-type conspiracy apparently overlook or avoid consideration of these telling details.

was faithfully reported. Huldah accepted it and so a major piece of Northern *torah* came to be put together with the Southern. Nor was that Josiah's only gesture to the North.

Like his great-grandfather, Hezekiah, he included Northerners in his Passover observance, a Passover the likes of which had not been seen in the country in 600 years if one can credit 2 Chronicles 35:18 ‖ 2 Kings 23:22; cf. 1 Esdras 1:20. This is not to say there had not been a Passover since Joshua's time, as some scholars suggest. It probably meant that Josiah was responsible for combining Passover, the celebration of spring lambing, with the Feast of Unleavened Bread[19]—and, of course, inviting for Northerners to share in it.

His gesture did not mean that the Northern remnant would have any sort of parity with the South. Josiah dug up the bones of Northern priests and burned them on their own altars, defiling both.[20] I suspect this "bone fire"—the original form of our "bonfire"—is the origin of the bonfires that Jews still light on the thirty-third day after Passover. As we will explore further below, customs may persist long after the reason for them has been forgotten.

It is Kings that gives the more thorough description of Josiah's moves to centralize worship around Jerusalem; Chronicles is more interested in describing Josiah's elaborate and unprecedented Passover celebration.

Josiah's obvious aim was to reunite the kingdoms under his own leadership. Here we should pause to note that the same Huldah who reported favorably on the Book of the Law also predicted—not entirely accurately, if the oracle is to be taken literally:

> Assuredly, I will gather you to your fathers and you will be laid in your tomb in peace. Your eyes shall not see all the disaster which I will bring upon this place. (2 Kings 22:20-21 ‖ 2 Chron. 35:28 NJPS)

Chronicles uses similar language, but also records a conversation between the Egyptian Pharaoh Neco (2 Chron. 35:20-21) and Josiah at Megiddo in which Neco declares he has no quarrel with Judah and merely wants to pass through Israel.

---

[19]Second Chronicles 35:17 might be read as suggesting that Josiah was the first one to combine the festivals of Passover (spring lambing) and Matzoth (first-grain harvest).

[20]Second Chronicles 34:5; cf. 2 Kings 23:20. His actions in the North were only slightly less drastic.

The device of spicing up historical writing by inventing conversations between principals was well known all over the eastern Mediterranean. Unfortunately, the use of this device means we cannot tell which conversations are real and which fictional.

Josiah was pro-Babylonian, but he could not have adopted Swiss-style neutrality even had he wished to do so. (For all that, as we have recently learned, neither could the Swiss.) Stepping aside would have been seen as an anti-Babylonian gesture.

Josiah died of wounds sustained in battle in 608 BCE, intercepting Neco's Egyptian army (2 Kings 23:29-30; 2 Chron. 35:20-24). Jeremiah composed laments for Josiah (2 Chron. 35:25). Those laments are now, alas, lost (but see Jer. 22:10).

From that time until the end of the kingdom, Judah was something of a political football, three of its four succeeding kings being appointed and deposed by Egypt or Babylon. The Babylonians exiled King Jehoiakim to Babylon in 597 BCE, where he lived another thirty-six years, as we know from Babylonian ration tablets detailing his household's allotments.[21] It might be wondered why they bothered to keep him alive, but one reason could be to hold out hope for a restoration to elements of the Judean community, and thus to secure greater cooperation from them.

As we saw above, Israel and Judah had long courted allies in each other's rear, so Babylon seems to have favored children of Josiah's Southern wife while Egypt preferred the son and grandson of the Northern wife. Presumably the families or clans from which these women came had definite political agendas of their own.

The fanciful idea that kings chose wives by whim or as the result of "beauty contests" such as we find in the Book of Esther will have been no more true in Judah than it was in Persia—or Great Britain. We may infer, then, from this alternation of king-candidates that if Judah was a political football, not all of its constituent members were on the same team.

Paul Johnson goes further, claiming that the Benjaminites submitted to Babylon in 588 BCE and consequently were not exiled.[22] If so, this

---

[21]Translations of the Babylonian ration tablets for the King and his retinue are found in ANET², 308.
[22]Paul Johnson, *History of the Jews* (New York: Harper & Row, 1987) 78. This position is supported by Abraham Malamat, "Caught Between the Great Powers," *Biblical*

"cowardice" would have stuck in the craw of those Judeans who only shortly thereafter came to collect and write their history. It would have produced an animus against Benjamin that seems to be felt—or even retrojected—into the time before the monarchy was established, as we will see in chapter 7, below.

In any event, we know that Judah met its own catastrophic end a scant thirty-six years after Josiah's reforms began and twenty-two years after his death. In 586 King Zedekiah (Mattaniah), a son of Josiah by his Southern wife ("Hamutal, daughter of Jeremiah of Libnah," 2 Kings 24:18 ‖ Jer. 52:1 NJPS), and uncle of his immediate predecessor (2 Kings 24:17),[23] tried to extricate himself from Babylonian overlordship by making overtures to Egypt. He was captured by Babylonians as he tried to flee his capital. After being made to witness his children's execution—the last thing he ever saw—Zedekiah was blinded, fettered, and taken to Babylon along with a large number of the inhabitants while Jerusalem and its Temple were destroyed.

§4. Rationalizing the Destruction

I heard upon his dry dung-heap
That man cry out who cannot sleep:
"If God is God, He is not good;
If God is good, He is not God. . . . "   —Archibald Macleish (in *J.B.*)

Just before 586, Jeremiah had excoriated Judeans for forsaking God and baking cakes for Astarte, the Queen of Heaven to whom Mesopotamians had prayed for more than a thousand years. (Molds for goddess statuette cakes have been found at Mari, a city on the Euphrates whose heyday was before Abraham's time.) The clear implication is that Judeans had never completely given up worship of other gods, and now their God had lost patience.

Archaeology Review 25/4 (July/August 1998): 34-41 and 64, esp. 41 and n. 10.
   [23]Chart 3.   Josiah's Family

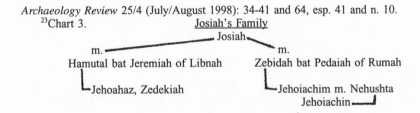

Following the cataclysm, the Judeans had to make their way out of the theological corner into which they had painted themselves. The South had, if barely, survived the Assyrian onslaught of 724–722 BCE that had carried off its sister kingdom, Israel, but it was a near thing. Kings reports a death-grip siege on Jerusalem in 701 that was broken, as if by a miracle, when the besieging Assyrian army suddenly disappeared, called back to put down a revolt at home.[24] Naturally, the Judeans would have seen these events as deserved punishment of the North and merited salvation for themselves.

An American immediately thinks of Francis Scott Key's inspiring words composed during the British shelling of Fort McHenry in 1812, which became the national anthem: "Our flag was still there. . . . " And it still is.

If the Judeans composed a song for their deliverance on that occasion we no longer have it and, in any case, their own precarious independence was relatively short-lived.

Fortunately, in a sense, the despised Jeremiah had also apparently predicted that Jerusalem would become "like Shiloh," a cultic center in the North destroyed some five centuries before.[25] This prediction had gotten Jeremiah thrown into prison at the time. Now the unthinkable had occurred: Jerusalem was destroyed. And yet all was not lost. A major consequence of the destruction was that prophets like Jeremiah became respectable because what they predicted was seen to come true.

Prediction of this sort was not the only or even the major function of prophets, as we will see in chapter 9. Moreover, this new respect was by no means universal. Some Judeans criticized Jeremiah, complaining that the calamity came upon them precisely for leaving off the sacrifices to Asherah. But the mainstream of Judean opinion seems to have regarded their fate as punishment for infidelity—the Bible often speaks of it in sexual terms—to the God identified by the Tetragrammaton YHVH. Paradoxically, even perversely, the destruction in 586 entrains the triumph

---

[24]Unfortunately the Assyrian Eponym List is broken just at this point and Sennacherib's Annals (ANET², 287-88), as might be expected, is silent on this point.

[25]Jer. 7:14. That Jeremiah even knows its name 500 years later is instructive and casts further doubt on the theory that the Bible is entirely a product of the Persian period. If that were the case, it would require that the composers still knew, or cared about, Shiloh 800 years after its destruction.

of Yahwism, at least in theory. This is the subject of chapter 12, "Jeremiah's Judah," but some account will be taken here.

Judeans adopted a particularly powerful rationalization for their own destruction, one that would haunt their descendants through all succeeding centuries. The destruction of the Temple, they said, was through and because of their own sin, in this case the apostasy of polytheism, and the consequent anger of the God they now recognized as being *One* or, as I prefer, *Alone*.

This rationalization should not be too surprising. The reader will remember that one of my premises (see chap. 1) is that all religion is anthropocentric: it revolves around those involved in it just as—they would have said—the sun revolves around the earth. The Moabite Stone[26] attributes Moab's defeat to the anger of their god, Chemosh. But although Israel's God used other countries as the "rod of his anger," he would continue to watch over Israel, his punished people.

Heartened by Jeremiah to "dig in" in the place to which many had been exiled in 597, to "seek after the good of the country in which you are put" (Jer. 29:7), worship of Israel's God survived. Psalm 137, the only demonstrably exilic[27] psalm, says:

> By the rivers of Babylon—
> there we sat down and there we wept
> when we remembered Zion. (137:1 NRSV)

Surely there were other exilic compositions, but, as Spinoza observed, time works against preservation of such fragile things. The important question here is, how long would Jewish identity in Exile—or anywhere else—have lasted?

A further casualty of the First Temple cataclysm seems to be the Jews' own sense of history. Prior to 586, I would argue, the overarching idea of history in the ancient Near East, one shared by Hebrews, is cyclical. Year by year everything returns like the stars in the sky and crops from the earth; stasis, stability, is what is desired. This is especially evident in Egyptian texts from the First Intermediate Period (after 2130 BCE) that lament the overturning of the natural order.

---

[26]The Moabite Stone, one of very few Moabite texts we have, was found by French archaeologists in 1868 and now resides in the Louvre, Paris.

[27]Previous scholarship held that all psalms were necessarily postexilic. Now only Psalm 137 may with confidence be so identified.

The destruction of 586 BCE said "good-bye to all that." Without a Temple, history suddenly acquired a "linear" dimension. Cyclicality remained, as it still does, in the cycles of day, week, month, year, Sabbatical, and Jubilee, and, perhaps, the "lifetime" of seventy years (or eighty, Psa. 90:10—counting this last makes for seven cycles . . . or is it eight?!). Overriding these cycles, however, is the linear idea that "God works in, through, and by means of History."[28] Mircea Eliade writes:

> With Judaism God enters history by caring for groups and individuals. The latter can attain union with God (mystics) or salvation, but the end of history will be salvation.[29]

Salvation, yes, but by what means, through what agency? A Christian tradition has it that Abraham knew of Jesus and was glad. I would say that until 586 the idea of any messiah, let alone a divine one, was completely foreign to Israel. As a noun it is not found in the entire Torah except in passages that clearly indicate consecration of priests.

> *Attempts by Christians and Jews to read Jesus or any messiah into texts that predate 586 are, I submit, expressions of theologies arrived at much later and read back or even inserted into the text. This, however, has not stopped both groups from doing so, often to their great loss.*
>
> *Rabbinic support for Simon Bar Kochba ("son of the star"), who led the Second Revolt against Rome (132–135 CE), was based on Numbers 24:17: "a star [kokhav] shall arise from Jacob." The Roman suppression of the revolt was so thorough that the world price of slaves was depressed because of a flood of enslaved Jews.*

Messiahs, that is, "anointed persons," such as kings and priests, had been known for centuries, but as long as David's line held the throne and the Temple stood, there was no need for any "savior." Even after 586, Israel's hopes were modest: restoration to the land, a new Temple, and a Davidic king—the exiled Jehoiakim or another—and these they got within three generations. Of course such a relatively speedy return to something like their previous situation could not have been widely expected at the beginning of the Exile, despite the predictions of some prophets.

---

[28] An idea popularized by the school of G. E. Wright.
[29] Mircea Eliade in Pals, *Seven Theories of Religion*, 158-97.

However, because the Exile did, in fact, only last about as long as the "seventy years" Jeremiah predicted and because that period is much closer to the beginning of Israel's history than it is to our time, scholars and religious people have not given due weight to the tragic and disorienting circumstances under which the Hebrew Scriptures were first called into being.

Furthermore, except for the hundred-year reign of the Hasmoneans (164–63 BCE), Judah never regained political independence; Bar Kochba controlled only a small area in the highlands and that briefly. The circumstances of continuous occupation by foreigners must necessarily have had its effect, a depressing one, upon the collectors of Scripture.

§5. Whose Bible Is It, Anyway?

"I'm Brian [of Nazareth], and so's my wife."
—Gregory (in Monty Python's *Life of Brian*, sc. 31)

It was during the Babylonian Exile that the first attempts were made to collect and canonize parts of Scripture. We know little of the process by which the Torah's various books or documents might have been blended. If the text sources commonly called J and E (after the names they each use for God) are as old as scholars think, that is, from around 950 and 850 BCE respectively, who wrote these passages, and when were they combined? Were there "learned councils" of sages editing, arranging, making decisions? If so, no "minutes of their meetings" remain. H. L. Ginsberg posits that D, the third document, took rise in the North around 740 as a result of early prophetic activities, such as those of Amos and Hosea. Further, he says it was these prophets whose words influenced the rise of prophecy in the South, which seems more than likely.[30]

Richard Friedman boldly proposed that the prophet Jeremiah wrote the Bible, or at least the Deuteronomic History.[31] This history includes not only most of the book of Deuteronomy, but also Joshua, Judges, 1-2 Samuel, and 1-2 Kings as well. Subsequently, Friedman left that position and now suggests that the fourth document—what Wellhausen labelled P (Priestly)—was the product of doubly disfranchised Northern priests.

---

[30]Ginsberg, *Israelian Heritage of Judaism*, 92-96. Also, see below, chap. 9.
[31]This idea derives from Wilson, *Prophecy and Society in Ancient Israel*, 303.

Ousted from office by Solomon, these priests confidently expected to be reinstated in the North when Jehu ended Omri's line. Disappointed, they wrote P, their account of how things were and should be, which may be characterized as "a pox on both your kingdoms." Remember that Jeremiah himself was a descendant of the Northern priests whom Solomon had exiled to the South. He was not forced into exile by the Babylonians because of his known pro-Babylonian stance before 586.

We have some clues to the collection process, though. The notation at the end of the twenty-fifth chapter of Proverbs states that they were collected by "the men of Hezekiah." This speaks to an ongoing process of textual accumulation, at least, even before the fall of Jerusalem. By the time the Torah and the Prophets were canonized, even messianic concerns would have found their way into Israel's thinking.

At the end of the day—a very long day indeed—what we are left with is the judgment that the major part of Scripture was made "official," and some of it written, between 586 and 450 BCE. In the first half of this period there was no temple, and throughout that period Judah was under foreign control. It is my belief that these were crucial, formative circumstances for the collecting, editing, and writing of much of what became the Jews' "Holy Scripture." I will return to this subject in chapter 13. Meanwhile, it is to this Hebrew Scripture, and its record of history, in the form that we presently have it, that we now turn.

Chapter 6

The View from Downstream

Introduction

As we saw in part 1, there are four "streams" that together flow into one side of the pool I have called Posttraumatic Hebrew Historiography. They are (1) Israel's physical landscape; (2) the "mental geography" that landscape conditions; (3) the language in which that geography is expressed; and (4) the religious ideas shaped by the language. From the other side of the pool flows Israel's—or now more properly speaking, Judah's— view of its own history, beginning in Genesis 12 with Abram and Sarai.

Modern scholars, skeptics, and liberal religionists agree that the stories of the founders in the Pentateuch, the first five books of the Bible, are not all of a piece. Rather they are a collection of conflicting accounts, memories, and even some pious fabrications designed to create the story of united Israel's origins and the emergence of Judah as its leader.

Judah's is the history of a covenanted people, uniquely singled out by a god who is not only their God, but ultimately the only real deity in the created universe. Far from being a dispassionate attempt to record history as it actually was, Judah's history is a tapestry of real history, sometimes well, sometimes poorly, remembered, and colored throughout by fantasy, polemic, and idealization.

In trying to imagine a plausible history of biblical Israel, the historian must steer a middle course between two-dimensional, traditional retellings of Bible stories and multiplex scholarly conjectures. The former are often simplistic to the point of distortion, the latter tedious. I offer the following reimagining with a confidence that I may not always altogether feel in service of telling a story that I hope may be read and appreciated by students of all persuasions.

§1. Patriarchs and Matriarchs, or One Man's (Dysfunctional) Family

> Abram and Sarai were sorrowful, yet their seed became as the sand of the sea, and distracts the politics of Europe at this moment.
>
> —E. M. Forster (*The Longest Journey*)

Forster might appreciate that even as I write this, Jews are jostling Muslims for a presence at what they, and Christians, consider to be the tombs of all the patriarchs/matriarchs (except Rachel) in Hebron while the Western world again holds its breath. All the parties agree on who these matriarchs and patriarchs were, but those entombed in Hebron number fewer than half of greater Israel's progenitors even by Scripture's own count. There are as many as nineteen people who might have been considered as Israel's eponymous (name-giving) ancestors, but the Bible is at some pains to reduce the number of venerated patriarchs and matriarchs to seven—a number that we saw in chapter 4 has its own symbolic significance. Who are the others and why are they not also in Hebron? This chapter will investigate the beginnings of Israel's self-understanding, the so-called "Patriarchal Period," as mediated to us by posttraumatic Jewish historiography.

Taking the Bible at face value for the moment, that the original Israelite "family" was what we would term dysfunctional is indicated by their fighting more among themselves than together against others: Sarah and Hagar, Esau and Jacob are two "family feuds" that come most quickly to mind. Joseph often fell afoul of his ten half-brothers, but it is Jacob's youngest son, Benjamin, who became the stormy petrel of his family—a harbinger of strife. (For more on Benjamin, see chap. 8.)

The patriarchal/matriarchal family tree begins with Abram, later named Abraham, whom Genesis 12 presents as springing theologically fullblown from God's forehead. Even if this were so, we want to know something of the parents from whom Abraham allegedly broke. Genesis doesn't say anything about their religion, a deficiency addressed by later *midrashim*,[1] but the biblical text does give us some hints.

As we saw in chapter 4, Ur and Haran, the cities associated with Abraham, were centers of moon worship. The names of Terah, Abram's father, and Jericho, the city of his nephew Lot, are both from the root √*y-r-h*, *yareah* (moon). Abraham's wife Sarah's name is also moon-related in Akkadian (*sarratu* = Ningal, wife of Sîn). Such evidence seems to suggest that Abram/Abraham's ancestors were moon worshippers, some-

---

[1]*Midrashim* (*drṣ*, "inquire") are later interpretations of biblical stories and events, usually with a moral message to impart. (The term *midrash* itself occurs at 2 Chron. 13:22 and 24:27 where it was [routinely] translated "story" [KJV, NJPS]. At 24:27, NRSV and NJB [accurately] render it as "commentary." For both occurrences, NIV translates as "annotations." Both NAB and NJB simply transliterate ["midrash"] at 13:22, as NAB also does at 24:27.) According to one *midrash*, Abraham's father owned and operated an "idol store," and it was there that Abraham became the first literal iconoclast.

thing that should come as no surprise so deep into the era that began with the "farming revolution."[2]

The mothers of Abraham's children were Sarai (later Sarah), her concubine Hagar the Egyptian, and Keturah. He had eight children by these three women but only one, Isaac son of Sarah, carried the Israelite patrimony. The Bible reports that disfranchising Ishmael, at Sarah's insistence, took an "act of God." This, however, may be a cover for another, later reason for exclusion.

Kidnapping people for sale into slavery is prohibited in Exod. 21:17, Deut. 24:7, and probably also in the Ten Commandments, where it is cryptically abbreviated as "do not steal." It may be that it was because Ishmaelites were involved in this "trade" that they were denied Abraham's patrimony. (See Amos's criticisms of Gaza, Amos 1:6.)

Isaac had one wife, Rebekah, who gave birth to the twins Esau and Jacob. The patrimony passed through Jacob to the twelve sons that he had with four different women: wives Leah and Rachel and concubines Bilhah and Zilpah. Clearly, our story—the Bible—is being told from the point of view of Judah, fourth-born of Leah. But why fourth-born?

After all, if these stories were later fabrications, why not make the story simpler? Why go to the trouble of inventing three older full brothers of Judah with superior birthright claims to family headship who then have to be disqualified? It rather reminds one of the Alec Guinness film, Kind Hearts and Coronets, in which the last person in line for the throne serially exterminates all those ahead of him—the whole lot being played by Guinness.

---

[2]My Abraham is almost contemporary with the stelae at Hazor, one of which shows hands raised to the moon. It would be difficult to believe that moon worship originated after Abraham's time. It certainly did not end there. See Julius Lewy, "The Late Assyro-Babylonian Cult of the Moon and Its Culmination at the Time of Nabonidus," *Hebrew Union College Annual* 19 (1945–1946): 405-90. Lewy's work was carried forward by Andrew Key, "Traces of Worship of the Moon God Sîn among the Early Israelites," *Journal of Biblical Literature* 84 (1965): 20-26. See also Agnes Spycket, "Le Culte du Dieu-Lune a Tell Keisan," *Revue Biblique* 80 (1973): 384-95. Spycket is also dealing with the early first millennium, and quotes the prayer of Nabonidus's mother: "I raise my two hands towards Sîn, king of gods, imploring with reverence" (author's translation). One cannot help but think of Aaron and Hur holding Moses' hands aloft during the battle with Amalek (Exod. 17:11-12). Key's article ends by noting "the continuing emphasis on lunar holidays and festivals which play so large a role in later Judaism."

The answer is that Israel in Canaan began not as one man's family, but as a loose-knit confederation. The *Encyclopedia Judaica* admits that even the tribe of Judah contained a large admixture of Canaanite elements and had a low social status; consequently, the "theme of brotherhood, a metonymy for the bond that links humanity, is handled with growing complexity from the beginning of Genesis to the end."[3] The early history of Israel might therefore be compared to that of colonial-revolutionary America and its slogan *E pluribus unum*, "from many, one."

Judah's rise to prominence, though devious, was a good deal less bloody than our revolution. Numerically the largest of all the tribes, Judah displaced small, Transjordanian Reuben, Jacob's firstborn. The ostensible reason that Reuben "deserved" displacement was that he tried to sleep with their father's concubine, thus asserting leadership. In actuality, the Reubenites disinclination to cross the river to fight alongside their brothers (Judges 5) led to a loss of any role in the governing coalition.

Similarly, Judah absorbed the tribe represented by another older brother, Simeon. Their story (Judges 1), thought to be an addition to the text, says Simeon "owed him one," for the assistance Judah had given in clearing Canaanites from Simeon's territory, but Simeon deserved to be eclipsed. The tribe may have fought alongside Judah, but he and Levi were both credited and displaced for killing all of the newly circumcised men of Shechem after Dinah's marriage to its prince (Genesis 34).

Levi was not absorbed but got no land. Levi's landlessness may represent a real memory of the tribe's having spent four generations in Egypt. By the time Levi came—or came back—to the land, it had been settled, divided. But Levites were the "shock troops" of Israelite monotheism, credited also with killing 3,000 of their brethren in the wake of the Golden Calf apostasy (Exod. 32:25-28), so they were appointed to serve as priests in the various Israelite settlements.

With the three ahead of him neatly disqualified, the next son in line was Judah. Tradition remembers Judah as the leading southern tribe, eventually giving its name to the area (Judea) and the people (*yehudim* = Jews) living there.

---

[3]Thus ends J. P. Fokkelman's chapter on Genesis in Robert Alter and Frank Kermode, *The Literary Guide to the Bible* (Cambridge MA: Harvard University Press, 1987) 53. See *Encyclopaedia Judaica* 10:326-28.

Our biblical history also includes other narrowly "national" or even tribal issues answering such questions as: What were the relations among Jacob's sons and how did his family "acquire" Shechem? How is it that, although many groups were related, some "relatives"—Edom, Amalek, Moab, Ammon—were not welcome in the Israelite community? But before we can sort out Jacob's family and their complex relationships, we must journey back into Israel's prepatriarchal past.

§2. Israel: An Etiological Appreciation

Unity in the family is created by the belief, even if fictitious, that all the members of the family are related.   —Joachim Wach (*Sociology of Religion*)

Whether one begins with Adam and Eve, Mr. and Mrs. Noah, or the Tower of Babel, the Bible presumes that, with the possible exception of the *rephaim*,[4] all humans are descended from common parents. Politically incorrect theories of multiple origin and concomitant "racial" inferiority[5] would scarcely have occurred to the Bible's collectors—though not for the sake of "political correctness." There could be no creation outside God's single creative act. In this light, the story of Adam and Eve can be seen as a complex of etiological, that is, "question-answering" explanations.

Rudyard Kipling's Just So Stories, *answering such questions as how the rhinoceros got his horny hide or the leopard his spots, are examples of tongue-in-cheek etiology. In an even lighter vein, so is Bill Cosby's Q & A: "Why is there air? Because you need something to fill a basketball with."*

How the first humans came to be, why they clothed themselves, why they had to work for their daily bread, why they died—and why we do— such questions are much graver. The traditional answers to most such questions involve the notion that they—and consequently we—are justly punished for our human failings, notably disobedience to God. It is important to observe that answers of this kind need to be treated with a certain caution if only because the recurrent false logic mentioned

---

[4]Deut. 2:20-22 identifies Ammon as the former home of the *rephaim*.
[5]As found in Carleton Stevens Coon, *The Living Races of Man* (London: Jonathan Cape, 1966) and Richard Herrnstein and Charles Murray, *The Bell Curve: Intelligence and Class Structure in American Life* (New York: Simon & Schuster, 1996).

above—"what comes after is necessarily caused by what comes before"—
is all too easily applied.

*The classical illustration of this is that the sun always rises after the
rooster crows, therefore, the rooster's crowing causes the sun to rise.
Similar to this is the belief that bad fortune or illness is the result of
one's or one's ancestors' sins.*

Noah's Flood is read as just such an example of divine response to
human failings. But the story is not unique to Israel and may be partly
borrowed or remembered from the Sumerian and Akkadian tales of
Utnapishtim, Ziusudra, and Atrahasis which also tell of great floods.[6]
Despite all such stories, it is wasted effort defending the idea of a real,
universal flood because there is overwhelming scientific evidence against
such an event.[7]

Moreover, these arguments point us in the wrong direction because,
ultimately, it doesn't really matter whether Noah was an actual historical
figure. The importance of Noah's story to its hearers was that it answers
such questions as when we became meat-eaters (Genesis 9), how we discovered wine—and its effects—and how the survivors of the Flood are
all related.[8] The Table of Nations in Genesis 10, which immediately
follows the Flood narrative, is Israel's view of the world's peoples
following the Flood. The Table recognizes seventy nations divided into
three distinct human groups: Semites,[9] children of Shem who inhabit
much of the present-day Middle East; Hamites, children of Ham who include Africans, mostly of North Africa; Canaanites; and Japhethites, children of Japheth. A few words about the last-named may be appropriate
here.

---

[6]The flood tales of Utnapishtim, Ziusudra, and Atrahasis can be found in any edition
of *ANET*.

[7]Evidence against a universal flood was found only four miles from Ur by Sir
Leonard Woolley—see his *Ur of the Chaldees* (London: Penguin, 1950)—but this has not
put the matter to rest. Modern expeditions to find the Ark, or claims that it has been
found, continue to occur.

[8]If Ryan and Pitman (*Noah's Flood*) are correct, the similarities among languages
spoken by people across a broad swath of the earth's midsection attests to a very close
relationship among their ancestors.

[9]The term "Semite" was first used in 1781 by the 18th-century Austrian historian/lin-
guist August Ludwig von Schlözer (1735–1809), who used it to designate descendants of
Shem in the Genesis list and then to identify the language family we still call "Semitic."

The majority of Japhethite names seem to come from an area that roughly corresponds to the land between the Black and Caspian seas. These people could have fled southward even as far as Israel from the Black Sea flood, or been gradually pushed out of their homes by those who did flee. We recognize others as eastern Mediterranean, such as those from the islands of Rhodes or Crete.[10]

In support of this notion, we might look at Joshua 16:3, which mentions "Japhletites," a group so insignificant that it does not rate a mention in the *Encyclopedia Judaica*.[11] Like many biblical names, it is transliterated from its unknown original without translation, but let us hazard one. The root is √p-l-t, "to flee" as from a disaster. We call such people "refugees." If this is a reasonable speculation, it might suggest that we also reinvestigate the name Japheth. Scholars derive Japheth from the root √p-t-h, "be spacious, wide, open" which fits eastern Mediterranean island dwellers. But this etymology rests on the wordplay of Genesis 9:27, "May God enlarge [*yapht*] Japheth" (NJPS),[12] hence the argument is circular and the identification suspect. More informative is the verse's continuation, "And let him dwell in the tents of Shem." Does this not suggest a memory of the Ionian sons or grandsons of Japheth: Cypriotes, Cretans, Rhodians, and others who might have had occasion to flee their land in the backwash of the explosion of Santorini? In that case, Japhlet would be a more appropriate name for Noah's third son.

If "Greeks" are present in the family of Noah, notably absent from the family are Asians. There are no Chinese of any sort here, no Japanese, Ainu, or Okinawans, Koreans, Vietnamese, Hmong, Laotians, Malaysians, Tibetans, Thais, or Cambodians. The Bible's apparent ignorance of any peoples living east of India reflects the fact that, even at the time of final editing, there had not been significant contact with these peoples.

---

[10]Cyrus Gordon and Gary Rendsburg identify Oholiab of Dan (Exod. 31:6; 35:34; 36:1, 2; and 38:23) as an Aegean craftsman, in "The Consistency and Historical Reliability of the Biblical Genealogies," *Vetus Testamentum* 40/2 (1990): 185-206, esp. 206. Robert Graves, *The Greek Myths*, 2 vols. (Baltimore: Penguin, 1955) 2:353, thinks the Gibeonites who tricked Joshua into an alliance were Achaeans, that is, Greeks. David's personal bodyguard were Cretans. More on this in chap. 8.

[11]"Japhletites" occurs only at Josh. 16:3. Mandelkern's *Concordance* separates it from people of the same name ("sons of Japhlet") mentioned twice in 1 Chron. 7:33. The only other occurrence of the progenitor Japhlet's name is 1 Chron. 7:32.

[12]The wordplay is deliberately preserved in *The Schocken Bible*: "May God extend/*yaft* Yefet, / let him dwell in the tents of Shem, . . . " (Gen. 9:27).

Also noteworthy, but not surprising, is the fact that Israel itself is absent from the list. Abram is a tenth-generation descendant of Noah. This chronology may be conventional, but it represents the compilers' knowledge that Israel is a relative latecomer. If the Table of Nations in its final form comes from early monarchical times, which very well may be, remembering to leave Israel out represents a fairly high standard of historical reporting.[13]

Scripture's brief history of the world before the Israelites entered the scene ends with the story of the Tower of Babel in Genesis 11. It is usually read as a cautionary tale warning people not to try scaling heights reserved for God, and it is indeed that. But Isaac Kikawada[14] observes that the whole of Genesis 1–11 may be read as a critical vision of the city-based world from which many proto-Israelites were refugees and outcasts.

Bab-el ("Gate of the Gods"), which represents the city par excellence, is the creation and home of the first murderer, Cain. Since Cain's victim, Abel, was replaced by another son, Seth, one has to ask why God didn't simply annihilate Cain and replace him with some less truculent individual? Even more so since Genesis 9:6 proclaims, "He who sheds the blood of a man, by man will his blood be shed" (my translation). One answer is that in this case strict retributive justice would have balanced the scales and leave unaccounted-for the evils that rural peoples associated with cities.

Plato speculates that the mountain shepherds who survived the great Flood would be naturally suspicious of city dwellers.[15] In the same vein, Giorgio Buccellati points out that, once established on the steppe, outcasts from riverine civilizations would develop a way of life that became increasingly estranged from its city roots.[16]

---

[13]Compare *The Sumerian King List*'s account of Mesopotamian origins, in Thorkild Jacobsen, *The Sumerian King List* (Chicago: University of Chicago Press, 1939).

[14]Isaac Kikawada, *Before Abraham Was: The Unity of Genesis 1–11* (Nashville: Abingdon Press, 1985). A narrower focus is employed by Jack M. Sasson in "The 'Tower of Babel' as a Clue to the Redactional Structuring of the Primeval History (Gen 1–11:9)," in *The Bible World: Essays in Honor of Cyrus H. Gordon*, ed. Gary Rendsburg et al. (New York: KTAV, 1980) 211-19.

[15]Plato, *Laws* 3:1272.

[16]Giorgio Buccellati, *Cities and Nations in Ancient Syria*, Studi Semitica 26 (Rome: Instituto di Studi del Vicino Oriente, University of Rome, 1967).

*If there is still mutual distrust between "hillbillies" and "city slickers,"
how much more so in earlier eras?*

Cities are by definition more cosmopolitan than rural areas. When
rural peoples took themselves and their wares to town, what they would
hear is people speaking many tongues. Genesis 1–11 ends with the "confusion of tongues" at Babel as God's answer to the overreaching of city
dwellers, but the pre-Abrahamic stories do not precede the rise of cities;
rather the opposite is the case. Cities were always polyglot. Isaac
Kikawada further observes that cities also feature such other "undesir-
able" elements as slavery, metal working—and music.[17]

The first-known instruments date to about 2700 BCE and come from
Sumerian Ur. Depictions of early musicians show some instruments being
played by naked women. They sometimes played while other people were
copulating, or while copulating themselves.[18] While David used music to
soothe Saul's savage breast, for some people, the power of music to
arouse is a greater danger to society than its therapeutic value is
beneficial.

*In fact, many types of music were initially derogated or outlawed. In
1914 the pope declared the tango to be "sinful" and it was duly banned
in Boston. In their times, the waltz, foxtrot, ragtime, jazz, jitterbug, rock
and roll, punk rock, gangsta' rap, and hip-hop have been derogated in
the West. To this very day Western music or dance is taboo in some
parts of the Middle East.*

According to Genesis 4:22, metallurgy was the invention of Cain's
descendant Tubal-the-Cain, that is, "Tubal-the-metalworker/smith,"[19] and
smithing has an enormous, if inadvertent, effect on social structures.

*One thinks of Britain's Luddites, an early nineteenth-century group of
workers who went so far as to destroy industrial machinery, fearing
(correctly!) that it would change their way of life.*

---

[17]Kikawada, *Before Abraham Was: The Unity of Genesis 1–11.*

[18]Ann D. Kilmer, "Music and Dance in Ancient Western Asia," in Sasson et al., *Civilizations of the Ancient Near East* 4:2601-13. The Bible's collectors would surely have
seen this as immodest, even scandalous.

[19]Gen. 4:22. The "Kenite Hypothesis," that is, the idea that Israelites learned smithing
from the Kenites with whom they intermarried, was very popular in the nineteenth and
early twentieth centuries. Since then, our increasing knowledge of metallurgy has required
that we look a bit further afield.

We saw this effect earlier in the change of name of Barzillai the Gileadite, who adopted his wife's name—Barzillai also = ironworker or "smith"—because of its status.[20] Like all advances, the new technology was accepted by some, resisted by others. Biblical opposition to the use of metal tools in shaping the stones of the altar may look like a desire to preserve the "virginity" of its stones, but it is also a way of precluding wielders of the new technology from sharing or usurping priestly power. For a while, anyway.

As economists say, "Bad money drives out good." On the profane level, new technology cannot be long resisted, and its unlooked-for ramifications may be enormous. We have mentioned the example of Elisha G. Otis, whose 1852 invention of the elevator incidentally made skyscrapers possible. Similarly, the development of military scimitars, ultimately derived from the Neolithic farmer's wooden or bone sickle, made possible the Assyrian military successes in the eighth century—no wonder they deified their weapons.[21] Needless to add, such transitions are often slow.

§3. The Rise of Cities

> Any city where the better sort are victorious over the masses and inferior classes may properly be said to be mistress of herself.   —Clinias the Cretan

The rise of cities and the emerging prominence of specialists such as smiths, scribes, musicians, and instrument makers caused a widening social chasm among classes of people. Urban lower classes tended to become submerged, a situation notarized by the religious belief that what happens to you for good or ill is reward and punishment for your own behavior or that of your ancestors.

Hierarchical social structures and the unequal distribution of the wealth it promotes eventuated in the institution of kingship, the form taken by urban-based government in Egypt as early as 3000 BCE. Kingship quickly gave rise to the dynastic principle, which dictates that rulers

---

[20]Neh. 7:63. Second Samuel mentions the name *Barzillai* seven times, as compared to the rest of Scripture's five times, and that in only three verses. We know that Israelites were late in acquiring iron technology. It was probably brought east by an Aegean group (possibly the Denyen, see below) and wasn't in wide use until ca. 800.

[21]Morton Cogan, *Imperialism and Religion: Assyria, Judah, and Israel in the Eighth and Seventh Centuries BCE*, SBL Monograph Series 19 (Missoula MT: Scholars Press, 1974).

are chosen by lineage and not by merit. This inevitably led to greater corruption and incompetence, as appointees were often those whose qualifications for preferment were limited to the fact that they were relatives of the king. We call this nepotism.

The full name of Iraq's present leader is Saddam Hussein al-Tikriti. The last element names the village he is from and, not coincidentally, the same village many of his supporters and officials also come from.

We may contrast kingship with the form of government in premonarchic Israel: there a regional or tribal leader's own abilities played a key role in his election and tenure. In chapter 7, we will investigate the two centuries of the "judges"; for now note that no judge was succeeded by his or her own offspring, avoiding the succession squabbles inherent in kingship (see chap. 8, below).

Opposition to dynasticism with its inherent corruption would necessarily give birth to dissidents. Job, even if fictional, represents the quintessential dissident. He didn't merely challenge the social order, but the justice of God himself.[22] And if God may be challenged, how much more a mortal monarch? But opposition is not without its hazards.

Elijah may be the prime example of an antiestablishmentarian in biblical Israel, but my feeling is that the *story* of Abraham, especially in forms like the late midrash about his idol-breaking activities, represents what happens to dissidents, to iconoclasts whose emperor has no clothes, and to those with certain diseases or physical conditions.[23]

It may be just as well that Job kept his complaints more or less to himself, but what happened to those critics and whistle-blowers who "go public"? They were not welcome. The person we know as the prophet Amos was expelled—elsewhere I have argued, exiled from his own

---

[22]Robert Redfield, *The Primitive World and Its Transformations* (Ithaca NY: Cornell University Press, 1953) 64-91. Norman Gottwald's work has advanced the thesis that Israel was basically formed by disfranchised and oppressed urban lower classes. For all Gottwald's avowed Marxism, the theory still needs to be taken seriously as a partial explanation for what happened.

Not everyone accepts the status quo in the world as being part of some divine plan. A particularly trenchant example of modern-day opposition to their fate is the phenomenon of Hindu untouchables in Tamil Nadu converting to Islam to escape their congenital status.

[23]Dissidents might be permanently expelled, but it is possible that one original use of the *herem* (banishment) was as a medical measure.

country[24]—and had to seek refuge in Judah because he publicly criticized his society's religious and social practices. Though the vagaries of history have caused him to be remembered as "the first literary prophet," my feeling is that any society would have produced its share of illiterate or anonymous Amoses. The question is: What did Bronze Age urban societies do with their Amoses?

If Amos's case is representative, dissidents were at least expelled, cast out. We know that city justice was conducted "in the gate." Those found guilty of certain infractions would be literally cast out and forced to make their way outside the city's protective walls. If they fled without waiting for a trial, they might be extradited and executed, as we know from the Esarhaddon Vassal Treaty.[25]

Until the development of deep-well technology allowed the outcasts to survive on the steppe, expulsion was probably tantamount to a death sentence unless the outcasts found refuge with an agrarian tribe, in another city,[26] or had the resources and resourcefulness to found their own.

Whole groups of people might be broken loose when their leader lost his bid for succession. The expulsion of the Sharif Husayn tribe from Mecca by the ibn Sauds in 1925 and their subsequent organization of Jordan is only one of many modern examples. The "Long March" of Mao Tse Tung fleeing Chiang Kai Shek in 1934 is another. The organization of *yamini* (southern) tribes in the time of Yahdun-lim and of Babylon by the "loser" in the Assyrian succession struggle (ca. 625 BCE) are ancient examples. Such things must have happened with some regularity.

---

[24]Stanley N. Rosenbaum, *Amos of Israel: A New Interpretation* (Macon GA: Mercer University Press, 1990).

[25]"The Vassal-Treaties of Esarhaddon" provide for the extradition of prophets (§10). See James Pritchard, *The Ancient Near East (ANE)*, vol. 2, *A New Anthology of Texts and Pictures* (Princeton NJ: Princeton University Press, 1975) 53-69. Just such a case of extradition is reported in Jer. 26:20-23. One Uriah ben Shemaiah was brought from Egypt, executed, and buried in a common grave.

[26]The story of Idrimi's flight and successful return can be found in *ANE* 2, *A New Anthology*, 96-98.

§4. Israel's Self-understanding

Only you have I cherished from among all the nations of the earth. (Amos 3:2)

Nations need histories for internal as well as external consumption.[27] As we just saw, the story of Jacob's family masks the underlying reality that Israel began as a congeries of disparate groups. Having a mythology that united its constituent elements into a family over against the other families of the earth was an important concept for maintaining separation. In Israel's case, a history justifying its own existence and divinely ordained right to the land would also be necessary.

Therefore, Israel came to see itself as chosen to follow a code of conduct that others did not, separate and distinct from the rest of the world.[28] Because of this, Max Weber identified Jews as a "pariah people" and Karl Marx excoriated his Jewish ancestors as "rootless urban cosmopolites,"[29] but these nineteenth-century sociologists were hardly the first to see Israel this way (see below).

Paradoxically, Israel's chosenness was not exactly of its own choosing. Proto-Israelite groupings will have included a lot of "outcasts and ne'er-do-wells,"[30] malefactors who probably joined themselves together through blood-brotherhood rituals. Then, as now, the blood brothers would be seen as excessively "clannish"[31] and feared, like old-time outlaws, pirates, and in our time the Mafia and the KKK. Also, their wandering lifestyle would be objected to by the very people who caused them to band together in the first place.

---

[27]See Hans Barstad, "History and the Hebrew Bible," in *Can a "History of Israel" Be Written?* ed. Lester L. Grabbe, JSOTsupp. 245 (Sheffield: Sheffield Academic Press, 1997) 37-64.

[28]Even today, the Jewish prayer response to the Sabbath blessing of wine includes the phrase, "For You have chosen us and sanctified us from among all peoples." This kind of "chauvinism," however, is hardly confined to Jews. Redfield, *Primitive World*, 64, reports: "The Negroes (of the Ituri forest) distinguish four ranks or orders of living beings: people, pygmies, chimpanzees, and other animals."

[29]Max Weber, *Ancient Judaism* (Glencoe IL: Free Press, 1952) 51, seems to have bought into Marx's notion and expands upon it.

[30]Donald B. Redford, *Egypt, Canaan, and Israel in Ancient Times* (Princeton NJ: Princeton University Press, 1992) 278.

[31]In Lawrence Boadt's words, they were connected more by faith than blood. *Reading the Old Testament: An Introduction* (New York: Paulist Press, 1984) 153.

At least some of the proto-Israelites followed flocks and herds because that is what seasonally rain-fed vegetation dictated. Suspicious of cities from which some of them had been cast out, proto-Israelites adopted a seminomadic (dimorphic) way of life that did not endear them to more settled civilizations. Robert D. Redfield writes,

> Egyptian Nilotic society had, since the dawn of time, given practical and moral superiority to sedentary life and poured contempt on the uncontrolled movement of people.[32]

In the oft-quoted Deuteronomy 26:5, "A wandering Aramean was my father," we should pay as much attention to the adjective as to the proper noun it modifies. Also note that this verse continues, "before going down to Egypt." The Egyptian term for "wanderers" *sh's*, *shasu* has a derogatory connotation, a connotation found in contemporary societies as well.[33]

Here is the opinion of Akhtoy III, father of Merikare of the Tenth Dynasty, about 1900 BCE, on the subject of pre-Israelite ancestors: "Lo, the vile Asiatic! . . . He never dwells in one place, but has been forced to stray through want, traversing the lands on foot."[34]

§5. What Is Remembered —Alice B. Toklas
[A]ll the guesses and legends, the stuff that comes before the facts. . . .
—Ursula K. LeGuin (*City of Illusions*)

The first Hebrew to go to Egypt, of course, was Abraham, who is also noted as the first person to practice circumcision.

> *It is unfortunate that Scripture does not often concern itself with its characters' states of mind, else we might have Abraham wondering why God did not order the procedure on Hagar's newborn child, since at the time there was no hint that Sarah would ever bear a child. Abraham was ninety-nine when he circumcised himself and both of his sons. Ishmael was thirteen, the age at which Muslims today perform the operation.*

---

[32]Redford, *Egypt, Canaan, and Israel*, 271. A similar view of "Amorites"—the generic term for "Westerners" once generally thought to have been the origin of the Israelites—was held by Sumerians. One of their complaints reads, in part, "who has no house in his lifetime." Ada Feyerick et al., *Genesis, World of Myths and Patriarchs* (New York: New York University Press, 1996) 96.

[33]For example, bedouin = "desert dweller" = wanderer. Compare French *pieds-poudre* < peddlar (W. F. Albright's "dustyfoots"), or North American "Blackfeet" Indians, who had migrated from the East to Montana, and hunted buffalo on foot.

[34]Redford, *Egypt, Canaan, and Israel*, 67.

If the outcasts were a diverse group, circumcision might have been one of their blood-brotherhood rituals. Despite its seemingly divine ordination, there is a question as to how widespread the practice was and how early it is found in the ancient Near East. There is evidence that it was done in Egypt to some priests in the Sixth Dynasty,[35] that is, in the late third millennium, but no indication that it was a universal practice. If not, Exodus 19:6—"but you shall be to Me a kingdom of priests and a holy nation [*goi kadosh*]" (NJPS)—takes on a different ring.

Egyptian circumcision seems to have been done at puberty and to have had some sexual implication, either as an "offering" to ensure virility or as a male compensation for the onset of female menses, two considerations that seem absent from the biblical practice of infant circumcision. Since various peoples circumcise males at different ages[36] (the mutilation miscalled "female circumcision" is not a parallel), we have to wonder what Abraham, or God, found to be so special about the procedure. Jewish tradition knows circumcision as the "sign in the flesh" of what later becomes Israel's covenant with its god, but it may have begun as something more modest, the sign of a human covenant.

We cannot leave this subject without a brief mention of various suggestions that removal of the foreskin was early seen to be a health measure. That the procedure, in fact, promotes better health is still hotly debated, but it is unlikely that it could have been seen as such three thousand years ago, any more than were the "symbolic wounds" we know from other societies.[37] Sepsis, that is, infection that may be caused by circumcision, might have been a greater health hazard than any medical benefit the procedure conferred.

Jewish tradition posits that Moses himself delayed circumcising his and Zipporah's son for such a reason (Exod. 4:24-26), and there is some

---

[35]Edgar Schoen, "On the Cutting Edge: the Circumcision Decision," in *Moment* 22/5 (October 1997): 44-45 and 68-69. Kent R. Weeks, "Medicine, Surgery, and Public Health in Ancient Egypt," in Sasson et al., *Civilizations of the Ancient Near East* 3:1793, says circumcision was for religious reasons, contra Herodotus's claim (*Histories* 2.37) that it was for reasons of health and cleanliness.

[36]Arnold van Gennep, *The Rites of Passage*, trans. Monika Vizedom and Gabrielle Caffe (Chicago: University of Chicago Press, 1960) 70-72.

[37]Bruno Bettelheim, *Symbolic Wounds: Puberty Rites and the Envious Male* (Glencoe IL: Free Press, 1954). See David Gollaher, *Circumcision: A History of the World's Most Controversial Surgery* (New York: Basic Books, 2000).

possibility that, after Israel became established, the practice of circumcision fell out of use. At least, some commentators read Elijah's complaint in 1 Kings 19:10 that Israel had "forsaken [its] covenant" as meaning that the Israelites had stopped circumcising, but the text is not explicit.[38]

§6. Patriarchs

Abram the Hebrew. (Genesis 14:13)

Traditionally, Israelite history begins with Abram and Sarai (Gen. 12), characters for whom we have as yet no extrabiblical evidence. Consequently, many early archaeological expeditions to the "Holy Land" were mounted and funded by Western people or institutions with religious agendas—desires to "prove" biblical truths or demonstrate the Bible's historical veracity.[39] Suggested dates for the beginning of the Patriarchal Period vary widely. Frank Frick gives three, all higher than the date I favor.[40] If the patriarchs are at all historical, they and their descendants likely lived towards the end of the Bronze Age(s), which we saw in chapter 2 is a 2,000-year stretch from 3200 to 1200 BCE.

Wherever we put him, it is not presently possible to determine whether there was a real Abraham; later Israel would have strong reasons for inventing one.[41] How much has simply been imperfectly remembered and how much invented? Before trying to answer this question we might wish to ask, Does it matter if there was a real Abraham? Yes, in the sense that "recall" of historical memories, however dim and confused, is of a different order than whole-cloth creation of national histories.

---

[38]Some Jews in Maccabean times did forsake it, or at least reverse its effects so that they could pass as Greeks, especially in athletic events which required that participants be naked.

[39]For example, John Garstang's "finding" of the wall at Jericho that Joshua allegedly destroyed. Sir Leonard Woolley solicited funds from pious widows, giving him some incentive for finding evidence to support the Bible, evidence with which his patrons would be pleased.

[40]Frank Frick, *A Journey through the Hebrew Scriptures* (New York: Harcourt, Brace, 1995) 156. Jan Alberto Soggin, *A History of Ancient Israel* (Philadelphia: Westminster, 1984) 89-91, suggests that the wide variation indicates a basic lack of historicity to the narratives as a whole.

[41]George Mendenhall suggests that the Abraham stories were grafted in to support the idea of kingly (Gen. 17:6) over priestly rule; also, we might add, they legitimize Jerusalem over Shechem as the seat of government. Mendenhall, "Tribe and State in the Ancient World: The Nature of the Biblical Community," in *The Tenth Generation: The Origins of the Biblical Traditions* (Baltimore: Johns Hopkins University Press, 1973) 174-97.

My assumption is that there are real nuggets of historical memory in the patriarchal narratives, though one may have to dig deep to find them, and even then not be sure of what one has found. At the same time, I keep in mind Barstad's observation, "Future studies must start from the presumption that 'truth' . . . and 'fiction' . . . is not a valid distinction anymore."[42] So our study does not stand or fall on the question of provable patriarchs.

The cautious Donald Redford thinks Abram (and Jacob) were actual Middle Bronze figures, and John Bright (an Albright student) reminds us, further, that Jews of later periods would hardly have invented ancestors who routinely broke the laws they themselves were trying to establish, such as Abraham's serving of both meat and dairy to his visitors, or Jacob's or Elkanah's marriage to sisters.[43] I would put the period of Abraham at about 1500 BCE.

Only forty years ago, William F. Albright was still drawing a fairly sharp-edged portrait of Abraham as a donkey caravaneer,[44] an idea that subsequent scholars have sneered at. But is there something to it? Already in the Old Assyrian period, well before Abraham's time on any but the highest chronological reckoning, there was a caravan route between Asshur and Anatolia (Kanesh), where tin and woolens were exchanged for silver and gold. The famous Egyptian Middle kingdom tomb painting at Beni Hasan is dated to the nineteenth pre-Christian century. It shows Canaanites bringing trade goods to Egypt.

Albright's identification of Abraham as one of these teamsters depends in part on his clever use of Genesis 49:11, suggesting that Judah, Abraham's great-grandson, got out of the teamster trade and took up viti-culture. We saw above that the Bible remembers cultivation of vines as a development within history, not found in man's original Edenic state. What would attract Judah to this "new" profession or what would cause him to leave his old one?

First, as we saw above, international trade depends upon the ability of nations to sustain and protect it. That ability seems to have evaporated

---

[42]Barstad, "History and the Hebrew Bible," 43.
[43]John Bright, *A History of Israel*, 4th ed. (Philadelphia: Westminster, 2000) 76-78.
[44]W. F. Albright, "Abraham the Hebrew: A New Interpretation," *Bulletin of the American Schools of Oriental Research* 163 (1961): 36-54. On donkey nomads, see Buccellati, *Cities and Nations in Ancient Syria*, 85-86.

toward the end of the Bronze Age; as Judges 5:6 cryptically remarks, "In the days of Shamgar [ca. 1100] . . . [the] caravans ceased." The economic vacuum thus created would have opened the way for independent "nomadic" traders. At some time, perhaps at many times, Tel Masos in the Beer-sheba valley in southern Canaan served as an entrepôt for these traders.

Second, just as America's canal boats were put out of business by railroads, and railroads seriously hurt by semitrailer trucks, so international donkey trade was eventually made obsolete by the advent of the long-ranging camel. Camels can eat almost any vegetation, go for up to three weeks without fresh water, and, if necessary, drink salt water. Camels can go across deserts, while donkeys, because they require water every three days, have to go around or carry their own water. With this improvement in the means of transport, the routes probably changed, too.[45]

The Bible obscures this development by ascribing camel use to the patriarchs. But that seems to be a glaring anachronism. Modern archaeological investigations suggest that camels don't appear to have been domesticated for haulage in Canaan until well into the Iron Age, and Judah—if he was in fact a real character—would have lived and died well before that time.

Camels seem to have been used in Arabia much earlier. In any case, historical compression might have collapsed the time between the story and its written preservation. Since the later collectors of these tales had had domesticated camels for time out of mind, they might well assume their ancestors had them as well.[46]

Assuming the use of camels also obscures the importance of Exodus 34:20's rule that the firstborn of a donkey is not sacrificed, but redeemed by a sheep: Why? If he owns one, the donkey is a caravaneer's livelihood, one of the "tools of the trade," and just as later Jewish law requires

---

[45]Like the Hanseatic League's improved Atlantic shipping putting Europe's north-south commercial land axis out of business, the Suez and Panama Canals, and the recently proposed flying directly over the North Pole, did or could radically change commercial routes.

[46]Evidence exists that camels were not domesticated for long haulage until the eleventh century, so that reference to them in the Patriarchal Period is an anachronism. The presence of anachronisms, however, speaks only to the period of text composition without precluding that the stories themselves are earlier. See Gaalyah Cornfeld, *Archaeology of the Bible Book by Book* (San Francisco: Harper & Row, 1976) 29.

that a doctor not be required to put up his medicine bag as pledge for a loan, so here, too, the cheaper, more plentiful sheep substitutes for the donkey.

I begin with Albright's Abraham, not because I think it is demonstrable that he existed, but because his circumstances are comprehensible within the framework of what we know. Documents from Mari and even more from Nuzi show that what Abraham did was comprehensible within a Middle-Late Bronze Age framework—something later Israelites or Judeans could scarcely have remembered.[47] What is posited of him effectively schematizes what the Bible's ultimate collectors obviously thought was the case (my level 2). It also served effectively to create a linear relationship amongst the various Israelite elements (my level 3).

What can we discern from the Bible's account of Abraham? Genesis 14:13 calls him "Abram *ha-ivri*," "Abram the Hebrew." What does this mean? Tradition connects the word *'ivri* with $\sqrt{}$*'-b-r* referring to his seventh generation ancestor, Eber, but this would hardly be of interest to anyone else. The word *'ivri* could derive from the verb "to cross over," assuming Abraham came from Ur on the Persian Gulf and had crossed the Euphrates (which I along with many others dismiss), or that he was *habiru*.

A connection between *'apiru* (the spelling varies) and Hebrews was suggested as early as 1911 by F. Th. D. Bohl.[48] Bohl maintained that all Israelites were *'apiru*, but not the converse. There likely was a considerable overlap between the two groups, but not as close as our use of "Hebrew" to transliterate *'ivri* makes it appear.

Jonah's introduction of himself as a "Hebrew" (Jonah 1:9) who worshipped the God of heaven has colored our appreciation of the term *'ivri* as it is used elsewhere in Scripture, making us think that in every case "Hebrew" is a faith-designation. This puts the cart before the horse. The

---

[47]There are names and name-forms in the Bible, some ending in *y*, such as *pdry* (found in Ugaritic), similar to Sarai's before it was changed, and some such as *Yakob-el* or *Yakob-har* at Mari that had fallen out of use, their places of origin destroyed before Israel came into being. (See n. 46, below.) Could Scripture have remembered such names when the names of the places they came from had been forgotten? On the other hand, Jan Soggin, *A History of Ancient Israel* (Philadelphia: Westminster, 1984) 396n.24, suggests that earlier claims of such close parallels have been exaggerated.

[48]Cited in Harold H. Rowley, *From Joseph to Joshua* (London: Oxford University Press, 1950) 45-47, who gives a detailed account of other opinions as well. The different spellings are inconsequential.

term likely refers to groups not bound by blood (or other) ties,[49] indicating that some sort of blood-kinship ritual might have been seen as necessary to bind them together. Malamat derives *habiru* from the root √*h-b-r*, "to unite, be joined," and says it "denotes a group of closely associated households, possibly within nomadic tribal confederations."[50]

Habiru are known over many centuries and locales. From the Amarna Letters of the fourteenth pre-Christian century, we learn that they were people who, if times were good, hired out as mercenaries or caravaneers. In bad times they might sell their children or even themselves as slaves in order to survive (Deut. 15:12-14; Exod. 21:2-11).

> *In any developed society, there are jobs that the "better people" leave to the poorer, as Palestinians did the menial work of Kuwaitis before the Gulf War; untouchables in India perform tasks thought to render them ritually unclean; and migrant workers, hobos, or—before the Civil War—slaves in the United States did and do the poorest paid, most arduous and dangerous work.*

With desperation, or sufficient numbers, the *habiru* might take to banditry. Are the 318 supporters of Abraham in Genesis 14 who defeated four kings such people? Authorities usually denigrate opponents, whether legitimate or not. Here again is Akhtoy:

> He never announces a day for fighting, like an outlaw thief of/or a (criminal) gang. . . . The Asiatic is a crocodile on the river bank; he snatches on the lonely road, (but) he will never seize at the harbor of a populous city.[51]

In the mid-fifteenth century, one Idrimi of Alalakh took refuge in Canaan, where he gathered a group of such adherents who later escorted him to a triumphal return. Similarly, the Bible refers to "worthless" or "godless fellows"—the etymologies of the two words are surprisingly close—in three places. In each instance they serve rivals for power, leaders whom the Judeans did not particularly admire: Abimelech and Jephthah in Judges, and Jeroboam I in Chronicles. (Compare David's earliest adherents.)

---

[49]Abraham Malamat, *Mari and the Early Israelite Experience* (New York: Oxford University Press, 1992) 40.
[50]Malamat, *Mari and the Early Israelite Experience*, 39.
[51]Redford, *Egypt, Canaan, and Israel*, 67.

Here we might note that *'ivri* from $\sqrt{}$*'-b-r* and $\sqrt{}$*'-p-r* < "dusty" might be from related, possibly even the same initially biliteral root; they can certainly be confused.

With our modern emphasis on individuality, we overlook the fact that many of our surnames are derived from professions, even if we no longer remember an ancestor who practiced them. Smith and Potter are two apparent names, but so are Fletcher (arrow maker) and Keebler (club maker). I suggest that something of the sort is also the case here. That is, Abraham was identifying himself by his profession, *habiru*, as a caravaneer. Compare Tubal *the* Cain = "smith" of Genesis 4:22, "who forged all implements of copper and iron" (NJPS).

That the running of caravans was decidedly low class we can see from Genesis 44:32, where the Egyptians wouldn't eat with Joseph's brothers.[52] Caravaneers were not like independent modern truckers—even when they owned their own donkeys. If they were like the people mentioned in the Hammurabi Code,[53] they were salaried workers responsible for the safe delivery of goods and could be liable to the owners for losses. There is a report of one Mesopotamian caravan of 3,000 animals returning empty-handed. (I wonder who stood the loss?) But even the profits of a safe trip might be eroded by unfair imposts.[54]

What with uncertain water supplies, wild animals, and the recurring threat of bandits, running caravans was and remains difficult and dangerous work.[55] Despite all this, "mule skinning" was probably better than

---

[52]Of course, the same might be said of Egyptians eating with any Asiatics. However, one of Seneca's letters urges people to be civil to slaves and puts donkey drivers first on the list of inferiors, indicating lowest status. See also Babylonian Talmud (BT) *Kiddushin* 42a.

[53]The relevant laws in the Hammurabi Code, nos. 102 and 103 (*ANET*[2], 170) differentiate between simple loss, for which the "trader" is responsible to his "seignior," and "theft," which is excused if corroborated by witnesses. Laws concerning trade are scarce in Scripture, leading some scholars to conclude that early Israelites were not much engaged in it.

[54]Ur-Nammu, founder of the UR III Dynasty, 2112–2095 BCE, claims that he took steps to free traders from burdensome imposts (*Ancient Near East* 2: *A New Anthology* [1975] 31-32; and Buccellati, *Cities and Nations in Ancient Syria*, 88-89).

[55]Jacob Neusner, *The Way of Torah: An Introduction to Judaism* (Belmont CA: Wadsworth, 1993) 42, cites Mishnah *Qiddushin* 4:14: "A man should not teach his son to be an ass driver." (In what must be one of history's more obscure ironies, during the First World War Joseph Trumpeldor led an Allied unit consisting of 150 Palestinian Jewish caravaneers known as the "Zion Mule Corps.")

some of the other *habiru* "occupations." The most serious drawback for caravaneers, however, and the reason they were so low in social status, was that they could die on the road. If that happened, they might not be buried in their ancestral home, or not buried at all, a far worse fate.

One of Pharaoh Pepi II's (twenty-third century BCE) ass caravans was set upon by Nubians, its leader killed and his corpse *held for ransom.*[56] *Ransoming corpses is no isolated, culture-bound phenomenon. Medieval Jews did this, for example, in the case of R. Meir of Rothenburg, and their secular descendants, the Israelis, still do. Most recently they traded eight live Syrians for one dead Israeli soldier.*

Both Jeroboam I and Baasha in Kings were threatened with nonburial of their corpses so that their spirits would not, might never be, at rest. Why? Because the wandering spirit had to depart this world from a designated place and, in some societies, at a certain time,[57] almost like a scheduled train leaving a railway station, in order to reach its preferred destination.

There is no lack of ancient Near Eastern material attesting to this belief. For example, we have noted that the "Tale of Sinuhe" relates the story of an Egyptian official who, though comfortable and prosperous in the Lebanon, gave up everything to be buried in Egypt. Similarly, Joseph, though honored in Egypt, insisted on having his bones brought back to Canaan. One Barzillai of Gilead refused David's invitation to come to Jerusalem, not all that far away, saying, "let me die in my own town, near the graves of my father and mother" (2 Sam. 19:38, NJPS).

If it is objected that these are only "tales," we can respond that, as in the case of Antigone's braving execution to perform ritual burial rites for her brother, such tales reflect actual customs.

§7. Matriarchs

A woman of valor, who can find? (Proverbs 31:10)

In a 1953 film, *Captain's Paradise*, Alec Guinness plays the skipper of a lake steamer who has a wife at either end of his run, each unaware of the other. In an ancient Near Eastern context this would not be altogether

---

[56]Redford, *Egypt, Canaan, and Israel*, 57.

[57]For the Celts, that day would be our November 1, which they called Samhain. All Saints' Day (1 November; and in some churches, All Souls' Day on 2 November) is the Christian "cover" for this day.

fanciful or anything to hide. Caravaneers might have wives in (all) termini of their routes, and since polygamy was not unusual,[58] they need not have been hidden from each other.

Something of the sort may be represented by the mothers of Abraham's children. Sarah, mother of Isaac, is the most famous of his wives/women. She was of the family and presumably of the same locale as Abraham. This might be Harran near the present Syrian-Turkish border, where, if local tradition may be trusted, some memory of their stay seems to be retained to this day.[59]

How Sarah acquired an Egyptian handmaid is not recorded, but Egypt was one of Abraham's termini. Carrying goods to Egypt, he twice identified Sarah as his sister, which she was: they had the same father.[60] Abraham's identification of Sarah as his sister and as his wife would have been familiar to royal Egyptians whose children habitually married half-siblings (of different mothers) for the same reason, to "keep it in the family."

The misleading identification of Sarah was allegedly done to avoid Abraham's being killed and his wife taken by his Egyptian host. Sarah, however, was sixty-five, so later Jewish midrash finds it necessary to assert that she was still beautiful, still desirable, a questionable judgment indeed, considering the probable effects of wind, sand, and harsh climate on her skin. Even so, it is highly unlikely that any pharaoh would unite with a desert sheik's woman, whether wife or not. It was as unusual for pharaohs to marry such women as it is for British monarchs to marry commoners.

Sarah, however, was the second of three women by whom Abram had children. Hagar, Sarah's Egyptian handmaid, produced Ishmael, his *first* child and the progenitor claimed by modern Muslims. Since we know from later Jewish (and Muslim) law that men might divorce wives for

---

[58]Carol Meyers, "The Family in Early Israel," in Leo G. Perdue, Joseph Blenkinsopp, John J. Collins, Carol Meyers, *Families in Ancient Israel* (Louisville: Westminster, 1997) 1-47, thinks polygamy was rare among pastoralists. She does not factor in what practices the prospect of death in childbirth might have necessitated.

[59]Feyerick et al., *Genesis, World of Myths and Patriarchs*, discuss the possibility that memories of the patriarchs are retained in some Turkish place names.

[60]Ephraim A. Speiser, "The Wife-Sister Motif in the Patriarchal Narratives," in *Oriental and Biblical Studies: Collected Writings of E. A. Speiser*, ed. J. J. Finkelstein and Moshe Greenberg (Philadelphia: Jewish Publication Society, 1967).

barrenness, this ancient form of surrogacy allowed the barren woman to maintain her place in society.

Ishmael's offspring were the Midianites who lived on the shores of the Gulf of Eilat, with whom Israelites had a number of important, though often hostile, connections. Joseph was sold by his ten *half*-brothers to Midianites who then sold him into slavery—something that, as we saw, later Israelite law forbids. This, however, did not deter Joseph's great-grandnephew Moses from marrying a Midianite, the daughter of Jethro. The bottom line here is that an Abraham-Hagar union can be seen symbolically to represent the trade that went on between Canaan and Egypt.

A similar situation obtains with regard to Abraham's third wife, Keturah. Her name actually means "incense" (Gen. 25:1). It is remarkable that the Bible doesn't note Abraham's advanced age (137) at the time he "mourned" the loss of Sarah by marrying again. And if Sarah was surprised Abram was still virile at the age of 100 when her only child was born, how much more might she marvel that Keturah had six children by him?

It is probable that *Keturah*/"incense" (frankincense, myrrh) represents what Abraham and fellow caravaneers brought to Canaan and, especially for embalming, to Egypt from Saudi Arabia. This probability becomes almost a certainty when we recognize that four of Keturah's children bore still-identifiable Arabian peninsula place names.[61] What all this says is that the Judean writers retain the memory that Abraham's adult life was spent caravaneering in the triangle delineated by Arabia and Egypt and North Syria. Here is a suggestion of what was on offer.

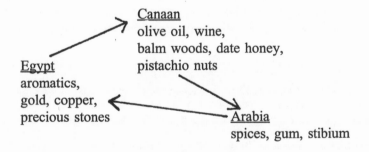

Canaan
olive oil, wine,
balm woods, date honey,
pistachio nuts

Egypt
aromatics,
gold, copper,
precious stones

Arabia
spices, gum, stibium

---

[61]Kamal Suleiman Salibi, *Secrets of the Bible People* (London: Saqi Books, 1988).

When Sarah died, Abram, by then known as Abraham, bought land in Canaan—which had become his home—in which to bury her. This was not a simple real estate deal. Burials establish claim to ancestral/arable territory, hence the protracted negotiations with Ephron the Hittite (Gen. 23). The name changes Abram/Abraham and Sarai/Sarah are here as elsewhere in Scripture indicative of a change of religious identity, perhaps tied to a change from a wandering to a more sedentary way of life.

If, as some minimalists suggest, Hebrew Scripture was the invention of the Persian period, it would be the better part of wisdom to omit the Keturah story altogether or, as they might say, not to invent it in the first place. Conversely, midrashic literature falls off the other end of the table by claiming that Keturah is none other than Hagar brought back to Abraham after Sarah's death. Rashi repeats *Genesis Rabbah* 61 that Hagar was called "keturah" because "her deeds were as beautiful (sweet) as incense" (*ketoreth*).[62] This is forced, but even if it were true, how old would Abraham have been when these six children were born?

Clearly, something about the traditional interpretation smells funny, but I find no reason to doubt that there is some historical truth here. Moreover, there is some intrabiblical reason for accepting it. Chronicles is so uncomfortable with the legal implications of this third family that it characterizes Keturah as a concubine (1 Chron. 1:32-33). This acknowledges a legitimate relationship but denies her parity with Sarah, or her children's with Isaac. Keturah's children get gifts, but are not counted as mainline descendants with claims on the land.

As we saw at the beginning of this chapter, Jews and Muslims base their claims to Israel in part on the alleged primacy of their respective biblical ancestors. If the later chroniclers of events were the Bible's actual authors and not merely its collectors/editors, they would simply have written Keturah out of the script.

If it is not a case of circular reasoning, we may infer that one thing that separates matriarchs from concubines is the power to act independently in matters of family or tribal policy. Both Rebekah and Rachel were active in this regard (more below).

---

[62]An accessible translation of Rashi is found in Morris Rosenbaum and Abraham Moritz Silbermann's *Pentateuch with Rashi's Commentary* (New York: Hebrew Publishing Co, 1938).

§8. Cousins in the 'Hood

We know where Abram settled, but where did he come from? Tradition links him with *Ur Kasdim*, Ur of the Chaldees, a city on the Persian (or Arabian) Gulf, but this identification is another glaring anachronism. The term "Chaldee" was not in use before 625 BCE, when Babylon established independence from Assyria. H. L. Ginsburg's view is that Abraham's connection with this Ur is late, exilic, and invented for hortatory purposes.[63] That is, just as our father Abraham was called from Ur, so we too, exiles from Israel living in his old neighborhood, will be called back.

It is more likely that Abraham or his ancestors migrated into Canaan from the north. As we have noted, Jacob says in Deuteronomy 26:5, "A wandering Aramean was my father." This would help explain why Abraham sent north to find a wife for Isaac, and why Jacob also went north to find his own wife. Abram probably had made his way south from Syria/Harran along the spine of the Judean hills, settling in the area between Hebron and Beer-sheba and becoming a southern Canaanite paterfamilias.

Returning to Israel's immediate neighborhood, we see that Moab and Ammon are *mispochah*, "family." Sons of Abraham's nephew, Lot, they are Jacob's sons' third cousins once removed. But because these two are incestuous offspring of Lot with his two daughters (Gen. 19:30-38), they are not mere "bastards." Bastards might be legitimized later by the formal union of their parents. *Mamserim* are children of a union that could never be consecrated under any circumstances, and by law they and their offspring can have no part in the Israelite community.

Generally, Ammonites and Moabites are ranked together (for example by Amos) with Edom. From an eponymous area in northwestern Saudi Arabia, Edomites are also the offspring of Jacob's twin brother, Esau, whom Jacob tricked to obtain the eldest's birthright. That Ammon, Moab, and Edom are considered family, even if estranged, is apparent in Amos's oracles as arranged by Botterweck.[64]

---

[63]So also Soggin, *A History of Ancient Israel*. Even before Alexander the Great founded and named thirty towns after himself, there were numerous examples of two (or more) towns bearing the same name. This is true even in a country as small as Israel itself. It is perfectly possible, therefore, that Abraham came from a more northerly Ur.

[64]Johannes Botterweck, "Zur Authentizität des Buches Amos," *Zeitschrift fur Alttestamentliche Wissenschaft* 70 (1958): 176-89.

Relations with cousins—some more than others—are uneven. Moab and Ammon were not attacked by Israel on its way in to Canaan, a fact that will assume greater importance when we discuss Joshua (chapter 8). Furthermore, Ruth of Moab is a celebrated link in David's ancestry. Apparently, the tradition is satisfied that Ruth's self-conversion removes the stain of foreign ancestry. Conversely, the hated Amalekites are Esau (= Edom) descendants, no doubt through his foreign wives (Gen. 36:2ff.) and thoroughly proscribed. Amalek is also accounted for in Deuteronomy 25:17ff. and in 1 Chronicles 4:41-43, accused of not only opposing Israel's passage from Egypt, but of falling upon and killing Israelite stragglers.

§9. Isaac

> I thought I saw an eagle
> Or it might have been a vulture
> I never could decide.   —Leonard Cohen song, "The Story of Isaac"

The story of the binding of Isaac (the *akedah*) contains an obvious "dispensation" from child sacrifice; there is even a midrash that Sarah died of joy on hearing the *akedah* did not end with death of her then-thirty-seven-year-old son. The Bible's story might in fact have been composed in response to King Manasseh's apparent revival of the practice in the seventh century. Despite Orthodox Judaism's strained denial, we know child sacrifice took place in Israel, and not only under Manasseh.[65]

Another minor tradition holds that Isaac was actually killed, went to heaven, and was resurrected.[66] If this minor tradition were correct, it would not be the first time that some scholars feel Isaac had been brought to life. They suggest that postexilic Jewish writers called Isaac into being to connect the Abrahamic/Amorite tribes centered on Hebron with those of Aramean Jacob in Shechem and Esau in Edom. To these scholars, Isaac is considered a fictive figure, whose "deeds," so closely paralleling those of his father, seem mainly designed to establish the legitimacy of his position as hinge between father Abraham and son Jacob. As examples we may mention the encounter with Abimelech at Beer-sheba,

---

[65]This is complained of in Psa. 106:37-39 and, as we know, was practiced during the reigns of Ahaz and Manasseh (late-eighth to mid-seventh centuries). For more on these kings see chap. 11, below.

[66]Shalom Spiegel's book-length study, *The Last Trial* (New York: Pantheon, 1967) is a complete account of the minor tradition.

where he seems to have lived, and his passing his wife off as his sister (both in Gen. 26).

Here, at least, the modern minimalists are flat wrong. They point out that Isaac is only mentioned in connection with another patriarch, but that is hardly surprising since he is the only one who is both son and father of a patriarch. Isaac's story is told mainly in chapters 24–28 of Genesis, but only in chapter 24, dealing with his marriage to Rebekah, and chapter 26, the incidents at Beer-sheba, is he a major actor. Isaac is more famous for what happened to him than for what he himself did. If Abraham's existence may be questioned, how much more so that of his son Isaac?

Despite the questioning, evidence for Isaac's existence is hard to deny. An intrabiblical knowledge of Isaac is detectable as early as the eighth century in the Book of Amos. Amos uses *Yishaq*, Isaac, as a parallel with Joseph, the northern kingdom, but "misspells" his name. The usual spelling is *Yizhak*. This variant spelling of the name, found twice in Amos (7:9, 16), once in Jeremiah 33:26, and in one identifiably Northern Psalm (105:9), argues strongly that Isaac stories were known in Israel before 760 BCE and hence could not have been invented later. If the Isaac story *were* a later fiction, why would his name be spelled in the same different way by the only four variant texts? Suggesting that Josiah's men, or anyone, could have "planted" these dialect variants is to imagine a hoax of such magnitude and delicacy that it is hardly conceivable.

An odd feature of the relationship among the patriarchs should be mentioned here. Although after the Flood the ages at death of named figures seems continuously to decline (as also in the Sumerian King List), Isaac's years surpass his father's by five, 180 versus 175. Never mind, for the moment, that both of these figures seem improbable to us. Grandson Jacob lives to be 147. Nahum Sarna points out that

Abraham's 175 is 5^2x7
Isaac's 180 is 6^2x5
Jacob's 147 is 7^2x3.[67]

In other words, there is a definite mathematical relationship among them. Can it be only coincidence? If not, what is it designed to "prove"? As we saw in chapter 4, numbers are more than a means of accounting for

---

[67]Nahum M. Sarna, *Understanding Genesis* (New York: Jewish Theological Seminary, 1966) 84.

commodities. But that brings us no closer to understanding this matter, so here we shall have to leave it.

§10. There Are Wheels within Wheels, Mr. Ezekiel

Whichever side one is on, I think arguments concerning the existence of Isaac are a useless distraction. Even the etiological explanation—why Israel does not practice child sacrifice—hardly exhausts the larger truths of the story. Recall that modern Jews use the divine call and answer of Abraham as a contrast with the call and answer of Jonah to indicate the range of human response to our apprehension of the divine. Abraham's readiness to heed the voice is remarkable because what he was really being called upon to sacrifice was his common sense. It is quite insane to suggest that Abraham will have a posterity if he kills his "only" son before that one has a chance to reproduce. And yet he agrees without hesitation.

> *Neither the Bible nor the midrashim report Abraham as thinking to himself that, obviously, God had decided to recall Ishmael to favor and simply hadn't gotten around to informing Abraham of this turn of events. This despite the rabbinic tradition that Abraham's consort after Sarah's death, Keturah, was really Hagar, recalled as wife.*

Monotheism itself does not depend upon accepting certain nonrational propositions as "mysteries of faith," but it is still, at base, counterintuitive and problematic. This may explain why many Israelites through history were so uncomfortable with monotheism that a thousand years after Abraham's time they were still worshiping other deities. There are so many "powers and principalities" at work in the world that it is hard to conceive of them as emanating from a single creator.

If there is but one creator, then that creator either intends or at least countenances evil, any evil, as part of the divine scheme of things. Job's "Should we accept only good from God and not accept evil?" (2:10 NJPS) is the most concise example of this theology that I know. However, Job's proposition is often difficult to defend. At best, it creates an "ethnocentric universe" in which Israelites or Jews are the only active agents, while the other peoples are merely instruments of God's will.

This is, I submit, a more positive response than that of religious fatalists, for example, Hindu untouchables who acquiesce in remaining forever at the bottom of the human heap. At worst, and a terrifying worst it is, it requires us to adopt a "blame the victim" mentality for those evil things that befall. The recent pronouncement of Israeli Rabbi Ovadiah Joseph that all the Jewish dead in the Holocaust were, necessarily, reincarnations of sinners is a logical, if outrageous, conclusion.

None of this proves that a historical Isaac existed. The evidence we have, though thin, is sufficient to convince me. If, in fact, he did not exist, then I think we must stand in awe of his human creators who have given us such an effective and enduring story.

§11. Double Trouble

Two nations are in your womb. (Genesis 25:23 NJPS)

To continue that story, Isaac was noted as the father of the twins, Jacob and Esau.[68] Esau, his favorite, was the ancestor of those people living immediately southeast of what would become Israel. He was called "Edom" (Red) because the reported redness of his complexion mirrored the reddish sandstone of Edom. Though the firstborn, he is not the designated heir. The question is, again, if these stories are made up, why not simply create one in which Jacob has initial primacy instead of showing him to be a sniveling, conniving coward?

What may be being heard here is a historical echo of the idea, supportable by several biblical texts, that Israel's God YHVH began his "career" as an Edomite weather god, hence the early primacy of the Edomite branch of the family. This possibility, which scholars increasingly recognize, is notably but not surprisingly absent from some recent popular "biographies" of God.[69] In any case, the Bible relates two stories that aim to legitimize Jacob's supplanting of his older brother.

One story concerns Esau's "sale" of his birthright to Jacob. The other represents Rebekah as concerned that Jacob not marry foreign women as his brother had done. Here we may note the active role played by a "matriarch" in determining the family succession. But this was not the first such intervention.

Fleeing Laban, Jacob's wife Rachel took it upon herself to steal and then conceal the family *teraphim*, variously identified as religious objects

---

[68]See Stanley N. Rosenbaum, "New Evidence for Reading *Ge'im* in Place of *Goyim* in Pss. 9 and 10," *Hebrew Union College Annual* 45 (1974): 65-70.

[69]Diana V. Edelman, ed., *The Triumph of Elohim* (Grand Rapids MI: Eerdmans, 1995); Karen Armstrong, *A History of God* (New York: Ballantine, 1993); Jack Miles, *God: A Biography* (New York: Alfred Knopf, 1995).

or things conferring family headship, like the "orb and scepter" of British monarchy. The Chalcolithic hoard of copper/bronze objects found at Nahal Mishmar would seem to contain not only military weapons, but also things the possession of which could be signs of tribal headship. It cannot be an accident that the same Hebrew word, *shevet*, can mean both "scepter" and "tribe,"[70] just what one would expect of totemic groups. Note, too, that in Amos's oracles against foreign nations, God's wrath is aimed at the "scepter bearer" (Amos 1:5, 8).

Father-in-law Laban tricked Jacob into marrying Leah before Rachel, so Rachel's act was poetic justice—the trickster tricked. It also demonstrates that what we would call duplicity is no group's monopoly, nor was it considered in the same negative light by the ancients as it is by us moderns.[71] And speaking of duplicity. . . .

The story of Dinah's alleged rape by the prince of Shechem effectively tells its audience why Jacob's family was entitled to take over there. It seems to be included only for that reason. But was Dinah in fact raped? This is a case that needs careful investigation.[72]

Shechem was vitally important because it controlled the major north-south Canaanite trade route passing between mounts Ebal and Gerizim. As people who have been to modern Nablus know, the pass between the mountains is so narrow that it is easily interdicted. Who controls the pass can levy taxes on whatever passes through. Among the items sent south to Egypt, as we saw, were (date) honey, pistachio nuts, balm woods.

The prince of Shechem's desire for Dinah is an example, however crude, of *connubium et commercium*, the idea that if members of two groups marry, their groups are then related and may do business "in the family." Lemche, doubtless following earlier anthropologists, avers that unmarried women are the "chief commodity" of some groups and that they have to trade in women, as it were, to be connected.[73]

---

[70]See Brown-Driver-Briggs, *Lexicon*, 986-87.

[71]Tikvah Frymer-Kensky, *In the Wake of the Goddesses* (New York: Free Press, 1992) 136-37.

[72]Frymer-Kensky, *In the Wake of the Goddesses*, 194, discusses whether or not Dinah was, or was viewed by Shechem ben Hamor to be, a woman who was free to consent to intercourse—that is, a prostitute. Aggadic midrash blames her parents for any wanton behavior.

[73]Niels Lemche, *Ancient Israel: A New History of Israelite Society* (Sheffield: Sheffield Academic Press, 1988) 94-95.

Various tribes may have practiced exogamy and have met periodically to swap marriageable girls,[74] discarding the old rape-marriage practice. Some meetings may have taken place at Gilgal, Israel's "Plymouth Rock," or as in Joshua 24 at Shechem, where the incident under discussion took place. The rape claim provided a good excuse for what Dinah's brothers, Simeon and Levi, did to the newly circumcised men of Shechem, but their response was disproportionate, given the mores of the time.

As Herodotus says regarding the cause of the Trojan War, "Thus far there had been nothing worse than woman stealing on both sides. . . . Abducting young women, in their [the Greeks'] opinion is not, indeed, a lawful act; but it is stupid after the event to make a fuss about it."[75] Before around 1183 BCE, then, it was common practice among Greeks and Trojans to carry off and physically take other tribes' girls as a form of marriage.

I assume it was the same way in Greece as in Canaan; cohabitation, even if forced, was a recognized form of marriage. Under ordinary circumstances, Bible-toting Israelites were admonished not to marry "them" (foreign men or women) (Deut. 7:3) whoever they are, but (later) Israelite law gives a raped woman the right to compel her rapist to marry her (Deut. 22:28-29). Later still, the Talmud allows that a rapist may be killed to prevent rape (BT *Yad* 10), but subsequent execution of the perpetrator, let alone murder of his entire tribe or city, is never condoned. (The situation in Judges 19 is entirely different. Here a woman is gang raped, making her permanently ineligible for any marriage.)

So the notion of Jacob's boys "avenging the family honor" is, if anything, a later idea that has been backread to justify the seizure of Shechem and maybe to ease the Israelite conscience. But the Bible cannot

---

[74]The subject of kinship and marriage, that is, whether tribes practiced exogamy or endogamy and, in the former case, what kinds of marriages were permitted, has its own literature. The "marriage" that is most immediately relevant here is Amnon's copulation with his half-sister, Tamar (see chap. 8, below).

C. H. J. de Geus writes that Jacobites preferred endogamy, marriage to a related person. De Geus, *The Tribes of Israel* (Assen: Van Gorcum, 1976) 81. Mara Donaldson imagines that there is a development toward (though often not practiced) cross-cousin marriage as opposed to the other sorts of endogamous unions. Donaldson, "Kinship Theory in the Patriarchal Narratives: The Case of the Barren Wife," *Journal of the American Academy of Religion* 49/1 (1981): 77-87.

[75]Herodotus, *The Histories* (Baltimore: Penguin, 1954) 14.

have it both ways. If the retaliation was justified, then Simeon and Levi should not have been punished for it by disqualification from family headship.

That Jacob himself went back to Aram to marry a daughter of Uncle Laban rather than just buying or raping some hapless local wench into matrimony makes Aram the likely place of origin of Abraham, his father's father. By such marriage, Jacob would further cement his claim to the patrimony, since brother Esau married several foreign (Hittite) women: Judith, Basemath—much to mother Rebekah's chagrin (Gen. 27:46)—Adah, and Oholibamah (36:2).

Of course, this could all be so much anti-Edomite polemic. I don't think so. But now—like Esau, so to speak—it gets really hairy.

Jacob's children were borne by four women, two primary wives and two concubines, who together gave birth to twelve males and (only) one named female, the unfortunate Dinah. There was a rivalry among these women, as between Elkanah's two wives later, to produce male children. So fierce was the competition that we learn in Genesis 30:9-20 that Leah gave her handmaid, Zilpah, to Jacob and had two more sons of her own, Issachar and Zebulun, *after she herself had stopped bearing* (Gen. 29:35 and 30:9).

Unlike Ishmael's children, all of Jacob's offspring were part of Israel. Counting all of the patriarch-matriarch/concubine unions before him, there could have been fourteen additional founders of Israel, nine male and five female. That this is not the case implies that arriving at the number seven for the patriarchs and matriarchs combined is deliberate. Is it more than coincidence that this number is also the sum of the sun, moon, and five "wandering stars"? (See above, chap. 4.)

To sum up, if one were to try to rebuild a mirror from shattered pieces, one would likely get a collage, overlapping in some places, missing pieces in others, reflecting light in many directions. So it is with the Bible's own accounts of its patriarchal origins. These stories are not history in our sense,[76] because their purpose is not so much to remember what actually happened as to establish Israel's claim to national coherence

---

[76]This is hardly surprising. See Charles Doria and Harris Lenowitz, eds., *Origins: Creation Texts from the Ancient Mediterranean: A Chrestomathy* (Garden City NY: Doubleday, 1976).

in, and ownership of, a God-promised homeland, and to establish Judah's preeminence within Israel.

Counting Abraham's three wives and their children, Rebekah and Isaac's twins, and all four of Jacob's wives, there could be nineteen Israelite patriarchs and matriarchs, but the Bible only "counts" seven. Interestingly, as we saw in chapter 4, there are seven times in each nineteen-year period when it is necessary to add a thirteenth lunar month. If this coincidence seems entirely far-fetched, we might also wish to repeat here that the 12/13 tribes of Israel, Jacob's children, match the 12/13 lunations in any given solar year. It is tempting, then, to read the patriarchal/matriarchal narratives as some sort of later monotheistic cover of an earlier moon-based religion.

Of course, our Jewish and Christian traditions have made of them the founders of a new people beginning what became a revolutionary religion. The name most associated with this new religion was a great-grandson of one of Jacob's children who, tradition recalls, began life in Egypt. He was called Moses.

Chapter 7

Moses/Exodus/Joshua

§1. Going Down to Egypt

In the Dreamworks movie *Prince of Egypt*, Moses grows up not knowing who he is, and palling around with *the* son of Pharaoh. This portrayal is not only impossible, but does a disservice to viewers who accept it at face value. To understand what might really have been the case, we need first to examine Egypt's situation and policies in the Middle Bronze Age.

The Nile is a much more reliable source of irrigation than rainfall in the region, so Egypt seldom suffered from food shortages the way Canaan did. Consequently, groups of drought-starved Asiatic or Aegean agriculturalists must have come into Egypt, the "breadbasket of the ancient Near East," on many occasions. If drought, with its accompanying famine and disease, compelled some migrants, others may have come as mercenaries drawn by the lure of empire. Still others were brought as hostages or slaves.

Egypt was not immune from deficient harvests, reminding us of the Joseph story.[1] We have, alas, only the Bible's word that Joseph existed, much less that he went down to Egypt and rose to a position of prominence there. Nevertheless, we may still mine biblical accounts and Egyptian records for clues as to which proto-Israelites went down to Egypt, when, and how long they stayed.

---

[1]Redford, *Egypt, Canaan, and Israel*, 61-62, reports famines at the end of the third millennium. The much-beloved story of Joseph in Egypt is a special case for its length and literary merit alone. Many scholars, however, suspect it is strictly literary, that no such person as Joseph existed. That Joseph was carried to Egypt by the Hyksos invaders who established mastery there around 1670 BCE seems unlikely. The biblical account bears no hint that such was the case, and the Hyksos date is far earlier, I think, than even Abraham was born. However, since "Asiatics" were often brought to Egypt, we are not compelled to argue for or against a particular date. Joseph's rise to administrative power, his marriage to an Egyptian woman, and his desire to have his bones returned to his homeland are elements that speak to some kind of truth in the story. At least the storyteller seems familiar with Egyptian customs. And the story brings some Jacob tribes to Egypt whence later tradition knew they came. (Compare the New Testamemt's story of Joseph and Mary journeying to Egypt so that Jesus could be called back from there.) It also establishes, albeit somewhat clumsily, a family pedigree for last-born Benjamin as full brother of the favorite sibling. Despite the awkwardness of Benjamin's birth narrative, here the family story succeeds in presenting a more convincing picture of the relationships. I wonder whether the author's purposes included legitimizing Benjamin, the last(?) group to join the coalition and last to be mentioned in the Blessing of Jacob (Gen. 49)?

We know from Egyptian name lists that as early as 2000 BCE a fair percentage of Egyptian household servants/slaves were Asiatics. Some time after 1450 BCE, the Pharaoh Amenophis II reports that among many people whom he brought back from Retenu there were "Canaanites: 640; princes' children: 232; princes' children, female: 323; . . . brothers of princes: 179"; and somewhat later, "Apiru, 3,600.[2]

Egyptians gave their servants Egyptian names as part of an attempt to civilize them.[3] The Bible knows this much because it reports that Joseph was renamed Zaphenath-paneah, "Life-giving North Wind" (Gen. 41:45). If Joseph began his Egyptian stay as a slave, he was not alone since even "princes' children" were involuntary guests, as were young Native Americans at the Carlisle, Pennsylvania Indian School (1879–1918). In the El-Amarna letters of around 1450 BCE, there is correspondence from one Abdi-khepa of *matat Urusalim* ("country of Jerusalem") indicating that he had been one of those "children of the chiefs" schooled in Egypt.[4]

§2. Moses Who?

If Moses *were* an Asiatic chief's son, his presence at the Egyptian court would illustrate the practice of many monarchies. Empires wish to produce provincial rulers sympathetic and loyal to their adoptive "mother" country who thus will help protect the empire's economic interests. The Bible, however, supports neither view, that is, that Moses was a prince or a slave. What can we glean from its account of things?

According to biblical tradition, Moses was the great-grandson of Levi, son of Jacob. Joseph, Levi's half brother and the first to go down to Egypt, died at the age of 110,[5] so we might expect to find Moses born while great-granduncle Joseph was still alive and influential at court.

---

[2]Memphis and Karnak Stelae, *ANET*[2], 246-47.

[3]A Thirteenth Dynasty list of these (mid-eighteenth pre-Christian century) is translated in *ANE* 2, *A New Anthology*, 87-89. The personal name Sekratu, related to Issachar, is found twice therein. The practice of renaming inferiors was employed by imperial Rome and by American slaveholders, though in the latter case the purpose was to obliterate the African culture of their thus Christianized slaves.

[4]*ANET*[2] 487-89.

[5]As we point out elsewhere, 110 is the ideal life span for an Egyptian, just as Moses' 120 represents the same in Israel. That the teller of the Joseph story knows this indicates, again, some familiarity with things Egyptian.

However, both the Joseph story and the Exodus narrative are silent on this point.[6] This casts doubt on Joseph, but not necessarily on Moses.

Despite the absence of extrabiblical records confirming the existence of any putative Israelite ancestors in Egypt, this study presumes Moses was an actual character, partly because Jewish tradition gives such a patently bogus folk etymology for his name. Exodus 2:10 reports that the Egyptian princess who allegedly found him floating among bulrushes called him "Moses" because he was "drawn up," $\sqrt{m}$-s-h, from the water. This is most unlikely.

For one thing, it would require that Egyptian royalty, male and female, knew the language[7] of people whom they considered barbarians. Also remarkable would be an Egyptian princess's independence and willingness to shelter a Hebrew child—at what risk to herself?—right after her father, the pharaoh, had decreed death for all newborn Hebrew males. Something is being hidden here, but it isn't baby Moses.

Is Moses' name simply another of the puns with no ulterior purpose, puns in which the Bible delights? This, too, is unlikely. As it stands, "Moses" is a perfectly good Egyptian hypocoristicon (shortened form or pet name), that is, a "god-bearing" (theophoric) name from which the divine element has been subtracted, such as Ah-mose or Ra-amses ("Child of Ah," "Child of Ra" or, usually, "Ra has begotten").

Examples of Hebrew theophoric names in the Bible include Daniel, "God is my judge," and Jonathan, "gift of God." "Dan" and "Nathan" are the hypocorisms, respectively.

If the Bible has deliberately and piously omitted the first syllable of Moses' name, this apparent cover-up is some evidence for the reality of the person it seeks to disguise, though no guarantee of his existence. Note, however, that other Levites do have Egyptian names: Merari, Hophni, Pinchas (from Egytian *per-nehasi*, Nubian = "black"?). Moses' name, then, suggests that he was an assimilated Asiatic. He may have

---

[6]I remember visiting a ninety-two-year-old great-grandfather. If any of my four great-grandfathers had lived to 110, they would have been around for my birth. And these were all Reform Jews, men who did not produce children in their teens as our biblical ancestors so often did.

[7]We know from the Bible that Hebrew and Egyptian were not mutually intelligible. It is inconceivable that Egyptian royalty would learn any language but Egyptian, and certainly not the languages of the Asiatics.

been one of the Asiatic "princes" brought to Egypt for schooling and to insure the loyalty of his father who, on this reading, would not have been in Egypt at all.

Were Canaan's local leaders worth cultivating, worth integrating into the Egyptian sphere? Apparently, the answer is yes. Israel in Moses' time was not a country and certainly not a nation, but its importance to Egypt and the rival Hittite empire lay in its resources and geographic position, so cultivating Canaanites would still be a factor in Egyptian foreign policy. Egypt certainly had an interest in controlling timber sources in the Lebanon and keeping open the trade routes to them.[8]

Jewish tradition takes further pains to suggest that the assimilation represented by Moses' Egyptian name is not his fault. It attaches to his birth a narrative very reminiscent of the birth travels of Sargon, circa 2350, the first Semitic dynast of Akkad. Sargon's mother, too, set him adrift in a reed basket, for reasons not given. If Moses was hidden in a basket, was it to protect him, as biblical tradition has it, or is there another reason?

If the birth-in-Egypt story has any historic truth in it, I suggest that Moses was deliberately exposed because of some congenital defect. More specifically, I suspect Moses had a cleft palate or harelip—defects some moderns still attribute to the Devil—because he grew up to be of "heavy mouth and heavy tongue" (Heb. *kabod peh, kabod lashon*, Exod. 4:10) or "uncircumcised of lips" (Heb. *arel saphahtaim*, Exod 6:12, 30). Moses was, respectively, "slow of speech and slow of tongue," "a man of impeded speech" (NJPS).

In most, perhaps all societies down to our own time, children born with certain congenital defects are considered evil or dangerous and consequently may be exposed or abandoned. Clubfooted Oedipus is a fiction, but his story represents Greek practice. Reading backwards from a literal interpretation of Exodus 20:5—"The sins of the fathers will be visited upon the children"—these unfortunates could be seen as receiving punishments for the misdeeds of parents, grandparents, or even great-grandparents. (See John 9:2.) Further, the practice of "passive"

---

[8]A cylinder seal of Atanah-ili, ca. 1900, from Taanach, is a hybrid of Babylonian cuneiform and the Egyptian *ankh*, indicating some sort of cultural mixing and, with it, rivalry for economic hegemony in the area. Later, in 1415 BCE, Egypt and Mitanni concluded an interdynastic marriage, presumably to keep the rivalry friendly.

*infanticide by casting a child adrift for the gods or fates to care for is
widespread throughout history. Compare the eponymous unwed mother
in one version of the folk song "Mary Hamilton": "I put him in a
cockle boat / and cast it on the sea, / that he might sink or he might
swim, / but he'd ne'er hae more o' me."*

Moses' "difficult speech" would also explain why Moses needed
older brother Aaron as his spokesperson;[9] Micah 6:4 gives Miriam and
Aaron "equal billing" with Moses. In any case, the claims of a Miriam
or a Korah might also be based on a real need to interpret Moses' difficult speech.

H. L. Ginsburg thinks Moses was young, barely out of his teens when
he led the Israelites out.[10] Ginsburg's hypothesis would explain why
Moses was not yet married, something that would be well-nigh unthinkable for a forty-year-old Israelite male. It also makes it less probable that
an even younger Joshua was his aide-de-camp (see below).

Moses is said to have forfeited his privileged position when he
impulsively killed an Egyptian who was beating a Hebrew, an act that fits
a younger man's disposition better than it would an established "old-
timer" of forty.[11] True or not, this episode indicates that loyalty to his
own people had not been completely replaced by gratitude for his
privileged upbringing.

After leaving court, Moses seems to have made his way across the
northern Negev to the east shore of the Gulf of Eilat and (finally) to have
married into people to whom he was already related. His father-in-law is
variously identified as Hobab, Reuel, and Jethro, leading one to suspect
that he had more than one wife. If so, he probably had other sons besides
Zipporah's, but she is the only wife who is mentioned by name.
Zipporah's story seems to have another purpose, namely, the introduction
of the rite of infant circumcision to a people who, one might assume, did
not previously know it.

Moses learned from his in-laws as well, for instance, to create a
juridical pyramid for classifying and trying cases. Moses stayed with his

---

[9]Of course, it is not unheard of for siblings or kin to be spokespersons for holy
leaders. James was Jesus' brother (or, with the Roman Catholics, his cousin); Muham-
mad's daughter, Fatima, was similarly active.
[10](Henry) William "Billy the Kid" Bonney was twelve years old when he first killed
a man; Joan of Arc was seventeen when she first led a French army.
[11]Thanks to my wife Mary.

new family for forty years (admittedly, another conventional number) before returning to Egypt. We would love to know what had been happening among the Israelites, to Joshua and Miriam and Aaron, during Moses' absence. But here the Bible is altogether silent.

§3. Egyptians, Hyksos, and *Habiru*

Accepting the tightest chronology for Israel's residence in Egypt, four generations, as opposed to the 400+ years of biblical tradition, Moses might have been born around 1360 BCE. He would have reached his eightieth birthday and returned to Egypt during the reign of Ramses II, generally believed to have been the pharaoh of the biblical Exodus (more below).

During this time some Asiatics would have had time to acquire positions of responsibility, even eminence. We do not know how easily Asiatics in positions of authority were accepted. Egyptians, like ancient Greeks and Empire French, were xenophobic, that is, suspicious of foreign elements in their midst. Since Egypt had been or would be invaded by Libyans, Nubians, and the "Sea Peoples," Egyptian suspicions are perhaps understandable.

> *America has had two foreign-born secretaries of state, Henry Kissinger and Madeleine Albright—both from Jewish roots, incidentally. Even in a dictatorship such as Nazi Germany's, Admiral Wilhelm Franz Canaris, a Greek, could be a member of the general staff. That Canaris was a traitor is instructive.*

The most successful invasion of Egypt was that of the Hyksos, a group of little-known Asiatics who established the Fifteenth Dynasty. They ruled Egypt from around 1670 to 1550 BCE before the Egyptians succeeded in expelling them. The Bible, then, might be looking down the wrong end of the telescope when it says the reason for expelling Hebrews was to prevent them from allying with *future* invaders. More likely, they had already done so. But it would be a mistake to forget that the Bible does not record even a tithe of what happened in any given period.

As we saw in the previous chapter, not all Asiatics are identified by ethnic group or geographical origin. The *habiru* among them were a low-status social class, imported to do menial jobs. Some *habiru*, of course, might have come to Egypt as auxiliaries of the Asiatic Hyksos, or thrown in with them some time before the expulsion. That *habiru* might change camels in midstream was common practice, as various documents attest.[12]

We might ask, if *'apiru/habiru* had supported the Hyksos, would not there have been lingering hard feelings? Perhaps. (Official Palestinian support for Iraq led to the wholesale expulsion of Palestinians from Kuwait after the Gulf War.) But we have to remember that *'apiru/habiru* is a sociological label designating a class of people, not an ethnicon. Later *'apiru* might have been from an entirely different locale than previous groups. Hence, it is no surprise that a century after the expulsion Amenophis II imported another 3,600 of them.

§4. *The* Exodus?

Memory is composed of "invention and interpretation."
—Mary Gordon (*The Shadow Man*, p. 38)

Genesis remembers that Jacob went down to Egypt with a family of seventy—another conventional number—but never mentions a particular pharaoh, so we cannot be certain when any of these events might have occurred. The problem is compounded by the fact that the Bible gives four chronologies for the period of "Egyptian bondage": 400 years, 430 years, 541 years, if we count with Judges, and "four generations."

The rabbis of Jewish tradition were very aware of these chronological discrepancies, since one Serah bat Asher is identified as both among those going down and those coming back! They responded by making her a figure of almost Elijah-like proportions.[13] But if there were several exoduses,[14] all these chronologies might be correct. Taking as our model the story of the Pied Piper (see chap. 1, above), I think we may posit that Asiatic people fled or were expelled from Egypt on many occasions.

---

[12]First Samuel 14:21 would seem to be one example. Here, "Hebrews" fighting for the Philistines turn to join Saul and Jonathan.

[13]Leila Leah Bronner, *From Eve to Esther: Rabbinic Reconstruction of Biblical Women* (Louisville KY: Westminster, 1994) 42-60. Jewish tradition noted this extraordinarily long life and ended up comparing her with Elijah, that is, making her immortal. But if you figure an ancient Near Eastern generation at twenty years—and that's generous—Serah bat Asher might have been no more than eighty-something on the return trip. (See Gen. 46:17; Num. 26:46; 1 Chron. 7:30.)

[14]Theophile J. Meek, *Hebrew Origins*, 2nd ed. (New York: Harper, 1950) 44, sees two "Israelite" incursions, one around 1400 BCE and one around 1200. M. B. Rowton, *Cambridge Ancient History* 2:239, substantially agrees.

Presently, the best guess is that Ramses II (1290–1226 BCE?) is the pharaoh of the central Exodus event because of the great building projects he undertook throughout Egypt. This work required conscripting large numbers of Asiatics for forced labor, leading Halpren to suggest that some Asiatics might have simply fled their homes in the eastern delta region during his reign to avoid what they felt was Egyptian oppression.[15] Though the Egyptians did chase runaway slaves, this sort of unofficial exodus might have gone unnoticed by history.

There are some problems with identifying Ramses as pharaoh of the Exodus. As we saw, the stele of Mer-ne-ptah, Ramses' son, claims to have destroyed an "Israel" around 1210 BCE, scarcely time for Moses & Co. to have gotten off the road. But this assumes a single Exodus and a unified Israel, something that, if it happened at all, came only much later. On the other hand, Dever suggests that a residence of as little as twenty to thirty years would have been sufficient to bring an "Israel" to Egyptian notice.[16]

This problem may be ameliorated, however, if we posit earlier exoduses or recall that some "proto-Israelite" Canaanite elements probably never went to Egypt in the first place, so that they would have been in residence during Mer-ne-ptah's campaign. Still, we know of none that called themselves "Israel" at this early period.

Three generations after Jacob's journey, the Book of Numbers (1:46) says 603,550 people returned to Canaan. These, however, are only "heads of households," men aged twenty and upward, and does not include wives, children, and the "mixed multitude" (other Asiatics) accompanying them, so that estimates of the refugee total range from two to fifteen million.[17] Miller and Hayes estimate that, walking ten abreast, it would take eight or nine days for the tail of such a column to pass the point

---

[15]Baruch Halpren, "The Exodus from Egypt: Myth or Reality?" in Herschel Shanks, William G. Dever, Baruch Halpren, P. Kyle Mcarter, Jr., *The Rise of Ancient Israel* (Washington: Biblical Archaeology Society, 1992) 86-18.

[16]"Is This Man a Biblical Archaeologist?" *BAR* 22/4 (July/August 1996): 30-39 and 62-63, esp. 36.

[17]The more fanciful figures are based upon ever-increasing estimates for the numbers of people in the "mixed multitude" that accompanied Israelites from Egypt. It should be noted, however, that whatever their number, the Bible is here giving testimony to a diverse group of Asiatics.

where its leaders had begun. And that would be over passable terrain, not what one finds in southern Sinai.[18]

What we have at this point is a story reminiscent of Dr. Seuss's *To Think That I Saw It on Mulberry Street*, a story that grows in the telling. Thus, the Book of Numbers' 603,550 heads of household yields population numbers that are entirely fabulous. Israel Finkelstein omits the zeros, effectively dividing it by 100—which, when multiplied by 6 (for other family members) plus 2,273 Levites (one of three proposed figures) yields a figure of about 40,000—an estimate that can be supported by his recently excavated Iron Age settlements in Israel.[19]

Finkelstein finds no archaeological evidence that suggests Israel is anything other than a largely native collection of pastoral people moving in from the eastern desert fringes[20] (not deep desert, where people could not abide for many years before their land was exhausted). He thinks that what later became the tribes of Ephraim and Manasseh and of Benjamin started out in the north-central hill country, assigned them by Joshua.

It seems likely, then, that those Asiatics whom the Bible remembers leaving Egypt were not the entire "family" of Jacob, but only elements of what became the four major southern or "Leah" tribes: Reuben, Simeon, Judah, and Levi. However, even if they did number as few as 40,000, we need to ask how they could have made their way across the "great and terrible wilderness" that Deut. 1:19 calls the Sinai Peninsula.

§5. Which Way Did They Go?

The Bible reports that the refugees avoided the direct route to Canaan, the "way of the Philistines," across the northern Negev, for fear their passage would be interdicted by Egyptian garrisons. This also argues for a smaller number of refugees: what army could stop 2,000,000 people or even 603,550? But which way did the refugees go?

---

[18]J. Maxwell Miller and John Hayes's logistical analysis in *A History of Ancient Israel and Judah* (London: SCM, 1986) 60, points to the impossibility of maintaining the "southern route." The mountains of southern Sinai, as I know from personal observation, would be virtually impassable for large groups of people.

[19]Israel Finkelstein's "zero-ectomy" is in his *The Archaeology of the Israelite Settlement* (Jerusalem: Israel Exploration Society, 1988) 330-34.

[20]Finkelstein, *Archaeology of the Israelite Settlement*, 355. See also his and Neil Asher Silberman's *The Bible Unearthed* (New York: Free Press, 2001).

Through four editions of Bright's history, the traditional southern route is still favored, but scholars have not come to any agreement on the way of "The Exodus."[21] A Red Sea passage itself is no longer favored, and not simply because of our modern disinclination to credit biblical miracles. Yam Suf (Exod. 13:18; cf. 10:19), the Bible's phrase identifying what the Bible's transmitters clearly saw as the place for a miraculous event, does not mean "Red Sea," but either Reed Sea, or as I think, "end sea" (from the Heb. √s-v-f = "end"). It could refer to either northern arm of the Red Sea, to Lake Menzaleh (Tjouf in Egyptian) in the Bitter Lakes region, or even to the Straits of Tiran. (This would put Mt. Sinai in present-day Saudi Arabia, which has been claimed with a certain plausibility.[22])

My own feeling, however, is that Yam Suf denotes Lake Sirbonis (Bardawil), a briny lake on Egypt's north coast east of the Nile delta. Sirbonis is separated from the Mediterranean by a low-lying strip of land and dominated by Mons Casius, which could be the Baal Zaphon ("God of the North") of Exodus 14:2. This latter identification is discounted, for example by the Oxford Bible Atlas,[23] because archaeologists have found no remains dating from the supposed time of the traditional Exodus.

Such a denial, however, is predicated partly on the assumption that there was only one Exodus. What I would like to call "the Yam Suf incident" is probably based upon some real memories, else it could hardly have survived so long, but these memories need not all be contemporaneous. What might have happened to produce the biblical account? The answer is: multiple exoduses. Meeks's suggestion, which Abraham Malamat picks up, entails that differing routes could represent multiple migrations, which seems likely.[24] My feeling is that the period from, say, 1670 to 1250 BCE saw a lot of movement both to and from Egypt.

---

[21]John Bright, A History of Israel, 4th ed. (Louisville: Westminster, 2000) 122-23. The northern route is cautiously supported by Yohanan Aharoni, The Land of the Bible, A Historical Geography (London: Burns and Oates, 1967) 179.

[22]Thus Julius Lewy, as reported by Andrew Key, "Traces of Worship of the Moon God Sîn among the Early Israelites," Journal of Biblical Literature 84 (1965): 23.

[23]Oxford Bible Atlas, 3rd ed., rev. by John Day (New York: Oxford University Press, 1984) 135, which also disputes the identification of yam suf with Sirbonis.

[24]In Abraham Malamat et al., A History of the Jewish People, ed. Haim Hillel Ben-Sasson (Cambridge MA: Harvard University Press, 1976) 44, where Malamat speaks of "waves of migration at different time intervals."

One of these exoduses could be contemporary with the explosion of Santorini (Thera) which, as we saw (above, chap. 2), is a volcanic island sixty miles north of Crete. Jaynes says Thera's tidal surge was seven hundred feet high and smashed inland for up to two miles.[25] On the basis of dendrochronology,[26] many scholars confidently assign the explosion to 1628 BCE. Others estimate 1550, which fits our theory even better. Recall that the Ahmose stele (ca. 1550) says, "Then every house and barn where they might have sought refuge [was swept away . . . and they] were drenched with water like reed canoes."[27]

In either case, when Thera exploded the north coast of Egypt would certainly have been affected. The dramatic "drowning" of an Egyptian force fits here, but no explosion-generated tidal wave is necessary to produce flooding at Sirbonis. Even abnormally high tides would make it impassable for chariots. A less dramatic, regular flooding of the Bardawil barrier strip is not out of the question.

The Bible further reports that the Israelites were led by a "fire by night and a pillar of cloud by day." This description could be derived from Thera's tremendous column of fire, ash, and smoke towering up through the stratosphere. How high? Well, Mt. St. Helen's 1980 eruption plume reached 15,000 feet and deposited ash in eastern Washington, three hundred miles away. Thera's blast was considerably larger. It would have been visible over an area that I estimate to be the size of Montana. And with a northwesterly wind behind it, the plume would soon have been visible as far as the northwest coast of Egypt, only some three hundred miles away, for many weeks.

---

[25]Julian Jaynes, *The Origin of Consciousness in the Breakdown of the Bicameral Mind* (Boston: Houghton Mifflin, 1976) 212. Jaynes apparently gets this figure from Spyridon Marinatos, *Crete and Mycenae* (New York: H. N. Abrams, 1960). It is supported by Richard W. Hutchinson, *Prehistoric Crete* (Harmondsworth UK: Penguin, 1962) 301-302. And see the detailed discussion (with illustrations) of William H. Stiebing, Jr., "The Volcanic Eruption of Thera and the Exodus Events," in *Out of the Desert? Archaeology and the Exodus/Conquest Narratives* (Buffalo NY: Prometheus Books, 1989) 102-13.

[26]Dendrochronology ("tree-chronology") is the establishment of absolute dates by examination and comparison of tree rings. The explosion of Santorini caused years of stunted growth because of reduced sunlight. William Ryan and Walter Pitman, *Noah's Flood* (New York: Simon & Schuster, 1998) 145-46, add that this date is supported by evidence obtained by accelerator mass spectrometry.

[27]Redford, *Egypt, Canaan, and Israel*, 420.

Scholars such as Redford, Miller and Hayes, and Halpren explicitly deny any connection between Thera and *the* Exodus and I concur; even a date of 1550 BCE is too early. But again, their position is based upon the Bible-based assumption that there was only one such event. If the Exodus story is an example of historical compression, then the Exodus was not as unique an event as our tradition remembers it to be.

Greta Hort goes further, suggesting that all of the first nine plagues were natural events, but connecting them with unusually heavy rainfall further south.[28] It makes more sense to try to interpret them as results of a volcanic explosion, to wit,

1. Blood—iron compounds from volcanic ash would color water red.
2. 3. 4. 8. Frogs, Gnats, Flies, Locusts—vermin deprived of natural habitat become more aggressive.
5. 6. Cattle disease and boils—caused by malnutrition accompanying crop failure: acidic fallout affects crop growth. (The explosion of the Indonesian volcano Tambora in 1815 caused crop failures in New England the same year.)
7. Hail—driven south by atmospheric disturbances or other detritus from the sky.
9. Darkness—Ahmose also records a period of "[x] days when no light shone on the Two Lands."

Miller and Hayes shy from "such marvelous correlations of coincidental factors,"[29] but even Redford thinks the connections are "more than fortuitous."[30] And recall Braudel's words, that "there is no society, however primitive, that does not bear the 'scars of events.' " Middle Bronze societies were hardly primitive; in 1550 Egypt had been a kingdom for over a thousand years, and this event happened well within reach of written as well as oral memories.

However we judge this, what can we say about the tenth plague, the death of the firstborn? There is nothing natural about this. Could it be that in the face of a series of natural catastrophes the Egyptians resorted

---

[28]Greta Hort, "The Plagues of Egypt," *Zeitschrift fur Alttestamentliche Wissenschaft* 69 (1957): 84-103; and *ZAW* 70 (1958): 48-59; discussed in Nahum Sarna, *Exploring Exodus* (New York: Shocken Books, 1986) 70-72.
[29]Miller and Hayes, *A History of Ancient Israel and Judah*, 65.
[30]Redford, *Egypt, Canaan, and Israel*, 420, terms these events "more than fortuitous."

to that most dire of apotropaic measures, sacrificing their own children?[31] Predynastic Egyptians had sacrificed slaves to guard the spirits of the dead or new buildings. This was different, and after weeks of reduced light and accompanying crop shortfalls, increased vermin, and diseases, the Egyptians might have been moved to try something not previously done, namely, sacrificing their own children in an effort to appease the gods (see chap. 9).

If so, what did their Asiatic "guest workers" do? On this reading, the "Israelite" lamb sacrifice and blood smearing might not be, as Jewish tradition has it, to let the Angel of Death know they were non-Egyptians, but maybe to fool the gods or at least to fool the Egyptians into thinking that they had done as their Egyptian hosts had. Alternatively, they might have seen the divine anger as directed primarily against their hosts, so that only a vicarious sacrifice was required of them. Redford points out that what from a Canaanite point of view would have been seen as punishment on the Egyptians could also be seen as "pressure exerted *to effect a release*."[32] Pressure by whom he does not say.

Finally, someone notes that the quails of Numbers 11:31 on their usual migration across the eastern Mediterranean to Egypt could be held up by adverse winds—caused by Thera's explosion?—and fall exhausted in the northern Sinai. How convenient that would be! Is it true? We don't know. This incident more likely comes from some time during the wanderers' long stay at Kadesh-barnea, an oasis in northeastern Negev adjacent to Israel.[33] However, the quail bounty does not have to be attributed to the volcanic disruption of flight paths. None of the plagues need be so connected.

My point in stringing them all together is not to prove, à la Immanuel Velikovsky,[34] that the biblical story of the Exodus is an accurate record of a singular, contemporary set of events. Quite the contrary. The very

---

[31]Special thanks to Andrew Byro and the members of the Dickinson-Beth Tikvah (Carlisle PA) Torah study group. I find how that the same suggestion was made by Ian Wilson, *Exodus: The True Story behind the Biblical Account* (San Francisco: Harper & Row, 1985) 126-17, as cited by Stiebing, *Out of the Desert?* 105n.12.

[32]Redford, *Egypt, Canaan, and Israel*, 420; emphasis in original.

[33]H. L. Ginsburg suggests they spent thirty-eight of their forty years of "wandering" at Kadesh-barnea. Lewy looks for the origin of YHVH worship there.

[34]Immanuel Velikovsky, *Worlds in Collision* (New York: Dell, 1965). Velikovsky's theories were and are widely—and rightly so—discounted; but like a stopped clock, he's right sometimes.

number of plagues itself might be artificial, inflated as a parallel with the Ten Commandments, then shortly to be given and certainly present in the minds of the Bible's later collectors and organizers. What I do mean to suggest is that various, even all, of the Exodus phenomena might be based upon real, if misremembered and conflated, historical events woven into a single story.

It is possible, then, that Thera was either the cause of, or at least coincidental with, one or another group of Asiatics making their way to Canaan. Signs such as the fire and cloud would be so monumental that, even if they didn't accompany *the* Exodus, the Bible's editors could have put them in for dramatic effect. However, there is more at stake than simply telling a rattling good story (see §7, below, "Moses and, Maybe, Monotheism"). Thera might even have been used by the Egyptians as a sign that it was a propitious time to expel the Asiatic Hyksos of Dynasty Fifteen and other foreigners, whether previously loyal or not. The real Exodus story is not monochrome, but a "coat of many colors."

§6. Whither Sinai?

We know the Semitic Hyksos rulers of Egypt were expelled by Ahmose around 1550 BCE. So, did any of them, their Asiatic allies or anyone else for that matter, ever go south into the Sinai after that? Halpren doesn't think so, and for good reason. The mountainous terrain doesn't easily support human life or even allow free passage. Here we have been too much influenced by the location of that Mt. Sinai which is adjacent to the Greek Orthodox monastery of St. Catherine.

> *Of the dozen or so proposed sites for Mt. Sinai, the most famous is the one in the southern end of the Sinai peninsula. It was established by Greek Christians only in the fifth Christian century, some 1700 years after Moses' time, and therefore would be of dubious authenticity even without the "miracle" that Greek tradition cites to authenticate its location.*

There are many places where one would expect to find Sinai mentioned in the Bible, such as Joshua 24:6-8 or Judges 11:16-22, but it is not. One thing is certain: Mt. Sinai is not in Israel. On the basis of Deuteronomy 33:2, where it is parallel with Seir and Paran in Edom, Sinai may be located in what is now northwestern Arabia, a suggestion Muslim scholars are particularly pleased to note.

In the Bible's so-called E document the mountain of revelation is called Horeb, not Sinai (for example, Exod. 3:1; Deut. 1:2). Jewish tradition equates Horeb with Sinai, but I think the Bible collectors are trying to mask the fact that various groups in Israel had *different* holy mountains, just as, later, the Northern Kingdom thought that Mt. Gerizim and Mt. Ebal in the North were "the place where God caused his name to dwell."

Either way, that different groups within Israel could have had different names for the same mountain, or different holy mountains altogether, is some proof that Jacob's "family" is a later, artificial creation. Saul Levin points out that none of Jacob's sons married kindred—Joseph certainly didn't—and Levin's reading makes Moses' own grandmother a goddess-named person.[35] How did monotheism emerge?

§7. Moses and, Maybe, Monotheism

Who is like you, O LORD, among the *gods*? (Exod. 15:11 NRSV, emphasis added)

Israel's religious uniformity is credited to Moses and later to Joshua, but despite traditional recastings we can see that there was initially no religious unity among Israelites. In the verse quoted above, universally conceded to be from the oldest stratum of biblical texts, Moses' rhetorical question implies that there are, in fact, other gods. And not merely the gods of other peoples. Psalm 82, a product of the Northern Kingdom, begins with God taking his place in "the divine assembly" (NJPS; NRSV "council"), but judging "in the midst of the gods" (NRSV). Micah in Judges 17–18 hedged his bets (see 17:1-6).

In Exodus 15:11 (see above), NJPS translates "celestials" (with note: *Others "mighty"*) where NRSV has "gods." Here, however, the Protestants are correct, while NJPS attempts a kind of euhemerization with colors reversed. That is, since later Jewish tradition denies any gods besides its own, even the most modern Jewish establishment translation cannot easily admit that Israelites ever thought otherwise. It is not so.

Either Yahwism did not forbid or could not immediately displace other religious elements within the constituent tribes/groups, such as the

---

[35]Jewish tradition on Asenath has it that she was the daughter of Dinah, and so "Jewish." To say otherwise would be to admit wholesale "mixed marriage" among Jacob's family, something that later Judaism fought hard to eliminate. Saul Levin, "An Unattested 'Scribal Correction' in Numbers 26:59," *Biblica* 71 (1990): 25-33.

bull, serpent, and various celestial deities.[36] Moreover the famous graffiti at Kuntillat el-Ajrud suggest that somebody believed Israel's God had a female consort. The Ajrud graffiti seem to identify a "YHVH of Samaria and his Asherah" and also a YHVH of Teman.

> Asherah, represented by green trees, is the earth mother who bore "the seventy gods"; her consort is El the bull, and her original Ugaritic name means "Lady Who Traverses [or Treads on] the Sea [Dragon]."[37] She associates with lions and serpents. Here we should remember that fertility is the most important function a god(dess) can have.

But whose graffiti are they, how early, and how representative of Israelite worship?[38] The present text is probably ninth century, but scholars think it originates in the twelfth to tenth centuries. Since Ajrud is more than "three days journey" from the Nile, we must ask: What religion had Aaron, Miriam, and the other once-and-future Israelites been practicing during their lives in Egypt? Aaron was eighty-three and Miriam presumably a bit older when their brother returned, unlooked for, after a forty-year absence. Had they customarily led certain Asiatics for three days off a year to worship in the desert, as the Bible implies? If so, what god or gods would have been involved? Ajrud provides more than one possibility. Alternatively, Sinai may be connected with Akkadian *sîn*, "moon," the deity we associate with Abraham's ancestors.[39] Aaron's actions at the foot of the mountain are comprehensible if he represents a bull/moon tradition.

This brings us to the question of how Moses became a monotheist in the first place. Some scholars connect it with Akhenaton's revolution of

---

[36]Of the various deities worshipped in the ancient Near East some, like Bull, Lion, and Scorpion, have both heavenly and earthly manifestations.

[37]Compare Ninurta, who is called Belit-ili. See Cyrus Gordon, *The Ancient Near East* (New York: W. W. Norton, 1965) 103. Roman Catholic churches often feature statues of Mary treading on a serpent, and while this motif goes back to the Catholic interpretation of Gen. 3:15, it is actually far older. (It is not snakes per se that St. Patrick drove out of Ireland, I surmise, but the snake cult.)

[38]The later (after 586) Jewish mercenary settlement at Elephantine in Upper Egypt seems similarly polytheistic, giving God a consort, Anat-Yahu. That could be due to local "contamination"; we have no way of knowing, but increasingly evidence points to a less than pure monotheism among many Israelites at all times and places.

[39]Thus Andrew Key, "Traces of Worship of the Moon God," in *JBL* 84 (1965), following Lewy, sees traces of Sîn (moon) worship among Israelite ancestors, especially Aaron (p. 23).

two centuries before, so that if Moses saw far it may be because he, too, stood on the shoulders of giants.[40] But it is hard to see that a revolution which was ultimately rejected by the Egyptians managed to hang on for so long among their Semitic slaves unless, of course, the seeds of it had been planted much earlier.

The traditional response, that monotheism was already his family's faith revealed directly by God to Abraham, has the advantage of simplicity, but we know too much about actual circumstances to accord it unquestioning allegiance. Long afterwards, Moses and Joshua both had difficulty in selling the idea to their brethren despite the colossal miracles allegedly wrought so recently by the god of their choice. In any case, traditional explanations founder on the incident of the Aaron-led apostasy of the Golden Calf.

It is amazing that Aaron wasn't cashiered for this; instead he became the progenitor of the Levitical priesthood while Miriam, whose "crime" seems much less grievous, got leprosy.

Section 39 of the Esarhaddon Vassal Treaty,[41] contemporary with Hezekiah, implies that the moon can give one leprosy. The full moon looks leprotic. So is leprosy what you get if you look at the full moon? The Talmud says you get leprosy from gossiping, something that is often associated with women. This looks very much like a late "cover."

It has been suggested that Moses and Aaron were not brothers, but represent two strands of worship, the bull and the snake. Aaron's rod comes immediately to mind, and Moses' "horns" (*karnaim*). The rays tradition says sprang from Moses' face after he saw God, may be patterned after the horned figure of Ugaritic El. Sister Miriam, then, might represent the moon worship that persisted from the time of Abraham's parents.

The above sketch is highly speculative, of course, and in the absence of any substantial evidence need not be taken seriously, but odds are that

---

[40]Among those making the Egyptian connection: Sigmund Freud's *Moses and Monotheism* (New York: Vintage, 1958 [1939]), and most recently with Richard A. Gabriel's "The Memory of Egypt in Judaism and Christianity" (unpublished manuscript graciously provided me by Prof. Gabriel). For a lavish journey into the history of ideas, at least of one idea, see Robert K. Merton, *On the Shoulders of Giants: A Shandean Postscript* (San Diego: Harcourt Brace Jovanovich, 1985).

[41]Esarhaddon Vassal Treaty, §39, *ANE* 2, *A New Anthology* (1975) 63.

Asiatics in Egypt—including those who followed Moses—were a diverse
and necessarily polytheistic group. This Moses, then: Could he have become a religious revolutionary? Why not? Ethical monotheism, the idea
that there is but one God and that he cares about what we do for and to
each other—not merely that he gets fed on time—is revolutionary.
Perhaps this is because its guiding idea is so counterintuitive.

Israelite monotheism further proclaims the following as truths.

1. That the cosmos is God created; if not, the world itself would be a
   rival power source.
2. That the universe is orderly; one can see order in the circumpolar
   sky.
3. That earthly order is in some sense knowable, for instance, in the
   reproduction of humans and animals "after their own kind." This
   must be ordained because it couldn't happen by itself.
4. That humans are the crown of creation, made in the image of the
   creator.
5. That Torah (broadly) is the record of revelation and fount of knowledge.
6. That, the divine will being knowable/revealed, it is incumbent upon
   us to observe the rules that God has apparently set up to govern it,
   rules which can be either seen or intuited.
7. That reward and punishment, good and evil proceed from the One
   God.

In monotheism, the real fight is for *exclusivity*. That is, it's not an
either/or choice, YHVH or the fertility gods, but the proposition that YHVH
is responsible for fertility and everything else.[42] *Everything* else. However
much we presently believe in the revealed religions of Judaism, Christianity, and Islam, the archaic religions that preceded them reflect human
observation of structures that people in those times and places saw, even
literally.

If we may skip ahead in our narrative, by Jeremiah's time the inade-
quacy of astral predictors and protectors was evident to some. Saggs
notes that already by then Assyrian astrology texts contain some pretty
dodgy explications,[43] but the human need for explanation, if not also for

---

[42]Hence the claim of Baruch Margalit, "The Meaning and Significance of Asherah,"
Vetus Testamentum 40/3 (1990): 264-95, that Israel's God had no need of a consort.

[43]H. W. F. Saggs, *The Greatness That Was Babylon* (New York: New American
Library, 1962) 461, writes, "Astrology is a part of the Babylonian legacy which Europe

control of life and nature, is strong. Israelites therefore continued to invoke various gods or practice the various divination methods noted above in chapter 4.

Israel's original contribution to the development of religion is taken to be "ethical monotheism," that is, the idea that the universe is created and directed by a single Being who wants us to behave in certain ways. Those who claim this obviously have no need of developmental schemes, but Hebrew Scriptures show signs that the new monotheism did not quickly or completely eclipse the older, anthropomorphic or nature religions.

At best, I think the tribal brotherhood initially accepted YHVH alongside the gods they had previously worshipped,[44] something for which the Book of Joshua provides further evidence. Joshua is the first Israelite whose name is paired with Yah (Numbers 13:16), hardly surprising when Exodus 6:3 reminds us that, before Moses, Israel worshipped El Shaddai (see chapter 4).

An obvious consequence of the shift to monotheism is the realization that a created universe must have an inherent order which the adept can understand—a notion we have characterized as treating reality as though it were a giant paint-by-numbers game. In the excursus to chapter 4 we saw how, with requisite "wisdom," one scrapes away the paint, as it were, and discovers the numerical substructure.

Monotheism, then, may reflect a quantum leap in human thought that indicates a cusp between a material-driven and a mentally propelled theology.[45] That is, like a rocket that needs to develop a certain amount of thrust before breaking free of earth's gravity, mankind piled up, sifted, and evaluated millennia of sensory and cultural experiences before, finally, becoming able to extrapolate from them and postulate what must

---

could well have been spared."

[44]Stephanie Dalley, "Yahweh in Hamath in the 8th Century B.C.," *Vetus Testamentum* 40/1 (1990): 21-32. She leaves undecided the question of how worship of Yahweh found its way to north Syria.

[45]This brings us close to the discussion of emics and etics, that is, the schools of anthropology that hold man is what he thinks of himself vs. those who think the influence of man's material culure is decisive. See John W. Rogerson, "Anthropology and the Old Testament," in *The World of Ancient Israel*, ed. R. E. Clements (Cambridge/New York: Cambridge University Press, 1978) 31-35.

be true. But If monotheism is not simply revealed, we have to ask: Who thought of it and when?

§8. Who Was that Levi I Saw You with Last Night?

Note that it was the Levites coming out of Egypt—where they had spent the previous four generations—who became the shock troops of the One God. On the road they slaughtered 3,000 of their brethren (Exod. 32:25-29) who were worshipping the golden calf that Aaron made. (This number comports well with the 40,000 refugees claimed by Finkelstein.) What could fuel such ferocity? The story gives witness to a compelling new ideology—monotheism—that allowed and even compelled people to kill their own kin.

> *This should in no way surprise us. Everything from the virulently pacifist Yippie movement to China's bloody Cultural Revolution has been carried out by people who believed, even desperately, in what they were fighting for. In the latter case, as in the French Revolution and the Nazi period, it was not unheard of for people to denounce friends, neighbors, or even kin, though these denunciations could mean death for those accused.*

If there were proto-Israelite Levites in Egypt at the time Santorini/Thera exploded, it may be that the idea of a single God was born among them at that time. Only such a One would be capable of dealing the unprecedented and completely devastating blow to Egypt and its manifold gods that Thera dealt.

If we count the lifetime of a person as a generation, a date of around 1550 for Santorini's explosion comports well with an exodus around 1290 undertaken by people who had been in Egypt for four generations. The view of Psalm 90:10, "The years of a person's life are three score and ten or, by reason of strength, four score," yields a period of 280 (4x70) or 320 years, either of which covers the time from explosion to Exodus.

That Levites were granted no land in Israel suggests that by the time they got there the land was already occupied, either by "native" Canaanites or by various Asiatic groups who had previously left Egypt.

Admittedly, this is speculative, and it leaves us with a problem: How does the One God who smote the Egyptians show up with a female consort in so many places afterward? Apparently, the idea that it must have been the One God who had visited disaster on Egypt did not immediately sweep all other religious beliefs away even among the

Asiatics. Nor did the group that left Egypt, which included the Bible's "mixed multitude," all report to the same place afterwards like tourists descending from a bus.

Different groups might very well believe that the One God went with them and settled where they settled. So we could have YHVH of Samaria, YHVH of Teman, YHVH from Seir, YHVH from Paran, and so forth. Multiple sites would be fertile ground for all sorts of development, especially that which upheld the essential dualism that Semitic language speakers saw all around them.

Not until the Fall of Jerusalem would the idea take hold that this one God, alone, was not tied to a particular place. In the meantime, the addition of a consort—if that's what the Kuntillet Ajrud graffiti indicate the various YHVHs have—shows just how difficult it is to sustain the notion of a single God, the more so when the restrictions of Hebrew don't allow for a genderless God.

The current movement within the Roman Catholic Church to ascribe to Mary the position of "coredemptrix" alongside Jesus is very instructive on this point.

§9. An Evolving God?

I appeared to Abraham, Isaac, and Jacob as El Shaddai, but I did not make myself known to them by My name יהוה. (Exodus 6:3 NJPS)

From the advent of agriculture, perhaps even earlier, it was the duty of the worshipper to serve the gods and goddesses by performing required rituals completely and punctually or suffer the consequences. Recall the basalt stele from Hazor: hands lifted to the moon, indicating a belief in sky gods. And why not? That's where the moon and sun are, and where rain comes from. So prayers were sent upward, along with the smoke of sacrifices and incense. We might say, then, that the "axis of worship" for early agriculturalists was "vertical."

Taking it one logical step further, the worshipper was not overly concerned with what happened to neighbors on either hand. Indeed, helping stricken brethren could be interpreted as interfering with God's will since, if they are suffering, they must have done something deserving of punishment. To ameliorate "punishment" is to condone or validate sin. If we still have a tendency to "blame the victim," how much more so under the old paradigm?

I found this sort of fatalism in Israel in the 1960s. Some Muslim women took offense at our waving flies off their babies' eyelids even though I think they knew flies carry the trachoma that ultimately can cause blindness. Whatever evil befell, it was the will of Allah. Similarly, in nineteenth-century America and England there was opposition to the use of anesthetics for women during labor precisely because in Genesis 3:15, the objectors said, God ordained that Eve and her descendants should suffer pain while delivering children. In modern America there are still those who object to attempts at treating or even researching the HIV virus, on the (selective) grounds that AIDS sufferers are sinners who have supposedly brought their condition on themselves.

As far back as Hammurabi's codex, there are admonitions to help those less fortunate, but how seriously were these entreaties taken? Babylonian society was stratified to the extent that thoroughgoing social justice was never even an ideal. The nature of the Mosaic "revolution," as I have come to understand it, in addition to its divine exclusivism, is nothing less than this: a complete ninety-degree paradigm shift, from the "vertical" to the "horizontal" as the main axis of worship. Moses himself set an example by defending women at a well from bullying shepherds (Exod. 2:16-19).

The Israelite belief offers some revolutionary ideas (not all of which need be brand-spanking-new) such as

- Love your neighbor as yourself.
- Equal justice from a law that is no longer a respecter of persons as Hammurabi's is. That is, don't favor the rich or the poor.
- There is one rule for native-born and the stranger.
- Not all slaves are chattels and even chattel slaves are entitled to rest on Sabbath.
- Female slaves, otherwise the lowest of the low, are entitled to certain rights and treatment that male slaves are not.

The "program" seems to reflect the desires of people who had spent generations on the bottom of the totem pole. Some Jews have always favored messianic figures who promised "the last shall become first," or schemes like Communism that promised amelioration of their situation. It's no wonder that those who benefitted most from Moses' daring scheme embraced it.

More than a thousand years after Moses, we have Jesus' parable of the "good" Samaritan, which shows that not all Israelites accepted monotheism's accompanying social program. The parable need not be seen only as extolling hated Northerners, of which Jesus was one, or common people as over against aristocratic Judean officials,[46] but rather a demonstration that what is now required is helping those in need. As Jesus later put it, "[A]s you did it to one of the least of these who are members of my family, you did it to me" (Matt. 25:40 NRSV).

There are two implied *a fortiori* arguments in the parable: (1) if even a hated Samaritan knows and does what is required of him, how much more so should Judeans, and (2) how much even more so priests and Levites. This social/ethical imperative is not new with Jesus. It goes back at least to Amos and Hosea, two other Northerners. The question I cannot answer with certainty is: Does this ethical/social imperative really go back to Moses himself?

One's final answer will depend upon how accepting one is of the tradition that the entire Torah, save the last eight verses of Deuteronomy, was given to Moses, even though they were not written down until centuries later. Here scholars and the faithful will politely part ways, but both will find my way objectionable. Those last eight verses, which speak of Moses' death, are assigned by Jewish tradition to Joshua, to whom we now turn.

§10. *Et Tu*, Joshua?

"[T]he great passions are antinomian." —Saul Bellow (*Ravelstein*)

With so much popular attention given to Moses before him and David after him—for example, in Thomas Cahill's recent *The Gifts of the Jews*—Joshua tends to recede into the background. Like the Lone Ranger's friend Tonto, Joshua is simply a fixture in the biblical narrative that, until recent times, few people inspected. There are, however, many aspects of Joshua, the man and the book, that need to be examined more closely.

The book called Joshua presents Israel's entrance into Canaan as an invasion by a large, and largely unified, group of people. Here we have the miraculous fall of Jericho and the sun standing still as Joshua-led Israelites marched victoriously up and down Canaan rooting out and

---

[46]This old favorite continues to generate much interest. See Stanley N. Rosenbaum, "A Letter from R. Gamaliel ben Gamaliel," in Beatrice Bruteau, ed., *Jesus through Jewish Eyes* (Maryknoll NY: Orbis, 2001).

routing the inhabitants and taking their lands, all on orders from God. This "Conquest," as scholars used to refer to it, may be just ancient Near Eastern braggadocio; it may also be later Jewish "bad conscience," or at least a desire to put Israel's claim to the land beyond dispute. It is certainly great public relations for Joshua, who, as we shall see below, would have needed it.[47]

Joshua's story stands in curious contrast with the more judicious evaluation of the conquest in Judges. Judges suggests the invasion was more of a long-term infiltration, probably into areas not previously or at least not heavily inhabited, only sometimes warlike, and then not always successful. Modern archaeology weighs in on the side of Judges. But whichever account is more correct, we have to wonder why and how there are two such disparate accounts as Joshua and Judges lying cheek by jowl. Since chronologies in the period between Moses and David are notoriously contradictory, it could be that the accounts concerning Joshua, somewhat magnified, took place before those in Judges. The natural compression that occurs when we look back at history through a fog of time might account for what is an uncomfortable and often contradictory juxtaposition of people and eras. Here again, it is not necessary and is perhaps a waste of effort to try to harmonize all the accounts.

Even if we could make sense of the competing accounts, the story of Joshua is more important as propaganda aimed at establishing him as the legitimate national leader, successor of Moses. Why, we may ask, was Joshua Moses' successor, and not Caleb? It is Caleb, after all, in Numbers 13:30, who exhorted Israel to attack, and Caleb who was singled out to see the Promised Land (Num. 14:24). Joshua was twinned with Caleb in Numbers 14:30, 38, but otherwise is not mentioned again until Numbers 26:65.[48] Yet in Judges all Caleb got was Hebron, a consolation prize comparable to that of a patriarch's concubine. Joshua went on to become the national leader.

As such, Joshua did a number of things parallel to Moses' mighty deeds, such as stopping the Jordan's flow and sending out his own spies.

---

[47]Moshe Weinfeld, "The Period of the Conquest and of the Judges as Seen by the Earlier and Later Sources," *Vetus Testamentum* 17 (1967): 38. Finkelstein, *Archaeology of the Israelite Settlement*, passim, prefers the word "Settlement" to "Conquest."

[48]*Encyclopaedia Judaica* (5:41) suggests that the original spy story did not include Joshua, but does not explain why.

This reminds us of Isaac's actions paralleling Abraham's, and Elisha's of Elijah's. In each case the parallels are intended to establish the "succession" beyond dispute. The intrusive Deuteronomy 34:9 also cements the succession of Joshua, but was Joshua the man something other than his book claims? To answer this question, we will need to inquire more closely into the "biography" of Joshua.

By some accounts Joshua was an Ephraimite, by others a Benjaminite/Benjamite. The Ephraimite identification rests on more solid textual evidence, including 1 Chron 7:20-27. Numbers 13:8 identifies a *Hosea/Hoshea bin Nun* as the spy/representative from Ephraim and Joshua 24:29 gives him an Ephraimite burial place at Timnath-serah (Timnath-heres in Judges 2:9). But this is not his hometown and, if it is not a completely circular argument, Joshua had to be given some acceptable Israelite pedigree. (Jericho, the city most closely linked with Joshua, was or became Benjaminite.[49])

Making Joshua, the first "national" leader, might pacify those Northerners who mistrusted the upstart Southerner David.[50] If Joshua were Benjaminite, I think there would be some reason to forget or suppress that fact. As we know, the Bible goes to some lengths to discredit the Benjaminite Saul and all who descended from him. It might be argued that Joshua came before Saul and so should escape Saul's taint, but this will not suffice, as we shall see in the next section.

§11. "What's in a name?" —Shakespeare (*Romeo and Juliet*)

The above minidebate overshadows some even more fundamental questions: What accounts for Joshua's rather strange name? When was he born, and why is it that he, rather than some son of Moses, succeeded to the Israelite leadership? To answer these questions I begin where Joshua ends.

At the end of the book that bears his name, Joshua declares his family's allegiance to YHVH as over against "the gods that your ancestors served beyond the River [Euphrates] and in Egypt," and exhorts all Israel to do the same (Joshua 24:14-15; compare 2 Kings 18:4 and 23:5). This implies there were still viable worship alternatives, or at least that on the

---

[49]Moshe Weinfeld, "The Tribal League at Sinai," in *Ancient Israelite Religion*, ed. Patrick Miller, Paul Hanson, and S. Dean McBride (Philadelphia: Fortress, 1987) 303-14.
[50]See Stiebing, *Out of the Desert?* 201.

very eve of their entrance into the Promised Land, elements of the invading people still worshipped other gods. (The traditional explanation that these gods had not been worshipped *since* the time of the ancestors is ludicrous.)

One of these gods was represented by a bronze serpent, *Nehustan*, that God had commanded Moses to make (Num. 21:8-9). How is such a thing possible? This very curious incident involved making a "graven image" so soon after the giving of the Ten Commandments that, as we have said, we might suppose there was still rock dust in the grooves of the two tablets. Making a bronze serpent was such a blatant contradiction of the law, concluded traditionalists, that it could only be done by divine warrant. This "explanation," however, makes God capricious or sets him above his own laws.

Second Kings 18:4 informs us that King Hezekiah destroyed the serpent that Moses made, and that people still offered incense to it five hundred years later. If so, whose god had it been? I think Nehustan was, in fact, one of the "foreign" gods already present in proto-Israelite circles in Moses' time, and that it was so firmly rooted that it could not simply be extirpated but had to be "kosherized."[51]

Snake images would have been almost a natural product of man's early attempts at smelting metal, if only because of the molten copper's own properties, but as we saw above in chapter 2, snake worship is far older than metallurgy. Creating snakes was no mere accident of the mining and smelting process. Bronze serpents have been found at Timna, not far from Midianite territory, where excellent copper work had been produced for more than two thousand years before. Bernhard Stade suggests that Moses could have picked up the technology, if not the worship, from Jethro and the Midianites.[52]

Alternatively, Nun is an Egyptian god's name, and the Sumerian *Ningiszida*—note the similarity in names—was an even older Sumerian

---

[51]Gösta Ahlström, *The History of Ancient Palestine* (Minneapolis: Fortress, 1993) 702n.2, feels that if Moses made *nehustan* then he couldn't have been a "pure-yahwist." Karen Randolph Joines, "The Bronze Serpent in the Israelite Cult," *Journal of Biblical Literature* 87 (1968): 245-50, thinks that *nehustan* was a foreign worship object, which is likely enough.

[52]The "Kenite Hypothesis" that Israel learned smithing from this tribe, like all the other theories of Israelite "borrowing," may be likened to so many blind people having hold of different parts of the same elephant.

"serpent-god of fertility, sunrise, and the building of cities symbolized by entwined serpents and the dragon."[53] This means, of course, that it long predates any Israelite entities.

I suggest the bronze serpent was in fact a god of the group Joshua represented and led. Further, I am convinced Joshua was an Ammonite who did not know Moses and did not join the invasion until it neared his native land, Ammon. Before investigating these unusual claims, however, it is necessary to determine how Joshua's story has been woven into the biblical narrative. To begin with, we may look more closely at his "biography," especially his entire given name, *Hoshea bin Nun.*

In this regard, Moses' change of Joshua's first name from the unexceptionable Hoshea to Joshua/Jehoshua in Numbers 13:16 is, to say the least, odd. None of the other spies whom Moses sent were similarly treated. Why Joshua and why just then, when tradition mandates that he must have been at least forty years old?

Rashi was apparently troubled by this, too, so he cleverly reads the verb "name" as "pray"—which is possible—and says that Moses prayed that Joshua wouldn't be swayed by the negative accounts of the other spies. But this solution is worse than the original problem; it requires that Moses knew in advance what the majority report would be, a difficult proposition.

Now, any change of name usually implies significant change of status, as, for example, at confirmation, when (some) women marry or enter holy orders, when men become pope or king, or when someone adopts Islam. Some such thing is operating here, as Joshua became the first male, perhaps the first person, to have the *Yah* divine element in his name.[54] This seems to imply a change of religious loyalty. If so, what was he before?

Numbers 11:28 says "he was Moses' servant from his youth," but whose youth? His or Moses'? The Hebrew is ambiguous, but the context strongly suggests it is Joshua's youth that is meant. If he were, say, twenty, before Moses left Egypt—and how could he have been much younger and still have served Moses there?—he would only have had ten

---

[53]Michael Astour, *Hellenosemitica* (London: Brill, 1965) 159.
[54]Unless that person was Moses' mother. See Levin, "An Unattested 'Scribal Correction' in Numbers 26:59," 25.

years at the end of his life to complete his part of the conquest,[55] hardly long enough to do all the Book of Joshua credits him with. If Moses' youth is meant, it would leave Joshua even less time in Canaan. Joshua 24:29 credits him with 110 years, the measure of a "perfect" life in Egyptian thought, just as Moses' 120 is the measure of a perfect life in Israelite thought.

Furthermore, we have to ask why the then, say, thirty-five-year-old Moses, still in the good graces of the Egyptian court, would have had a Hebrew servant. Who were his servants before that time? Admittedly, this asks the text to provide details regarding which it simply is not interested.

Some scholars have cut this Gordion knot by concluding that Joshua simply did not exist. But if Joshua did not exist, why go to the trouble of inventing him? Disregarding the lifespan numbers (above), would it not still have been cleaner and simpler to have Moses' own family carrying on his work, as Aaron indeed did? The very trouble that tradition takes to integrate Joshua into the narrative is some proof that there is a real, historical person hiding somewhere in the story, but who was Hoshea/Joshua bin Nun?

Tradition carefully retains *bin*, "son of" (compare Arabic *'ibn*) instead of the customary *ben*, which is also odd. Moreover, Joshua's is the only biblical name that is consistently "misspelled."[56] Now *ben/bat* can be tribal, not simply patronymic. If so, what tribal affiliation is here hinted at? Levin suggests it as originally *BN-YHVH*, ben-Yahweh, later changed by pietists who would not have used the Tetragrammaton this way.[57] I suggest that it is, rather, the tribe or cult of Nahash, the serpent, that accounts for Joshua's name *nun*.

There is no evidence for the Bible's making single-letter abbreviations unless it is here, but the letter *nun* (נ, ן) itself is ideographically identified as "serpent" as early as the proto-Sinaitic script (around 1900

---

[55]In the twelfth-century *Book of Tradition* (Philadelphia: Jewish Publication Society, 1967) 9, Abraham ibn Daud gives Joshua twenty-eight years in Canaan, not seeming to notice that this means Joshua could not have come to know Moses before his first, precipitous flight from Egypt.

[56]Curiously, James Barr, *The Variable Spellings of the Hebrew Bible* (London: Oxford University Press, 1989) omits discussion of Isaac, *yisaq/yishaq*. He is extremely cautious on the subject of dialect (20-21).

[57]Levin, "An Unattested 'Scribal Correction' in Numbers 26:59," 33, thinks the change was made to avoid the suggestion of divine sexuality.

BCE) and the Egyptian "alphabet" on which it rests. In addition, we should recall that Hebrew *Nehuštan* (from √*n-h-š* = "serpent") is also the name of the bronze serpent made by Moses.

In support of this idea, we note that at least one king of the Ammonites bore the name Nahash (1 Sam. 11:1ff.), and his reign seems to have been at the end of the Conquest, suggesting a connection that wants investigation. Note also that the Joshua-led Israelites did not conquer Ammon, because God reminded them that Ammon was given to the children of Lot, Abraham's nephew (Deut. 2:19). Paradoxically, as we saw, these Ammonite relatives were considered ineligible for membership in the Israelite community for the selfsame reason: they were, allegedly, children of Lot's incest with one of his daughters. (The Moabites are the other "misbegotten" offspring: Deut. 23:3-4; and see Gen. 19:30-38.)

King Nahash of Ammon, an enemy of Saul, enjoyed good relations with David, possibly because this king was the father of David's sister Abigail. After all, Jerusalem and Rabbah/Rabbath ("Heights of") Ammon, the capital of Ammon, are only thirty-five miles apart—less than two days by donkey. So Nahash was a Saul enemy, a David ally. David's grandson, Rehoboam, Solomon's sucessor, married Na'amah, an Ammonitess. It would be nice if we knew whether or not David had a hand in choosing her, and who her parents were. In any case, despite a questionable paternity, Ammonites were spared and good relations with them were possible. So far, so good. What would change things?

For one thing, the Bible reports numerous attacks on Israel by . . . whom? In translation, for instance in Judges 10:9, *bene 'ammon* is usually rendered "*the* Ammonites" (thus RSV, NRSV, NJB, REB, NAB, NJPS), but that is terribly misleading. The Hebrew term *bene 'ammon* means "children (sons) of Ammon" (as in KJV, ERV) indicating a rather loose group united only by geography. In contrast to *the* Moabites, and others, Hebrew Scripture almost never uses the definite article with Ammonites and, even if it did, we should not suppose that this would refer to *all* the Ammonites. After all, why should they have been any more unified than the Israelites were?

That some Ammonites attacked Israel would not, therefore, have made Israelites the implacable enemies of all of them. Relations between Israel and various Ammonite groups were obviously an up and down affair.[58] Still, there may be a compelling historical reason for disguising Joshua's Ammonite origin, a reason that would have emerged not long before the time the Former Prophets were being collected and canonized. We know that after the fall of Jerusalem in 586, a King Ba'alis of Ammon encouraged, and then gave shelter to, one Ishmael ben Nethaniah of Judah, who killed Gedaliah ben Ahikam, who had been appointed governor by the Babylonians. This happened sometime between 586 and 582 BCE. Though not of David's line, Gedaliah represented the last shred of Judean independence. Here, then, we have a literal "smoking gun," a solid historical reason for excluding Ammonites from the community.

Certainly, Genesis's allegation of Ammonite illegitimacy would effectively mask this more sensitive reason and set the cause of the estrangement well back in the national history. Too far. If the Ammonites were excluded as *mamserim* in Abraham's time, David should not have engaged in cordial relations with them, the strange bedfellows of politics notwithstanding. This may be the motivation for 1 Chronicles (2:13-17) and the Septuagint "translation" of 2 Samuel 17:25 changing the father of Abigail from Nahash to Jesse, a change in no way dictated by the text itself.

Astonishingly, we have an account of the Ba'alis[59] conspiracy only from Jeremiah, who tells the story at great length (40:5–41:18). Kings omits the Ammonites' part in it, and Chronicles, in fact—though it carries the history beyond that in Kings—never mentions Gedaliah at all. Could it be that Israel-in-exile found it politic to efface any connection between Ammon and Joshua?

Here is another place where the editors, who were not *the inventors of Scripture, failed to cover their tracks. The official accounts directed attention away from Ammon, but the text of Jeremiah likely could not*

---

[58]If Israelite politics are hard to figure out, Ammonite politics, with no surviving records except those in the Bible, are more so. Colin Renfrew, *Archaeology and Language* (London: Penguin, 1987) 65, puts his finger on the problem when he writes, "It is one of those unfortunate conventions of archaeology that each culture and each language must have a name." Jephthah conducts a successful campaign against some Ammonites in Judges 11. Later, David apparently prefers one son of Nahash, Shobi, to another son, Hanun, who had befriended him during his own dynastic struggle.

[59]A seal bearing the name of this king has recently been found. See Robert Deutsch, "Seal of Ba'alis Surfaces," *Biblical Archaeology Review* 25/2 (March/April 1999): 46-49 and 66.

be eviscerated because it was already public record, "the truth," and,
at least in the popular mind, canonized.

To return to our question: Why did Moses change Joshua's name in Numbers 13:16, and why did he have to when, apparently, the new moniker had been used already? Numbers 11:28 informs us that *Joshua* (called here by his new name, though it had not yet been given) had served Moses since he (Joshua) was a lad in Egypt. If, as Ginsburg suggests, Moses was a teenager himself when he left, it makes Joshua's putative position even less tenable. I suspect Joshua, whom tradition saw fit to place with Moses in Egypt, has been grafted into the Moses-Exodus story at a point earlier than he originally entered it.

For support of this idea, consider the following. When Moses returned to Egypt after forty years absence, Joshua was curiously absent. The Bible assumes Joshua was born in Egypt, so forty of his years would necessarily have been spent there while Moses was in Midian; what was he doing during this time or the subsequent forty years in the Wilderness? Joshua's first post-Egyptian appearance is not until Exodus 17:9, where he led a successful battle against the hated Amalekites, a people who would have lived near what I postulate was his native Ammon.

Joshua's name is not found in Exodus 24:9 alongside those of Aaron, Nadab, and Abihu and the seventy elders, as we might expect. Exodus 24:13 does contain a phrase that indicates Joshua went at least part way up Sinai with Moses, but if the phrase, "with Joshua, his assistant" is omitted, the passage reads more smoothly. It continues, "He [Moses] said to the elders. . . . " The verbs in the Hebrew text are singular. The plural is read only in the LXX.

Rashi muses, "I am not sure in what capacity Joshua appears here," and is compelled to imagine Joshua pitching his tent, alone, at the foot of the mountain, then waiting forty days for Moses to reappear. It is to be hoped that Joshua brought a plentiful food supply with him . . . even so, one wonders how long he would have been prepared to stay on alone awaiting Moses' return.

For Joshua to succeed Moses, it was useful to get him out of the camp as Exodus 24:13 does. He thereby avoided any responsibility for the Golden Calf, association with which might have been seen as a disqualification from further leadership. It would also be necessary to disconnect him from any later idolatry, for example, the Bronze Serpent in Numbers 21. It is Moses, then, who is credited with the creation of a

Bronze Serpent (Nehustan), following God's orders. Making Moses or, even better, God, responsible for the bronze serpent certainly takes the onus off Joshua. As with so many things, legitimacy is best established if it can be shown that "it was already so" far back in time, and has an unassailable pedigree.

Returning from the mountain, it was Joshua who is said to have mistaken the noise of idol worship for the sound of battle. His ears apparently weren't as good as eighty-year-old Moses', nor perhaps his eyes, either. Joshua would have been the first to see Moses' irradiated face and yet it was Aaron and the elders who seem to be first to have noticed this remarkable change.

There are causes for which a person will cross a border, even an ocean, to fight. The names of Von Steuben, Kosciusko, and the Marquis de Lafayette come to an American's mind. Joshua not only joined Moses' cause, he saw fit to give up his Ammonite religion, and "convert" to Moses', as the change in name indicates. Taking all of this together, I think we can say that, yes, sometime around 1240 BCE the mantle of leadership passed from Moses to Joshua the Ammonite.

Joshua succeeded Moses because he was a *strategos*, a brilliant military leader. Later Jewish historians, under the peculiar pressures of their own time, found it convenient to forget that Joshua had ever been anything else than an Israelite. As such, he led a confederation, albeit fragile and short-lived, of disparate, displaced groups united more by a desire to obtain land than by any ideology or ethnic affiliation.[60]

I deliberately use the amorphous term "groups," not "tribes," because it is impossible to tell in most cases just who they all were and how organized. Some people try to make a hierarchy out of the terms *mishpachah*, "family," *shevet*, "tribe," *bet 'av*, "father's house(hold)," but others say these terms are too mixed up to separate. Is the "clan" or "extended family" the organizational basis? To what extent can we read social change out of change in burial mound practice? Does it look as though larger groupings (with bigger chiefs) came to replace smaller ones because farming requires greater social cooperation than hunting and gathering? We cannot yet say.

---

[60]In this effort he may have been moved and helped by the contemporaneous collapse of the Canaanite city-state system.

The people Joshua led, then, were probably not organized in tight-knit tribes and included brigades of brigands and collections of outcasts banding together like Apaches in the American Southwest (or in the purlieus of Paris in the 1920s). We can say that the groups' very disunity might have been a good thing in the long run because "tribalism is an evolutionary cul-de-sac."[61] It would take another two hundred years for this proto-Israel to transcend its own tribalism and, even then, theirs was a temporary success.

§12. System Collapse

In those days there was no king in Israel; every man did what was right in his own eyes. (Judges 21:25 RSV)

International trade broke down rather badly at the end of the thirteenth century BCE when the traders could no longer project military power to protect the routes or apprehend brigands. Without trade revenues, the small cities of Canaan could no longer hire mercenaries, so their *habiru*, like the unemployed *Freikorps* in Germany after World War I, might have made themselves available to whoever could pay them, as they did later to judges Jephthah and Abimelech, and to King Jeroboam of the Northern Kingdom and David in the Southern Kingdom.

The period between Joshua and Saul, Israel's first king, began around this time and lasted for two centuries—about the same length of time that the United States has been a country. Much of Judges is taken up with wars between Benjamin and "the rest of Israel" that almost led to Benjamin's annihilation. That it should have taken almost two centuries for such diverse and fractious groups to achieve any sort of unity is, therefore, no surprise.

Even with two biblical books, Joshua and Judges, devoted to it, this period remains one of the dimmer stretches in Israel's history. We know that Israel's wars against "natives" were never carried on by the whole confederacy. Not only were Southern tribes reluctant to help Northern brethren (see Judges 5), we have to ask how brotherly, in fact, these

---

[61]M. Fried, quoted in De Geus, *The Tribes of Israel*, 131. Charles Montesquieu, in *The Spirit of the Laws* (New York: Hafner, 1949; orig. 1648), proposed that geography and climate have profound effects on the kind of government people choose. He should, therefore, have been impressed that Israel was able to overcome its tendency toward fragmentation even if only for a while.

groups ever felt during the period of the Judges? For all its superficial evenhandedness, Judges seems to be written from a Southern viewpoint. It features criticisms of the Northern tribes for failure to conquer allotted territories, and of Benjamin in particular for failure to take out the Jerusalem Jebusites, reserving Jerusalem's conquest for David.

Is it noteworthy that Jerusalem is in Benjamin's territory? Yes, because that makes Benjamin's failure and David's success more pointed. In Judges 1, apparently added on, it is Judah (again) who is successful in capturing Jerusalem,[62] along with older brother Simeon, who "owed him one" for coming back to rescue him in Egypt. (Simeon then conveniently disappears, that is, reference to Simeon is not found in Moses' blessing of "the tribes" in Deuteronomy 33; compare Jacob's blessing in Genesis 49.)

Joshua's immediate successors, the "judges," are chronicled in the Bible's seventh book. The name "judge" is a misnomer because the twelve or thirteen so named were more situational military chieftains than regular legal or religious leaders. Hence, Sir James G. Frazer's remark concerning Samson, that "he hardly adorned the bench" is clever, but rather off the mark.

More is known of some judges than of others, a few being represented by single verses. Even from this paucity of information we can glean a few things. The thirteen named individuals did not all come from the same tribe and not all tribes were represented, indicating that no tribe during this time exercised anything like national leadership. Only two, at most, were Judean, the rest Northern or Transjordanian.

Some, like Othniel, the text's first judge, had recognizable Yahwistic names. Others did not. Putting Othniel's judgeship first may indeed be a later editor's attempt to promote the primacy of Yahwism in Israel. Other judges, such as Shamgar ben Anath (note the goddess matronymic), "who killed six hundred of the Philistines with an oxgoad" (Judges 3:31), seems to have been Hittite (as was Uriah, of David's bodyguard).[63] Were all judges actual historical figures? On one hand, thanks to Halpren's mag-

---

[62]Contra Margreet Steiner and with Jane Cahill and Nadav Na'aman, I think Jerusalem existed in David's time. See their articles in *Biblical Archaeology Review* 24/4 (July/August 1998): 24-44.

[63]Stephanie Dalley identified Shamgar with Sheger the moon god in a seminar talk I heard in Oxford in 1992. The *mem* is an infix. All commentators agree Shamgar was foreign, but suggest differing points of origin, Hatti being one.

nificent reconstruction,[64] we have every reason to think that Ehud of Benjamin, the second (or was he the first?) judge, who is remembered for his treacherous murder of a king of Moab, was a real historical figure. On the other hand, Samson, the last judge, and the one to whom most space is given (four chapters), is the least likely to have been historical. The others fall somewhere in between.

Of the judges mentioned, three surely stand out: Samson, because of his bizarre exploits, and Deborah/Barak. Nineteenth-century scholars noted that the name Samson has the same root, √š-m-š, as the word for "sun," and concluded that Samson was a sun myth. Right church, wrong pew. As we saw, de Santillana and von Dechend make a convincing case for Samson's being an Orion figure.[65] Either way, it is instructive that this Hebrew Hercules should be from the tribe of Dan; it makes Dan "part of the family" and thus satisfies Wach's criterion.[66]

The story of Deborah and Barak is noteworthy for two reasons. She is the only female who might be considered a judge—at the least a leader of Israel—in this period. And her "song," Judges 5, is generally conceded to be almost contemporary with the events it describes. The later prose version that precedes it (Judges 4) shows just how little the Bible's collectors understood some of the material they were collecting.

Serious collection of the various tribal stories might have begun during the monarchy, so it is to that period that we now turn.

---

[64]Baruch Halpren, *The First Historians* (University Park PA: Pennsylvania State University Press, 1988) 39-104. On linguistic grounds, Ahlström, *History of Ancient Palestine*, 38n.2, does not think Ehud a Benjaminite, but an Asherite from southern Ephraim. However, most scholars (e.g., Day, *Oxford Bible Atlas*, 65) locate Asher on the coast north of Mt. Carmel, and it is Benjamin that straddles the Ephraim/Judah line. Moreover, it is Ehud's politics that make him acceptable to Eglon and this speaks to his "Benjaminism." (The phrase is Michael Astour's.)

[65]Hertha von Dechend and Giorgio de Santillana, *Hamlet's Mill* (Boston: Godine, 1977) 165-78.

[66]Joachim Wach, *Sociology of Religion* (Chicago: University of Chicago Press, 1944) 108.

Chapter 8

Of David and Jonathan, Saul and Solomon

§1. The Birth of Two Nations

Nations emerge through time. In the late nineteenth century, the chancellor of Germany, Prince Otto von Bismarck, sneeringly dismissed Italy as "nothing more than a geographical expression." The same thing, however, might have been said of his Germany or, indeed, of most European nations at one time. A hundred years later, we can still see that the majority of countries are composed of diverse nationalities or regional ethnic groups.

Multiethnic countries, however, are essentially artificial and often exhibit enduring animosities that tend toward fragmentation. Canada, Czechoslovakia, Italy, Iraq, the Philipines, Indonesia, and many African countries are examples. The case of former Yugoslavia represents only what happens when these tendencies reach their final and desperate conclusion: civil war. Curiously, many national fracture lines occur on a north-south axis: that is, the animosities are felt between Northerners and Southerners. Again, Germany and Italy are examples, but so are Norway, the United States, Korea, and Vietnam.

The success of nation-states depends largely upon building a common sense of nationality among all their inhabitants. This may occur through war, as it did with the various Christian inhabitants of the Iberian peninsula in the long centuries of the Reconquista, or with the Dutch who broke from Spain in the sixteenth century. I think Germany itself became a united nation only during and because of the war of 1914–1918.

Unity may also be achieved through the efforts of a charismatic leader such as Marshal Tito of Yugoslavia or David in biblical Israel. In such cases, the nation often does not long survive the death of the unifying leader. Such was the case in Israel, whose fragile empire fractured with the death of David's son, Solomon. On the Israelite popular level, however, the various parts of the kingdom were never very close. In 931 BCE that situation was notarized by their formal separation.

That some modern scholars such as Siegfried Herrmann and Bernhard Anderson feel otherwise—that is, that Israelites always felt basically united—may reflect an uncritical acceptance of the tradition-hallowed account of Israel as, willy-nilly, one big family. On this view, Joseph's forgiveness of his half brothers for selling him into slavery represents a sort of bottom-line sense of family that nothing could finally destroy. As we saw in chapter 6, however, the family relationships among tribes claimed by the Bible are largely spurious.

Furthermore, they seem to have stopped fighting among themselves only when presented by outside threats, and not always even then. The notion of essential Israelite unity is inferred from such depictions as royal marriages between the two ruling houses, joint commercial or military ventures, and the commission of Amos, held to be a poor, shepherd Southerner, but able to command an audience in the North.

Amos, however, as I have shown elsewhere, was not a Southerner (nor poor, nor a shepherd), but a native of the North. The joint ventures were sporadic and opportunistic and, in most cases, it was the North that coerced or cajoled the South into cooperating. As to royal marriages between the two kingdoms, it is true they were sometimes arranged in an attempt to reunify them. Royal marriages might be expected to usher in a period of peace and prosperity between the two contracting people, at least what the Romans would later call *connubium et commerciam* (something like "Let's get married and then our families can do business").

Such unions might also facilitate other common aims, as the marriage of Ferdinand and Isabella enabled Christians to expel the Moors—and Jews—from Spain.

In order better to understand the situation in monarchic Israel, we must first attempt to determine the identity of its constituent parts. As we saw in chapter 6, they were already in the Bronze Age a diverse group. Egyptian documents mention peoples living in Retenu (Canaan) whose names are tantalizingly like those of some that we associate with Israel or its constituent elements, such as the Asheri (Asher).[1] The Mer-ne-ptah Stele of circa 1210 BCE mentions an "Israel" there,[2] but this cannot be the

---

[1]Canaanites known as "Asheri" are mentioned in Papyrus Anastasi I. See Gösta Ahlström, *The History of Ancient Palestine* (Minneapolis: Fortress, 1993) 278. Two Asiatics named Sekratu, a name related to Issachar, are found in a list of Asiatic servants who have been given Egyptian names. See "Asiatics in Egyptian Household Service," trans. John A. Wilson, in *ANE* 2, *A New Anthology* (1975) 88. Translator Wilson notes (87) that this list may indicate a "trade in Asiatics carried on by Asiatics themselves," which reminds one both of the Joseph story and of the subsequent prohibition against kidnapping in the Bible.

[2]The well-known and widely discussed Merneptah Stele, ca. 1210 BCE, mentions an

later biblical nation because that would not come into being for another two hundred years. Foreign annalistic documents scarcely mention an Israel of any sort before the mid-ninth century BCE,[3] and for them the Northern kings Omri and his son Ahab are more important than David and his successor, Solomon.

Considering how relatively unimportant the whole country had been except as a transit point for traders or armies, this is not surprising. Now we may address the political situation that obtained when Israel emerged, albeit briefly, as a kingdom.

§2. "Who are those guys?" —Butch Cassidy

There are three reasons the need for a history might have been felt as early as the days of David's patchwork kingdom. (1) It provided some ideo - logical justification for a monarchy in the face of stiff opposition; (2) if that form of government were accepted in principle, it explained why kingship should be dynastic; and (3) it justified why the dynasty should spring from David son of Jesse and not Saul son of Kish. For Israel itself—especially the South and its later descendants—David's Jerusalem is the sun around which everything else revolves. This gives the Bible's history, its self-portrait, a "spin" that we must constantly keep in mind.

David the Imperialist, Founder of the Dynasty, Singer of Psalms, is the hero par excellence of the Judeans.[4] So popular did he become that his penchant for duplicity—notably demonstrated in his adultery with Bathsheba and complicity in the death of her husband, Uriah the Hittite— while remembered in Kings, is somehow not held against him. In Chronicles it is not even remembered, and in the Talmud it is explicitly denied.[5] This progression should warn us that the collectors and editors

---

"Israel" in Canaan, but uses "a people" rather than "a nation" as determinative in the identification. If Meek is correct and there was more than one exodus of Asiatics from Egypt, the problem of Merneptah being too close to Moses' time to allow for an Israel in Canaan disappears.

[3]The most famous of these is the Black Obelisk, also known as the Taylor Prism, that shows Jehu accepting Assyrian overlordship in 841 BCE.

[4]David's name and even his existence have been questioned, but the recent discovery of an Aramaic stele at Tel Dan, though its reading has been debated, seems to prove his existence. See Avraham Biran, *Biblical Dan* (Jerusalem: Israel Exploration Society, 1994) 275-78.

[5]The Talmud says Uriah gave his wife a conditional divorce document, a *get*, which effectively dissolved their marriage until his return. But such documents were not known

of Israel's history were less concerned with passing down an intact factual framework and more concerned with supporting an ideological agenda previously arrived at.

It is probable that the first text, the "J" document of Wellhausen's Documentary Hypothesis, was begun under, perhaps even commissioned by, Solomon. R. E. Friedman and Harold Bloom both think they see a woman's hand in its writing. If so, it would not have been the first time a woman was prominent in literature—far from it.[6] In any case, J is *Judean* Torah, favorable to the House of David.

For the earliest history of the Israelite monarchy, we are almost wholly dependent upon the Bible's own record, the account in Samuel being the most complete and literarily commendable. As such it has been the subject of much attention.[7] Kings and Chronicles were written, respectively, some 450 and 550 years after some of the events they describe, that is, after the monarchy split and both kingdoms were overrun. Chronicles, likely written after the return from Exile, has a particular, Southern viewpoint. Before trying to reconstruct all of that, however, we need to say a few words about how Israel developed a monarchy in the first place.

In political development, Israel seems to be about 2,000 years behind the Egyptians, who achieved a unified government about 3000 BCE under the legendary King Menes. Some Mesopotamians opted for a temporary, crisis-management sort of kingship in the late third millennium under Sargon, the first Semitic ruler. Emerging much later and caught between bigger, more powerful, and more efficient governments, the loose-knit Israelite confederation was, like eighteenth-century Germany, unable to defend itself from foreign incursion or even to control its own trade routes.

When not actually under foreign control, Israel/Canaan's governments had always been local or, at best, regional and reactive. Israel's constitu-

---

until centuries after David's time and would certainly not excuse adultery by wives whose husbands did return.

[6] The Sumerian poet/priestess Enheduanna, daughter of Sargon of Agade and author of numerous poetic works and hymns that were still being taught two thousand years after her death, is the subject of William W. Hallo and J. J. A. Van Dijk, *The Exaltation of Inanna* (New Havenn CT: Yale University Press, 1968).

[7] Most recently Robert Alter's new translation and commentary, *The David Story* (New York: W. W. Norton, 1999).

ent elements, what we casually refer to as tribes,[8] were never completely united. Only in times of external threat did smaller conglomerates elect temporary war leaders whom we know as judges. Some, like Abimelech, may even have "elected" themselves and hired *'apiru* mercenaries to support their warlord-like leadership (Judges 9). At no time did all join together even to fight a common enemy; more often they fought amongst themselves. As we will see, the Benjaminites seem to have been most often out of step with the rest of the family. But here we get ahead of ourselves.

Monarchy was ultimately chosen not because of any divine command, but because it was a more effective way of dealing with foreign powers and problems concomitant with settlement. Alternatively, Frick thinks the choice of monarchy had more to do with internal than external pressure.[9] Either way, the choice was made over the protest of Samuel, the man chosen to implement it.

Samuel, Israel's first "national prophet," threatened dire consequences from instituting a monarchy. The previous mode of governance, while ostensibly egalitarian, was subject to corruption by the very people who led it. Samuel's own sons are painted in the same less-than-glowing colors as are the sons of Eli, whom Samuel seems in some measure to have supplanted (1 Sam. 8:1-3). Hence, his warning fell on deaf ears.

Samuel's initial anointments were not done in public because there was strong antimonarchic sentiment in Israel, especially in the North. It was the Northern Kingdom, Israel, that later seceded from the union on the twin bases of unfair taxation and opposition to David's dynastic leadership—only to make more and worse errors than those it had condemned.

---

[8]For decades biblical scholars threw around terms such as "tribe," "clan," "family," and "father's house" without due attention to determining the precise social structures they singly and collectively identify. Recently, however, anthropologists have been working to clarify this aspect of Israelite life. Rogerson, "Anthropology and the Old Testament" (28) extols Niels Peter Lemche, *Early Israel: Anthropological and Historical Studies on the Israelite Society before the Monarchy*, VTSup 37 (Sheffield: Sheffield Academic Press, 1985) as superceding "everything previously written on the subject."

[9]Frank Frick, *A Journey through the Hebrew Scriptures* (New York: Harcourt, Brace, 1995) 288-96, feels that monarchy was less a divine command than a response to external and internal pressures. See also Frick, *The Formation of the State in Ancient Israel* (Sheffield UK: Almond, 1985) 29-30.

At one point Deuteronomy also warns against monarchy, but then says that the king should not be a foreigner (17:14-20). I think this exclusion (vs. 15b) is a deliberate anti-Saul insertion of later editors. Tipping our hat toward Wellhausen, we may posit that Josiah's people could have made this "prepublication" change without challenge because Deuteronomy would precisely not just then have been on everyone's coffee table. The question is, why, so long after Saul's fall, would it still have been necessary to derogate anything identifiably "Benjaminite"?

Here we must remember that the leadership was often contested, especially when the ruling king died. Such families as the Tobiads of Trans jordan, whose East Bank estate 'Iraq el-Amir ("Fortress of the Emir") is still an impressive ruin, were perennial contenders for national kingship or foci for threats to form their own breakaway kingdoms, as happened in Transjordan shortly before the fall of the North. (For more on the Tobiads, see chapter 10.)

So we have stories like that of one Sheba ben Bichri, well-known "worthless fellow and *ish yamini* (Benjaminite)" who gave the call, "Back to your gods [*'elohehem*], O Israel" in Samuel (2 Sam. 20:1 ‖ 1 Kings 12:16; cf. Deut. 5:30 [Heb. 5:27]). The present text reads "tents" (*'ohelehem*) for "gods." That "gods" is the probable original reading is confirmed by the context: who lived in tents besides Rechabites? The call is followed by Jeroboam I's erection of golden calves throughout the North.[10] Sheba also cursed David for executing members of Saul's house, no doubt putting himself on the "enemies list."

Dying David instructed Solomon (1 Kings 2:8-9 and 36-46) to keep an eye on one Shimei ben Gera, another Benjaminite separatist. Solomon did better than his instructions, first restricting Shimei to Jerusalem and then executing the man for leaving town to pursue runaway slaves, an offense we would see as scarcely graver than a parole violation. Apparently, for a very long time Benjaminites were out but not down, so it was necessary to preclude them from ever again exercising leadership.

---

[10]The change to "tents" is a *tikkun sopher* (scribal correction) unmarked by *Biblica Hebraica*. Key, "Traces of Worship of the Moon God," 23, correctly observes that Jeroboam's religion was ancient.

§3. "Son of my pain. . . . " —Rachel (Genesis 35:18)

The story of Benjamin is blended into the patriarchal narrative to give this originally "foreign" tribe a legitimate place in the family. The key text is Genesis 35, Benjamin's birth narrative. It's wildly out of position, four chapters distant from the births of the other sons. The Bible suggests that the name Benjamin was given by his father to mask the one given by dying Rachel—surprisingly enough, the only biblical figure to die in childbirth. It is alleged to be a gloss on her phrase *ben 'oni*, "son of my pain": what Rachel exclaimed during her difficult labor.

Mary Lefkowitz observes, "The Greeks always used what we would now call puns to explain the etymology of words."[11] Lefkowitz cites two examples concerning Odysseus. But there is more at stake here. The Hebrew pseudoetymology is obviously made up, and not just to shield the boy from later psychological trauma. It is an attempt to legitimize the Benjaminites as Jacob's offspring. This is one factor that leads me to suspect that Benjamin is a late addition to the lists. There are others.

The idea that the name Benjamin (*ben yamin*, "son of the right hand" = Southerner) derives from the tribe's having been the southernmost tribe of the Northern Kingdom (see Judges 5:14), is not convincing (though if Astour is right, Benjamin is a constituent element of the North).[12] Elsewhere, the name *bene yaminu* (sons of the South; compare *bene simallu*, Northerners) is well attested as the designation of Jaminite states under Jahdun-lim.[13] They were Mesopotamians living in the area of Mari on the middle Euphrates in the early second millennium, noted for their resistance to central government. In periods of central government strength such as that under Ashur-uballit I, around 1365–1330 BCE, some of these tribes could have been pushed to the margins of Mesopotamia and thence departed for greener, or at least freer, pastures.

---

[11]Mary Lefkowitz, *Not Out of Africa* (New York: Basic Books, 1997) 64.

[12]Michael C. Astour, "Bene-Iamina et Jericho," *Semitica* 9 (1959): 5-20. The pioneering work in this field is Jean-Robert Kupper's *Les nomades en Mésopotamie au temps des rois de Mari* (Paris: Société d'Édition "Les Belles Lettres," 1957).

[13]Astour thinks there were four Yaminite states, Buccellati three. See also Robert M. Whiting, "Amorite Tribes and Nations of Second-Millennium Western Asia," in Sasson et al., *Civilizations of the Ancient Near East* 2:1231-42. The question is whether descendants of any of them could have persisted long enough to retain some ethnic identity at the time of the "Conquest."

With a five-hundred-year gap between the texts from Mari and our Bible, a direct connection is hardly demonstrable. Our Benjamin is probably descended from these Mari tribes. This supposition is based not merely on the claim that their names are similar, a claim that is itself disputed. However, to establish anything like a real connection, we need first of all to examine the biblical text's uses of the name.

The name Benjamin occurs about 160 times in Scripture. One-fifth of the occurrences of the name are in Ezra, Nehemiah, or Chronicles, and mainly concern lists and genealogies. Kings makes Judah and Benjamin a tandem (1 Kings 12:21), and indeed the myth of the "Ten Lost Tribes" generates from this time. After all, two from twelve leaves ten. (For more on these tribes and their fate, see chapter 10.) Judges 5:14 links Benjamin with Ephraim, but after the Return the tribe is connected with Judah, reflecting a postexilic situation.

A fourth of the occurrences are clustered in Judges 19–21. A key text here is Judges 20:16, which notes that the Benjaminites[14] fielded seven hundred left-handed soldiers. Why is this noteworthy? Left-handers not only had an advantage in single combat, as they still do in fencing and boxing, they were also useful as assault troops against walled cities.

City gate defenses were usually constructed with outer "corridor walls" that constrained infantry attackers to come in from the right. Since right-handed infantry necessarily carried shields on their left arms, this exposed their right sides to stones and arrows cast or shot from the city walls. Left-handers, with their shields on the right arm, would be protected when attacking from the right.

Halpren notes three biblical references to "left-handed" Benjaminite soldiers: Ehud the judge and the "700 picked men" (Judges 3:15 and 20:16); of course David's "mighty warriors" in 1 Chron 12:2—albeit not specifically left-handed—were *ambidextrous* Benjaminite archers.[15] It may also be the case that Ehud's tribal origin enabled him to get closer to the Moabite King Eglon than someone from another tribe could have. I mean

---

[14]Even the spelling, *benei yamini*, betrays an older stratum, while retention of this variant indicates some lack of detailed editing.

[15]Baruch Halpren, *The First Historians* (University Park PA: Pennsylvania State University Press, 1988) 40-41. "In no other text," Halpren points out, "does handedness figure" (41). Ahlström (*The History of Ancient Palestine*) does not think Ehud was a Benjaminite, but his identification of Ehud's territory is so close to that associated with Benjamin that such a judgment cannot be made with certainty.

to suggest that at this early point in the history Benjamin might not have been regarded as an organic part of the Israelite confederation, so Benjamin's loyalty to "greater Israel" would not have been taken for granted. This fits in with what we know of the *bene yaminu*.

Mesopotamian Benjaminites, if I may call them by that name, had resisted control by central governments in regard to such things as census, corvee, and taxes until the reign of Samsi-Adad I (1814–1782 BCE).[16] After that they suffered a gradual loss of autonomy. What is likely, then, is that during succeeding periods of Assyrian central government strength some displaced *bene yaminu*, having recently been forced or migrated far to the west, made their way toward the Mediterranean, where they joined a loose confederation of "Leah-tribes" on the eve of their entry into Canaan.[17] Astour points out that Jericho/Yericho/Yarihu is the name of one of the Benjaminite tribes, and biblical Jericho is in the Benjaminite tribal territory.

§4. Good King Saul

The first Israelite to be anointed, around 1020 BCE—whether he was "king" or "chief" is a matter of discussion—was Saul, identified as a fifth-generation Benjaminite. The Bible's Benjaminites were known as warlike or at least skilled in warfare, as were the *bene yaminu* of the Mari texts. Genesis 49 "celebrates" the tribe's voraciousness, so, insofar as it was necessary forcibly to dispossess earlier inhabitants, Benjamin would have played a key role.

The empire that the Bible credits to David was, in fact, largely Saul's doing. From his base in the central highlands, Saul successfully rebuffed an Ammonite threat in Transjordan. It was this success, perhaps, that caused him to come down to fight the Philistines instead of harrying them from the hills. Along with son Jonathan, he lost his life at the Battle of Mt. Gilboa.

Why was Saul chosen? The Bible reports that "from his shoulders and upward he was higher than any of the people" (1 Sam. 9:2 KJV). But

---

[16]H. W. F. Saggs, *The Greatness That Was Babylon* (New York: New American Library, 1962) 503 and passim.

[17]Dimorphic chiefdoms contain nomadic elements. See M. B. Rowton, "Urban Autonomy in a Nomadic Environment," *Journal of Near Eastern Studies* 32 (January-April 1973): 201-13.

the real reason he was elected captain (and played "center") is that his
team owned the ball. That is, they had fighting skills most other tribes
lacked.[18] During the long period of the Israelite organization of Canaan,
Benjamin could have provided the cadres necessary for training and
leading groups of agricultural or pastoral people who had little skill in
warfare for those situations in which war was necessary.

Unfortunately, such skills were not always directed at Israel's enemies. Most of the references to Benjamin in Judges and Samuel concern
fighting between Benjamin and assorted other Israelites, or between Benjamin and all the others together. So fierce were the animosities that, ultimately, "all Israel" rallied against them, but that was not until after Benjamin had reportedly made an ugly slaughter of those initially sent against
them, despite having been outnumbered by fifteen to one (Judges 20).

In the third round of their conflict, the other Israelites used a strata-
gem to defeat Benjamin and allegedly killed 25,000 of them (20:46).
After that, Israel took an oath not to intermarry with Benjamin—another
indication, too often ignored by scholars, of the tribe's essential foreignness—but then undertook a razzia against Jabesh-Gilead to provide the
endangered Benjaminite remnant with wives. A doublet of this story
follows. In it, "Israel" instructs Benjamin to abduct women from Shiloh.
The question in both cases is, Whose tribe's women were these?

This confused, confusing, and contradictory narrative cries out for
explanation. If it was composed after the event—even after Saul's death,
as I suspect—it might have the purpose of discrediting Benjamin and pre-
venting any future Benjaminite leadership, on whatever basis that might
be claimed.

To shift metaphors somewhat, Benjaminite leadership had represented
a marriage of convenience. True, they were the group with the best military skills, but the others were not happy being thus "betrothed" to Benjamin, and relations were tenuous at best. The strange episode of the
Levite's concubine (Judges 19) offers a pretext for Benjamin's ostracism,
but to me that story is a red herring. The Judeans, editors of Scripture

---

[18]First Chron. 5:18 credits Gad, Reuben, and half-Manasseh with 44,760 warriors.
Other Gadite fighters are mentioned in 1 Chron. 12:9ff. See also Deut. 33:20. Most of the
time the king, or as Frank Frick prefers, "chief," would be involved in domestic questions
of land acquisition, cultivation, and division. See Frick's *The Formation of the State in
Ancient Israel: A Survey of Models and Theories*, Social World of Biblical Antiquity
series 4 (Sheffield UK: Almond, 1985).

and inheritors of Saul's kingdom, wanted an ironclad reason why Benjamin deserved to be put down and kept down.

Saul's accomplishments, for example, his going to the relief of Israelites in Jabesh-gilead, might not be gainsaid, but even Saul's war record was eclipsed by the brave Judean David, who killed Goliath and "ten thousands" of enemies, as compared with Saul's paltry "thousands" (1 Sam. 18:7). One might think that Saul's heroic death, if not the life that preceded it, would be worthy of fond remembrance in Israel, but it was not. By the time the national history came to be written, Benjaminite leadership had been thoroughly discredited. Why?

If Paul Johnson is correct, the Benjaminites made a separate peace with invading Babylon right before the destruction of Jerusalem,[19] that is, not too long before the second section of TaNaKh was canonized. Judean survivors/editors would then have had a strong and current reason for excoriating them. When this happened, not only the contemporary male-factors were vilified, but their ancestors and their progeny as well—"root and branch," to borrow a phrase from Amos.

Benjamin's "defection" was, no doubt, opportunistic, but it emphasizes Benjamin's essential and continuing foreignness within Israel. For one of the constituent tribes to have had and maintained its own "foreign policy" would have been as useless and divisive as the city of Cleveland's having its own navy with which to menace Canada.

Consequently, reasons to change the ruling house while accepting the dynastic principle itself had to be found. If we credit the biblical account, Saul proved limited in several ways. He was apparently very moody, possibly bipolar—if one may hazard a "diagnosis" of a man dead three thousand years. Perhaps, too, Benjaminite tribal leadership had not evolved to the same point as in the other tribes. Saul did not observe the separation between king, priest, and prophet that had apparently been becoming the norm.[20]

Another infraction: Saul consulted the dead Samuel, by means of a spirit-medium, right after he himself is reported to have forbidden Israel from just such "consultations." Of course, this is just the kind of thing

---

[19]Paul Johnson, *History of the Jews* (New York: Harper & Row, 1987) 78, and Abraham Malamat, "Caught between the Great Powers," *Biblical Archaeology Review* 25/4 (July/August 1999): 41 and n. 10. There is what may be a hint of this in Jer. 6:1.

[20]Simon Maccabee made the same mistake almost 1,000 years later.

pro-David polemicists might have invented against Saul, but the story is odd enough to have the ring of truth. The woman Saul consulted raised Samuel's shade, but also roused his ire against Saul, and not for the first time. Saul's sparing of the Canaanite "king" Agag against Samuel's explicit orders, was, from a contemporary standpoint, quite objectionable (though the incident may take quite a different cast when viewed through modern sensibilities).

Even Saul's religion was suspect, especially to later Israelites. At one point, he appealed to Samuel to pray to "your god," not "God," or "our God," indicating perhaps that Samuel's god was not his. Though one of his sons was named Jonathan, a kosher Yahwistic name, another was named Ishba'al, "man of Ba'al," and Jonathan himself had a son who was named Meribba'al, "Ba'al is (my) advocate." Later, the -ba'al element in personal names became so repellent that Jews who edited Samuel and Chronicles would not write it, in some places spelling the theophoric element as bošet ("shame"). This, of course, represents another later judgment.

Alternatively, did Saul have more than one wife? Probably. David had ten and Solomon allegedly had seven hundred, including an Egyptian princess and a Yemenite queen. The children's names could indicate different ethnic origins within Saul's family. Or was Saul himself a polytheist? Lemche is correct in pointing out that the Judge Gideon's other name, Jerubba'al, cannot mean "he fights against ba'al," but "let Ba'al contend," because the theophoric element is grammatically never an object.[21] From the Samarian Ostraca we may infer that -ba'al or 'egel (calf) were legitimate Israelite name elements, especially in the North, but this merely points up persistent regional differences.[22]

Finally, Saul did his own prophecy. "Is Saul also among the prophets?" (1 Sam. 10:11, 12 and 19:24), is not admiration, but later "Bible-speak" for "Who does he think he is?" Putting all these elements together forms a kind of indictment or disqualification of Saul, his family, and his whole tribe from leadership. When we add that such luminaries as Moses, Jacob, and David himself were younger or youngest sons, the desire to disfranchise Benjamin becomes even more understandable.

---

[21]Niels Lemche, *Ancient Israel* (Sheffield UK: Sheffield Academic Press, 1988) 225.
[22]Thomas, *DOTT*, 206.

The feisty tribe was not "rehabilitated" until the Persian period, the time of Benjaminite Esther and her Uncle Mordecai, when danger to national survival outweighed old hatreds, fears, and prejudices. It is probable that, by the Persian period, the tribe of Benjamin had dwindled into insignificance. Ehud (Benjamin) becomes an eponym in 1 Chronicles 7:10, a late text from the time when the anti-Benjaminite animus may have cooled somewhat.

§5. Bedfellows Make Strange Politics

All that remains of David and Jonathan is a few scraps of poetry.

—E. M. Forster

Shakespeare, apparently, wasn't Jewish. In *Julius Caesar* he wrote, "The evil that men do lives after them, / The good is oft interred with their bones" (3.2.80-81). By the time Chronicles was written, the good that David had done was remembered and the evil interred with his bones. If we did not have the accounts of Samuel and Kings, David might have been thought the most virtuous man in Israel. The only mistake otherwise recorded of him—allowing a census of Israel—is characterized as prompted by Satan (1 Chron. 21:1) and so not entirely his fault. Moreover, he bravely accepted responsibility for it, sparing Israel from more disaster than that already visited upon them.

Here we have to ask why the Bible's editors didn't cover their tracks better. The parallel account in 2 Samuel attributes David's actions to "the anger of the Lord." What would readers think who knew both accounts, much less those who had both in front of them?

One modern translation of 1 Samuel 16:12 says David "was ruddy, and had beautiful eyes, and was handsome" (RSV = NRSV). Today we could call David charismatic, but in truth he was a charming scoundrel or worse. As one Nabal complains, "Servants leave their masters [to follow him]" (1 Sam. 25:10). Servants and debtors—the two groups would have overlapped—and malcontents of various sorts, no doubt including *habiru*, made up the first band of four hundred that the Bible says gathered around David. But that wasn't the entire retinue.

David himself was attracted to other men's wives, such as the afore-mentioned Nabal's spouse, Abigail. He married her after the convenient death of her husband. Bathsheba, whose husband's death he engineered, was having an adulterous relationship with him while her husband was still alive.

However, he was skilled in the tactics and strategy of warfare and his reflexes were quick enough on two occasions to dodge Saul's thrown spear. Tradition also credits him with composing almost half of the canonical Psalms, and while this has been disputed it seems likely enough. Skill in poetry and music making is almost a liability for leadership in most modern Western countries. (George M. Cohan won the Congressional Medal of Honor for his songs, but it was George Patton who led the Third Army.) Both talents were most essential for an ancient Near Eastern leader. Amos remembers David's music making (6:5) and his playing had the power to soothe Saul's savage breast (1 Sam. 16:23).

Here again one has to accept inner biblical evidence for David or else credit later editors of Amos with a deviousness that would have excited Machiavelli. If Amos 6:5 isn't genuine, it must be planted.[23] *But people clever enough to do this would surely have had the sense to harmonize the accounts of David's census that we just mentioned.*

Recognizing David's popularity, Saul alternatively tried to get him killed, to kill David himself, or to marry him into his own family. At one point Saul promised his daughter Merab to David, but then married her off to someone else. David then married another of Saul's daughters, Michal, but she too was given to someone else during the conflict between David and her father. After becoming king, David remarried Michal, whom he forcibly took from her then-husband. This was more than garden-variety lust, however, as she had helped David escape from one of her father's attempts on his life; there is a practical resonance as well.

Politically, a son of David by Michal would have had a powerful claim to the throne of Israel, and one that could be accepted by both Judeans and Benjaminites. In the end, of course, the succession went to Solomon. (We are told that Michal had no children, as a punishment for her levity at David's honoring of the Ark in 2 Samuel 6:20-23. But the

---

[23]There is a third possibility. Wellhausen was so convinced that Israelites had no artistic talents that he emended "like David" to "banging potsherds." Thus the "Higher Anti-Semitism" complained of by Schecter.

incident might also reflect Michal's allegiance—inconsistent with David's agenda—to the goddess shrine at Bethel, for example.)

Another family relationship of which Saul could not approve was that between his son, Jonathan, and the young upstart, David. Jonathan is portrayed as a daring, even foolhardy leader, at one point going with a single retainer to a Philistine encampment and killing twenty of the enemy (1 Sam. 14:1-15). That Jonathan should have aided and abetted his father's and his own potential rival bespeaks more than a casual relationship.

Robert Alter characterizes Jonathan only as "well meaning and naive";[24] he offers no other reason why Jonathan would love David "as himself." But I have to ask, were David and Jonathan lovers? When Jonathan was killed, David lamented that his love for Jonathan "surpassed that of women," whatever that meant in Israel.

Plato's Greeks understood that in a culture in which women are kept strictly separate from men (and often prevented from developing intellectually), bonds between people of the same sex can be profound in a way that bonds between those of opposite sexes could not. Our tendency to fix impermeable boundaries between various kinds of sexual preference may prevent us from appreciating the nuances of more fluid understandings.

The Bible's own texts are not much help here. First Samuel 18:1 is ambiguous, as is the long narrative in chapters 20–21. All we can say is that David and Jonathan had an especially close, possibly physical relationship.[25] In the NJPS translation of 1 Sam. 16:12, the phrase "had beautiful eyes" (as in RSV and NRSV), referring to David, is translated as merely "bright-eyed," but this merely shows that modern translators, too, have agendas, and the possibility remains. If so, it would seem to indicate a passing youthful passion rather than what our culture identifies as homosexuality per se: both had families, and of David we know that he had ten wives and at least seventeen children.

---

[24]Robert Alter, *The David Story* (New York: W. W. Norton, 1999) 123n.2; see also 112n.1.

[25]This subject is so emotion-laden that conservative Christians and Jews dismiss any suggestion of homoerotic relations between David and Jonathan out of hand. On the possibility of such, see Thomas Horner, *Jonathan Loved David: Homosexuality in Biblical Times* (Philadelphia: Westminster, 1978).

David's skills were not limited to music and warfare. As king he refused to drink water that some of his soldiers had foolishly risked their lives to get, apparently so as not to encourage such behavior (compare Alexander, almost a millennium later, pouring out a similar offering to the gods). He refused the gift of Araunah's threshing floor, saying, "I will not offer burnt offerings to the LORD my God that cost me nothing" (2 Sam. 24:24 NRSV). David's most astute gesture, however, came in response to Saul's having declared him an outlaw.

This is the only case in Scripture where one Israelite declares another *'oyeb*, "enemy," a term customarily used to identify foreigners, for example, in Lamentations 1:10. When Saul considered David an *'oyeb* who therefore might be killed on sight (1 Sam. 18:29), David acquired the right of self-defense.[26] But David repaid Saul's attempts to kill him with pointed forbearance. He had three opportunities to kill Saul, but declined to do so on the grounds that Saul was "the LORD's anointed." David went further, killing the Amalekite who reported that he himself had delivered the fatal stroke to the wounded king at Saul's urgent request (2 Sam. 1:1-16).

This story, with which 2 Samuel begins, is at variance with the story of Saul's death that ends 1 Samuel. There it is said that Saul fell on his own sword after his armor bearer, terrified, refused to kill him. Whichever story is true, the one in 2 Samuel advances the notion that the person of the king is sacrosanct, a good precedent for David to have set.

And it worked. David's dynasty endured for 350 years, and except for Queen Athaliah (see chapter 10), Joash—murdered after a forty year reign (796 BCE), and Amon (ruled 642–640 BCE), the Southern kingdom was free from the assassination of its kings.[27] In the North, political assassinations became routine. The year 885 saw three different kings rule because of two assassinations. Consequently, the average reign of Northern kings was about ten years, while in the South it was about seventeen; the latter figure would have been higher were it not for the three foreign interven-

---

[26]Stanley N. Rosenbaum, "Israelite Homicide Law and the Term *'eyvah* in Gen. 3:15," *The Journal of Law and Religion* 2/1 (Winter 1984): 145-51.
[27]Amaziah of Judah was murdered in 767 BCE, but I think he was no longer king, having been replaced by his son Uzziah during the time of his ten-year detention in Israel. Edwin Thiele, *The Mysterious Numbers of the Hebrew Kings*, 2nd ed. (Grand Rapids MI: Zondervan, 1983) 115, concurs, saying, "Amaziah returned to Judah but did not reoccupy his throne."

tions in Judean politics in the twenty-two years that followed Josiah's death.

David began as a local leader in the area of Hebron, where he held sway for seven and a half years. Before this time he had an up-and-down relationship with the region's dominant Philistines, during one period joining them because of the need to escape Saul's jurisdiction. Here, too, he played a double game. At one point he feigned madness in order to avoid being sent into battle; at another he falsely reported having attacked Judean towns so that his Philistine overlord would think David had permanently alienated himself from his own people. He was, as noted, a charming scoundrel.

Taking advantage of political weakness in Egypt and Assyria, the two traditional rivals for Palestinian hegemony, David was able to expand onto both sides of the Jordan river the modest empire that he had inherited from his once and future father-in-law. He showed no concern for any prohibition against fraternizing with Ammonites or Moabites, using both countries as refuges when fleeing from Saul or from his own son Absalom.

In the case of Ammon, this could have been because, as 2 Samuel 12:30 suggests, he might have previously made himself king of part of Ammon. Even so, we have to ask why ruling the offspring of the incestuous Lot would have seemed desirable to him. Just as likely, David was the guest of and enjoyed good relations with that King Nahash of Ammon who was the enemy of his enemy, Saul.

As we noted in chapter 7, the same Nahash may have been the father of David's sister Abigail. If so, that would help explain why David apparently had no objection to Solomon's marrying an Ammonite. Of course, one might respond, Who did Solomon not marry? But this woman was the mother of Rehoboam, who next ascended the throne, making her the queen mother. As for Moab, David's great-grandmother was Ruth, the celebrated Moabitess who converted herself to the religion of her mother-in-law, Naomi. Obviously, the exclusion of Ammonites and Moabites was often winked at.

§6. Solomon: Wise, Yes; Smart, Maybe Not

Just as there are two Davids—the one in Kings and the one in Chronicles—so there are also two Solomons. Kings has Solomon attending to his father's last shrewd political instructions concerning whom he should reward and who kill. Chronicles makes it appear as if there was never a question as to who would succeed: the rivals' names are not even mentioned. This raises two questions.

How did David get conned—there's simply no other word for it—by Nathan and Bathsheba, into selecting Solomon? It will not do to say that David must, indeed, have made such a promise earlier, because, had he done so, the text would certainly contain it; important officials such as General Joab and Priest Abiathar would have been consulted; Nathan and Bathsheba would not have had to conspire as they did; and, on the other hand, the actions of David's son Adonijah would have been seen as a conspiracy against Solomon.

The second question is how the organizers of Scripture could allow two such glaringly contradictory accounts as Kings and Chronicles to inhabit the same volume, but we'll have to wait until later (chapter 13) to address this.

It is possible that the loyalty David commanded from his common soldiers was not shared by all his top commanders, especially by those who, like Joab, had their own ambitions for leadership. On the other hand, like some modern-day Afghans, generals Abner and Amasa came over to David after having fought for Saul and Absalom respectively. Even from the bare bones of biblical narrative, then, we get a picture of intrigue, envy, and constantly shifting loyalties.

With the Davidic kingship of such recent origin that proponents of Saul's leadership were still quite active, and with others in Israel, no doubt, still opposing the principle of kingship, weakness at the top was an invitation to civil war. In such a situation, any son of David who wished to be king would have been almost compelled to make moves that, authorized or not, established him as the successor. That is what Absalom did.

Absalom edged toward the kingship by putting on various trappings of the role, enlisting or trying to enlist the support of such powerful people as Joab who were close to David (2 Sam. 14:28–15:12), and finally acting as de facto king (1 Kings 1:5-53)—for *four years*.

Another possibility in explaining the succession struggle would be to posit that the same circulatory illness that made David feel physically cold toward the end of his life also caused his mind to experience periods of confusion. He was, after all, at least in his sixties and had had a difficult and stressful life. Some form of dementia is certainly possible and it might have been manifest for much longer than the brief account in 1 Kings 1:1-4 would lead us to believe. How else explain Adonijah's four years of virtual usurpation?

§7. Uneasy Lies the Head That Would Wear the Crown

David is not noted for parenting skills, but then he had multiple wives and concubines who produced seventeen named male offspring. We don't know which of the mothers was initially the favorite wife, nor the order of all their sons' births, but the first six male children were: Amnon, Chileab/Daniel, Absalom, Adonijah, Shephatiah, and Ithream (2 Sam. 3:2-5; 1 Chron. 3:1-4). Which one would succeed him?

We may assume that the same sort of "harem intrigue" that Albert Olmstead talks about in his *History of Assyria*[28] would be present in any polygamous monarchy, so that any child who lived might be a contender. However, stories concerning only how three were disqualified are found in Scripture.

Amnon, though he was firstborn, apparently was not automatically assured of the succession because, for one thing, the principle of dynastic succession had not been established. He therefore tried to "marry" his half-sister, Tamar, using a ruse to cohabit with her over her protest. This was not the simple, lust-inspired rape claimed by modern feminist interpretation, and her plea that an appeal to David might gain royal permission was not a ploy to buy time as some have suggested.

Israelite law allows a woman to claim as her husband a man who has had relations with her, even if he raped her. Amnon knew this. So, heeding the counsel of his "crafty" (NRSV; NJPS "clever", 2 Sam. 13:3) cousin Jonadab, a son of David's brother Shimeah, he was trying to strengthen his claim to the throne by forcing marriage on a woman who was also David's daughter. Doubtless cousin Jonadab hoped to enjoy a privileged position in the ensuing Amnon regime, which is probably why he suggested the plan in the first place.

Marriages between children of the same mother had never been countenanced, but children of the same father by different mothers might marry. This was certainly permitted in Abraham's time—hence, his deception of Pharaoh. Passing Sarah off as his sister aroused the ire of

---

[28]Albert T. E. Olmstead, *History of Assyria* (Chicago: University of Chicago Press, 1923).

Pharaoh and of many readers of Scripture, modern and ancient. However, this type of union was not contrary to Israelite law until prohibited in Leviticus 18:9. How old is that piece of legislation? Sometime between Abraham's time and David's any half-sibling marriage had begun to be seen as borderline incestuous and therefore illegitimate, so only royal permission might grant an exception.

> *Jacob's marrying sisters, and Moses' father marrying his own aunt, are other examples that tell against the patriarchal stories' being nothing but late fabrications. Who would attribute such illicit activities to the founders of their line?*
>
> *Perhaps the prohibition of half-sibling union came about because the results of narrow inbreeding had noticeable and ultimately predictable results. Congenital deformities such as we may deduce from the realistic portraits of Pharaoh Akhenaton's reign—at a time when some proto-Israelites resided in Egypt—might have caused the practice to be proscribed eventually.*

The real problem here is that modern translations do not recognize that what Tamar actually says to Amnon is not "Do not do this wanton folly" (2 Sam. 13:12 RSV; NRSV has "anything so vile"; NJPS, "vile thing"; Robert Alter, "scurrilous"), but "Do not do this *impious* thing." That Hebrew *nabal* can bear the meaning "impious" we can see from Psalm 14's *hannabal* [NJPS: "benighted person"] *amar b'libbo 'ain 'elohim.* "The *nabal* says in his heart, 'There is no god.' " Saying "in your heart," that is, silently to yourself, that there is no God *is* foolish because Jeremiah 17:10 shows that Jews have long acknowledged that God is "a searcher of hearts." But denying God, even silently, is more than foolish, it is gross impiety.

Additional proof may be had from Micah 7:6, where a related form of the word characterizes sons' actions toward their fathers. The context tells us that the action is bad, wrong, and so the modern translations duly translate it as "despise," "spurn," "hold in contempt," and so forth. But Proverbs 17:21b's "The father of a *nabal* has no joy" is something of an understatement. It is the "b" clause in a verse that parallels *nabal* with *c'sil.* The 1917 JPS translation of this verse, which uses "fool" and "churl," respectively, is better than the NJPS's "dullard" and "villain." But again, there is more at stake here. Such a flagrant violation of the commandment to honor one's father, Israel's strongest example of "Black Letter Law," is gross impiety.

By David's time, so also was marrying your half-sister.
Tamar continues, "This [half-sibling marriage] is no longer done in Israel" (my translation). Would it have been possible, even after the law forbidding half-sibling marriage was in effect, to get some sort of royal dispensation from it? Perhaps. Note Genesis 29:26, where Laban says, "It's not the *practice* to marry off a younger sister before an older one." This verse, too, uses the same Niphal of √*y-s-h* to indicate customary use. (David himself is offered Saul's elder daughter first.)

Absalom's subsequent rejection of Tamar was probably a projection onto her of his own feelings of self-loathing, common enough in such cases—here even more so, as Amnon was himself enticed into it by his clever cousin. Nonetheless, the ploy might have ultimately succeeded if Tamar's full brother, Absalom, had not had Amnon killed *two years later*.

Here again, what we have is not an avenging of the family honor. If that had been the case, retaliation should have been swift, especially since Absalom was also a favorite of his father. And where was father in all this? The Septuagint of 2 Samuel 13:21 (not in RSV but included in NRSV as "reading with the LXX") reports that while David "was greatly upset, he did not rebuke his son, Amnon, for he favored him, since he was his first born." However, when Amnon was killed, the Hebrew text says that David mourned him, but finally yearned for Absalom who had fled to Geshur. Absalom's response, then, was a carefully crafted counterplay on the part of one who had his own legitimate claim for the kingship to press.

Absalom seems to have been most like David himself. *People Magazine* might have featured him as "the sexiest man alive," because the Bible says as much. He was only third in line for the throne, but the second-born son, Chileab ("Daniel" in 1 Chron. 3:1), simply disappears from Scripture after his initial listing in 2 Sam. 3:3-4. He may have died in infancy. Probably even before the succession was in question, Absalom embarked on a long and complex campaign, like that of a modern office seeker, to win the hearts of enough and of the right people so that he could obtain—and hold—the throne.

As I indicated above, Absalom's strategy might have been partly motivated by David's failing health and increasingly ineffectual leadership, and the fear that the country might break up if the succession question were not settled before the old king died. Despite having been David's then-current favorite, he ultimately overplayed his hand. On the advice of friends and counsellors, one of whom was an agent of David, Absalom tried a naked usurpation of power. He publicly had intercourse with some of David's concubines, a standard symbolic claiming of the kingship.

Absalom subsequently drove his father from the city: so David was out, but he was not down. Just as the Union's General George Meade failed to pursue Robert E. Lee's Confederates after Gettysburg, Absalom listened to the counsel of David's agent, Hushai, and failed to follow up his advantage. In Meade's case, this merely delayed the Union success; in Absalom's case it was fatal—to him. After an initial military success, Absalom's attempt failed and he was killed. Despite this disloyalty, David was so distraught at Absalom's death that he had, finally, to be upbraided by Joab, David's nephew and commander-in-chief of his army, for "loving those who hate you and hating those who love you." After that, David returned to Jerusalem.

Adonijah, David's fourthborn, waited until David was close to death (1 Kings 1) before having himself proclaimed king. But the last-minute intervention by Solomon's mother Bathsheba, guided by David's advisor Nathan the prophet, managed to thwart Adonijah even in the midst of his feasting. Bathsheba "reminded" David that he had promised her that Solomon would succeed him, a promise of which we have no record. But the king responded as though it were the case. David gave orders for Solomon to be anointed king, and so it was.

Even then, Adonijah didn't give up. Dethroned, he still asked Bathsheba for the rights to Abishag, the Shunamite woman who had last warmed David's bed. Like the public intercourse with David's concubines, this was *lese majeste*, an attempt at usurpation; one wonders why Adonijah thought he could get away with it. Did he not at least know the story of Reuben, a firstborn who was nevertheless disqualified from family leadership for the same reason? One might infer from this that the stories of the Patriarchal Period were not widely known.

What is interesting here is that Adonijah sought Bathsheba's assistance and that she agreed to intervene on his behalf. A woman who was clever enough to obtain the throne for her son by bluffing a king who might have had her killed would not casually give away what with so much risk she had just gained. Was Bathsheba, like her murdered husband, a Hittite, and so assumed to be ignorant of Israelite law and practice? Alternatively, as queen did she have jurisdiction over the harem? We don't know. I think she agreed to carry Adonijah's request to Solomon precisely because she knew what her son's reaction would be.

If there were any lessons learned from the struggle to succeed David, perhaps the most important was that the king should publicly appoint his successor while still in control of the country. Succeeding Southern monarchs were able to do this on six separate occasions, making the transition between rulers smoother and maintaining the Davidic dynasty throughout the South's independent political history.

§8. Queen of Hearts—and Minds?

This episode speaks to a power that Bathsheba wielded within the government, and we have to wonder what part was customarily played by the favorite wife/queen or queen mother. In that regard, we usually think of Jezebel, the foreign wife of Ahab, but we should remember that of the nineteen queen mothers mentioned in Scripture, seventeen (including Athaliah) were Southern, indicating they were considered important enough there to be remembered.

Bathsheba was the first of them and, as we saw above, had both hands up to the elbows in palace politics. But what functions—social, political, or religious—did the queen mother customarily play?[29] To answer this it might be best to start with the case of King Asa's (911–870 BCE) mother Ma'acah. (There is some confusion as to whether this Ma'acah was also a daughter of Absalom, named for her grandmother—one of David's wives. If so, she might have carried the hopes of the "Absalom faction" for an eventual return to power.)

What's noteworthy about Ma'acah is that both Kings and Chronicles agree that Asa stripped her of the rank of "queen mother" (*gebirah*) because she made, or caused to be made, an Asherah image. What, then, makes this such a grievous offense, and what kind of powers did the queen mother *ex officio* normally exercise?

As we saw concerning Hannah (chapter 4), a woman's position in ancient and even in some modern Middle Eastern societies depends upon

---

[29]For a recent discussion, see Carol Smith, " 'Queenship' in Israel? The Cases of Bathsheba, Jezebel, and Athaliah," in *King and Messiah in Israel and the Ancient Near East*, ed. John Day (Sheffield UK: Sheffield Acacdemic Press, 1998) 142-62, and the sources named there.

her production of male heirs.[30] So, in addition to the "national" religion, if there were one, women might have recourse to any god or goddess who could promise them fertility. Women, then, were likely to retain forms of goddess worship along with whatever else they did, and no amount of official condemnation seems permanently to have put an end to it.

If that's true, the mother of the current king and wife of the previous king would necessarily have had a high place in the Asherah cult. Her own fertility would have been symbolic, that is, a sign of increase and stability for the whole nation. She also might have had a say in the succession, as Bathsheba and Athaliah (see below) did.

The biblical *asherah* seems to be related to Assyrian *ashirtu*, a feminine fertility deity, and to have been represented in Israel by a pole or stripped tree trunk. The phallic nature of such a pole[31] is obvious; devotees would pray that the "seed" implanted in them would bear fruit. I think we have to assume that Asherah worship was something that Ma'acah, like queen mothers before her, was accustomed to practicing. Otherwise, the story sounds about as likely as a tale of some Orthodox rabbi returning from vacation to find that his mother has, suddenly, put up a Christmas tree in his own living room window.

We may speculate that, since religion is inseparable from politics, the move against the asherahs—not the only such move that Asa made—was part of a campaign to secure his own power. This action was made necessary by the ascendancy of his mother during the early years of his long reign when he was, presumably, a minor.

Why his mother, rather than some other family member or a group of "elders," would have been regent is another of those unanswerable questions. It may be that as high priestess of Asherah she already had leverage in ruling circles. Apparently, highly placed women such as the

---

[30]For example, Soraya, former queen of Iran. The fact that Reza Shah Pahlavi consistently eschewed cross-tribal marriage alliances may have contributed to his downfall. See Mara Donaldson, "Kinship Theory in the Patriarchal Narratives: The Case of the Barren Wife," *Journal of the American Academy of Religion* 49/1 (1981): 87-98. In some present-day African societies, women are not considered truly married until they have given birth.

[31]May Day celebrations have a long history in England—and were forbidden as idolatrous under Cromwell. Two maypoles are erected every May Day at Bryn Mawr College (Pennsylvania), as I had occasion to witness when my daughter matriculated in 1980.

queen or queen mother had a place in what we may loosely call "women's religion"; the biblical text gives some evidence that this might have been the case through the stories of Jephthah's daughter and Michal, Saul's daughter. This is not to say that women had a religion different from men, as Greek women did, but that they almost certainly had a cult which they practiced in addition to the state religion.[32]

Solomon is criticized for allowing asherahs, but if the practice were illegitimate, when did it become so and why? The Bible claims that it was among many foreign imports allowed by Solomon only when weakened by old age (1 Kings 11:4), but this explanation reflects a position that was arrived at much later; it's an obvious, bald-faced attempt to exonerate Solomon from any complicity. Interestingly, the two national deities that are mentioned here, the Phoenician Ashtoreth and Ammonite Milcom, are likely not chosen at random. The former is a concomitant of Solomon's close relations with Hiram of Tyre and the latter was the god of that wife who bore his successor, Rehoboam.

Later reform-minded Southern kings Hezekiah and Josiah, obviously influenced by the free prophets—who, I must say, would have a place on the religious spectrum similar to the *hezbollah* ("the party of God") in Islam—tore down the poles. But note that they did so at an interval of some hundred years. Obviously, like a cancer only partly eradicated, the evil practice grew back. Jeremiah complained of similar activity within a few years of Josiah's death. Note, however, that not all prophets condemn the practice.

---

[32]Traditionally, one of Solomon's many wives was the queen of Sheba. If so, we may presume she was not a Yahwist. Another, for whom we do have textual evidence, was the infamous Egyptian princess for whom Solomon built a shrine in Jerusalem so she could worship as she was accustomed to do. "And he did the same [built "high places"] for all his foreign wives who offered and sacrificed to their gods" (1 Kings 11:8 NJPS). We have no evidence that Solomon's foreign wives' devotions were "open to the public," but, presumably, they were not the only persons in attendance.

Frymer-Kensky holds that asherahs were viewed as no threat to Yahwism, merely a sort of harmless private worship indulged in by women, but even this judgment seems too mild. Competing cults would be seen as a threat. The Kuntillet Ajrud graffiti indicate that in some circles, at least, Asherah was Yahweh's consort, clearly a concept that strict Israelite monotheism would ultimately have to reject. To put it another way, the private religious practice of women would not explain why King Asa deposed his mother from the office of queen mother.

§9. The Shrewdness of Solomon

Solomon is well known for the "heart of wisdom" for which he prayed (1 Kings 3:9; 2 Chron. 1:10), but there was another side to him that was not wholly forgotten, the side of *Realpolitik*. Obtaining the succession was one thing, staying on the throne was something else again. To consolidate his position he needed powerful allies in the army and the cult, and he needed to neutralize rivals and those who had opposed him by backing other king-candidates.

David, of course, knew this, so on his deathbed the king recounted to his son a number of their enemies and appealed to Solomon's "wisdom" to deal with them as they deserved. The charge, which Robert Alter terms "worthy of a Mafia chieftain," included Adonijah, Joab, and Shimei ben Gera, but we may suppose that there were others on the "hit list" whom the Bible does not remember. In any case, the "house cleaning" had begun earlier; Saul's "sons" had already been given over to the Gibeonites who slaughtered seven of them (2 Sam. 21:1-9).

Adonijah was the easiest rival for Solomon to justify killing. As we have seen, he had made a backdoor move to usurp Solomon by trying to get rights to Abishag, the last woman with whom David had slept. This *lese majeste*, a crime against the ruling sovereign, cost Adonijah his life. It may be, however, that Solomon would have contrived to have this half-brother killed in any event, because that is what he did with the other rivals.

Dying David accused Joab of avenging in peacetime blood that had been shed in war, thus justifying his forfeiture of sanctuary even on the horns of the altar. Joab had been loyal to David through the Absalom affair and had, in fact, killed Absalom though David told him not to. So cousin Joab was murdered on the horns of the altar by another army commander, Benaiah, leader of Cherethite (Cretan) mercenaries serving as David's bodyguard. The choice of a foreigner is instructive: Benaiah would not himself have been a candidate for the throne.

Modern translations of 2 Samuel 20:23 do not notice that the "and" in the phrase describing Benaiah's command, "the Cherethites and the Pelethites" might and should be read explicatively, yielding "the Cretans, that is, the escapees/refugees," and connoting Cretan mercenaries. This possibility is noted in Encyclopedia Judaica 13:403.

It was Joab who had carried out the orders that led to the death of Uriah, opening the way for David to marry Bathsheba and, no doubt, giving Joab considerable political leverage with Uncle David. It was Joab, too, whose siege of Abel Beth Ma'acah had led to the death of Sheba ben Bichri. The Bible characterizes Sheba as a "worthless fellow" in much the same way that Soviet Russia labelled dangerous political opponents as "hooligans." Sheba was a supporter and possibly a relative of Saul, and likely wanted to reestablish Saul's line in the North.

The tale of Joab's victims also included men David deemed worthy: Abner son of Ner and Amasa son of Jether. Abner had been Saul's army commander but defected to David. Obviously, his position and experience made him a potential rival to Joab. Amasa was another of David's nephews and had commanded Absalom's army in the revolt, but David nonetheless made him commander of his own army, replacing Joab, who then threw his support to Adonijah. I say "then," but the events may not have happened in just the order I suggest.

The important point here is that David's lingering illness and death put the throne up for grabs among his many male heirs and kinsmen. Joab himself might have had designs on the throne, and why not? He was a son of David's sister, Zeruiah, and David was greatly in his debt for carrying out the orders that killed Uriah. We are left to wonder how men such as the well-connected Adonijah or the politically powerful Joab did not have their own loyal troops to defend them at the last, but with no help from Scripture we must be content merely to ask the question. Later Jewish tradition seems satisfied with explaining how the losers got what they deserved.

Shimei ben Gera, like Sheba ben Bichri, was a Benjaminite. The former was on the enemies list for allegedly cursing David on the way up from Mahanaim. David promised not to kill him and we should not wonder at that: cursing someone is never listed as a capital offense. And why would David have wanted him dead, when having to witness the king's triumph would surely be worse punishment? But Shimei was no isolated malcontent. Like Sheba, he was a Benjaminite leader whose wish to reinstate Saul's family or at least to proclaim himself as king over Benjaminite territory threatened the unity of David's fledgling empire.

In any event, Solomon put Shimei under "house arrest," confining him to Jerusalem where, presumably, Solomon's people could keep an eye on him. When Shimei left Jerusalem to pursue runaway slaves,

Solomon had him killed. As I have noted, such a stiff punishment for what seems to us little more than a parole violation seems excessive. Of course, it is also possible that Shimei was trying to escape Solomon's jurisdiction and concocted the story of the runaway slaves, but, if so, one would think the Bible might label the story a lie. Shimei must have represented a political threat.

The one conspirator who did escape with his life was the Nobite priest Abiathar. (We should be indebted to Solomon for his forbearance in this case, because one of Abiathar's descendants was Jeremiah: had Jeremiah held a position in the establishment priesthood, he might never have been moved to prophecy.) A priest from the line of Eli, Abiathar had remained loyal to David during Absalom's revolt, but then, along with Joab, he threw in with Adonijah. For this he lost his priesthood and was confined to a family estate at Anathoth, then about three miles northeast of Jerusalem.

David left instructions to reward friends, too, though the only one mentioned in the deathbed list is Barzillai the Gileadite. He was among three who brought food and supplies to David during the Absalom revolt, but one wonders if his help was more than that. Barzillai, as we have seen, means "smith," so it is possible that he supplied David with weapons at a critical time. If this is not so, why were the other two supporters not mentioned by dying David?

I have discussed these matters in some detail because the standard works, especially those used as textbooks, pay scant attention to Solomon's part in palace intrigues. They usually concentrate on the good things, of which there is no lack, that are attributed to him. He was no doubt quite a boon to the construction industry and to those engaged in international trade. He was, as well, personally talented and discerning, as the story of the baby claimed by two prostitutes shows. But even Solomon's glorious success carried within it the seeds of its own failure.

It may be, of course, that the warning words of Samuel were written after Solomon's time, but Solomon's was the kind of monarchy against which Samuel warned. Solomon was an apt student of monarchical systems, dividing the country into twelve administrative districts and extracting human and material resources from all. Even if the Bible's account of things is exaggerated, so much of the country's wealth was sucked up to support this regime and its attendant bureaucracies, religious and civil, that the gap between rich and poor must necessarily have widened.

Unfortunately, the economic lessons of his reign were not taken to heart and taught to his son. Solomon's successor, Rehoboam, promised to increase rather than decrease the tax burden, leading to Jeroboam's revolt and the secession of the eight Northern tribes.

Chapter 9

The Breakup of Their Camp

§1. The House of Joseph

Government depends upon the consent of the governed. —Thomas Jefferson

The burden of this chapter is to show that during the two hundred years of the divided monarchy it was the North that was of greater importance in international affairs. I ask the reader's indulgence for not including accounts of all the kings of Israel and Judah such as larger treatments of the subject can afford, and also for having to "back up" well into the premonarchic period to gain perspective.

Israel, the Northern Kingdom, has its own peculiar history. The Bible tells us that it largely comprised tribes named for Joseph's sons, Ephraim and Manasseh, with the younger, Ephraim, getting grandfather Jacob's blessing over Joseph's protest (Gen. 48). In the following chapter, called "The Blessing of Jacob," the patriarch does not seem to know that son Joseph has divided into Ephraim and Manasseh—even though Jacob had just adopted them!

Adoption would seem to have been unnecessary, since they were his own grandchildren. However, by thus "promoting" members of this next generation to full sonship, Israel might have been trying to avoid a Benjaminite claim based upon ultimogeniture. Ultimogeniture, the practice of favoring the last-born in inheritance, was a common biblical occurrence.[1]

With Judah dominant in the South and Ephraim in the North, there would be no room for a Benjaminite kingdom west of the Jordan. The

---

[1]Accustomed as we are to the principle of primogeniture, the opposite tack, favoring the last born, seems odd. But Esarhaddon of Babylon brags about being the youngest of his sibs and the Bible itself is replete with cases of younger sons—such as Abraham, Jacob, and Moses—or youngest sons such as David becoming their people's leaders. Why should this be?

There are two reasons. First, as the Bible relates concerning Jacob's love of Joseph, "sons of old age" are proofs of their fathers' virility, a factor that continues to be of paramount importance even in modern Israel among those of Middle Eastern origin. (Note, however, that the same joy that greeted Joseph's birth was not repeated at the birth of Benjamin.) Second, since firstborn sons would likely be only fifteen to twenty years younger than their fathers, a "son of old age" would likely have a longer, hence more stable, reign as king. That the last should become first remains a staple of much religious thought.

Northern family, however, had its own internal problems. Ephraim occupied much of the central hill country north of Bethel and west of the Jordan, while Manasseh was divided into groups living—much like present-day Palestinians—on both sides of the Jordan. For most of its length the river was more a psychological barrier than a physical obstacle.

However, that was not the case in Judges 12. Here Ephraimites crossed the river to attack Judge Jephthah's Gileadites and then got cut off at the river when they retreated. The ostensible reason for the Ephraimite "invasion" was pique at not having been invited to help in a war against some Ammonites. Jephthah claimed that he did call on his brethren for help, but that they did not answer (Judges 12:2); so, after a long and carefully reasoned argument attempting to dissuade the Ammonites from attacking him, he thrashed them with his own forces. After that, Jephthah defeated the Ephraimites.

Here we find the famous *shibboleth* incident, which indicates that Israelites probably spoke differing dialects, but it tells us more than that. It tells us that relationships even among closely related Northern groups were tenuous. The text of Judges 12:4 is confusing, but NJPS translates, "You Gileadites are nothing but fugitives from Ephraim—being in Manasseh is like being in Ephraim." Now, if this intramural invective is found among northern groups, how much more might animosity obtain between Northern and Southern groups?

The point I should like to make here is this: the kingdom of Israel itself was an uneasy alliance among disparate, occasionally desperate peoples. Choosing monarchy was not the result of divine decree or democratic deliberation, but a response to external and internal pressures. When the former abated, the latter expanded. The language of 1 Kings 12:16, "We have no portion in David, No share in Jesse's son; To your gods [see previous chapter for discussion of this translation], O Israel," is very reminiscent of 2 Samuel 20:1, in which these words are the call for a Benjaminite-led revolt. Taken together, I think they offer evidence that dynastic monarchy, even monarchy itself, did not sit well with many of Israel's constituent groups, not only with the Rechabites.[2]

---

[2]A brief discussion of the Rechabites is found in chap. 10, below.

§2. The End of Empire

Israel the empire was a fragile thing. Born in a power vacuum unusual for the area, imperial Israel held together for less than a century. Like Yugoslavia under Marshall Tito, it was an artificial creation and destined to fracture from its own internal stresses. For most of its brief existence, its success was due in large measure to the military skills of Saul, the charisma of David, and the ruthlessness of Solomon. When the monarchy broke up after Solomon's death in 931 BCE, it was the Northern Kingdom, Israel—with eight of the tribes and most of the good land—that seceded from the union.

Solomon's son, Rehoboam, went north to Shechem for his coronation. Going to this "queen city" of the North might have been done in order to show the North that he was indeed in control, or it might have been a sop to Northern sensibilities. The former seems more likely since, once there—against the advice of his older counsellors—he declined to alleviate the heavy tax burdens needed to sustain Solomon's empire; so the North revolted. Other reasons for the split were cultural, political, and religious, the last two being intertwined.

On the political side, there was still opposition to kingship in principle: to dynastic kingship in general and to the Davidic dynasty in particular. Religiously, the major difference between North and South was that the North still used bovine images in worship and a liturgical calendar that differed from the Southern by a month.

Calendrical correctness was no minor matter, as we may infer from the different dates for Christmas and Easter in Greek Orthodox and Roman Catholic circles. Neither side would willingly adopt the other's calendar nor would they be inclined to "split the difference" in the name of Christian unity.

In Israel, major festivals were celebrated a month later in the North than in the South—not surprising if one considers that crops would mature faster in the south. As we have discussed, Hezekiah's later celebration of Passover according to the Northern calendar,[3] a bold step

---

[3]Southern Passover is in Nissan, Northern in Abib. See *Encyclopaedia Judaica* 14:742 and Jacob Ben-Ezzi (Shafik) Cohen, *Who Are the Samaritans: Their Religion, Customs, and History* (Nablus: privately printed, 1968) 8-9.

which did not sit too well with some of his own people, was never repeated.

It's hard to get beyond the Bible's own story of what happened after Solomon's death, because there are so few extrabiblical accounts we can go to. Neither Israel nor Judah was initially big or important enough to warrant anyone else's attention. However, this soon changed. The Shalmaneser III Inscription of 853 BCE[4] gives a list of the north-Syrian states arrayed against him. In it, King Ahab of Israel is listed third, though his force included half the coalition's chariotry.

The Bible blames Jeroboam the son of Nebat, Israel's first king, for the split and for inventing the golden calves erected in Dan in the North and in Bethel on the Israel-Judah border. The pair Dan—Bethel is a hendiadys, like our "A to Z," indicating that calves were used throughout the North. Here Scripture conveniently forgets that this icon had a long— if not always appreciated—history going back to Aaron and resting, as we have seen, on millennia of ancient Near Eastern practice.

Note that Amos is silent on the subject of "ba'alism," indicating that still in his time (around 760 BCE), it was a legitimate part of Northern worship. It is highly unlikely that any king in Israel or Judah could simply change the people's religion by royal fiat. It was later Judaism that regarded bovine images as idolatry, making it easy to indict the North for an ex-post-facto crime.

Jeroboam is identified as "an able man" in Solomon's service who had charge of the forced labor. His elevation to ruler of the North seems to be a promotion he did not seek. Rather, it was foisted upon him by a prophet named Ahijah, who claimed that Solomon had forfeited leadership by allowing or even facilitating worship of other gods. In the light of Solomon's many marriages, this seems like a reasonable claim.

Ahijah, however, was not a disinterested, itinerant prophet. He was from Shiloh, the city that had been Israel's cultic center before it was moved to Jerusalem. He might therefore have expected Jeroboam to right this wrong; when he did not, Ahijah predicted the death of the king's son and the decline of the North.

Here I should mention Richard E. Friedman's attractive theory that what is identified as the P (Priestly) Document is the composition of

---

[4]Shalmaneser III Inscription, *ANE* 2, *A New Anthology* (1975) 188-92.

doubly disfranchised Northern priests.[5] Left under- or unemployed by Solomon, they fared no better under Jeroboam who, moreover, is faulted (1 Kings 13:33-34) for appointing unqualified people to the priesthood. As a consequence, the disappointed priests wrote a screed that says, in effect, a pox on both your royal houses. It would not take much editing to make this document simply anti-Northern and hence worthy of integration into the Torah. The story of the anonymous "man of God" in 1 Kings 13 is an obvious anti-Jeroboam interpolation (see §3).

Within a century of the split, the North probably began to write, or write down, its own Torah, Wellhausen's so-called "E Document."[6] The magic of writing would itself have been a potent force, maybe outweighing conservative opposition to the new technology's replacing oral recitation. It is also possible that Northerners were influenced by "tales out of the South," and felt the need to protect themselves from having the national memory falsified by Judeans. It is an irony of history that Judah, the weak Southern kingdom, survived to collect the stories of its own and Israel's past.

Imagine if the American North, the Union, had acquiesced in allowing the Confederate South to write or edit all the accounts of that nineteenth-century conflict which the two sides did not even call by the same name.

§3. Musical Thrones

When Jeroboam died, the North disintegrated. The tale of one son's, Abijah's, death following a prophetic prediction is told in 1 Kings 14. Another son, Nadab, succeeded him, but reigned for less than two years before being assassinated by one Ba'asha of Issachar during a siege of Philistine Gibbethon. In rejecting the dynastic principle, the North had opened itself up to just such a situation. This would not be the last time there were several kings in quick succession. In 886/5 BCE there were four. To put it another way, during the reign of Asa of Judah alone, seven kings sat on Northern thrones.

---

[5]Richard Friedman, *Who Wrote the Bible?* 2nd ed. (San Francisco: Harper Collins, 1997) 188-89 and 206-16.

[6]The most likely patrons of the Northern history would have been the Omrids (885–841 BCE), the dynasty whose most famous and successful king was the above Ahab (874–853 BCE).

Of the seven, Ba'asha ruled longest, twenty-two years. During this time the two kingdoms were so often on the verge of war that Asa made a political alliance with Aram/Damascus in Israel's rear, threatening war on two fronts. Though Chronicles later chastises Asa for this "disloyalty" to God, Chancellor Bismarck's observation to the effect that, "You must be aware of the importance of a party of three on the European chessboard,"[7] would have applied equally well in the checkerboard days of the divided monarchy.

Ba'asha's son, Elah, ruled for less than two years; his assassin Zimri, commander of half of Israel's chariot forces, killed himself after only one week when it became apparent that his rule could not be established. At that point Israel's loyalties divided, some following Tibni, an army commander, and others Omri. The latter won out. (Omri's rival died four years later. The Bible does not say how, but we may surmise it was not a natural death.) Omri succeeded in founding the first real dynasty in the North, one which lasted through four generations, though less than fifty years all told. Still, in that time Israel became sufficiently strong that it became known abroad as the "House of Omri" even after that dynasty's demise.

Half of the period in which the Omrids sat on the throne was the reign of the infamous King Ahab (874–853 BCE) and his hated Phoenician wife, Jezebel. It would be unusual indeed if Ahab were monogamous, but if he had another wife, the Bible doesn't mention her. Later Jewish tradition is surprisingly kind to him, saying that, except for the incident of Naboth's vineyard, his good deeds would have outweighed the bad.

The incident with Naboth, however, is worth examining. Naboth had a vineyard that Ahab wanted to buy or trade for. When Naboth declined, Jezebel hired people to accuse him falsely of a crime. He was duly executed and his lands taken by the state. Jezebel has had "bad press" for this ever since. In her defence, it may be noted that she was likely operating under an assumption that she brought from her native Tyre: namely, that a king's "request" might not be declined—especially in the matter of land ownership, widely held in the ancient Near East to be

---

[7]For the recollection of Bismarck's observation, my thanks to the late Prof. K. Robert Nilsson of Dickinson's Political Science Department.

crown land, only held in fee by commoners.[8] On this view, Naboth was guilty of treason and hence deserved death.

Compelled to observe the external trappings of Israelite law, Jezebel suborned perjury from the required two witnesses and effected the conviction/execution of Naboth. Whatever the truth of this reconstruction, it shows that some queens in Israel and Judah were not simply brood-mares for the production of the kings' children.

But we may wish to ask why Jezebel and Ahab were so greedy: Didn't they have enough wealth already? To answer this we need to examine Israel's internal structure, the international economic situation, and the cultural differences that, increasingly, separated the North from the South.

By Ahab's time, Israel and Judah had had separate monarchies for nearly sixty years. These kingdoms required revenues with which to pay their armies, and land upon which to settle soldiers after they mustered out. Land was also needed to grow the chief export items that upper-class people traded for, the imported items that only they could afford.

As we know from the famous Megiddo and Samaria ivories, the residents of the North developed a taste for luxury goods. To obtain these goods, the Northerners needed something to exchange. Now Israel did not produce much in the way of precious metals as Egypt did, nor precious stones as the Mesopotamian kingdoms did. It did not make fine pottery to rival Greek wares. Israel did produce foodstuffs, but its two biggest export items were olive oil and wine.

Olive trees take a long time to "come on line," but vineyards could be up and running in less than ten years. To reach exportable production levels, landowners needed extended holdings. This they could accomplish most easily by expropriating small family subsistence farms and planting them with wine grapes. Hence the desire to acquire more land, to "add field to field" (Isa. 5:8, also 3:14). Amos already alludes to this when he warns, "You have planted pleasant gardens, but you will not taste their fruit" (Amos 5:11, my paraphrase).

As Philosopher George Santayana observed, "Those who cannot remember the past are condemned to repeat it."[9] The same sort of dis-

---

[8]Cyrus Gordon (private communication).
[9]From chap. 12 of *Reason in Common Sense*, vol. 1 of his *The Life of Reason* (1905–1906).

location has been and is being caused in the United States today by modern corporate farms that buy up small family farms. A "supermarket to the world" might help us to enjoy lower prices, but it does serious damage to the social fabric of communities that displaced small farmers are compelled to leave.

International trade brought with it a growing cosmopolitanism that was felt much more in the North than in the less agriculturally valuable and more geographically isolated South. But the North had a head start toward cosmopolitanism anyway, because many of its constituent elements were Canaanite in origin. The tribes that biblical genealogy assigns to Jacob's concubines—Naphtali, Issachar, Zebulun, and Asher—were probably autochthonous peoples or groups who migrated into Israel some time before it took shape, bringing their religions and customs with them.

Putting all of this together, it is easy to see why the North and South—even when they shared the name "Israel"—were really two different countries. Both will have had complaints about the other, but the Bible increasingly reflects a Judean viewpoint. Chronicles simply doesn't mention any Northern kings at all.

To return to Ahab, his "good deeds" seem to have included playing a key role in organizing the north-Syrian coalition that withstood Assyria until 841 BCE, some twelve years after his death in battle. Shalmaneser III claims a victory at Qarqar in 853,[10] the year Ahab fell, but it would be another four years before Assyrians ventured westward again, and the coalition held them off three more times before it broke up.

Ahab had made peace with Judah, and his Phoenician marriage-alliance gave him some protection in that quarter. It was just as well that he was so politically adroit, because during this time he was having his own troubles with the kings of Aram-Damascus. The Arameans often used the periods of Assyrian inactivity to attack. At one point Ahab captured his rival Ben-hadad but, rather than killing him, he simply exacted some economic concessions—which seem never to have been delivered. Ben-hadad repaid this generosity by having his soldiers seek out and kill Ahab in their next battle.

Jezebel continued to exercise some influence for the next twelve years, that is to say during the reigns of her sons Ahaziah and Joram. But

---

[10]See William W. Hallo, "From Qarqar to Carchemish: Assyria and Israel in the Light of New Discoveries, *Biblical Archaeologist* 23/2 (May 1960): 33-61.

Ahaziah was fatally injured in an accident and lived only until 852; Joram, the last of the Omrids, ruled until 841 BCE. This is the time of the prophet Elijah of Gilead and his disciple Elisha, the well-known opponents of the regime, with whom I deal at some length in the next chapter.

During the Omride period, it was the North that took the lead in Israel/Judah. Ahab invited Jehoshaphat of Judah to join him in the attempt on Ramoth-gilead that cost Ahab his life. His son, Ahaziah, invited Jehoshaphat on a joint expedition to get gold from Ophir when Jehoshaphat's own ships were wrecked. Jehoshaphat declined, but it is important to note where the initiative came from. When, later, the South invited the North on a joint expedition to recover Edom, the result was a disaster for the South. Before that occurred, however, momentous changes had taken place in both kingdoms.

§4. Athaliah Redivivus

Truth is the Daughter of Time. —Old Proverb

Israel may have been born in a power vacuum, but that was a temporary situation. When they recovered, the bigger powers had an ongoing interest in the area. In 841 BCE Shalmaneser broke the north-Syrian coalition, apparently by wooing away Hamath, thus opening the road to Damascus and points south and west. Astour thinks the Assyrians reached the Mediterranean coast at Mt. Carmel, but not before destroying Betharbel (perhaps Arbela in Gilead, modern Irbid?) in Transjordan with such ferocity (see Hosea 10:14b) that its name remained a byword in Israel for a hundred years.[11]

Assyria's sudden success caused major changes in the royal houses and foreign policies of Israel and Judah. Jehu, a chariot commander, hurried back from the Aramean front and assassinated the king of Israel and his Phoenician mother, Jezebel. He also killed the king of Judah and then forty-two Judeans—2 Kings 10:13 calls them "kinsmen of Ahaziah"—who happened to be visiting in the North. (For more about them, see below.)

With Elijah's blessing, Jehu made himself king of Israel and accepted vassalage to Assyria, as shown on the famous Black Obelisk. Since the

---

[11]Michael Astour, "841 BC: The First Assyrian Invasion of Israel," *Journal of the American Oriental Society* 91/3 (1971): 383-89. This position is now generally accepted, for example, by Miller and Hayes.

Arameans were pressing him hard, he had no other choice. It is some measure of the wisdom of this course that his dynasty lasted longer than any other in the North: four kings who reigned a total of ninety years.

However, Israel paid a heavy price for survival. The kingdom would be bullied and pummeled by Aram for forty years before Assyrian power could put a stop to it. Israel also lost control of Moab, and even a joint venture against that Transjordanian kingdom by Israel and Judah could not recover it.

The story of Moab's revolt (2 Kings 3) includes the account of its king's sacrifice of his own son (vs. 27), or so most read the text. If so, it is another example of child sacrifice in time of emergency that harks back to my suggestion that the Egyptians sacrificed their firstborn in an attempt to appease whatever god they thought had afflicted them in the aftermath of the Thera explosion.

The history of this period is complicated because of the uncertainty concerning whether Joram of Israel (reigned 852–841 BCE) and Jehoram of Judah (853–841 BCE) are two persons or one. The Bible thinks there are two, but their dates of rule are congruent, their names virtually interchangeable. Second Kings 8, in fact, uses the full spelling, Jehoram, for the Northern king's name. If the South *had* put its ruler on the Northern throne, the Bible might well be expected to take notice, while if the opposite were the case, that fact might be suppressed because it would have meant a break in the Davidic dynasty.

Taking the Bible at face value, I conjecture that an attempt to join the two ruling houses was made by marrying the Northern princess Athaliah to Jehoram of Judah. In one place (2 Kings 8:26), Athaliah is referred to as the daughter of Omri, but in another (2 Kings 8:18) as the daughter of Ahab. She is of the House of Omri in either case, but since Ahab had only one known wife, 2 Kings 8:18 would make Athaliah the daughter of Jezebel, a connection that Jewish tradition also might not care to remember. The Syriac of this verse emends the text to read that Athaliah was Ahab's sister, showing a continuing inclination to distance her from Jezebel.

There is no reason to suppose that royal marriages effectively unified Judah and Israel any more than Hamor of Shechem's "marriage" to Dinah or the more conventional marriage-union of Assyria and Babylonia in the fourteenth century made their two peoples one. Miller and Hayes acknowledge this by titling their book A History of Ancient Israel and Judah, *but even they do not recognize how serious and abiding the divisions were.*

Following Jehu's bloody purge, Athaliah, widow of Jehoram and grieving mother of slain Ahaziah, took the reins in Judah in 841 BCE. She was the first woman to rule an Israelite kingdom in her own right; there would be only one other and that not for almost eight hundred years. Athaliah is castigated for continuing the religious practices of her father's house, but it may be that she was more loyal to Judah than tradition remembers. After all, by then she had lived in the South for many years.

In consolidating her power she allegedly killed a number of would-be successors—that is, her own grandchildren.[12] One has to wonder, however, whether this story is not a fabrication such as that which Matthew's Gospel (chapter 2) attaches to King Herod or, again, whether Jehu (above) hadn't already done much of the killing: How many heirs to the throne were among the forty-two slain princes? Closer to home, killing erstwhile rivals for the throne is, in fact, what 2 Chronicles 21:4— with no hint of disapproval—says Athaliah's own husband Jehoram had done when he became king.[13]

The cold-blooded murder of children strikes us as revolting, even inhuman. It reminds us of a beehive wherein the first queen to hatch mindlessly kills the other potential queens. On the other hand, leaving live contenders for the throne, especially those who might be upset at having been passed over, is a recipe for turmoil. What had happened in David's time must have been fresh in the minds of the royal family, and we should remember that brothers, half-brothers, uncles, and nephews, as well as children of all the king's wives, had theoretical claims to the throne.

In Judges 9, Abimelech suggests to the citizens of Shechem that rule by one alone is better than rule by "seventy." Agreeing, they give him money with which he hires followers who assist him in killing his

---

[12]H. Tadmor finds this unlikely: in Abraham Malamat et al., *A History of the Jewish People*, ed. Haim Ben-Sasson (Cambridge MA: Harvard University Press, 1976) 126.

[13]Since these stories are precisely that, they might be influenced by myths such as that of Cronos, who eats his children so they will not supplant him. It makes a difference, of course, whether Jehoram's bloody deeds were directed at his own house or that of his rival.

seventy brothers. (The hired men are not called habiru, *but* habiru *did hire out as mercenaries.)*

How many Athaliah allegedly killed is not known, nor do we know whether any were old enough to serve as king—or if too many were. The Athaliah story reads as though the queen went round all by herself murdering children in secret, a serial-killing Lady Macbeth whom everyone else consequently despised. This cannot be. She must have had some supporters even if she had to pay them, and with what? Unfortunately, the Bible does not tell us who her adherents were or what their motives might have been except "wiping out the house of Judah." But this polemic makes no sense.

For one thing, if destruction of the Judean royal house were the aim, why not step aside and invite Jehu and his Israelite gang to complete the dirty work? For another, accepting Chronicles, note that Ahaziah, her son, was forty-two when he took the throne; Athaliah herself must have been nearing sixty. Even reading with Kings, as Thiele prefers, that Ahaziah was only twenty-two and his mother, therefore, about forty,[14] what would the destruction of the royal house accomplish? If she was not pure evil or simply crazy, there must be something else going on here.

The Bible records that Athaliah "overlooked" one potential monarch, the infant Joash. As the son of her half-sister and the High Priest Jehoiada, he probably had the strongest claim to the throne, and yet he was the only one she failed to kill. Moreover, the baby was hidden for six years right next door, as it were, in the Temple precinct—by her own stepdaughter acting in concert with the high priest. Along with Ahlström, I find this story "incredible."[15] Wouldn't Athaliah have been on guard against just such a thing? Would she not have had spies or informers to bring her word of this treachery?

The story of one legitimate heir escaping is so frequent in ancient literatures, for example, Abimelech's story in Judges, that it is almost a cliché. But perhaps she *did* know that one heir survived. If she knew that an heir lived, and held her peace, it could only mean that she was

---

[14]Edwin Thiele, *The Mysterious Numbers of the Hebrew Kings*, 2nd ed. (Grand Rapids MI: Zondervan, 1983) 218.

[15]Gösta Ahlström, *The History of Ancient Palestine* (Minneapolis: Fortress, 1993) 599-601. In fact I owe this idea to my wife, who developed it while writing a novel about Athaliah.

colluding with the Judeans. Let us now more closely examine Athaliah's situation.

As a daughter of Ahab, she might have been expected by other Northerners to take advantage of the death of her husband and son and "deliver" Judah to the North. She did no such thing, just the opposite. By acting as she did and "holding the fort" for seven years she probably preempted a Northern takeover,[16] though her own reputation was inevitably tarnished and her life ultimately shortened by doing so.

What an irony it would be if the woman who kept David's dynasty alive when its fate hung by a thread, the most important heroine in all of Israelite history, is remembered instead as a tyrannical child killer. But, as Josephine Tey so eloquently demonstrated in her tale of Richard III, truth may be buried for a long, long time.[17] I do not suggest that Athaliah conspired in her own overthrow. More likely, her actions failed to ingratiate her with Judean authorities even as they alienated her from her own people, leaving both political flanks unprotected.

Admittedly, there is little evidence for my position, but there isn't much evidence against it, either. Second Kings' account of Athaliah is confined to sixteen verses, of which fourteen tell of the plot that killed her. The narrative leaves out a whole lot more than it includes, for example, the motives that these people had for their actions, moving us to try to fill in some of the blanks. The story in 2 Chronicles adds only an indictment, blaming Athaliah for counseling her son Ahaziah to join with his uncle Jehoram, the son of Ahab, in his war against Hazael of Aram, which resulted in Ahaziah's being murdered along with his father by Jehu.

Our job is made somewhat easier by remembering that the family squabbles of Israel and Judah were not simply a private affair. They took place against a background of international political movements, a background that all too often intruded itself into the foreground. The real

---

[16]Carol Smith, " 'Queenship' in Israel?" in *King and Messiah in Israel and the Ancient Near East*, ed. John Day (Sheffield UK: Sheffield Academic Press, 1998) cautiously concludes that "Jezebel and Athaliah were opposing dissident elements within their nations in order to avoid a serious threat to stability" (159).

[17]Josephine Tey, *The Daughter of Time* (New York: Berkeley, 1951). This historical mystery, sifting fact from fiction concerning Richard II's alleged murder of his nephews, should be required reading for all beginning history students, if not all students in the social sciences.

reason Jehu usurped the throne, I suspect, was that he had been engaged in a battle with Aram that he knew he could not win, but might very well lose. When the Assyrians showed up virtually on his doorstep, Jehu subjected himself to Assyria, thus averting immediate catastrophic defeat, but causing the precipitous decline of both Israel and Judah.

Whether forty-two or not, the princes of Judah mentioned above were probably a delegation from the anti-Assyrian faction in Jerusalem. Since the days of Asa, Judah had courted Damascus as a counterpoise to Israel. Some in Judah again wanted to ally with Damascus and Israel against Assyria, forming a south-Syrian coalition that, they must have felt, would be as successful as the earlier north-Syrian coalition had been.

They would have held that an alliance with Damascus could withstand Assyrian might. While that might have been true in theory, if the Arameans double-crossed their partners and made a separate peace, the full force of Assyrian arms would have fallen first upon Israel and then on Judah. This had very nearly occurred when Irhuleni of Hamath defected from the earlier coalition. Certainly, neither Israel alone nor Aram/Damascus by itself had sufficient forces to withstand Assyria, so the coalition strategy was something that Jehu decided to avoid as simply too risky.

This also reflects what I take to have been the underlying foreign policy of Elijah—Jehu's anointer—and of Elisha, the prophet's disciple. As Northerners who lived under the threat of Damascus, their natural inclination would have been to seek help in Aram's rear. Strength in Assyria would have provided that help.

Thus the pro-Aramean Judean delegation died. Whether or not they were the same "boys" who had taunted Elisha cannot be determined. In any case, an Assyrian alliance became the cornerstone of Israelite policy; to implement it necessitated having someone on the throne of Judah who would accept such a move. Athaliah made herself that person—for a little while. But the situation changed rapidly. The last years of Shalmaneser III's reign were marked first by a continuous struggle with Urartu for control of valuable trade routes, and then by a series of revolts at home. With Assyria occupied elsewhere, the high priest brought seven-year-old Joash forward—perhaps sooner than he had expected to—and had him proclaimed king. Athaliah was summarily executed.

Again, we are left to wonder why no one openly supported Athaliah, or died in her defense, or went into exile because she had been overthrown. She might have been resented as a woman or suspected as a Northerner, but she had held the throne for seven years. If her support came strictly from the North, why were there no Northern soldiers present when she was killed, and why did Jehu so suddenly abandon the person who had supported his pro-Assyrian policy? We are left with the conjecture that Athaliah's origins made her suspect in Southern eyes, while her policies alienated her from the North. Since she had a secure footing in neither camp, it was comparatively easy for the high priest and his political cronies to engineer her murder, and even easier for the later Judean collectors of Scripture to put the cry of "Treason! Treason!" in her mouth.

Still, she must have had some support to have held the throne for seven or eight years. The likeliest scenario is that both the army and the city of Jerusalem backed her. We can surmise the former from the fact that Jehu was rampaging through the North during this period, killing whoever stood in his way, but evidently never attempted an assault on the South. The latter supposition comes from the sentence that closes the passage in 2 Kings (11:20) dealing with Athaliah's life: "And the city was quiet after Athaliah had been killed with the sword at the king's house" (NRSV); "All the people of the land rejoiced, and the city was quiet. As for Athaliah, she had been put to the sword in the royal palace" (NJPS). This is ordinarily interpreted to mean that, with the death of Athaliah, peace reigned. However, there is a perfectly good word for peace in Hebrew that isn't used here. We might read, a bit euphemistically, that the city was "pacified." It seems likely that here we have another example of the perennial conservative-country/liberal-city polarity. The elaborate description of how the *'amei ha-'aretz*, "people of the land" (at this period, "landed gentry" or "rural nobility"), were brought secretly to the Temple precinct for the installation of seven-year-old Joash and the assassination of Athaliah would seem to corroborate this reading. And compare NJB: "All the people of the country were delighted; the city, however, made no move."

In any case, Athaliah did not live to see her one surviving grandson take the throne.

Despite its soap-opera beginning, the reign of Joash was among the longest of any king of Judah or Israel, and he is well regarded by Kings and Chronicles for attempting to refurbish Solomon's Temple, even riding herd on his officials to make sure the money for the job got to where it was intended. But he also is reported to have given a massive bribe to Hazael to avert Judah's destruction, and his reign ended when he was murdered by a conspiracy of his own counsellors, probably angered by his craven foreign policy, in 796 BCE.

§5. The War between the States

The incipient civil war that had been brewing between the two Hebrew kingdoms ever since Solomon's death broke out in earnest in 792 BCE. At that time, King Amaziah of Judah engaged Israelite mercenaries to help him in a campaign against Edom, but changed his mind at the last minute and dismissed them. Enraged, the Israelite soldiers rampaged through Judah on their way back to Israel. This was both injury and insult to Judah's honor, and could not go unanswered. Amaziah opened battle against Israel despite King Jehoash's warning of disaster (2 Kings 14:8-10) and was roundly trounced. Jerusalem was attacked and Amaziah himself was brought captive to the North, where he was held prisoner for ten years.

In Amaziah's absence, his sixteen-year-old son Azariah (Uzziah) became king. Ten years later, when King Jehoash of Israel died, the old Judean king—he was all of thirty-nine—was amnestied, but despite the Bible's crediting him with a twenty-nine year reign, I agree with Thiele that he never regained the throne.[18] Fifteen years after returning to Judah (767 BCE), Amaziah fled to Lachish, where he was murdered. That he had to flee indicates that he didn't have the military protection one would expect a king to have. Nor was this likely the first attempt on his life. Whoever killed him was probably exacting revenge for the disastrous war that had seen Jerusalem attacked and plundered. Such an action would have been parallel to the assassination of Joash for bribing Hazael of Damascus (above).

After 792 BCE, then, the relations between Israel and Judah must have been akin to that between the American North and South after our Civil War (also called by some Southerners "The War of Northern Aggression"). Perhaps because outside forces have so often compelled Jews to band together despite their differences, scholars have not adequately

---

[18]Thiele, *The Mysterious Numbers of the Hebrew Kings*, 115. Stanley N. Rosenbaum, *Amos of Israel* (Macon GA: Mercer University Press, 1990) 21-23.

appreciated that bad blood marked relations between the two kingdoms even during periods of superficial amity and cooperation.[19]

> *Part of the problem, I think, is that Jewish scholars tend to reflect tradition-shaped views of "Israel" vs. the Nations," while Christian scholars have too often seen all of Israel's story merely as prologue. The fourth edition of Bright's History still ends with the old epilogue entitled "Toward the Fullness of Time," which looks to Judaism's fulfillment in Christianity.[20] What, I wonder, would Solomon Schechter say?*

§6. The Last Days of Israel

After nearly a century in power, Jehu's dynasty ended in 752 BCE. Amos's prediction (7:17), that Jeroboam himself would die in exile, did not come true.[21] Zechariah, Jeroboam's son, succeeded him but was usurped and assassinated within a month. His assassin, Shallum, was in turn assassinated within six months. The North was breaking up. Did I say two kingdoms? The Hebrew kingdoms had almost as many fault lines as the underlying land itself. It wasn't long after this that a split-off of the Transjordan occurred. There is suggestive evidence in Hosea 5:5 (compare Ps. 78:67 and the *Annals of Tiglath Pileser*) that mentions Judah, Israel, *and* Ephraim, as though the last two had become separate entities. I think they had, and maybe not for the first time. Recall the Ephraimite invasion across the Jordan in Judges 12.

One Northern successor, King Menahem, ruled for eleven years, but only in Samaria, while one Pekah son of Remaliah held sway across the river.[22] Menahem continued Israel's pro-Assyrian policy, but Pekah allied himself with Rezin of Damascus as each jockeyed to gain an alliance that

---

[19] A contributing factor to this misapprehension of relations between Israel and Judah is the traditional view that Amos, a "poor Judean shepherd" had unhindered access to Northern holy places where he preached against the government. In my earlier work, I hope to have demonstrated that Amos was a Northerner, thus knocking out one of the props under this view of Israel/Judah relations after the monarchy divided.

[20] John Bright, *A History of Israel*, 4th ed. (Louisville: Westminster/John Knox Press, 2000) 464.

[21] The presence of this homely prophetic error and others like it is some proof against the hypothesis that the Bible was concocted at a late date. Jeremiah's prediction concerning Jehoiachim—"Record this man as childless" (Jer. 22:30 NRSV; "without succession" NJPS)—came nearer the mark.

[22] Thiele, *The Mysterious Numbers of the Hebrew Kings*, 132.

would threaten its rival on a second front. Isaiah 9:19-20 indicates that skirmishes, if not war, characterized the triangular relationship of Ephraim, Manasseh, and Judah.

Pekah's Transjordanian state seems to have stood for only twelve years, though powerful clans across the river, notably the Tobiads, continued to scheme for independence for centuries (more in chapter 11). I think we may also infer that there were other fractures, the knowledge of which has been swallowed by the sands of time. But the Northern Kingdom had begun its decline even before Assyria again rose to preeminence.

Left to themselves, the little states would, no doubt, have continued the internecine warfare that characterizes Israelite history, but their local conflicts were swallowed up by the emergence of a newly invigorated superpower, Assyria. Assyria had been having its own difficulties, with Urartu in the north and Babylon in the south. Eventually, however, these troubles subsided and Assyria turned westward once again, putting the Syrian states under its sovereignty and installing kings who consequently would be loyal to them. When Pekah proved unreliable, his share of the pie was given to Pekahiah, the son of Menahem.

The south-Syrian states chafed under Assyrian rule, and often tried to reconstitute some semblance of the glorious alliance that had proved effective in the previous century, but even a unified Israel/Judah/Aram/Transjordan could not stand against the power that had arisen in the East. For support they often applied to Assyria's natural rival, Egypt, but the Egyptians always promised more than they delivered. Isaiah 36:4-5 quotes the words of the "Rabshakeh" (ambassador from Assyria; NJB "cupbearer-in-chief") against "relying on that broken reed, Egypt, which pricks and pierces the hand of the person who leans on it" (NJB).

Matters came to a head after 727 BCE, when Tiglath-Pileser III, the Assyrian king credited with Assyria's resurgence, died. His death gave hope that the ensuing struggle for succession would leave the Syro-Palestinian states free to pursue their own courses. King Hoshea, who had taken the throne in Israel five years before, applied to Egypt for aid, but his hope was dashed when Shalmaneser V gained firm control of Assyria. Second Kings 17:4 reads:

> But the king of Assyria caught Hoshea in an act of treachery; he had sent envoys to King So of Egypt, and he had not paid the tribute to the king of Assyria, as in previous years. (NJPS)

Rebellious Samaria was besieged in 724; in 722 BCE, after a siege lasting three years, Samaria fell. Here, apparently, Amos had predicted things more accurately. His mocking lament (5:2), composed in the *kinah* (funeral-dirge) meter of 3+2 beats, came to pass:

> Fallen, not to rise again,
> Is Maiden Israel;
> Abandoned on her soil
> With none to lift her up. (NJPS)

Two years after the destruction, Samaria—its name changed to Samarina—was annexed and put under direct rule by Assyria.[23] The Northern tribes never again enjoyed political autonomy.

As we have noted, the myth of "Ten Lost Tribes" comes from this destruction and the subsequent listing of Benjamin alongside Judah: twelve minus two equals ten. But Simeon had long since been absorbed into Judah, and shadowy Reuben was never a Northern tribe. The Northern tribes numbered eight at most.

For reasons of clarity, this discussion has not included an extensive discussion of the part played in Israelite politics and religion by its prophets. It is to them and especially to Israel's first national prophet-hero, Elijah, that we now turn.

---

[23]This is well presented by Morton Cogan, in *Imperialism and Religion: Assyria, Israel, and Judah in the 8th and 7th Centuries B.C.E.*, SBLMS 19 (Missoula MT: Scholars Press, 1974).

Chapter 10

Elijah and the Rise
of Israelite Prophecy

§1. The Party of God

"Is that you, you troubler of Israel?" —Ahab (1 Kings 18:17 NJPS)

The subject of prophecy in Israel is so complex that any attempt to treat it as a chapter in a larger work may be questioned. There are individual volumes on even minor prophets such as Amos that are longer than the present work. Other books of equal length explore the phenomenon of prophecy itself.[1] How then shall we proceed?

My object here is to identify what I take to be Israelite prophecy's ultimately central and rather revolutionary theme (elaborated in §9, below). I do not intend to chronicle all of the prophets, but I will try to give special attention to the place of prophecy during the divided monarchy, with something of an overview of the place of prophecy in Israel-Judah as it developed over a long time.

Long indeed. Prophecy is "officially" present in Judaism from Moses to Malachi, a period of some eight hundred years.[2] And that period could be extended by several centuries if we take seriously the Bible's single identification of Abraham (Gen. 20:7) as a prophet.

Curiously, during this entire period the Bible names only about two dozen people as authentic prophets, often in contrast with derogatory references to *benei nebi'im*, "sons (disciples) of prophets" or those court prophets with whom Jeremiah disputes. A few anonymous individuals, notably the "man of God" of 1 Kings 13, are also chronicled, leaving us to wonder whether or not there was much more prophetic activity that simply went unrecorded. To speak of a prophetic "movement" would make little sense if its members were confined only to those whose names or stories we know.

---

[1]Much of the early literature on prophets and prophecy was written by religious people whose goal was to make the subject "relevant" to their own communities: for example, Abraham Joshua Heschel's *The Prophets* (New York: Harper, 1962). More recent studies such as Robert R. Wilson's *Prophecy and Society* have begun to examine the prophets in their own social and religious contexts.

[2]Later Judaism decided that prophecy of the biblical type had ceased with Malachi in the mid-fifth pre-Christian century. One wonders what exactly prompted this decision.

Most "prophets" would have been local or at best regional figures[3] as Samuel was, at least initially. For all his later national stature, his circuit—between Gibeah, Mizpeh, and Ramah—was confined to territory north of Israel"s "Mason-Dixon Line." For most prophets, their village or area function would probably have been even more physically circumscribed and largely limited to interpreting the signs educed through various divinatory practices.

Even national prophets such as Jeremiah were probably little known until well after the collection and canonization of the second part of TaNaKh. Even Jesus has been vastly overpublicized, I think. Few Jews and fewer non-Jews were aware of Jesus during his brief public career.

The majority of *benei nebi'im* prophets (see below for a discussion of terminology) would have been attached to and sympathetic with the institutions or individuals they served, temple or shrine, governor or king. They usually got "press" only as foils bested by iconoclastic hero-prophets, such as Elijah. For example, the 450 Baal prophets and 400 Asherah prophets whom Elijah confounded at Mt. Carmel were maintained by Jezebel.

Similarly, the name of the priest Amaziah of Bethel would not be known to us but for his run-in with Amos (Amos 7:10-17). Ironically, or perhaps sarcastically, Amaziah advised Amos to go to Judah and "earn your bread there" by hiring on as a court prophet for the Judean kings.

Elijah's most famous exploit, of course, was his contest at Mt. Carmel. Though tradition credits him with a stirring victory there, he subsequently had to flee for his life to escape the royal wrath of Ahab and Jezebel. This flight took him south of Beer-sheba; his route, I surmise, was later followed by many Israelites and Judeans as a pilgrimage destination—or so I read Amos 5:5 (more below).

§2. A Prophetic Who's Who

A thoroughgoing study of Israelite prophecy should also include a look at similar phenomena among neighboring peoples. Some of these, such as Mari, also had prophets. As early as the reign of Ur-Nammu (around

---

[3]Joseph Blenkinsopp, *A History of Prophecy in Israel* (Philadelphia: Westminster, 1983) 60.

2100 BCE), the monarch claims that in his time "the orphan was not delivered up to the rich man, the widow to the mighty man, or the less wealthy to the more wealthy,"[4] indicating that these had previously been common practices.

The code is too badly broken up to tell if there were divine directives behind this benevolence, and there are no surviving daily newspapers or court records of the time to indicate whether these instructions were faithfully carried out. However, the idea of social justice lies at the heart of Israel's prophetic vision, indicating a likely linkage of desired effect if not of motivation.

> *Mesopotamian prophetic phenomena seem much closer to the Israelite than Egyptian prophetic forms do, which seems odd if the people going up to Canaan had been in Egypt for the previous four hundred years.*

We should also examine the vocabulary that can be said to belong to the wider semantic field, prophecy. Mesopotamian prophecy can be roughly divided into two types, *bârû* and *mahhû*, which seem, respectively, to indicate revelatory and ecstatic prophecy. While these terms are not found in Scripture, there has been much discussion concerning whether they apply to Israel as well.

Israel, because of its relatively late development and polyglot origins, probably shared in all or most of the mantic prophetic forms we find elsewhere. For all but the most modern cultures, any "vision" or "audition" might come from a god. How not? Former nun Karen Armstrong, author of the popular *A History of God*, calmly reports "flashes of vision that I knew to be a mere neurological defect,"[5] that sometimes accompany her epileptic episodes. This reminds me of Numbers 24:16's description of Balaam, the foreign prophet who is called upon to curse Israel, as one who

> beholds visions from the Almighty,
> Prostrate, but with eyes unveiled.

> (Thus NJPS; RSV and NRSV are similar, but NJB completely masks the verse. Why?)

---

[4]*ANE* 2, *A New Anthology* (1975) 31-34, the Ur-Nammu Code.
[5]Karen Armstrong, *A History of God* (New York: Ballantine, 1993) xvii.

Ancient peoples would not have been able to dismiss epileptic visions as matter-of-factly as Armstrong does. It is even possible that epilepsy-induced visions—in free people anyway[6]—were considered valid messages from God or the gods.

Some ecstatics induced visions by oxygen deprivation accompanying wild dancing, from cutting themselves (producing loss of blood?), and, I think, by the use of hallucinogens. Though of this last there is scarcely a trace in the Bible,[7] various forms of *cannabis* are native to the Near East, as are opium poppies. Saul may have overstepped, dancing with a band of ecstatics, but such bands or individuals certainly existed and were countenanced at least until the time of Saul and Samuel, which is also, maybe, the time of the emergence of the *nabi'*.

The key text in any discussion of Israelite prophecy is 1 Samuel 9:9, which says, "Formerly in Israel, when one wanted to inquire of God one said, 'Let's go see the seer'; now we say 'Let's go see the prophet' " (my translation). The verse is probably interpolated, but it hardly matters when it was written; it shows there was some evolution of the prophetic function. Gad, the advisor to David, is called both *hozeh* and *nabi'* in 2 Samuel, indicating a transition period of uncertain duration. The real question is: Why is 1 Samuel 9:9 put in the text just here?

The context of the story is Saul's search for his father's lost asses. We need not retell the story here, rather we should infer from it that some in Israel were thought to possess the power to determine where lost or strayed objects/persons/animals were.

This should hardly surprise us. We still have many people who do likewise; they usually call themselves "psychics." And lots of them have 900 numbers. Probably 99.9 percent of these folks belong in the entertainment industry, but, noting their popularity, that is of no consequence.

---

[6]Apparently, the same condition in slaves was of no account. Wolfram von Soden, *The Ancient Orient* (Grand Rapids MI: Eerdmans, 1994) 75, says that an epileptic slave could be returned to his/her seller within 100 days of purchase. Or was it seen as the same condition?

[7]Only Job's question (6:6b)—"Is there any taste in the slime of the *purslane?*" (RSV, emphasis added; NJPS "mallow juice"; NRSV "mallows")—offers a possibility of referring to mind-altering substances: the root *hlm* ("to bind (firmly)"; by impl. "(to be) plump") also yields "to dream" (in the figurative sense of "dumbness"). Absence of any other direct reference is, I think, accidental and not the result of conscious suppression.

There are numerous examples of kings consulting prophets to determine whether or not to go to battle.[8] These "war prophets" were the type we would now call "clairvoyants," and we still have them, too: Edgar Cayce and Jeane Dixon come to mind, not to mention palm readers, phrenologists, and astrologers. Making use of the stars for religious purposes is at least as old as the Egyptians, who used them to align their pyramids northward—to that part of the sky where the stars die not.

If Israel shared in all or most of the mantic prophetic forms we find elsewhere, various "diviners" might also have used one or another of the "-mancies" discussed in chapter 4. Today we may dismiss such procedures as vain or silly, but they were and are a serious business. In our desire to find a way through life, we seek help in both the spatial and the temporal spheres. I propose that before the emergence of the *nabi'*, the two major Hebrew terms, *hozeh*, "seer" = "visionary" and *ro'eh*, "seer" = "psychic" denote people whose jobs, respectively, were to map out time and space.

The casual use of the same English word for both Hebrew words is a problem in most translations, but if the two Hebrew words are used interchangeably it may be because by the time the Bible came to be written no one knew or cared any longer what the distinction had been.

The first term, חֹזֶה *hozeh*, might better be rendered "future-teller," as in the priest Amaziah's characterization of Amos (Amos 7:12). The *hozeh* is almost always associated with a king, hence Amaziah's "advice" that Amos go to Judah to earn his prophetic living there. The רֹאֶה *ro'eh*, on the other hand, is more like our "psychic," and this is the term that 1 Samuel 9:9 says is replaced by the "new" term נָבִיא *nabi'* "prophet."[9]

There is, however, another dimension, which we might call the "ancestral." As we saw, Saul provides a biblical example of this, going to a spirit-medium at En-dor to contact the ghost of recently deceased Samuel (1 Sam. 28:7-25). This reminds us of the practice, going back to Neolithic times, of burying skulls under thresholds or bringing skeletons of dead ancestors back into one's house (see chapter 4). Samuel's shade was angered by the summons . . . but come he did. As we have noted, if

---

[8]In the Zakir Inscription, *ANE* 2, *A New Anthology* (1975) 501-502, the king prays to his god for reassurance before going to battle.

[9]This is cognate with Akkadian *nabium*, "the one called."

the biblical text may be trusted, this was just after Saul himself issued a decree forbidding such activity.

We may ask why Saul felt the need to contact Samuel; after all, did he not also have the power of prophecy? No, or at least, not fully. As we saw in chapter 8, the question "Is Saul also among the prophets?" (1 Sam. 10:11, 12 and 19:24) is later "Bible-speak" for "Who does he think he is?" It probably also reflects the very fluid situation of prophecy in early Israel, a situation in which the functions of king, prophet, and priest were not yet fully separated.

§3. God's Spokespersons

Discounting Abraham, Moses was the first *nabi'* and *the* prophet par excellence (Deut. 34:10). How odd, then, that Moses is identified as prophet/*nabi'* only in Deuteronomy 34:10-12 and probably 18:15-22. The root √*n-b-'* occurs two times in Exodus, once in 7:1 where it terms Aaron Moses' *nabi'* = "spokesman" (see Exod. 4:16) and once of Miriam, Moses' and Aaron's sister (15:20). But how can Moses have been anything else but a prophet? Unlike the *ro'eh* or *hozeh* whom the petitioner asked to inquire of God, the *nabi'* was a person to whom God spoke—at random and arbitrarily it would seem. Not only did God speak to Moses, Moses saw God "face to face" and lived.

One did not have to be known as any sort of prophet, as Amos—much less the then-ninety-nine-year-old Abraham—was not, to be spoken to by God. Why not? Because the God of Israel had other things on his mind than the location of lost donkeys or who would win the Super Bowl. The "vision" given the *nabi'* was of larger things.

God gave Moses a blueprint for the proper running of a society based upon equal justice. Ideally, government should be the rule of law, not the rule of human beings. Punishment should fit the crime and not be tailored to the social disparity, if any, between perpetrator and victim, as was the case in earlier, Mesopotamian law codes such as Hammurabi's. This is the burden of the much-quoted and much-misunderstood Leviticus 24:20, "an eye for an eye, a tooth for a tooth" (cf. Exod. 21:23-25).

Most people do not understand that retribution is more a synonym for justice than it is for vengeance. Vengeance is violent revenge—for example, what Jacob's sons did at Shechem. When Isaiah 63:3 proclaimed, "I trod out a vintage alone [says the Lord]" (NJPS), it meant that only God may choose violent revenge. (Deut. 32:35 is more specific:

"Vengeance is mine [says the Lord]"—quoted at Rom. 12:19 with the elaboration "I will repay, says the Lord.")

A human judiciary is constrained to aim at balancing the scales of justice, not tilting them in favor of the party who was first injured. The famous Micah 6:8, "Do justice, love mercy . . . " puts justice first. These are some of the truly revolutionary ideas of all time.

The prophets whose words we pass down insisted that any society that failed to uphold these principles was doomed. Consequently, the downfall of the Northern Kingdom in 722 BCE was no surprise to some in Israel. Amos and Micah (especially Micah 1:6-7) had predicted the disaster less than forty years before, well within the lifetime of many still living when it occurred. Like Jeremiah's, the soundness of their visions probably played a part in the rise to canonical status of the books of *nebi'im*.

Just as the 1906 British Dreadnought battleship made all other warships obsolete, the Hebrew nabi'-prophet did the same to all other forms of prophecy in Israel, at least in theory. In practice, prophets were roughly received. Long before Israel's fall Amos had been exiled to Judah, something that Jesus, himself a Northerner, probably knew of when he said, "Prophets are not without honor except in their own country and in their own house" (Matt. 13:57 NRSV).

Israel's down-the-line insistence on social justice that included even "strangers," foreigners who lived among them (Num. 15:14-16), may be another innovation. If so, it is hardly to be wondered at. Israelites were people many of whom began at the bottom of the socioeconomic ladder, people whose existence was pockmarked by oppression, expulsion, and slavery. Because their community was originally, and for a long time thereafter, multiethnic, it needed an "inclusivist" social policy framed and reinforced by an "exclusivist" theology. That is, Israel needed legal/religious fences to build and nurture community unity while denying any value even to those religions which various Israelite groups had previously professed.

In response to the injunction to leave the "corners" of their fields unharvested so that their poor might glean with dignity (Lev. 19:9-10; 23:22; Deut. 24:19-22), the Talmud (Mishnah *Peah* 1:1) later set a minimum leaving of one part in sixty, then said that anyone who did only so little was not truly observing the law. Still, as Frymer-Kensky wryly observes,

We can only imagine the bewilderment of farmers who are told that the earth will be fertile so long as farmers remember to treat the poor correctly.[10]

Nebi'im, then, were spokespersons[11] for God. With variations, all proclaimed what God had told them: Worship God, alone, and establish a society based upon equal justice for all. In other words, what the prophets "preached" was an exclusive and ethical Yahwism, two ideas which their brethren were slow to accept. Monotheism, as we saw in chapter 3, is a counterintuitive proposition. That, no doubt, is one reason why the Bible reports it as revealed by God rather than discovered by humans.

§4. Also in the Cast Were . . .

If the prophets were God's "preachers," they were not the only group in Israel that promoted monotheism. Two others that we must consider are the Rechabites and Nazarites/Nazirites. The former seem to have been people who rejected the urban, cosmopolitan way of life and even the Farming Revolution. They lived in tents, avoided wine—they were forbidden even to own vineyards—and planted no seed. Usually, they seem to have avoided "contamination" from the general public, coming to Jerusalem in Jeremiah's time (chapter 35) only for fear of the Babylonian army. We find Rechabites first in Jehu's time, where they cooperated with him in his campaign against Ba'alism, leading some to suggest that they were a kind of clan *qua* military unit.

Rechabites may have been a family; Nazirites were not. Nazirites— the Hebrew root means "consecrate," and is related to √*n-d-r* "vow"— could volunteer or be dedicated by their parents. The Bible's two most famous examples are Samson and Samuel.

Many scholars see the Nazirites' function as ecstatic war prophets. (In Samson's case, berserker, in the original Norse sense of the word, seems closer the mark.) That they might have had some prophetic function seems apparent from Amos's criticism (2:11-12) linking Nazirites and *nebi'im* as having been equally rejected by his Samarian audience. But

---

[10]Tikvah Frymer-Kensky, *In the Wake of the Goddesses* (New York: Free Press, 1992) 153.

[11]Named female prophets are rare. Miriam ("Aaron's sister," Exod. 15:20 + 13 t.), Huldah (lit. "weasel," only 2 Kings 22:14 ‖ 2 Chron 34:22), and one Noadiah (only Neh 6:14) are the only three in Scripture.

there may be something else involved here: a link between Nazirites and Rechabites.

More than half of the references to "Nazirites" are in Numbers 6. There Nazirites are instructed not to drink wine or other intoxicants, not to cut their hair, and not to come near corpses, even those of close family members. I suggest this last prohibition has been misunderstood.

Priests (*cohanim*) lived under the same prohibition, and even ordinary Israelites who came into contact with corpses were "unclean until evening." It makes more sense to suggest that Nazirites were forbidden to come near the corpses of animals—that is, to eat meat. Samson, of course, seemed to violate this prohibition by eating honey from the carcass of a dead lion. But Samson's behavior would hardly have been normative in any respect, the less so if he is completely nonhistorical.

If the third prohibition makes Nazirites vegetarians, it comports very well with the first two decrees. All three things denote conditions that were present in the Garden of Eden. Adam's hair was long because metal, from which razors were made, was first smelted by Tubal-Cain. Noah planted the first vineyard; desert-dwellers drank an intoxicant made from dates rather than grapes. Finally, it was only after the Flood that God allowed people to eat meat. The asceticism of the Nazirites, then, symbolized a desire to live as though we had not been expelled from Paradise.

Positing these same things of Rechabites makes sense if we make the term from √r-h-b, "chariot." They might then have been chariot-soldiers who felt that these and other expressions of "purity" would make them successful in battle. In support of this we may cite the example of Uriah, who declined to have relations with his wife even when home on furlough from the front.

§5. Prophetic Continuity

Samuel began his career not as a prophet but as a *nazir*, apprenticed to Eli, the priest at Shiloh whose place he later took. Samuel appointed his sons not as priests or prophets, but "judges." (They were discredited after his death and, except for the *hozim/nebi'im* Gad and Nathan, David's advisors and sometime critics, no other prophetic activity is recorded until Elijah about seventy years later.) Samuel himself is called a "prophet" in 3:20, but his functions do not seem to have had the same parameters as Moses'. His prophetic "portfolio" included the power to anoint kings, which he did twice. (Similarly, Ahijah anointed Jeroboam and Elijah anointed Jehu.)

We have noted that the span from Moses to Samuel is a period of approximately the same length of time the United States has been an independent country (225 years), so it's more than curious that the Bible is virtually silent on the subject of prophecy during that period. What became of prophecy *between* the times of Moses and Samuel? Judges 6:8, which looks like another insertion, is the only verse in Judges or Joshua to mention prophets in general. Assuming that the verse is genuine, Deborah is still the only person in the period so to be identified, and that only once (Judges 4:4).

Moses died without setting foot in Israel. Rabbinic tradition (TB *Pirke Avoth*) says that what Moses passed on to Joshua was then passed on to the "judges" who followed, and from them to Samuel, but such a claim smacks of the much-later theology of those making it, namely, creating an unbroken line of tradition. Scholars, I think, make the same mistake when they speak of Israelite (or Ephraimite) prophetic "tradition" (see below).

At this point, we have to pause and ask just how "plugged in" was each succeeding prophet to the work of those who had preceded him/her? Until recently, treatments of the subject seemed unconsciously to assume that each prophet knew the entire preceding prophetic corpus as we moderns know our religious histories. But did Ezekiel, for example, have copies of Amos, Hosea, Isaiah, and Micah on his table? This would have been possible only if scrolls of prophetic writings—assuming that prophets could read—or oral accounts retained by disciples were in general circulation for the centuries between their first utterances and their final canonization.

In some cases, we are able to detect the influence of earlier upon later prophets: of the "writing prophets" Amos obviously influenced Micah and Isaiah; Hosea did the same for Jeremiah—that is, if what we take to be influences are not later editorial insertions that aimed to provide continuity. I think it fair to say, however, that "real" prophecy begins with one prophet who wrote no book, Elijah.

§6. My God Is YHVH

Eliyahu ha-nabi,	*Elijah the Prophet,*
Eliyahu ha-tishbi,	*Elijah the Tishbite,*
Eliyahu, Eliyahu, Eliyahu ha-gil'adi.	*Elijah, Elijah, Elijah the Gileadite.*
Bim heira b'yameinu yabo eileinu	*May he come soon in our time,*
Im Mashiach ben David,	*and bring Messiah son of David.*
Im Mashiach ben David.	—song for the end of Sabbath
	and Passover

Samuel was right: one hundred seventy years of monarchy had produced an increasingly stratified society in which the regime requisitioned people, land, and material resources from the country. In a certain sense, what we call "free" prophecy was called into being in Israel because of the inequities that both monarchies, the Israelite and the Judean, perpetrated.

As we saw in chapter 9, Solomon's Judah and Omri's dynasty in Israel found themselves increasingly drawn into the wider, eastern Mediterranean economic community. Solomon had an ivory bed overlaid with gold. While this degree of opulence was probably not common, there was an increasing demand for such luxury goods as the Samaritan ivories[12] (mentioned above), by which the richer people distinguished themselves from the poorer classes.

Remember that Israel's contribution to trade consisted mainly of wine and olive oil, and that while it takes decades for an olive tree to reach production, vineyards could produce commercially valuable quantities in about ten years.[13] Of course, the process might be shortened if one took over producing vineyards, hence, as we saw, Ahab's offer to buy or trade Naboth for his.

To participate effectively in international trade, an entrepreneur might need to consolidate many of these smaller holdings, but how was he to do so, how tear up the patchwork quilt of small family farms and those tended by generations of tenant farmers? To answer this question we can turn to the indictment against Northern society leveled by Amos around

---

[12]Pictures of Samaritan ivories may be found in Anton Jirku, *The World of the Bible*, trans. Ann Keep, World Ancient Cultures series (Cleveland: World, 1967) illus. 35-38, between pp. 138 and 139; and *ANE* 2, *A New Anthology* (1975) 293.

[13]I owe this information to Dr. Craig Houston, vintner, and emeritus professor in Dickinson College's Department of Economics.

760 BCE (below), but first we need to consider the man who, more than any other single person, was responsible for Israelite prophecy: Elijah.

Those familiar with Genesis 20:7 would have had the assurance that *nebi'im* such as Elijah were found to go back to Abraham's time, giving the "movement" an impeccable pedigree. It may be, however, that this verse, the only one that identifies a patriarch as a "prophet," is a later insertion designed to produce just such an impression. As we noted above, Elijah-type prophets were thin on the ground before the creation of the monarchy.

Elijah began his activities within seventy years of the division of Solomon's kingdom and was active in the North during the reign of the Omrids, especially Ahab. Even before the Bible came to be written, Elijah's career was a lens through which social concerns could be backread.

Here we must distinguish between Israel's concerns before and after the settlement in the land. Before the settlement, these concerns would have concentrated on obtaining justice for a sojourning, minority people who made something of a fetish of remembering their former status as aliens. After the settlement, when this people had itself become the Establishment and fomented some of the same injustices, prophets would inevitably have arisen who called their own regimes to account.

§7. "Pure" Yahwists

"I alone am left. . . . " —Elijah (1 Kings 19:14 NJPS)

Elijah seems to have been the first of the "pure Yahwists," though perhaps that distinction should go to the parents who named him "My God is YHVH." Unfortunately, their names are not remembered. They lived in Tishbe in Gilead, a little town on the western edge of the Transjordanian plateau about twenty miles south of the Sea of Galilee. Though the North was the locus of Elijah's activities, he is remembered as the preeminent prophet in all Israel, its first truly national—even international—prophet, so much so that his name is still invoked at the end of every Sabbath and Passover, to herald and hurry the coming of the Messiah. What accounts for this enduring fame?

Elijah left no first-person accounts, but 1 Kings devotes a lot of space to him. He multiplied scarce food and raised a child from the dead, an act that convinced the child's mother that he was, indeed, a true prophet. Why such a sign was necessary and why Elijah had the confidence that he could effect a resurrection the text doesn't say. The same two deeds, in equally close proximity, figure in the career of Elisha, his disciple. (Joseph Blenkinsopp thinks Elisha's farm background may have been a factor in his becoming Elijah's chosen disciple.[14]) The deeds figure again in the better-known career of Jesus—but nowhere in between.

Elijah was active not only in Israel's political life, but in Syria's as well. However, it is his spirited opposition to the religious situation of the North in the time of Ahab and Jezebel, notably his famous contest with prophets of Ba'al on Mt. Carmel, for which he is most remembered.

Here God demonstrated that he, and no other deity, had power. This monotheistic exclusivism, even three hundred years after Moses' time, was a "hard sell." As Barstad put it, the contest was not between God and the fertility gods, but advanced the claim that YHVH *was* the fertility god.[15] What other deity, exactly, did the Ba'al prophets represent? It's hard to say, because the Bible has adopted the name *ba'al* as a kind of generic name for any non-Israelite religion. However, the contest did take place in the North, and Jezebel, Israel's Queen, was from farther north than that, so maybe I can hazard a guess.

As we saw in chapter 3, the bull was often used as the symbol for the Ugaritic and Canaanite deities El or Baal, typically represented wearing bull's horns. Rulers were often represented wearing horns or were called "the Mighty Bull," and priests or even commoners might also have donned bull's horns for ritual purposes, including promoting fertility by sympathetic magic practices. I think it's a fair guess that that Ba'al whom Elijah's God bested was a bull-god, whether representing himself or Taurus or the moon is hard to say.

As we saw in chapter 4, the *ba'al*/bull is a hybrid of the constellation Taurus and the largest and most powerful of domestic animals, the ox. The Sumerians knew Bull, Lion, and Scorpion constellations, our Taurus, Leo, and Scorpio, respectively, reminding us that anything with strength, sexual potency, or life-taking ability has to be respected. In any event, Elijah's fiery success at Carmel should not distract us from the underlying social and political situation that, I think, gave rise to his activities.

First, note that four centuries after Moses' death, Israel had still not given up polytheism. This phenomenon is often and unfairly blamed on

---

[14]Blenkinsopp, *A History of Prophecy in Israel*, 73-77.
[15]Hans Barstad, *The Religious Polemics of Amos*, VTSup 34 (Leiden: E. J. Brill, 1984) 10; see also 82-89.

foreigners such as Solomon's wives or Ahab's Jezebel or "innovators" like Jeroboam I. However, it was endemic in Israel and Judah, too, at all levels of society. If the North was more pluralistic, this will have been a natural consequence of its having been composed of so many disparate ethnic elements from the beginning, and of its geographical situation, straddling more routes important to international trade.

The Bible's picture of the YHVH-Ba'al conflict is painted almost exclusively in religious terms because it reflects the concerns of later writers and collectors. But much more is at issue here. Religion was not a private affair, not merely a matter of which church one patronized, which theology one subscribed to. The religious establishments of the various deities necessarily competed for economic support from their would-be congregants. In a polytheistic society, every deity would get a share of the goodies, even if not a fair share. But a dramatic shift to one and away from all others would leave the latter with a shrinking base of support.

A similar situation exists in the USA today, with old-line denominations such as Presbyterians shrinking while Mormons and Muslims, to name two of the most thriving new or imported religious groups, are increasing at a great rate.

Peasants who chose YHVH to the exclusion of other gods would have been less able and less willing to bear the taxes and other imposts levied by regimes that used their resources to support *ba'alim*. So the contest on Mt. Carmel, whether or not it actually happened, is symbolic of the competition for allegiance that would ultimately have dictated which religious institutions, which priesthoods, received material support. In this struggle it appears that the polytheistic preferences of the Northern regime were at odds with a growing popular support for Yahwistic monotheism.

Elijah was the first prophet to draw a sharp distinction, but he was an outsider, both geographically and politically. Amos was the person who first called to task a regime of which he was a privileged part. As I hope to have shown elsewhere (see chapter 6, n. 21), the real Amos was a middle-level government functionary and, like his contemporary, Hosea, a Northerner.

§8. Amos of Israel, Social Critic

Therefore, because you trample on the poor. . . . (Amos 5:11 NRSV)

Amos (around 760 BCE) was the first "literary prophet," that is, one who has left us prophetic writings that he or others collected into a book.[16] Judeo-Christian tradition makes of Amos a lowly Southern shepherd, but this "tradition" dates only from the time of Augustine, 1,000 years after Amos. A Talmudic reference nearly contemporary with Augustine refers to Amos as "a wealthy sheep-owner," which is closer to the truth, but doesn't make as good a basis for those who like to fashion David-vs.-Goliath-type sermons.

Amos himself was probably brought up on stories of the great prophets, Elijah and Elisha, and their fight against Ahab's house. Note that Elijah was no further back in Amos's time than Teddy Roosevelt, the great "Trust Buster," is in ours. And, like Elijah, Amos was a Northerner.

To us, Amos's spiritual descendants, he has been a prophet for a long time, at least as long as the time in which his words were included in the canon. However, the "real" Amos as I have come to know him was a middle-level Northern bureaucrat, a district overseer of royal sycamores and sheep, as he says in the admittedly difficult 7:14. His trenchant criticism of a government and social system from which he personally benefitted made him something of a "traitor to his class," if not to his country. He was, in fact, accused of treason—not "conspiracy" as some commentators have it[17]—by the Northern Establishment.

If biblical Hebrew had a word for "conscience," we could have called Amos a "man of conscience." His main concern, like Elijah's, was the escalating impoverishment of the poor by the wealthy, whose habits he seems to know in some detail. Amos's description of the *marzeach*[18] as a kind of combination country club and burial society (Amos 6; see also Jer. 16:5) shows how well the rich lived, often at the expense of the poor whom they exploited, and how intimately Amos knew it.

---

[16]Chapter 1:1 of Amos had been added, but I think that the Book of Amos largely escaped the recurrent editing that marks other prophetic books such as Hosea and Isaiah.

[17]See Rosenbaum, *Amos*, 39 (chart 2. "Treason") and comments there.

[18]See Jonas Greenfield, "The MARZEAH as a Social Institution," in *Wirtschaft und Gesellschaft in alten Vorderasien*, ed. Joseph Harmatta (Budapest: Akademiai Kiodo, 1974) 451-55.

If we carefully examine the roster of crimes in chapter 2 that Amos accused people in the North of committing, we can see that most of them were economic in nature. They sold impecunious freeholders for want of a "sandal strap," that is, they foreclosed loans on the flimsiest of pretexts. If there was no available pretext, they perverted justice through bribery (or suborning perjury, as Jezebel did). They simply evicted tenant farmers, abrogating the accepted practice among the landless of "bequeathing" use of the land that they did not in fact own to their children—that is, if they were not forced to sell their children or even themselves into indentured servitude for debt relief.

Amos's "They [the rich] pant [hunger] after the *dust . . . on the head of the poor*" (Amos 2:7 KJV ERV ASV) is a brilliant trope: this dust is the last little bit of land the poor possess.

Displacement from the land of farmers who did not own it was reprised when Zionist settlers bought land in Palestine from absentee landlords in Lebanon, Syria, and Egypt who legally owned it—thus displacing the people who had farmed the land, sometimes for centuries.

In 5:26 Amos accuses Israel of also worshipping Saturn, one of the names that has deliberately been revocalized with the vowels for "detestable thing" (NJPS note). Saturn/Cronos, whom the Greeks thought preceded Olympos, is a god closely associated with child sacrifice, as we have seen. One must wonder, then, whether this practice had not crept back into Israel even before the time of evil Ahaz (735–716 BCE). The point of these references, of course, is to deny independent power to any celestial objects.

Since constellations were known by Sumerians as long before as 2000 BCE, it is no problem if Amos, 1,200 years later, knew that the order of succession of constellations determined planting times and that the heliacal risings of Aries, Taurus, and Scorpio were reliable signs for plowing/planting in spring, summer, and fall respectively.[19] Amos 5:8, however, proclaims that the Lord made the Pleiades and Orion and, in the

---

[19]With at least eight "seasons," constellations or individual stars would have been useful in determining proper planting and harvesting times. See Willy Hartner, "The Earliest History of the Constellations in the Near East and the Motif of the Lion-Bull Combat," *Journal of Near Eastern Studies* 24/1-2 (January–April 1965): 1-16. Al Wolters, "The Riddle of the Scales in Daniel 5," *Hebrew Union College Annual* 62 (1991): 155-78, identifies the scales as the constellation Libra.

admittedly difficult v. 9, context leads me to believe he also mentions Aries and Capricorn.

In 6:13, Amos's disparagement of *karnaim*, "horns," and *lo-debar*, "nothing," that Israel took to itself, were long thought to refer to small towns west of the Jordan recently recaptured in the interminable wars with the Arameans. They may be that. But Amos delights in paranomasia (plays on words) and "horns" have long had a sexual/cultic referent: our use of "horny" as "lustful" is still found in the dictionary. Amos's Northern hearers would also have recognized this, especially if they were familiar with representations of Ugaritic Ba'al as a bull mounting a heifer.[20]

Was this disparagement an indirect attack on Northern state religion, and, if so, why would Amos have been devious just here? Amos attacked his fellow Northerners for maintaining the primacy of regular ritual over helping those in need, and attacked them for practicing ritual prostitution as a fertility rite, but said nothing directly against any sort of "ba'alism" per se. This again indicates to me that he was a Northerner and that, in the North, some use of bull-bovine symbols even in service of YHVH was still legitimate.

Seen in this light, even Moses' "horns" (Exod. 34:29-35) take on a new meaning. The apparent intention, that his face radiated light from the encounter, may be supported by reference to a similar description of Dan'el in Ugaritic myth. Unfortunately, Michelangelo's literal crafting of horns on his great statue of Moses for the tomb of Pope Julius III has obscured the Bible's dexterous transfer of all power from the Bull of Heaven to Israel's God.

Amos did not write the first verse of his book, but *dibrei 'amos*, "the words of Amos"—not "word of God" with which most prophetic books begin—must have given powerful impetus to the Southern prophetic movement as a whole. The Isaiah of chapters 1–39 (active circa 720–675 BCE) and Jeremiah (627–580 BCE) both show knowledge of, and dependence upon, Amos. Also, the short oracle against Judah in Amos 2:4-6 may well be one of the editorial additions spoken of above to make the text more relevant in the South. If so, it masks the fact that 3:1-2's "Only

---

[20]Cyrus H. Gordon, *Ugarit and Minoan Crete* (New York: W. W. Norton, 1966) 23n.15.

you have I cherished among all the families of the earth" (my translation), was originally meant to apply to the North.

Hosea begins in the same vein, complaining that "the land commits
great whoredom by forsaking the LORD" (1:2 NRSV). Here, again, I think
the verse is meant both figuratively and literally. This is a dominant
metaphor in Hosea's early chapters. If for the "party of God" any
credence given to other deities was the religious analog of adultery, how
much more so even ritually prescribed sex?

Hosea is hard to make sense of because the text, as we have it, has
apparently suffered extensive editing. Thus, the first part of chapter 2, if
it is Hosea's, must come from another time, since it completely vitiates
what the prophet has just said. I have no desire to get into close-order
textual dissection, but it seems apparent from Hosea 5:5 that his text was
still fluid from the time that the North split into two kingdoms, about 740
BCE, until after 722 when Samaria fell to the Assyrians.

This distance in time means that Hosea could be more forthright than
Amos in his criticism of Israel for ba'alistic religious practice if, indeed,
those references are original Hosea. But the prophetic "revolution" that
both men represent is far more profound even than an insistence upon
exclusive monotheism.

§9. Changing the Axis of Worship

Notre Père, qui êtes aux cieux / Restez-y. . . .
Our Father, which art in heaven / Stay there. . . .
—Jacques Prevert ("Pater Noster," 1949)

We come, finally, to what I think is the revolutionary core of Israelite
prophecy: the idea that it is incumbent upon all of us to help each
other—in a word, altruism. Nowadays, such an idea seems a truism,
doesn't it? But we need to imagine how it must have been received by
those who were raised in a millennia-old tradition that said just the
opposite.

Scholars and preachers have long noted the prophets' opposition to
"empty, formalistic practice" and their championing of "justice" (Amos)
and "steadfast love" (Hosea). Conversely, I think many modern clergy
and liberal rabbis often underestimate the importance that properly per-
formed ritual had in and for the ancient world, a world whose beginnings
hark back to the Farming Revolution.

Perhaps from as far back as 8,000 years before Amos's time, people all over the Near East had, as they thought, "insured" the return of migrating fish, seasonal rains, and their crops by performing rituals that became time-honored, unchanging. They offered up sacrifices and prayers to their gods at the ritually prescribed times.

When we consider how much modern opposition there has been to developments such as nineteenth-century Reform Jews' deviation from full-Hebrew service, the post-Vatican II Roman Catholic Church's changing from the Latin mass, or the Episcopal Church's ordination of women, we can appreciate peoples' reluctance to change practices that had "worked" for them for uncounted centuries.

Concomitant with this "vertical" axis of worship was the idea that crop failure, illness or disease, even death were the gods' punishment on worshippers for sins or deficiencies. This is a thesis that the Book of Job hotly disputes, but Jesus' "Take heart, my son, your sins are forgiven" addressed to a paralytic in Matt 9:2 (RSV) shows that Job was not much in vogue then. So for one more fortunate to come to the aid of an afflicted person would be to contravene the will of the gods. Let the diseased or wounded man lie; better, as we say, "not to get involved."

If this sounds like a prelude to Jesus' Parable of the Good Samaritan, it is. But the message that Jesus articulated, care for one's neighbor, is one that by his time was already eight hundred years old, going back at least as far as Amos.

§10. Prophecy in Judah

"Would that all the LORD's people were prophets. . . . "
—Moses (Numbers 11:29 NJPS)

Prophecy may initially have been less prominent in the South because Judah adopted dynastic succession, or because it was less involved in international import-export trade. On my reading of Amos, the prophet was exiled—not deported—to the South. Judah provided fertile soil for the growth of prophecy because the same social inequities complained of in the North were present there as well.

A longer version of Amos's oracle against Judah (2:3-5) was probably added to the text (but later eviscerated) in order to make his prophecy relevant there. To what extent, then, is that prophecy which we can call "social criticism" a Northern phenomenon that migrated south in the last half of the eighth century, a migration personified by Amos's banishment?

Hosea and Amos were both Northerners, as were Jonah ben Amittai and Obadiah, assuming that the latter was the advisor of Jeroboam I (which is highly doubtful). Jeremiah's family was of Northern—priestly origin, too, but Judah produced its own prophets as well. First Isaiah[21] and Micah, contemporaries of Amos, who lived a day's walk southwest of Jerusalem and had complaints similar to Amos's, were the first indisputably Southern prophets.

The Book of Micah is most like a sheaf of notes whose student-author never got round to making into a term paper. Another way of looking at it—assuming the verses all come from the same approximate period—is that they are like shards of a broken mirror glued together in the order they were picked up, giving us a blurry picture of Judean society. Succeeding generations of documentarists smear Micah's verses ever closer to our times—as shown by Max Margolis, who disagrees with them.[22] But even the conservative Margolis has trouble maintaining that Micah is an organic whole, and modern scholars think only the first three chapters are indisputably from his pen.

§11. Isaiah ben Amoz

There is a tantalizing similarity between Amos's name (עָמוֹס *amos*) and that of First Isaiah's father (אָמוֹץ *amots*). The spelling variants are no obstacle, as spelling in Israel as reflected in the Bible was never standardized, and the chronology of their lives fits very well. It is tempting, then, to see the Amoz who was Isaiah's father as having been our Amos. Unfortunately, despite their many similarities of theme and even vocabulary, no tradition remembers such a relationship. *Lev. Rabbah.* 6:6 and *Pirke de R. Eliezer* 118 claim that Isaiah's father was also a prophet, but if that prophet had been Amos this surely would have been remembered. Still, there is little doubt that the words of Amos exerted great influence on this "son of Amoz" and on Jeremiah.

---

[21]This is the scholarly designation of the first thirty-nine chapters of Isaiah. At least two other "Isaiah's," the authors of chapters 40-55 and 56-66 respectively, have been posited.

[22]Max Margolis, *Micah* (Philadelphia: Jewish Publication Society, 1908).

Isaiah's sixty-six chapters offer us comparatively great scope for sociohistorical reconstruction, but it must be noted that there is strong evidence to suggest the book has at least three authors and was collected over a period of more than a century. Isaiah 45:1, which names Cyrus of Persia as a "savior" of Israel, must have been composed after 539 BCE. Even so-called First Isaiah is not all of a piece, nor are its parts in an order that we would call coherent.

We can say that Isaiah was involved in the political turmoil that surrounded Judah. Beginning about the time that the Assyrian empire began its rise under Tiglath-pileser in 745 BCE, Isaiah saw Assyria as the "rod of God's wrath" that would itself be chastised by and by. He counselled Ahaz and son Hezekiah to trust in the Lord and eschew politics, to "beat their swords into plowshares" (2:4), but as we saw in chapter 5, Swiss-style neutrality was not an option. If you sit long enough on railroad tracks, sooner or later you won't have to decide to get off.

It was to Ahaz that Isaiah gave the famous "Immanuel prophecy" that Christians later took to indicate the birth of Jesus. On its face, the text (7:14) seems only to indicate that the expected birth was that of Ahaz's son, Hezekiah—a potent sign indeed if the king had already sacrificed an heir. But Ahaz was not convinced.

As Jehu had done long before, Ahaz adopted a pro-Assyrian policy, hence Isaiah may be seen as anti-Assyrian, as was Jeremiah later. But Babylon was not on the stage in Isaiah's time. Was Isaiah more anti-Assyrian than simply against all foreign entanglements? Isaiah's main concern seems to have been, like Amos's, the mistreatment and expropriation of the poorer classes by the rich, and he uses language often reminiscent of Amos or Hosea in describing this. Whether these similarities are original—indicating that Isaiah knowingly followed in the footsteps of his slightly older contemporaries—or the product of a later, editorial homogenization cannot easily be ascertained.

From a combination of biblical and nonbiblical sources we can at least frame the situation that Isaiah saw and responded to during a prophetic career of as much as forty years. Under the shadow of growing Assyrian strength, some of the south-Syrian states, notably Damascus and Israel, attempted to re-form the coalition that had successfully opposed Assyria in the ninth century. To join or not to join?

Meanwhile, opportunities to participate in international trade beckoned, leading to the creation of large income-producing estates at the expense of small freeholders and tenants.

This is not so different than our government's right of "eminent domain," but while our government cannot simply seize land and must in theory and in law compensate owners fairly for land it confiscates, the rulers and aristocrats of Israel often winked at such laws as they had.

The influence of prophecy upon politics and morals was felt, though never as strongly as the prophets would have wished. Those prophets whom tradition canonized were preserved because they were uncompromising Yahwists. The "flip side" of monotheism was, so to speak, that just as God rewarded good behavior, he punished the evil, whether it be social injustice or the apostasy of polytheism. So far so good; the logic was impeccable, reinforced by the fall of Samaria and Judah's miraculous escape from Assyrian conquest some twenty years later. But the Judeans were not Greeks; their logic held a flaw.

Formally, it is called the fallacy of Excluded Middle, a modern example of which would resemble the following syllogism.

Love is blind. [Major premise.]
Stevie Wonder is blind. [Minor premise.]
Therefore, Stevie Wonder is Love. [Conclusion.][23]

Transposing to a biblical key, these monotheists could say:

Evil is punished.
We are being punished.
We must be evil.

Monotheists necessarily live in a universe in which they are at the center, the crown of creation. Everything that happens to them is dictated by their god—for there are no legitimate others, no powers to contest God's will—and he is responsive to their actions. Individual voices such as Ecclesiastes' "the race is not to the swift, nor the battle to the strong, nor bread to the wise . . . but time and chance happen to them all" (Eccl. 9:11 NRSV) might occasionally be raised, but the writer is late, Greek-influenced and . . . he was not a prophet.

---

[23]For this syllogism, my thanks to Ms. Amanda Smith, one of my students at the University of Kentucky.

Chapter 11

Judah Alone

§1. Assyria Renascent

In this chapter we look principally at the surviving Hebrew kingdom, Judah, in the critical period from the fall of its Northern sister in 722 BCE until the death of Josiah in 608 BCE. Obtaining precise dates for Judean rulers in this period is still a matter of scholarly debate,[1] which is unfortunate because it is important to know just what the world situation was that each king faced at his accession. A recurring question here will be: How much did renascent Assyrian power cast its shadow before it?

Some framework for the period is given by the Assyrian Eponym List, a record of people and events that, though fragmentary at both ends, preserves valuable information about Assyria from 892 to 648 BCE and, incidentally, about surrounding countries as well.[2] For our purposes the List's most important dates are 724–722 BCE, the dates of the siege and fall of Samaria. But the Assyrians did not use our calendar. How do we know those were the years?

In the entry that is thirty-nine years before the siege began, the List notes "In the month of *Simanu* an eclipse of the sun took place." Taking a modern model of the solar system and running it backwards, we determine that this eclipse must have happened in June 763 BCE. Thus the Assyrian conquerors of Samaria have provided us with a framework within which to understand their activities. The most important of these activities center around the man who revitalized Assyria, Tiglath-pileser III, who took the throne in 745 BCE.

The first sign of Assyrian resurgence was the defeat of its longtime northern rival, Urartu, in 743 BCE.[3] With the northern threat removed, Assyria was free again to turn its attentions to the west in ways it had not

---

[1]The debate over dates began in 1945, when William F. Albright arbitrarily changed some of the Bible's numbers because he couldn't make them fit. Most moderns follow Thiele, but J. Maxwell Miller and John H. Hayes, *A History of Ancient Israel and Judah* (Philadelphia: Westminster, 1986) 296, leave some dates blank.

[2]See Edwin Thiele, *The Mysterious Numbers of the Hebrew Kings*, 2nd ed. (Grand Rapids MI: Zondervan, 1983) 221-26.

[3]A massacre in Urartu in that year is reported in the Assyrian Eponym List (Thiele, *The Mysterious Numbers of the Hebrew Kings*, 224). Boris Piotrovsky, *The Ancient Civilization of Urartu* (New York: Cowles, 1969) 201, reports that the kingdom endured until ca. 585 BCE.

been able to do for sixty years. The first such incursion happened in 738 BCE. How would the western states respond?

Northern Kingdom Israel and Damascus responded by initiating a confederacy to oppose Assyria. Moved perhaps by memories of the grand coalition that had withstood Assyrian might four times in the previous century, they prepared, like the British and French of the 1930s, to "fight the First War over again." They may have had an exaggerated notion of their own strength or have critically underestimated that of their foe.

At the same time, Israel and Damascus were not content merely to rely on their own armies, but cast about for allies in the region; additional armed strength would never be unwelcome. Assyrian inscriptions that list the empire's north-Syrian opponents usually mention a dozen or more opposing "kings." If the confederates could not enlist all of them, they wanted at least to neutralize neighbors that might make separate deals with Assyria, as Irhuleni of Hamath had done in the ninth century, destroying the north-Syrian coalition of that day. One of these small but important neighbors was Judah.

As bad luck would have it, Judah's King Uzziah had only recently died.[4] His fifty-two-year reign had given Judah more strength and stability than it had enjoyed in more than a century. Chronicles is particularly lavish with praises of his military accomplishments, especially in the areas of increasing the army's size and the measures he took to insure Jerusalem's defense. (Recall that in his father's time the city had been successfully attacked by the North.)

Uzziah might have been impressed by his own success because, Chronicles continues, he tried to offer incense on the incense altar of the Temple itself. It is interesting to see how often in Israelite history the theoretical "separation of powers" between king and priesthood is transgressed, usually by a king who wants more power or thinks he deserves to be priest as well as king. Negative accounts of this, especially the later ones, might be suspected of having a "priestly agenda."

In one of these accounts, 2 Chronicles 26:16-21, Uzziah was confronted by priests; the result of this confrontation was that "leprosy broke out on his forehead" (26:19). This effect would seem very unlikely, possibly something made up later by religious authorities to show that

---

[4]Uzziah died in 740/39 BCE. The reason for the uncertainty is that scholars are not sure whether the year was accounted as having begun in spring or fall.

they had been in the right, but the leprosy itself is not fiction; archaeologists recently recovered the plaque that sealed his tomb with cautions that the bones not be moved.[5]

It could be that the priests claimed he was leprotic because this, they knew, would force him to withdraw from the sacred precincts. Alternatively, the king's leprosy might have been backread into the story. Or, it is within the realm of possibility that in those days of uncertain diagnosis, Uzziah had a chronic skin condition exacerbated by stress—and no cortisone. Be that as it may, Uzziah died in 740/39 BCE, and was succeeded by that son, Jotham, who had been made coregent with him ten years before.

Neither Kings nor Chronicles has much to say about Jotham. He is credited with some success against neighboring tribes and some building projects. He didn't make serious moves against "the shrines," but he did have the good sense to stay out of Temple affairs. Kings adds (2 Kings 15:37): "In those days, the LORD began to incite King Rezin of Aram and Pekah son of Remaliah against Judah" (NJPS).

The Bible reports that this Pekah was an aide to the previous king, Pekahiah, who had usurped and murdered his master after only two years of rule. Their names are close enough to be interchangeable—the theophoric element being optional—and their dates are so hard to reconcile that some scholars simply rearrange them arbitrarily. However, it may make sense if we posit that one of these kings—Pekah, in my opinion—was king in Transjordan and that the reigns of Menahem and Pekah begin at the same time. After all, this was the time (752 BCE) when the Jehu dynasty ended and Northern kingship went up for grabs.

Two hundred years later, the Bible's Judean collectors might not have remembered that their greater homeland had once contained three kingdoms. My conjecture, the "Pekah-variation," is strengthened by noting that the Bible identifies Pekah's supporters/henchmen as Gileadites: in other words, men from across the river. This would indicate that the anti-Assyrian coalition that pressured Jotham included Arameans, Israelites, and related Transjordanians. Eight years after taking the throne, Jotham died. Like Penelope, he had successfully held his suitors at arm's length, neither joining nor defying them.

---

[5]A picture of Uzziah's burial plaque may be seen in Miller and Hayes, *A History of Ancient Israel and Judah*, 310.

*This situation reminds one of King Hussein's Jordan in the Gulf War.
Caught between Iraq and a hard place, he joined neither the Iraqis nor
the coalition of states arrayed against Iraq, satisfying neither party,
perhaps, but keeping his throne and his head. His balancing act was a
feat of considerable statesmanship.*

The death of Jotham brought his son Ahaz to the throne. Ahaz had
been made coregent when he was about sixteen, at about the same time
he produced the child who might succeed him (see below). When Ahaz
became sole regent he was twenty, neither old nor young by ancient Near
Eastern standards. He seems to have been old beyond his years in
political sagacity, but could not indefinitely put off his political suitors as
his father had done.

When Ahaz declined to join the anti-Assyrian coalition, the confederates plotted to overthrow him and put one of their own on the Judean
throne in his stead, one ben Tabeel. It is difficult but useful to try to
determine just who this king candidate was. Following Benjamin Mazar,
I suggest that Tabeel is a/the name of the Tobiads[6] whose famous
fortress, Iraq el-'Amir, still stands east of the Jordan.

*Later, in the Second Temple period, the Tobiads were still major
contenders for national leadership. They were active in Israel's politics
well into Hellenistic times, though by then the family had divided into
factions and was fighting with itself.[7]*

In Isaiah 7:3-9 the prophet counsels Ahaz not to fear the plot. The
text includes the peculiar advice that "within sixty-five years" (vs. 8; vs.
9 in NJPS) the two plotting kingdoms would be destroyed. Such pinpoint
predictions are not usual in prophetic literature, and besides, the predicted
time frame makes little sense as well as being of little comfort to
beleaguered Ahaz. I wonder, then, if somehow, the text should be understood to mean "within five or six years,"[8] indicating an imprecise but
short period.

---

[6]See Victor Tcherikover, "Social Conditions," chap. 4 in *The Hellenistic Age: World
History of the Jewish People*, ed. Abraham Schalit (New Brunswick: Rutgers, 1972) 96-
105.

[7]Victor Tcherikover, *Hellenistic Civilization and the Jews*, trans. S. Applebaum
(Philadelphia: JPS, 1959; repr.: Peabody MA: Hendrickson, 1999) 357.

[8]As suggested by Edward J. Kissane, in *The Book of Isaiah*, vol. 1 (Dublin: Browne
& Nolan, 1941) 1:78-79, 82.

This would compare with Amos's warning to the Israelites of a generation earlier: "You have planted delightful vineyards, / But shall not drink their wine" (Amos 5:11, NJPS), referring to the period of eight to ten years that it takes to get a vineyard on line (see also Isaiah 8:4). Given even the approximate dates for Ahaz's reign and firm ones for the siege of Samaria, it seems entirely likely that the advice was indeed given about five or six years before the Assyrian axe fell.

§2. Under the Shadow of Assyria

One consequence of Assyria's resurgence might have been that a trickle of Northerners entered Judah to escape Assyrian pressure. And they would have been let in, if not exactly welcomed. They were renegades and apostates, perhaps, but they were not the later Northerners whom the Assyrians so mixed with other peoples that, according to Southern reckoning, they were no longer "Jews." The Torah that these early Northern refugees brought was allowed to be deposited in the Temple. For all that, the Southern refuge would ultimately prove as perilous for them as France did later for German Jews fleeing Nazi persecution.

The Bible does not deal kindly with Ahaz. It remembers him as someone who stripped the Temple treasury and reinstated or imported abominable Aramean or Assyrian practices into Judah. One of these practices necessitated sacrificing his own son—obviously not Hezekiah. That he did sacrifice a son makes the "Immanuel prophecy" of Isaiah chapter 7 the more poignant. The "young woman," whom Jewish tradition sees as Hezekiah's mother, was pregnant; the succession was assured and, even more, God had promised Judah's king that the threat of invasion would be lifted soon.

> *Until the early twentieth century, Christian translations of the text insisted on reading "a virgin" for "the young woman" and claimed that the text pointed ahead some seven hundred years to Mary the mother of Jesus. James Moffatt's translation ("Old Testament" 1922, 1924) was the first generally accepted Christian translation that promoted "young woman" over "virgin." Moffatt was followed by Goodspeed's "American Translation" in 1927, then by the Revised Standard Version in 1952. (The [American] Catholic version NAB and most "conservative" Protestant versions [e.g., NKJB, NASV, NIV] retain "virgin.")*
>
> *Part of the problem is that Christians were referencing the Latin Vulgate's* virgo, *an unfortunate translation of the Greek* parthenos,

which can mean either "virgin" or "young woman." The other, major part of the problem is what German scholarship calls tendenz, *the desire that religious translators have to translate in line with their preconceived theologies. I mention this example of theologically driven interpretation to show that if it still existed in our lifetime, how much more so in the time of the Judean collectors of Scripture?*

Ahaz was not impressed. Was he a weak, sycophantic king or did he not rather, as they say in poker, get dealt a weak hand which he perforce had to play? Was he gambling on his ability to play both sides or, at worst, choose which side would win? If he cozied up to Damascus, Ahaz still could not but have been aware of the growing power of Assyria. He would therefore have faced the classic dilemma of a smaller state caught between two larger and more powerful ones. But Ahaz seems to have hedged his bets and taken some thought for putting Jerusalem in a better position to withstand a siege, improving on the defensive measures his grandfather had taken. It was not enough.

When Rezin made territorial gains south of Judah, Ahaz finally made a choice. He put himself and his little kingdom under the "protection" of Assyria and, indeed, the Assyrians quickly relieved the pressure on him. They also relieved the Temple of its treasure as payment for their services, something the Bible complains of—rather unfairly I think.

When Assyria smashed through its foes and captured Samaria, the trickle of Northerners seeking refuge in Jerusalem would have become a flood. As we have seen, it is from this event, the fall of Samaria, that the myth comes of the "ten lost tribes," from whom so many modern peoples have claimed descent. Perhaps the most bizarre claim stemming from this is Arthur Koestler's in *The Thirteenth Tribe.*[9] He postulates that all the Jews of Europe are descended from Khazarian (Crimean) converts who had been proselytized by Israelite refugees who fled northward to escape the Assyrians.

Koestler's claim is specious, the others false because the tribes were not lost, nor were there ten of them, as we have seen. Moreover, Judah had long since absorbed Simeon, while Transjordanian Reuben is more

---

[9]Arthur Koestler, *The Thirteenth Tribe: The Khazar Empire and Its Heritage* (New York: Random House, 1976). Koestler's ironic conclusion is that the murder by the Nazis of six million Jews was a big mistake because European Jews were not "racially" Jewish at all.

Southern than Northern, presuming, of course, that it remained a part of the tribal confederation at all. Moses' brief wish for Reuben's continued existence in the venerable Blessing of Moses, Deuteronomy 33:6, suggests the tribe was already dwindling.

The number of deportees from the North is known from two Assyrian inscriptions. One puts it at 29,270, the other at 27,290.[10] The population of the North at this time is estimated at more than 750,000 persons; if so, those taken amounted to less than four percent of the whole. It was, however, the most important four percent: the aristocracy, priests, military leadership, and even whole army units—subsequently integrated into the Assyrian army—were deported.

The Assyrians settled most of these people in the Gozan region on the Habur River, and in their stead imported similar populations into Israel from the other countries they had overrun. This tactic of population exchange, however much we might deplore it, served to preclude future revolts by separating potential leadership classes from their land base and from those who might be expected to follow their lead.

From a later Jewish point of view, motivated as much by political as religious considerations, the mixed peoples that resulted from Assyrian policy in the North were no longer Jews. This is despite, or even because of, the Bible's detailed account of groups of foreigners appealing to the Assyrian king to send back a "priest from the place" to teach them local religion and thus save them from a plague of lions. That one returning priest might be sufficient to do the job also indicates that we are not dealing with large numbers of forced emigrants.

Another thing we may glean from this story is that for many people, perhaps most, gods were still seen as local in scope. If that is the case, the popular view will have changed but little from that of the earliest, topocosmic settlers. The Northern tribes, then, were never lost. Rather, their identity was permanently compromised, at least in Judean eyes, and they never again succeeded in establishing any semblance of native government—as the South did later, after their own exilic sojourn.

I had the pleasure of visiting with the high priest of the Samaritans, Jacob ben Uzzi ha-Kohen, at their Passover in 1969. At that time he feared for the continuing existence of his community, then no more than

---

[10]Thomas, *DOTT*, 59.

7,000 souls, because the Israeli victory in the 1967 war meant that Samaritan young people were now free to settle throughout Israel and, ultimately, to assimilate. What the might of Assyria failed to do, the bright lights of Tel Aviv were accomplishing.

For all his undeniable ruthlessness, Tiglath-pileser III may have been the first ruler in the Near East with a real empire ideology, as opposed to a mere tyrant who used his strength to exploit and rob others to aggrandize himself. The Assyrians made Aramaic the *lingua franca* of their empire. This is noteworthy because Aramaic was not the native language of Assyria, and to choose a language other than one's own as the international language shows a certain breadth of vision. By way of contrast, remember that imperial Egypt despised all non-Egyptians and their languages; the Greeks actually called foreigners by a name, "barbarian,"[11] taken from their mockery of what non-Hellenic language sounded like to them.

Tiglath-pileser III did not live to see Israel fall, having died in 727 BCE. If the North saw this as an opportunity to wiggle out from under Assyria, they were disappointed. Succession in a polygamous kingship may be dicey, but this time it went smoothly.[12] His successor, Shalmaneser V, continued Tiglath-pileser's policies, and it was Shalmaneser who oversaw the end of the Northern kingdom, though he himself died the year Samaria fell.

This coincidence would have been seen as a "sign from heaven"—as the death of Franklin D. Roosevelt in April 1945 was seen by the Nazis—and led elements in the North to try to reverse recent history. They, too, were disappointed.

Two restless years after Samaria fell, the Assyrians were compelled formally to annex it to their empire as the province of Samarina. This put recalcitrant Samarians under Assyrian law. It also meant that now Assyria itself was now Judah's next-door neighbor. What we have seen previously in this chapter is a long, but necessary, prelude to understanding how things fared for Judah alone.

---

[11]That is, the Unintelligibles, the Stammerers. Compare "babble," "babbler."

[12]H. W. F. Saggs, *The Greatness That Was Babylon* (New York: New American Library, 1962) 116-17.

§3. Living Next Door to a 400-Pound Gorilla

Plus ça change, plus c'est la même chose.
The more things change, the more they remain the same.
—Alphonse Karr (*Les Guêpes*, 1849)

Scholars are divided over which Judean king sat the throne when the North fell, Ahaz or his son Hezekiah, a problem I cannot solve. I can say that Ahaz is remembered as evildoing while Hezekiah "gets marks second only to David,"[13] and this seems paradoxical. According to Ahlström, Ahaz adroitly protected Judah both from Assyria and the states that opposed her, while Hezekiah's actions almost wrecked the kingdom on two occasions. What accounts for this inversion of memory?

First, we have to note that all Judean rulers now faced the same challenge: how to survive the massive pressure of having Assyria on their very border. Even if the North had deserved its destruction, it was a bitter blow, ripping away from greater Israel the better part of the land the Judeans held to be theirs through divine promise. Judah was now the only independent state between Assyria and Egypt.

On the other hand, nothing had changed. How to manage the classic dilemma? It would be marvelous if we could determine just how small states collected the intelligence to decide what foreign policy to adopt. Did they interview traders and travellers to foreign lands, or even send paid agents to spy out the land, as Joseph accused his brothers of being? The Joseph story, whether true or fictitious, was written during the monarchic period and tells us, among other things, that countries were accustomed to spying on each other.

Some sort of intelligence-gathering activity must have been undertaken, because the stakes were so high that guesswork or emotion-driven decisions would lead to disaster sooner rather than later. In 712 BCE Hezekiah acquired enough intelligence to dodge a bullet. Hezekiah was apparently approached to join a revolt led by Ashdod against Assyria; after initially agreeing to do so, he backed out. In the event, the revolt was a local phenomenon and quickly put down.

Seven years later Hezekiah wasn't so lucky.

---

[13]Gösta Ahlström, *The History of Ancient Palestine* (Minneapolis: Fortress, 1993) 42-43.

In 705 BCE the Assyrian King Sargon died on campaign in the east. More significant, his body was not recovered. We have seen how important proper burial was viewed to be by all ancient Near Eastern peoples, so this fact was widely taken as a sign that Assyrian power was coming to a swift end. Hezekiah threw in with the anti-Assyrian forces. These included Merodach-baladan, the Babylonian leader who seized this moment of instability to reassert his rule over parts of Babylon, and also included the anti-Assyrian Nubian dynasty that ruled Egypt.

Both 2 Kings 20:12-19 and Isaiah 39 report that Hezekiah entertained the Babylonian king and even gave him a personally guided tour of the Temple and its treasures. This made Isaiah furious; he predicted that those treasures and even some of Hezekiah's children would be taken to Babylon. The king, however, put his own positive spin on Isaiah's words saying, in effect, that he would have peace in his own time. The first eleven verses of 2 Kings 20, the illness and recovery of Hezekiah, make this point.

Everyone has 20/20 hindsight. It is easy for us to criticize Hezekiah because we know how his story turned out. But from his own contemporary perspective, he must have thought that the Assyrians, already in some turmoil, could not manage a two-front war. If he sided with them he would be harshly dealt with by the soon-to-be victorious Egyptians, who were his immediate neighbors to the south. But, like his father and grandfather, he was not content with trusting his alliances to save his kingdom.

To make Jerusalem safe from a long siege such as Samaria had endured, he ordered the construction of a tunnel that would bring water from the Gihon spring outside the city to a point within the city walls. (The Siloam Tunnel Inscription, found in the tunnel in 1880 and now residing in the Turkish Museum in Istanbul, is one of the longest and best nonbiblical texts we have.[14])

The tunnel itself was long thought to be a miracle of ancient engineering. As with our Transcontinental Railway, the builders began at both ends and met in the middle. The trick here, though, is that while our railwaymen labored above ground, the Siloam Tunnel follows a crooked path of nearly one-third of a mile through solid rock. (It feels like a lot

---

[14]Thomas, *DOTT*, 209-11.

longer when one walks through it.) How then did Hezekiah's crews come within four inches of a perfect joint?

The answer seems to be that the tunnelers simply followed a karst line in the limestone, that is, a narrow channel that had already been eaten out by centuries of water trickling between rock layers of differing hardness, a common occurrence in limestone country.[15] Even so, one has to marvel at the endurance of men who were, finally, more than eight hundred feet from the entrances at either end laboring in very cramped spaces and competing for oxygen with their own oil lamps.

Prepared as he was, Hezekiah came close to losing the kingdom a second time when the Assyrian army made its appearance. First, the Assyrians met the Egyptians at Eltekeh, nearly due west of Jerusalem, and apparently fought them to a draw. This left Assyria free to invest Judah, which they promptly did, defying Isaiah's prediction in 2 Kings 19:32ff. (∥ Isaiah 37:33ff.) that Sennacherib, whom 2 Kings mentions by name in 19:36 (= Isa. 37:37), would not come to Jerusalem, much less beseige it. Sennacherib, who had succeeded his father, reports capturing forty-six Judean towns before besieging Hezekiah, shutting him up "like a bird in a cage" in Jerusalem in 701 BCE.[16]

Hezekiah sang. He admitted that he had "done wrong" by seeking alliance with Egypt (Isaiah 30, 31) and gave the Assyrians a massive payment in silver and gold and other "valuable treasures," including, according to Sennacherib's annals (but not in 2 Kings 18–19), some of "his (own) daughters."[17] Yet that did not get Assyria to call off the campaign. It is from this siege that we have the story of an Assyrian emissary, the Rabshakeh, speaking Hebrew ("Judean" NJPS; "language of Judah" NRSV) to the people on the walls of Jerusalem in order to convince them that further resistance was futile, and the emissaries from Hezekiah imploring him to speak rather in Aramaic, which they—but not the people—understood. One thing that we may glean from this account (2 Kings 18:26ff. ∥ Isaiah 36:11ff.) is that the installation of Aramaic as the language of empire had proceeded apace.

---

[15]Dan Gill, "How They Met," *Biblical Archaeology Review* 20/4 (July/August 1994): 20-33.

[16]Sennacherib, "The Siege of Jerusalem," *ANE* 1, *Anthology of Texts and Pictures* (1958) 199-201; "bird in a cage" on 200.

[17]Ibid., 201.

It is easy to sympathize with overrun countries wanting freedom, but the revolts against Assyria were opportunistic and ill-conceived. The far corners of the empire could hardly know when a particular king would die. Unless they had arranged an assassination or mutually agreed upon a date,[18] it would be near impossible for conspiring countries to coordinate their efforts. Appeal to Egypt was a constant in revolutionary calculations, but while Egypt had economic interests in Palestine, it always promised more help than it could deliver.

One is reminded of the Hungarian uprising of 1956. The United States secretly fomented it but, during the event, stood by while the courageous revolutionaries were penned in and exterminated by Russian soldiers.

Not all looked to Egypt for help, and with reason. Isaiah 36:6 (∥ 2 Kings 18:21) quotes Assyria's ambassador to Israel, the Rabshakeh, who characterizes Egypt as "that splintered reed of a staff, which enters and punctures the palm of anyone who leans on it" (NJPS). But Isaiah was no Jeremiah; that is, he does not seem to have been so much a political partisan as what we would call an isolationist. And a thoroughgoing Yahwist.

The continued survival of the South in the face of the more powerful Northern kingdom's demise could only be—a miracle. But such miracles were contingent upon Judah's placing exclusive trust in YHVH and "avoiding all foreign entanglements," as some of our country's founding fathers put it. The book that scholars call First Isaiah (most of Isaiah 1–39) is a good representative of the prophets as "the Party of God." This is understandable.

Hezekiah got the required miracle when the Assyrian army decamped, as the Bible says, overnight. Second Kings 19:35 tersely reports that an angel of the Lord entered the camp and struck down 185,000 men, causing the rest to depart. (Who, I wonder, counted the bodies and where were they buried? A cemetery of the requisite size would have been a landmark for generations.) Chronicles expands on this, saying that the Assyrians' disgraceful defeat was what caused Sennacherib's subsequent assassination.

In fact, the sudden departure of the besiegers followed Sennacherib's reception of a message saying that the army was needed at home to quell

---

[18]This happened in 595 BCE. See the next chapter, below.

a revolt. He was subsequently assassinated, but that event didn't happen for another twenty years. This again shows how history may be compressed, especially when "historians" have a reason for compressing it.

§4. Hezekiah's Reforms

The Bible's favorable treatment of Hezekiah—2 Chronicles devotes four chapters to him—despite his policies having come so close to losing the kingdom on two occasions no doubt stems from the (priestly) editors' favorable views of the king's religious reforms. In Chronicles we find a long and loving description of all the actions Hezekiah undertook to purify the Temple and the priesthood. But even Kings lauds him for dismantling or destroying objects that Yahwists would have seen as idols competing for Israelite allegiance: shrines, pillars, the asherah, and—most significantly—2 Kings 18:4 reports that Hezekiah destroyed the bronze serpent that Numbers 21:6-9 claims Moses had made. If this verse is factual,[19] it means that some form of serpent worship had been continuously present in Israel for five hundred years.

Unfortunately, we cannot refine the chronology of events to the degree we might wish. We would like to know whether Hezekiah's reforms were a response to the destruction of the North and Judah's narrow escape, or preceded any of those events. In either case, the "party of God" would see Judah's survival as a reward, just as they saw the North's destruction as punishment for apostasy.

Despite or because of this, Hezekiah tried to effect a reunion with the North. Second Chronicles 30:1-2 reports that the king sent letters "also to Ephraim and Manasseh" inviting them down to Jerusalem for a Passover in "the second month." There are two interesting things here. The first is that the dual invitation may indicate that Ephraim and Manasseh, while the former and half of the latter were annexed to Assyria, were under separate domestic management, as they had been

---

[19]Ahlström, *The History of Ancient Palestine*, 702, proposes the following dilemma: if the bronze serpent were Moses', Hezekiah shouldn't have destroyed it; if it were not, then Moses himself was not a monotheist. Ahlström does not seem to admit here the possibility of a pious fiction to make serpent worship acceptable. Karen Joines, "The Bronze Serpent in the Israelite Cult," *Journal of Biblical Literature* 87 (1968): 245-50, argues that the serpent was not Moses'. Considering the age and ubiquity of serpent worship, this would not be surprising.

shortly before the Assyrian conquest. The second is that Judean Passover is always in "the first month."

The reason given for the unusual delay was that there were not enough sanctified priests and "the people" had not assembled in Jerusalem, but we have to ask what year this was and why this year was different than all the previous ones. I think the real reason for the change in date was that the second month is the time Samarians traditionally celebrate Passover. In that case, Hezekiah will have used their date as a sop to Northern religious sensibilities.

Despite this, 2 Chronicles 30:11 reports that his gesture was generally rejected, and only a few from Asher, Manasseh, and Zebulun came. But later the same chapter reports that a "multitude" from Ephraim, Manasseh, Issachar, and Zebulun took part. Moreover, the account says they were allowed to do so even though they had not been cleansed in the prescribed fashion.

Presuming that the Chronicles account is basically factual, Hezekiah's actions were undertaken in an attempt to reunite the kingdoms, religiously if not politically, under Judean leadership. To us such a goal might not seem reasonable, but Hezekiah, I think, believed his own "press notices." After all, was he not the living embodiment of the sign that Isaiah had promised his father? And had not the South survived while Israel had not?

Whatever Hezekiah's religious success, the basic political fact had not changed. Assyria was still the reigning superpower, and as such continued to exert decisive influence on Judean foreign policy. Nowhere is this more apparent than in the long reign of Hezekiah's son, Manasseh.

§5. Evil Manasseh

If the figure for his reign is accurate, Manasseh's fifty-five years on the Judean throne make him the longest reigning king of either kingdom; in fact, half of the period between Samaria's annexation and Josiah's death is taken up by his reign. He is a target for much biblical invective, so much so that it is hard to know how much is deserved. One of the eighteen recognized "scribal corrections" mentioned in *Midrash Tanhuma*[20] even changes the name "Moses" to "Manasseh," diverting the

---

[20]The verse is Judges 18:30. Abraham Cohen, *Joshua and Judges* (London: Soncino, 1950) 296. Conversely, the Talmud is at pains to explain if not excuse Manasseh's

attribution of idolatry from a grandson of the prophet onto an easy target. What might have given rise to all this? Two things come to mind, but before we come to them, we should look more closely at Manasseh's historical circumstances.

Manasseh was twelve when he became king in 697 BCE. So he would have been only four during the Assyrian siege of Jerusalem, not old enough to have formed an opinion of its whys and wherefores. He gained the throne four years later, still in the backwash of Judah's near escape from the same fate that had overtaken Samaria. He, or his advisers, needed to ensure that such a catastrophe did not happen again.

For their part, the Assyrians wanted only political and economic loyalty from their vassals; even in annexed territories they did not impose their religion upon the conquered. Therefore, one way to court favor with the Assyrians would have been by the voluntary adoption of some of their rituals and practices. On the other hand, according to Cogan, adopting foreign worship reflected a situation in which some Judeans, at least, were disenchanted with their God and that this "abetted the assimilation of [such] foreign ritual."[21] In other words (Guinevere's in *Camelot*), they intended "to pray to someone else instead."

For Americans nowadays, changing churches is usually not a big deal. But Manasseh did more than that. He has an evil name in Israel's history, specifically, for the charge that he practiced child sacrifice, a practice that Judeans, if they knew Genesis 25, could say was made unnecessary already in Abraham's time.

> *Notwithstanding the protest of some Orthodox Jews, the phrase "he made his children pass through the fire" can only have one meaning. In 2 Kings 23:10 there is explicit reference to Josiah defiling Topheth, the place where child sacrifice was done, "that no one might burn [NRSV pass through fire] his son or his daughter as an offering to Molech" (RSV; NJPS is slightly less explicit).*

It is nice to have one person to blame for all of our, or our nation's, troubles, but Manasseh could hardly have survived as long as he did without some popular support. Moreover, the same charge of child sacrifice in even more direct language is made against his grandfather Ahaz

---

idolatry by claiming that he found it impolitic to swim against the current of his times.

[21]Morton Cogan, *Imperialism and Religion*, SBLMS 19 (Missouola MT: Scholars Press, 1974) 113.

(2 Kings 16:3). I think that, just as the rise of Nazi Germany called forth latent fascist elements in surrounding European countries, Assyria's presence, power, and success made it attractive to Judahite elements that were not, perhaps, as committed to monotheism as our later tradition wants us to believe.

Still, there may be worse that can be said of Manasseh. We know that in the half century before he became king, Judah was required to pay an exorbitant price for the "protection" given by Assyria. Both Ahaz and Hezekiah are reported as having done so, Hezekiah even stripping gold from the doorposts of the Temple (2 Kings 18:16) to satisfy Assyrian rapaciousness. But Hezekiah was also trying to buy an alliance with Babylon.

As noted above, when Babylonian envoys brought him a gift to celebrate his recovery from illness, Hezekiah showed them the Temple treasures, for which he was angrily rebuked by Isaiah. The prophet predicted that everything the kingdom had would one day be carried off to Babylon—something that would be easy to write in the light of subsequent events. But it is likely that these preexilic Babylonians did not go away from their visit empty-handed.

The question that suggests itself then is, What did Manasseh have, or have left, with which to pay tribute to the Assyrians? Neither Kings nor Chronicles provides any information, but Jeremiah contains more than a hint that Manasseh was compelled to strip the gold cherubs and gold cover from the very Ark of the Covenant to meet his obligations. Or worse. It is possible that the Ark itself was given into the hands of the Assyrians.[22]

He could hardly have done this all by himself, but if 'twere done 'twas best done quietly. It is easy to see why official versions of events would want to suppress this knowledge. If known, the loss of the Ark might provoke spontaneous insurrection, anarchy, and the inevitable Assyrian occupation. And if that doomsday scenario seems implausible, here is another. Loss of the Ark might convince great numbers of people that their God had been vanquished by the Assyrians' and cause mass

---

[22]I now find that this suggestion, which I owe to my wife's research, was earlier made by Menahem Haran, "The Disappearance of the Ark," *Israel Exploration Journal* 13 (1964): 46-58.

desertions from the faith. We know from history that this is a common enough occurrence.

So except for Jeremiah's dark—and as yet unpublished—hints, the secret would keep until 586 BCE. The "up side" of the wreck of Jerusalem was that it effectively masked the fate of the Ark. Of course, this still leaves the question of why the Bible's final editors did not either "come clean" or edit Jeremiah more assiduously. But this question must be left until the next chapter.

§6. Amon and Josiah

Amon has the distinction of having been born latest in the life of any reigning Judean monarch: his father was 45 when Amon was born, so he was definitely a "son of old age." No other king had been more than thirty-three when his successor saw the light. Manasseh had held the throne so long he doubtless outlived many of the children born earlier. The Bible doesn't mention any, leaving us to guess the number of those unnamed who were sacrificed to Molech. It is likely the Bible's editors were not interested in details that were recorded elsewhere, the more so since Amon's two-year reign was followed by that of his illustrious son, Josiah.

Amon had twenty-two years in which to observe his father's pro-Assyrian policies and evidently found no reason not to continue them. In 663 BCE the Assyrians under Ashurbanipal had made a successful incursion deep into Egypt; there would be no succor from Assyria to be found in that quarter. It was a difficult situation at best.

Kings offers only the expected criticism, but Chronicles calls Amon worse than his father in that he didn't "humble himself before the LORD" as Manasseh had done. Still, that's a harsh judgment to render against a man who ruled for only two years as compared to his father's fifty-five. Being further from events, the Chronicler probably feels freer to heap obloquy on the head of beloved Josiah's immediate predecessor. In any case, the pro-Assyrian policy and concomitant spread of polytheism must have produced a growing opposition, because the king was murdered in 640 BCE when his son and heir was only eight.

Second Chronicles 34:3 reports that Josiah "began to seek the LORD" when he was sixteen, but it was not until four years later that he began religious reforms. The timing is not accidental. Josiah, or those around him, wished to revive Hezekiah's policy of reuniting with the North. This they could not do with impunity while Assyria was strong. So they waited. By the time the king reached twenty-one years of age (627 BCE), the political situation was beginning to change.

The king of Assyria, Ashurbanipal, died and his sons fought over the succession, leading to the complete separation of Assyria's southern part, Babylon. (In only fifteen more years Babylon would become the dominant power in Mesopotamia.) As a consequence, Assyria was preoccupied with its internal division and could spare less effort to contest what were, after all, only religious reforms in Israel/Judah.

Chronicles, then, has twenty-year-old Josiah making thoroughgoing religious reforms in Jerusalem, going so far as to disinter the bones of idolatrous Judean priests and burn them on their own altars, desecrating both (2 Chron. 34:5). After that, Josiah went North to do likewise. Kings takes some account of these reforms, but begins its account with the more important finding of the "Book of the Law"—two sides of the same coin.

§7. A "Book of the Law"

Most scholars agree that what was found in the Temple is at least the core of our Deuteronomy, chapters 12–26. It is called *Deuteronomy*, "second law," because it repeats so much of what the first four books of the Torah say, notably a second version of the Ten Commandments. Much earlier in this book, I noted Wellhausen's take on its finding: Josiah's men found it in the Temple, he claimed, because they had planted it there. What's more, they had written it themselves, a "divine warrant" to secure popular support for what they had already decided to do, centralize worship around Jerusalem.

This uncharitable view of events strikes wide of the truth, but it may not miss it entirely. It is at least possible that Josiah's religious officials knew that some Northern torah had been deposited in the Temple a century before by refugees from the North. If H. L. Ginsberg is correct, this would have happened shortly after this torah was written down, that is to say, during the time when both Northern and Southern *torah* or "teaching" were still in a fairly fluid state. If Josiah wanted to reestablish some sort of religious, not to say political, unity with the North, it would be useful to create a unified, capital-T Torah, one that preserved elements of both.[23]

Examined closely, the story of this book's acceptance is some proof of its extra-Judean origin. For one thing, as we have seen, Josiah did not send the book to Jeremiah, his friend and the leading prophet of the era. Jeremiah had known pro-Babylonian leanings, so his judgment would have been politically suspect. But then, so would almost anyone else's. To guard against this, Josiah sent the book to one Huldah, a female prophet of presumably neutral politics—outside of royal females, we don't know how political ordinary women were at the time—and he sent it in the hands of a five-man delegation: two known pro-Babylonians, two known pro-Assyrians, and his own servant, Asaiah, to act as a sort of referee (2 Kings 22:11 ‖ 2 Chron. 34:20).[24]

Huldah pronounced it legal and binding, which must have pleased the king, and also sent back word that Josiah would "be gathered to your grave in peace" and not see the destruction that God would wreak "upon this place" (2 Kings 22:20 ‖ 2 Chron. 34:28). While it is true Jerusalem did not finally fall for another thirty-four years, Josiah died as a result of wounds taken in battle in 608 BCE, hardly what I would call being gathered to his fathers in peace (unless one can presume that, having achieved his aim in delaying the Egyptian army, he died at peace with himself).

Josiah died at Megiddo, the city guarding the most usable pass on the north-south road. (This place, called Armageddon in Greek, is where some Christians confidently expect the "last battle" between Good and Evil to be fought.) Josiah interposed himself and his army between an army out of Egypt on their way north to join their new-minted Assyrian allies.

Only fifty years after the Assyrian invasion of Egypt, the two long-time foes had become allies united by a common desire to head off Babylonian hegemony. Whatever Assyria thought of Egypt, the new policy was dictated by the fall of Asshur in 614 BCE and of Nineveh in 612 BCE, the latter event commemorated with approval by the prophet Nahum.

---

[23]Israel Finkelstein and Neil Silberman's theory, in *The Bible Unearthed* (New York: Free Press, 2001), is a lineal descendant of Wellhausen's.

[24]I owe thanks to Prof. Nahum Sarna (private communication) for analysis of the political composition of the deputation to Huldah.

Josiah's regime was pro-Babylonian. Therefore, despite the fact he had no quarrel with Egypt, as Pharaoh Neco points out in a one-on-one dialogue reported in Chronicles,[25] to stand aside would have been seen as an anti-Babylonian act. As we have seen many times in this study, real neutrality was never possible. If I may use Jesus' later words, "He who is not for me is against me." Josiah's was a futile gesture, but not an entirely useless one. The Egyptian force made short work of his army; however, they arrived too late to assist Assyria against Babylon.

Thus passed Josiah son of Amon, possibly the most capable king Judah would ever have, after a reign of thirty-two years. His friend Jeremiah composed a lament for him which, alas, is no longer extant (2 Chron. 35:25). We do, however, have the Book of Jeremiah with which to shed light on the last days of Judah.

---

[25]In the ancient world, inventing conversations between historical figures was a well-known literary device for establishing verisimilitude. It is our modern misfortune that, especially in regard to biblical tests, we so often assume that the speeches put in the mouths of the various figures are in fact their exact words. This suggests the continuing power of the written word.

Chapter 12

Jeremiah's Judah[1]

§1. Political and Family Background

In the half century or so before Jeremiah was born (about 648 BCE), Judah's situation had become precarious. Long gone was the "fleeting wisp of glory" that had been David's and Solomon's empire. The Northern Kingdom itself had been overrun (724–722 BCE) and then annexed by newly resurgent Assyria in 720 BCE. Judah barely escaped a similar fate in 701.

Assyria then carried its fight with Egypt onto Egyptian soil. Memphis came under Assyrian attack and then control in the first part of the century, and Thebes was sacked in 663 BCE. Though considerably weakened, Egypt was also interested in reasserting control over the Philistine lands. Caught again, as usual, between the hammer and anvil of two bigger powers, Judah had to fabricate an effective foreign policy, allying itself with one or the other.

A third foreign-policy option, earlier espoused by Isaiah, to avoid foreign entanglements, not trusting in "the broken reed that is Egypt," and trusting in the Lord instead, had not been heeded by Ahaz or his son Hezekiah, the kings to whom he gave this advice. Indeed, few Judeans of any sort would have accepted it. "Unilateral disarmament" when surrounded by adversaries seemed a surefire path to national destruction.

As an Assyrian vassal, Manasseh, king of Judah since 697 BCE, would have given any Assyrian army uncontested right of passage on its way south.

Jeremiah was born toward the end of Manasseh's reign, probably in Anatoth, a small village about three miles northeast of Jerusalem. (In modern 'Anata there is a modest grave said to be his.) He was the son of one Hilkiah, a priestly descendant of the disfranchised Northern priestly family of Abiathar. Recall that, though loyal to David through the Absalom revolt, Abiathar had the misfortune of backing the wrong candidate—Adonijah—to succeed David. When Solomon won the throne, he moved the potentially disloyal Abiathar family closer to Jerusalem, where he could keep an eye on them. Solomon's judicial execution of the Benjaminite Shimei for what we have characterized as no more than a parole violation shows how closely political enemies might be monitored. Yet, as we shall see, this history did not entirely dissuade Jeremiah and perhaps other members of his family from engaging in politics.

---

[1]Thanks to my wife, Mary, who responded to my complaint that there was nothing in English about Jeremiah by taking the next four years to write a novel about Jeremiah and his times.

§2. A Curse in Disguise?

If there can be such a thing as a curse in disguise, Judah's escape from the Assyrian invasion of 701 BCE might qualify. Jeremiah articulated what I have argued many Judeans doubtless felt, namely, that the fall of the North effectively demonstrated that the Judeans and not their Northern brethren were the real elect of God. He says of Judah, "You say, 'I have been acquitted; / Surely, His anger has turned away from me' " (2:35 NJPS).

The context of this remark, indeed of much of Jeremiah's early chapters, is a reflection on the fall of Samaria and Judah's survival. It would be easy to conclude that they themselves could do no wrong or, at worst, God would exonerate them from the wrong they did; in any case, "No evil will come upon us" (5:12 NRSV). Few people saw as clearly as did Jeremiah that this view was a recipe for disaster.

Paul Johnson calls Jeremiah "the first Jew," and Richard E. Friedman once claimed that it was Jeremiah who wrote the Bible.[2] These modern encomia may be a bit over the top; it is certain that in his own time and place Jeremiah was often, as Jesus observed of all prophets, "not without honor except in his own country." His fights with other prophets and with government officials no doubt contributed to this lack of appreciation. Jeremiah's many angry tirades and unpopular predictions have given us our word for such things: "jeremiad." In retrospect, however, Jeremiah appears to be the sanest of the three major prophets. His writing is clear, unlike Ezekiel's, and only his God-ordained celibacy represents exceptional behavior. Jeremiah once illustrated a prophecy by buying, wearing, burying, and then digging up a loincloth (13:1-11); by way of contrast, Isaiah illustrated a prophecy by going around naked (and barefoot) for three years.

At fifty-two chapters, the Book of Jeremiah contains the biggest assemblage of text that we can cautiously assign to a single author.[3] The book has a good deal to say about his life and circumstances. However, the Jeremiah material

---

[2]Richard Friedman, *Who Wrote the Bible?*, 2nd ed. (San Francisco: Harper Collins, 1997) 149 and elsewhere; Paul Johnson, *History of the Jews* (New York: Harper & Row, 1987) 76. The Babylonian Talmud (*Baba Bathra* 14b-15a) had already credited Jeremiah with the authorship of Kings.

[3]The LXX's Jeremiah has 100 words not found in so-called *textus receptus* (TR, the received [Hebrew] text), but lacks 2,708 words that are found there. Certainly not all of our present text is authentic Jeremiah—see Robert Wilson, *Prophecy and Society in Ancient Israel* (Philadelphia: Fortress, 1980) 231-35, and the scholars cited there—but I think a large proportion of it is. Alternatively, there may have been more than one version of Jeremiah in circulation.

does not seem to be in completely chronological order. I therefore feel free to use pieces as they seem to fit various times and situations.[4]

§3. The Ark of the Covenant

[People] shall no longer speak of the Ark of the Covenant. (Jeremiah 3:16 NJPS)

When Jeremiah was born, Judah was still ruled by Manasseh. During that king's fifty-five-year rule (697–642 BCE), he became a vassal of Assyria. This was no crime in itself; such strategems had been the cornerstone of much Israelite foreign policy from the time of Jehu. But Manasseh went so far as to ape Assyrian religious practice by reinstituting augury and divination (if, indeed, these had ever stopped), and countenanced the abhorrent practice of child sacrifice, starting with one or more of his own sons. This would have been enough in itself to merit the crushing doom that Jeremiah predicted for Manasseh in chapter 15:1-4, but it was not his only crime. In Jeremiah 3:16 we read:

> In those days . . . men shall no longer speak of the Ark of the Covenant of the LORD, nor shall it come to mind. They shall not mention it, *or miss it, or make another.* (NJPS, emphasis added)

I surmised in the previous chapter that Manasseh allowed himself or was forced to surrender the gold covering the Ark of the Covenant, and probably the Ark itself, to the Assyrians as tribute. I also argued that the government would have reason to suppress the fact of the Ark's loss, just as King Zedekiah suppressed the results of his meeting with Jeremiah in chapter 38. Admittedly, there is no direct evidence for this crime, but unless the above passage is wildly out of place, it can hardly be read as postexilic. That is, it cannot refer to events after 586 BCE.

Later Jewish tradition, written when it might have been safe to reveal the truth, offers me no support, but that is no surprise. There is a Jewish legend that Jeremiah himself spirited the Ark out of Jerusalem and buried it on the way to exile in Egypt. Today the rumor persists that the Ark resides in a small Christian church in Ethiopia. While unlikely, this speaks to a continuous popular desire, both Christian and Jewish, to deny that the Ark has gone out of physical existence.

When Manasseh died, old and full of evil years in 642 BCE, Jeremiah would have been about six years old (roughly the same age as Manasseh's grandson, Josiah). Manasseh was succeeded by the "son of old age" he sired at the age of

---

[4]Here I followed John Bright's *Jeremiah*, Anchor Bible 21 (Garden City NY: Doubleday, 1965) lv-lvii, who also does this rearranging.

forty-five, Amon. We don't think of forty-five as particularly old, but at forty-five Manasseh was twelve years older than any other Judean king had been on producing his heir. This lends additional credence to the charge that Manasseh practiced child sacrifice.

Amon, beginning his rule at age twenty-two, apparently had no qualms about continuing his father's religious and political policies. Jewish Aggadah, following Chronicles, labels him as even worse than his father, a characterization hard to credit to one whose reign lasted less than one twenty-fifth the time of his father's. In any case, Amon's actions were too much for certain Israelites and he was murdered after only two years of rule. We do not know who the assassins were; in Kings and Chronicles, they are identified only as "courtiers." I assume that they were at odds with the pro-Assyrian policies of Amon and Manasseh.

Now, several of Jeremiah's relatives have names identical with those of cult and court officers. If, like Jeremiah, they had pro-Babylonian positions, the death of Amon would have served them. This does not mean that any of them took part in the assassination, but such a scenario might explain why Josiah was so close to Jeremiah.

(Amon's killers were themselves killed by *'amei ha-'aretz*, "people of the land." The usual English translation of the term masks the fact that these were people of substance, not merely a popular mob, as the term had come to mean by Jesus' time.)

§4. The Boy King

Josiah, son of Amon, was only eight, then, when he was propelled onto the throne. Jewish tradition treats him as arguably the best king in Israel since David. At first the kingdom's governance must have been in the hands of regents or elders, because Chronicles reports that Josiah "began to seek the God of David his father" when he was sixteen: that would have been right after the birth of his first son. One hopes he was a better father than David had been. On the evidence of their actions as adults, however, one suspects that the mothers had more influence in shaping the characters of the royal heirs.

> Obviously, by fifteen he had at least one wife. She bore the first son—
> who, however, would be his father's second successor. Two years later
> he had the son who would become his immediate successor, by another
> wife. The Bible knows only these two wives, Hamutal and Zebidah,
> about whom it says very little, so we can only wonder what the
> relations between these women and their families were as the "hope"
> of one was displaced by the scion of the other (see §3).

The religious reforms for which Josiah is so admired were not undertaken until some four years later, that is around 627 BCE. The timing is not accidental;

it coincides with the latter days of Asshurbanipal when Assyria began to experience internal dissension. We have seen that Josiah first purged Judah of all the idolatries that could be found, going so far as to burn the bones of idolatrous priests on their altars, defiling both. Then he moved North and did similar things "in the towns of Manasseh, Ephraim, and Simeon, and as far as Naphtali" (2 Chron. 34:6 NRSV).

In this he was supported by Jeremiah. Although Jeremiah was the descendant of Northerners, he nevertheless upheld the exclusive Yahwism now at home in the South. Unlike Amos, he excoriated the use of Ba'al in Israelite worship and practice (2:9). His urging of Ephraim to "come back," especially in terms such as chapter 31:18's characterization of Ephraim as being "like an untrained [or untrainable?] calf," is particularly audacious, since the persistence of bovine elements in worship was what the South most held against the North.[5]

If Josiah's government disliked Assyria—for whatever reasons—it would have been natural for them to turn to Egypt for support. But Egypt still had not recovered from Assyrian depredations. It was shortly after this that a new contender for Near Eastern hegemony loomed, Babylon. Almost at the same time that Urartu in the north ceased to be a contender for world power, the southern part of Mesopotamia, Babylon, developed independent power under Nabopolassar (627–605 BCE). It was just about this time, too, (627 BCE) that Jeremiah's voice was first heard in public. Already in 2:16 and v. 36, assuming that it represents an early utterance, he inveighs against Egypt and Assyria.

So strong was the southern threat that Assyria ultimately made common cause with its longtime enemy, Egypt, against the Babylonians and their Eastern allies. We don't know exactly when Josiah adopted a pro-Babylonian policy, but he did so. Jeremiah, who was a close confidant of Josiah, adhered to a pro-Babylonian policy in adult life. As the descendant of Northerners, Jeremiah would have been schooled to seek an ally on the other side of Israel's main antagonist. Jeremiah's pro-Babylonian position, therefore, is no surprise.

What is surprising is that his political position was so well known that when the "Book of the Law" was found in 622 BCE, it was sent for evaluation, as we have seen, to Huldah (whose husband had the same name as a cousin of Jeremiah).

---

[5]One of the names found on the Samaritan Ostraca is 'Egelyau (Thomas, *DOTT*, 206). This pairs the word "calf" with a theophoric element that indicates Jeremiah's own God, YHVH.

§5. Responding to God's Call

"You seduced me, Yahweh, and I let you. . . . "

(Jeremiah 20:7a, John Bright's translation)

Like all prophets from Moses to Jonah, Jeremiah initially tried to evade the call. He may have known, probably did know, of Amos's exile to the South a century before. The extradition from Egypt and murder of the prophet Uriah by Jehoiakim had not yet taken place, but, as we saw, "doom prophets" could expect such a fate. At the least, a person who felt constrained to a lifetime of relaying divine rebukes could hardly expect to have a pleasant time of it.

In 1:6 Jeremiah therefore declines the call, saying, "For I am still a boy [*na'ar*]" (NJPS). Like most Hebrew nouns, *na'ar* has a wide range of application, but its modal distribution in Scripture puts him in the age range that we would call "teenager," at least someone under the age of military service at twenty. Thus we come again to the idea that Jeremiah and Josiah were born close together, perhaps in the same year. If so, it is noteworthy that the king was a father by the time he was fifteen, while Jeremiah, before his call at age twenty, was still unmarried and would remain so (Jer. 16:2).

Jeremiah 16:5 contains the injunction that Jeremiah not enter a *bēt-marzeach*, routinely but incorrectly translated as "house of mourning" (NJPS and NRSV; cf. [also incorrect] NJPS note: "*lit. religious gathering*"). Only recently have we come to recognize that these were not simple community organizations that any Jew in good standing could enter, like a modern-day synagogue or community center, but exclusive gatherings of the well-to-do.[6] True, one of their functions *was* to ensure proper burial of the dead because this is the foremost obligation of any Jewish community. But for the most part they were dedicated to the pursuit of pleasure, as their description in Amos 6:1-8 (and possibly verses 9 and 10 as well) makes clear. Recent discoveries indicate that such organizations were widespread, known from Ugarit to Palmyra and from the fourteenth to the third centuries.

That Jeremiah is forbidden to enter a *bet-marzeach* indicates that prior to his call he had sufficient standing to belong to a *marzeah*, which I earlier identified as a combination "country club and burial society." The family was not poor. When called upon to redeem a piece of family property, Jeremiah had the wherewithal to do so, indicating sufficient wealth to pay *marzeah* dues as well. But as a member of a priestly family with Northern roots, he would not have automatic entree there, I think, unless members of his family were active in

---

[6]See above, chap. 10, n. 18 and Stanley N. Rosenbaum, *Amos* (Macon GA: Mercer University Press, 1990) 64-67.

Judah's religious and political life. Once he began to prophesy doom he would have made himself, like Amos, a traitor to his class, and so unwelcome in the club. In 20:10 NJPS has him saying, "All my [supposed] friends / Are waiting for me to stumble," but I think "erstwhile friends" would be closer the mark. Jeremiah's initial reaction to God's call stemmed in part from his realization that answering it would inevitably forfeit his social standing.

History is replete with examples of such dedicated men and women, from the Buddha to St. Augustine and Teresa of Avila to Albert Schweitzer, all of whom voluntarily gave up privileged positions, but they were not also social critics. In our time, I think Ralph Nader comes closest to Jeremiah.

Whatever the case may be, we have seen that when Josiah's men produced that famous "Book of the Law" from their Temple restoration project in 622 BCE, it could not be sent to Jeremiah for evaluation. At the same time that the Assyrian empire under Asshurbanipal died of indigestion, having gobbled up more territory than it could successfully assimilate, Jeremiah had established a reputation as pro-Babylonian. As he became more and more convinced that Babylon was unstoppable, so his "reading" of the Book of the Law would be politically suspect, and if what had been found was Northern *torah*, religiously suspect as well.

In mentioning Jeremiah's personal politics I am asking the reader to look behind the two-dimensional figure of "prophet" that our religious education usually saddles us with. Some prophets, the benei nebi'im, *seem to have been little more than court-supported sycophants whose job it was to tell the king what he wanted to hear. At least this is the picture we get from the story of Ahab and Jehoshaphat's "consultations" with court prophets, as opposed to the "free prophet" Micaiah ben Imlah before the disastrous battle of Qarqar (853 BCE).*

Jeremiah had similar struggles with men—both in Jerusalem and later during the Exile—who are called prophets and who seem to be court-supported or, in some cases, self-appointed.

Jeremiah's public career had begun around the thirteenth year of Josiah's reign and just about the same time that Asshurbanipal died. Two of that king's sons contested the Assyrian succession in 626 BCE. The unsuccessful one, Sin-shar-ishkun, established his own kingdom in Babylon, the southern part of Mesopotamia. He was soon ousted by a Chaldean general, Nabopolassar, but in turn ousted his own brother Asshur-etil-ilani and took over Assyria. Still Babylonian power grew. In 614 BCE the city of Asshur itself fell, and in 612 Nineveh, the Assyrian capital, was destroyed in only three months, forcing the

Assyrians to flee north and west. The prophet Nahum's book rejoices at Nineveh's fall, but at the time probably few knew how portentous this change in the balance of power would be for Judah's future.

§6. Grandpa Josiah and the Mrs. Josiah

The "big news" in Judah had happened in 615 BCE when Josiah's firstborn son himself became a father. At this point we might wish briefly to return to the subject of the influence of women in government and religion that we looked at in chapter 8 and consider what effect, if any, the families of the queens had in Judah's political life.

The Bible usually attributes no direct policy influence to queens, but there are a number of interesting exceptions. One is Athaliah who, though Northern born, ruled Judah for six years, 841–835 BCE. The only other reigning queen is Salome Alexandra, wife of Alexander Janaeus, who ruled Judah after the death of her husband, from 76 to 67 BCE. These two represent isolated exceptions to the norm, but if there could be queens who ruled in their own name, we suspect that even "ordinary" king's wives, the favorites in any case, could and did wield some power, as did Bathsheba and Jezebel.

Jeremiah 13:18 yokes the king with the queen mother, saying:

Say to the king and the queen mother,
"Sit in a lowly spot;
For your diadems are abased,
Your glorious crowns" (NJPS).

In the case of Josiah's wives—Hamutal and Zebidah, both of whom became queen mothers—the only further information Scripture gives is their fathers' names and the towns they came from—standard information but not to be lightly passed over for all that. Esarhaddon of Babylon, who came to the throne in 680 BCE—after two elder brothers killed their father, Sennacherib, and were themselves killed—prevailed despite the objections of high government officials; he was no doubt aided by the powerful family of his mother.

Susan Ackerman notes that of nineteen named queen mothers, seventeen are Judean.[7] The power of the queen mother, I think, derived from the fact that she was the acme of successful fertility; she had pulled off a coveted "triple play" by having a child, a son, a king. (If Jesus' mother still occupies an exalted position among Roman Catholics, how much more so the mothers of Judean kings of 2,500 years ago?) It is also worthy of note that so many Judean kings

---

[7]Susan Ackerman, "The Queen Mother and the Cult in Ancient Israel," *Journal of Biblical Literature* 112/3 (1993): 398-99.

followed policies that differed from, in some cases reversed, those of their predecessors. Whoever was influencing them, it was evidently not their fathers exclusively.

Despite Isaiah's and Jeremiah's trenchant, often sarcastic criticisms,[8] Israelite women had never stopped baking crescent-, that is to say, moon-shaped cakes to Ishtar/Astarte/Anath, the Queen of Heaven. Later historical books may have blamed Israel/Judah's neighbors for introducing, if not actually imposing, these practices on Israel, but the prophets knew better. And so should we.

In one form or another, goddess worship has been with us for 30,000 years (see chapter 4). The prophets could not have known that, of course, but of all the "foreign" objects of worship— Sun, Moon, Venus, Bull, Lion, and Serpent—the Great Goddess is probably the oldest and most widely venerated. Her artifacts abound throughout the region.

One piece not in Marija Gimbutas's *Language of the Goddess* is a mold for making female goddess statues that was found in Mesopotamia dating from 1800 BCE. In other words, worship was not only religion, it was also commerce, business. One is reminded of the *midrash* that identifies Abraham's father as proprietor of an "idol shop."

> *In Jerusalem today, two churches claim to have the head of John the Baptist. My former college town of Carlisle, Pennsylvania is one of three places claiming to have the remains of "Molly Pitcher" of Revolutionary War fame, a major tourist attraction. Similarly, the post-Vatican II Catholic Church was slow to inform the town of Mugnano near Naples that their local saint, Philomena, had been struck off the rolls because the town derived so much revenue from her shrine. Religion is, willy-nilly, a business.*

Here I would like to introduce "Rosenbaum's Axiom," namely, Prohibition Presupposes Previous Practice. In other words, the prophets' very criticisms demonstrate that worship of astral or other deities persisted down to the fall of Jerusalem, that is, at least seven hundred years after Moses' time. In discussing Israelite prophecy, then, what we are dealing with is not simply an attempt to purge Israel of "foreign" influences; it also reflects a long, ongoing paradigm shift away from the Great Goddess and toward God the Father.

---

[8]Jon Levenson, "Is There a Counterpart in the Hebrew Bible to New Testament Anti-Semitism?" *Journal of Ecumenical Studies* 22 (1985): 242-60.

§7. On Backing the Wrong Horse

"You're either part of the solution or you're part of the problem."
—[Leroy] Eldridge Cleaver (speech, San Francisco, 1968)

Nahum's rejoicing over Nineveh's fall shows that there were some in Israel whose hatred for Assyria needed to be written down. Southerners would have reason to blame Assyria for something far worse, or so they might have said, than the mere destruction of their kingdom, namely, the importation of foreign and idolatrous religious practices. Already in the time of Tiglath-pileser III, King Ahaz ordered Uriah to build an "Aramean altar" patterned after one he had seen in Damascus (a tall, tower-like edifice rather than the familiar four-horned stone table familiar in the region) to replace the "bronze altar." The bronze altar he reserved "for me to inquire by" (divination?) (2 Kings 16:10-16). In the eyes of some, no doubt, anything would be too much. If, however, Nahum was not merely anti-Assyrian but pro-Egyptian, he would not have liked what happened next.

Egypt could see that only an alliance with Assyria, its recent enemy, had any chance of stopping the Babylonians. Jeremiah criticizes Judah for alliances with both Egypt and Assyria (2:16-18), but we don't know where this criticism is aimed. It could be the usual political/prophetic advice to "avoid foreign entanglements," but politics is inseparable from religion and the free prophets, the "party of God," could not countenance mixing Yahwism with anything else.

It may be that Josiah saw in Babylonian hegemony hope for a respite from Assyrian pressure. If he had been careful not to anger Egypt, he now saw a chance to escape both. Backing Babylon, however, cost Josiah his life. He was killed in 608 BCE, under circumstances described in chapter 11.

His body was brought down by chariot from Megiddo, where the battle took place, and buried in Jerusalem, showing again how important it was to have proper burial. (By way of contrast, Asshurbanipal had pointedly refused burial for the body of one Nabu-bel-shumati—sent to him preserved in salt for just that purpose—who had committed suicide rather than allow himself to be sent alive to Assyria.[9])

I have mentioned that the Bible reports Jeremiah as having composed a lament for Josiah that 2 Chronicles 35:25 says "is sung to this day" (that is, in the exilic period). If Josiah's death was a national disaster for Judah, it was also a personal tragedy for Jeremiah. Four successors, offspring, or descendants of Josiah by both of his wives followed each other in quick succession as Judah became a political football.

---

[9]Saggs, *The Greatness That Was Babylon*, 141.

Jehoahaz (Shallum—his personal name—in Jeremiah and Chronicles), Josiah's son by his wife Hamutal, daughter of Jeremiah of Libnah, succeeded his father, put on the throne by "the people," by which we should again understand people of substance. He continued his father's foreign policy, hardly a matter that would have been decided by popular vote. But the king—not young by then-current standards; he was twenty-three when he began to rule—held the throne for only for three months before being deposed by Egypt and replaced by his older half-brother, Eliakim, age twenty-five.

When Jehoahaz was deposed, however, Jeremiah lost his standing at court. He almost lost his life as well. As his book reports, Jeremiah immediately fell afoul of the new regime.

Libnah, the hometown of Jehoahaz's mother, Queen Hamutal, is in Judah, south and west of Jerusalem. Rumah, the home of Queen Zebidah the mother of Eliakim, is in Israel, the North. By marrying women from both North and South Josiah had already signalled a desire to reunify the country in the manner of his illustrious great-grandfather, Hezekiah. Northerners could hope that "Northern blood" would one day sit upon the throne in Jerusalem, which is indeed what happened, albeit briefly. Northern families might also be expected to have a pro-Egyptian stance because the North's erstwhile ally, Assyria, had been the author of the kingdom's destruction.

Southerners, by contrast, would likely have a pro-Assyrian attitude because they had often needed a northern ally, Assyria or Aram/Damascus, behind Israel to keep Israel in check, and because Egypt's history of invading their country far predated Assyrian incursions. Solomon's father-in-law, Shishak of Egypt, had invaded almost before Solomon was cold in his grave. The recent Assyrian over-lordship, for all its bad religious effects, had done its job in protecting the country. As the Russian proverb has it, "Better the terror that you know than the terror that you do not know."

It may be, then, that policies of the kings who succeeded Josiah were in part informed by the families and regions their mothers came from. In any case, we may posit that with so many factions crowding Palestine's political stage, choosing one willing to rule as a catspaw—of whichever cat—was not difficult.

This first change in leadership dictated by a foreign power obviously meant that the new king had an acceptably pro-Egyptian policy, whether natural or coerced. His given name was Eliakim, but the name under which he ruled, Jehoiakim, was given him by Egypt, a sign of his dependence upon Pharaoh Neco, who had appointed him. Brother Jehoahaz was first imprisoned and then taken to Egypt, whence he could be brought back if the new king proved untrustworthy. Jehoahaz died in Egypt.

*Jeremiah 22:11-12 predicts Jehoahaz's demise, but we cannot be
certain whether these words were uttered before or after the event
because the circumstances of Jehoahaz's death are not given. If spoken
before the event, the words would be ill-received by the pro-Babylonian
faction; since Jeremiah himself shared that view, his words here have
an authentic ring.*

It was in Jehoiakim's fourth year, according to Jeremiah 36, that Jeremiah
hired Baruch ben Neriah, son of a prominent family, to act as his scribe and record the public remarks that Jeremiah had been making for the past quarter century. Whether or not the timing of this move was connected with the Babylonian
triumph at Carchemish I cannot tell. It is worth noting that Baruch's agreeing to
work for and with Jeremiah again indicates that the prophet's social standing was
based in part on his family background, not merely on what he said.

*The final text of Jeremiah is replete with Ephraimite speech forms that
must be Jeremiah's own, rather than his Southern scribe's, and contains
several references to Ephraim that point to a residual longing for his
ancestral homeland. Considering how long his family had been in the
South, this is remarkable. Then again, the South had become a political
maelstrom in which Jeremiah had very nearly drowned.*

In one of the Bible's more famous scenes, the new king listened to the scroll
being read and, as each passage was finished, cut it off and threw it in his fire.
For this, Jeremiah predicted that the king would be cut off, would have no one
to sit his throne after him—a prediction that wasn't exactly fulfilled, as we will
see.

Jeremiah's bearding the king in his own den almost led to his death; only
the protection of a powerful holdover from Josiah's regime, Ahikam ben
Shaphan, son of one of the five who had carried the Book of the Law to Huldah,
kept him from the fate urged by some of the new king's retainers. Later—though
this episode is reported in chapter 20—Jeremiah was flogged and briefly jailed
by one Passhur ben Immer, identified as a "priest who was chief officer of the
House of the LORD" (20:1 NJPS).

*It must be asked why powerful people went to bat for Jeremiah when
he was clearly out of favor. With our latter-day esteem for the prophet
we unconsciously assume that "right-thinking" people have a common
bond. The full answer, I think, is not only that they shared his religious
and political views, but that his family had held important government
and religious positions, giving him what modern Israelis call protectzia.*

Jehoiakim ruled for eleven years (608–597 BCE). Though he was an Egyptian appointee, the Bible reports that he served Nebuchadnezzar of Babylon for three years (2 Kings 24:1). This will have happened around 605–602, because in 605 the Babylonians succeeded in vanquishing their Egyptian-Assyrian rivals at the decisive battle of Carchemish on the Orontes. Second Kings 24:7 reports, "The king of Egypt did not venture out of his country again, for the king of Babylon had seized all the land that had belonged to the king of Egypt, from the Wadi of Egypt [el-Arish] to the River Euphrates" (NJPS).

We may infer that sometime after 602 BCE, Jehoiakim again dallied with Egypt.

§8. The Last Days of Judean Independence

If Nebuchadnezzar couldn't return to Jerusalem to corral his wayward vassal right away it was just as well; Judah had all it could do to defend itself against the usual local foes. But in 597 BCE Nebuchadnezzar did return and depose Jehoiakim in favor of Jehoiakim's son, Coniah, whom Nebuchadnezzar renamed Jehoiachin. Chronicles reports that Nebuchadnezzar fettered Jehoiakim to take him to Babylon as prisoner and hostage (2 Chron. 36:6 ‖ 1 Esdras 1:40), but we do not know whether the king actually arrived there. Kings, in fact, reports that Jehoiakim died (598 BCE) but does not say the succession was imposed by the Babylonians (2 Kings 24:6).

In the Book of Jeremiah there is a letter to the Jews who by then had already been exiled to Babylon, exhorting them in God's name, "But seek the welfare of the city where I have sent you into exile, and pray to the LORD on its behalf, for in its welfare you will find your welfare" (Jer. 29:7 NRSV), and promising that the exile would not last more than one human lifetime—a prediction that seems to have been uncannily accurate, as we shall see.

The new king's mother was one Nehushta, daughter of Elnathan of Jerusalem. It is curious that any woman should be given a name associated with the bronze serpent, Nehustan, that Hezekiah had destroyed. Susan Ackerman connects the name with Asherah worship.[10] That Nehushta's family was Southern indicates, as we have suggested, that they could be expected to have a pro-Babylonian or at least an anti-Egyptian bias. Whether or not this was so, Nehushta's son proved unsatisfactory to his overlords, and "at the turn of the year" Nebuchadnezzar came back, deposed the new king, and took him back to Babylon. This we know both from Jeremiah 52:31-34 ‖ 2 Kings 25:27-30 and from corroborating Babylonian records of the rations allotted to Jehoiachin and his family for the next thirty-seven years. Eighteen when he came to the throne,

---

[10]Ackerman, "The Queen Mother and the Cult in Ancient Israel," 399.

Jehoiachin had reigned only three months (2 Kings 24:8). Jeremiah's prediction to his father was that close to being a hundred percent accurate.

The Babylonians also helped themselves to the Temple treasuries, which were to prove a point of contention between Jeremiah and other "prophets" in Jerusalem.

Nebuchadnezzar's next choice was to go back to the other side of Josiah's family. He picked Mattaniah, a twenty-one-year-old son of Josiah by his Northern wife and hence half-uncle of deposed Jehoiachin. They gave him the throne name Zedekiah. He had been ten years old when his father was killed, old enough, perhaps, to have absorbed some of Josiah's political ideas. He seems to have remained loyal to Babylon through the first nine years of his reign despite the "prediction" of one Hananiah ben Azzur that the Babylonian rule would end two years after it had begun (Jer. 28:3).

Hananiah's prophecy, we now know,[11] was the result of what we would call "insider information." He was party to an international conspiracy that was planning for a general revolt against Babylonian rule to begin in 595 BCE, hence the unusual preciseness of his prediction. In the event, however, most of the plotting nations didn't rise and the Babylonians were able to deal easily with the few that did. (This shows the uncertainty attendant upon multistate coalitions against powerful empire nations.) This result kept Zedekiah in line, for a time. Eventually, however, he tried to evade his obligations by making overtures to Egypt.

When Nebuchadnezzar subsequently laid siege to Jerusalem, Zedekiah asked Jeremiah for guidance, hoping the prophet could intervene with God on his behalf, but Jeremiah prophesied nothing but doom and defeat. Because of this he was jailed for a long period and eventually put in a muddy pit to die. Royal officials had accused him of disheartening the population and Zedekiah, in effect, washed his hands of the obstinate prophet, saying, "He is in your hands; the king cannot oppose you [the officials] in anything" (Jer. 38:5 NJPS).

Nonetheless, Zedekiah allowed Jeremiah to be rescued and secretly spoke to him again, after Jeremiah exacted a promise that he not be killed or given over to his political enemies. His worry was legitimate, but Judah had not long to wait before its own political independence came literally to a crashing end. When Babylonian sappers undermined the walls of the lowest course of the city on its eastern side, not only the wall but the whole section of the city came cascading down the steep hillside.

When Judah was overrun in 587/6 BCE, Jeremiah "reported" for exile to Babylon. However, he was excused by the commanding army's general, Nebuzaradan (Jer. 39:11-14), because of the prophet's steadfast political support

---

[11]I owe this insight to Nahum Sarna, private communication.

of Babylon, support which by then had covered a period of about forty years. It is interesting to note that the Babylonians apparently knew who their friends in Judah were.

As a friend, Jeremiah was given the opportunity to come along as a sort of guest, or, if he remained in Judah, advised to seek the protection of Gedaliah the son of Ahikam the son of Shaphan, whom the Babylonians had enlisted to act as their agent in Judah. The Shaphan family had been adherents of Josiah and remained protectors of Jeremiah. Jeremiah stayed.

Gedaliah rallied all the pro-Babylonian elements, some of which had apparently scattered into the countryside to avoid fighting against Babylon. But by agreeing to govern on behalf of the Babylonians, he marked himself as a quisling in the eyes of Babylon's opponents, the pro-Assyrian and pro-Egyptian factions. Curiously, Jeremiah's is the only book we have that details the plot by one Ishma'el son of Nethaniah, aided by King Ba'alis of Ammon, to kill Gedaliah (Jer. 40:7–41:18).[12] Kings has only a few verses on the subject (2 Kings 25:23-26). Chronicles omits any mention of the plot, even though it carries the story of the Judean monarchy a further forty years. Warned of the plot, Gedaliah chose not to believe it and hence lost his life (Jer. 40:13-16).

§9. Jeremiah in Egypt

The assassins of Gedaliah fled to Egypt to escape the vengeance of the Babylonians and their supporters, but not before asking Jeremiah for a word from the Lord. They promised not to disobey it; that they asked him at all shows that his influence went beyond the pro-Babylonian faction. But when the word came down, some ten days later, they went back on their own words and took Jeremiah and Baruch with them to Egypt. Jeremiah's word had threatened that all who went to Egypt would die there, but the plotters concluded that this was a ploy to help the influential Baruch who, presumably, would be one logical choice of the Babylonians to govern and implement their policies in Judah.

Jeremiah himself died in Egypt (though one tradition places his end in Babylon), a relatively old and embittered man. In several places he curses the day he was born; he complains to God in chapter 20:7, "You enticed me, O LORD, and I was enticed" (NJPS, so also NRSV; RSV "deceived"; Bright's "seduced" is a better translation). Though he predicted the ultimate demise of Babylon and the return from Exile, Jeremiah did not live to see his words vindicated. Exiles were only allowed to return after 539 BCE. A second temple was begun in 520

---

[12]The historicity of Ba'alis is now confirmed by the finding of a seal. See Deutsch, "Seal of Ba'alis Surfaces," *Biblical Archaeology Review* 25/2 (March/April 1999): 46-49 and 66.

and dedicated in 515 BCE, dates that squarely bracket Jeremiah's seventy-year prediction. I trust he would have at least smiled to see it.

If Ginsberg is correct,[13] the words of the prophets as collected and augmented by their disciples led to the canonization of Scripture, first with the Torah—canonized within two generations of Jeremiah's death—and, a century later, the words of those prophets who were judged worthy.

Thus we come to the end of our metahistorical narrative. The need for a national history will have greatly increased after 539 BCE, with the return of the exiles from Babylon. If there was any chance that the disparate groups that constituted early Israel could again cohere, they would need a story that showed what their God intended. What remains to examine is how Jewish tradition put their Humpty Dumpty back together again.

---

[13]Harold Ginsberg, *The Israelian Heritage of Judaism* (New York: Jewish Theological Seminary, 1982) 97-99.

Chapter 13

The Way Back into the Ground of Jewish Metaphysics[1]

§1. Both This and That

"Only you have I cherished from all the nations of the earth."

(Amos 3:2, my translation)

We began this study with the question asked by Pontius Pilate, albeit in a rather different context, "What is truth?" (John 18:38). In some measure, religious truth is what later religious faith communities wish us to believe. Hence, Jewish tradition holds that Moses received the entire Talmud from the mouth of God even while writing down all of the Torah except the last eight verses of Deuteronomy, but this is clearly a partisan position. Even at that, by Jesus' time Jews could claim a history that reached back over 1,000 years—some would say 2,000. Thus, the religion's antiquity and even more the singularity[2] of its message stand at the center of the Jewish view of the universe, what I like to call Jewish metaphysics.

Classical metaphysics is that branch of philosophy that asks, What is Real? To ask this question, however, is to be brought to another question, because it assumes that there really is something we could call Absolute Reality. In fact, Reality, like Beauty, seems to reside in the eye—or other senses—of the beholder. Franz Rosenzweig's admonition, "It were folly to imagine that we have to pluck them [our eyes] out in order to see straight,"[3] is worth remembering, but it does not alter the fact that each of us, or each group of humans, has its own version of a reality that revolves around us. In other words, reality is largely if not completely subjective.

One Algonquian tribe that lived in Delaware and New Jersey before white settlers arrived called themselves *Lenape*, "genuine people." Some more-modern Americans, who ought to know better, have auto license

---

[1]The title of this chapter alludes to Martin Heidegger's essay, "The Way Back into the Ground of Metaphysics," in *Existentialism from Dostoyevsky to Sartre*, ed. and trans. Walter Kauffman (Cleveland: World, 1956) 206-21.

[2]Unless one holds that Judaism, and Christianity too, are derived from other cultures, as does Richard Gabriel, *The Memory of Egypt in Judaism and Christianity*, Contributions to the Study of Religion 67 (Westport CT: Greenwood Publishing Co., November 2001).

[3]See above, 15n.35.

plates that read "USA #1." These assertions are expressions of tribal or national chauvinism that are, however, far tamer than that of the character Nicolas Chauvin, for whom the word is coined. In Cogniard's play *La Cocarde tricolore*, Chauvin was an officer in Napoleon's army who was so patriotic that he voluntarily accompanied his emperor into exile. If mongrel nation-states or their nationals exhibit this kind of pride, this view of "reality," how much more so groups that were, or thought themselves to be, more closely tied by blood and language?

Like our United States, ancient Israel was its own "mixed multitude," a pluralistic society that brought unity out of its diversity, or tried to. By the time Israel created its biblical canon—or even "the Law and the Prophets" that Jesus knew—its people would have had plenty of reason to think of themselves as singled out, special, chosen by God to spread the "gospel" of monotheism. Orthodox Jewish and many modern Christian scholars argue that Israel was so isolated that its theological ideas remained unique. That evidence from the Bible's own language, as well as from archaeological discoveries, increasingly indicate that this was not so does not impress the faithful.

The proposition that Judaism represents a complete and clean break with previous cultures has been a staple of Judeo-Christian "reality" for more than two millennia. The influence on Israel of contemporary or preceding cultures was therefore seen as a contamination, a sinful backsliding or succumbing to temptation as in the case of sick, elderly Solomon giving in to his foreign wives.

Actually, even to speak of foreign cultures begs the question; it preserves the rather fictitious boundary between Israel and other groups. Many of the practices that the Bible deplores were originally legitimate expressions of its various constituent groups. Like Rumpelstiltskin spinning straw into gold, the Jews took over pagan pre-Israelite festivals and spun them into their own national history. This is not to say that contemporary foreign influences played no part.

Hellenism, the culture of art, architecture, athletics, drama, and—most dangerously—philosophy was brought east by Alexander the Great and his followers after their defeat of Persia in 333 BCE, but ideas from the Greek and Semitic worlds had been influencing each other for centuries before that time. (In fact, during the Bronze Age the major flow of influence was east to west.[4])

Greek culture was adopted on a grand scale. The Maccabees, intolerant and ruthless nationalists whom Rabbi Robert Gordis neverthe-less calls "the first freedom fighters," all carried Greek names even as they pried Israel from the Hellenized-Syrian ambit in the period from 168 to 164 BCE, setting the stage for the Temple's rededication that has metamorphosed into the modern Hanukkah.

The logic Judaism exhibits, however, is decidedly un-Greek, even anti-Greek. Axioms of Aristotelian logic such as "A is not not-A" would have been rejected by biblical Hebrew speakers and thinkers. Rabbi Akiba (second century CE) said, in response to the Greek conundrum/ question as to whether everything is determined or man has free will, "Everything is determined, but mankind has free will." Or we might cite the response of R. Nathan of Gimzo. Faced with two competing interpretations of a text he said, "Both this and that (*gam zu v'gam zu*) are the Words of the Living God." For this his colleagues punned on his name, Gimzo, calling him Nathan Gam Zu.

§2. "Who's on first?"   —Bud Abbott and Lou Costello

Two of the biggest problems in interpreting biblical texts are, (1) to deter-mine the age and extent of "foreign" influences, and (2) to decide whether to read the Bible in the form we have it as a single document emanating from the time of its final compositors, or to attempt to identify and hence understand individual texts as the product of particular times and places.

Various authors have claimed that the Bible essentially derives from Egyptian or Mesopotamian or Greek sources. Horace Kallen claims[5] that the Book of Job was a late composition and modeled on Greek tragedy. My feeling is that Job is a book with early, perhaps pre-Israelite roots, but was finally edited late enough that it may be read as an essay in epistemology.[6]

---

[4]This is the burden of Michael Astour's *Hellenosemitica* (Leiden: E. J. Brill, 1965).

[5]Horace Kallen, *The Book of Job as a Greek Tragedy* (New York: Hill and Wang, 1918).

[6]A careful study of the vocabulary in the semantic field we might call "Wisdom" in Job, especially the words *hokmah* ("wisdom"), *binah* ("understanding"), and *da'at* ([experiential] "knowledge") indicates that they are being used with philosophic precision.

We have noted that epistemology is that branch of classical meta-physics that asks: How do we know what we know? In the case of the Bible as a whole, we complicate things by reading the Bible's texts synchronically, that is, as though it were all written within a short space of time, by few authors or even by a single hand. It is true, of course, that the "final edition" does come, ultimately, from a single time, but that does not guarantee that all of its constituent parts do likewise.

Do we then read the Bible as though it emanated from a single time—say, that of the last people to edit it—or do we try to unravel across ten centuries (from around 1200 to around 160 BCE) the many strands that make up the whole? This is what scholars call the "synchron-ic-diachronic" problem. When I trained at Brandeis in the 1960s, I was taught that the text was written diachronically, but we read it synchron-ically. This simply will not do.

If we read Scripture synchronically, there is no filter to keep us from using the meanings that words have at one time and reading these mean-ings into either earlier or later texts. This word-study method has been a staple of scholarly writing for 1,000 years and it often produces sharp insights. The question is whether these insights are "biblical truth" or just midrash, commentary on the text with its own moral agenda.

To understand that agenda, we ought to pinpoint the period of the text's collection, but that, too, is not easy to do. There were as many as five occasions on which the text was reworked, and these reworkings were not like successive paintings of a house in which each layer remains separate and can be uncovered by a careful peeling away of what lies above it.

On the other hand, if we try to read diachronically, we have at all points to determine when a text was written and when it was available to the people who populate the Bible's stories. For example, could Elijah have used Numbers 15:15's "There shall be one law for you and for the resident stranger" (NJPS) as a basis for his universalist populism? It's hard to say. Worse, if we accept the Documentary Hypothesis, a text that is old enough to have been known at a certain time might not, probably

---

Poetic parallels among them produce the proposition that while humans have experiential knowledge, only God possesses wisdom. This is not the view of Proverbs, which again shows why citing texts chronologically makes more sense than citing verses across a range of books.

would not, be known universally, but only in the circles from which it came.

We need to note that the Documentary Hypothesis involves a lot of circular reasoning. It assumes that various groups within Israel were, at an early period, essentially monotheistic and had only one appellative for their God. Hence, the Elohists could not use the Tetragrammaton, and Yahwists would never use "Elohim." This does not begin to solve the problem of the many names for "god" found in Scripture. Was each of them, then, the province of one particular group? Did no one think also to refer to God by an aspect, such as Islam's "the Merciful and Compassionate," by an appellative, or even a euphemism like "the Name" or "the Place"? In fact, they did just that. Job alone has about thirty-six different epithets for God, and though this is clearly exceptional, there are many names that were in general use.

Israel's surviving religion, Judaism, represented a significant break from man's deeper religious past; in theory, if not always in practice, Israelites were monotheists. Their god, under whatever name, was the only genuine God and hence both controlled nature (never capitalized) and ordered history. No part of nature, no other god, and certainly no human ruler could be accorded the praise due to God alone. The Book of Daniel, though—or even because—it is a fictional work, makes this abundantly clear, as does later Jewish resistance to placing statues of the Roman emperor in the Temple precincts.

When pressed, intransigent Jewish monotheism moved them to armed revolt and/or suicide, singly or in groups, such as at Masada. This is not to say that Jews, even the majority of them, did not mix—the prophets would say adulterate—their monotheism with other practices. In its formative period Israel had adopted, adapted, or coopted earlier practices, old skins in which to pour their new wine. One thinks of Nehustan, the bronze serpent; Samson, the Hebrew Hercules; or the eight-point calendar later masked as two intersecting squares and called by some the Seal of Solomon (see below).

§3. A Star to Steer Her By.   —John Masefield ("Sea Fever" st. 1)
Israel is immune from planetary influences. (BT *Shabbat* 156a)

At many points, Jewish tradition gives evidence that other peoples' beliefs were still influential. The Talmudic phrase quoted above comes from a millennium or more after Moses. A thousand years after that,

Yalkut Shimoni artlessly asserted that the standards of Israel's twelve tribes corresponded with the zodiac's signs. *Shimoni* is a midrashic anthology variously dated between the thirteenth and fifteenth centuries CE. This makes it nearly contemporary with Nostradamus, the French/Jewish astrologer who remains popular even today.[7]

Why, so many centuries after the advent of monotheism, was there any need to deny "planetary influences"? We may infer that the biblical Israelites' diaspora descendants still felt the powerful pull of religious ideas generated in the slow millennia before Israel emerged as a people or a nation, and which continue to exert a pull even today.

Texts such as Psalm 148:5 and Genesis 1:16 inform us that Israel's God, alone, created the "great luminaries," the sun and the moon, to regulate "times and seasons." And then, in an audacious act of theological arrogance, the creation of stars—which Aristotle later said had originally been gods—is relegated to a dependent clause, a kind of cosmic throw-in. Why, then, did Israel need the Talmud's "booster shot"? From what was it being immunized?

Jewish tradition would like us to believe that monotheism is revealed, not the result of an evolutionary development, and that Israel's subsequent and persistent backsliding is obstinate, sinful disobedience, usually, if not always, brought about by its whoring after other people's gods. By the time the Bible was finally collected, there were, at least officially, no other gods. In service of this idea, texts such as Psalm 121 state that adherence to Israel's God offers protection from the sun and the moon, but this "insurance policy" implies that heavenly bodies have power from which we need protection.

Now to answer our earlier question: What was it Israel wanted immunization from? As we saw in chapter 7, section 39 of the Esarhaddon Vassal Treaty,[8] roughly contemporary with Jeremiah, implies that the moon can "clothe you in leprosy," apparently if you look too long at the full moon, or worship it, or if the moon is angry at you. Remember that Miriam was stricken with leprosy for her part in the Golden Calf episode.

---

[7]Some people think Nostradamus correctly predicted Hitler and some of Hitler's officers were so fond of a particular Hungarian astrologer that the Allies, knowing this, planted false suggestions in the astrologer's newspaper column. Much like Caesar's wife, Nancy Reagan, wife of the former American president, consulted an astrologer before advising her husband.

[8]*ANE* 2, *A New Anthology* (1975) 63.

Continuing the theological line of Genesis 1, Hebrew prophets such as Amos and some psalms,[9] too, attempt to reinforce God's superiority over the celestial bodies.

It follows from this discussion that the Talmud's claim of immunity for Israel scores a decisive "own goal." It tacitly admits that planets (and stars) worshipped by other peoples were regarded, even if not officially, as having efficacious power among Israelites and their descendants. This remained true well into modern times, as we saw in the tradition of forbidding marriages on Mondays because Monday is "governed" by the moon. Even today, some Jews regard Mondays as unlucky.[10]

Similarly, Orthodoxy encourages married Jews to have conjugal relations on the Sabbath. It's easy to see this as a way of honoring God, which it is, but Friday in the classical world is Vendredi, Venus Day, and Venus is the Goddess of Love. Here, then, it would seem that we have another example of a later tradition "covering" a much earlier practice.

This "covering" or co-opting of previous practices is especially evident in the Jewish liturgical calendar represented in the "compass rose" on the following page.

As we saw in chapter 4's excursus on numerology, the primacy of the numeral 8 is reflected in the major festivals of Passover/Matzoth, Succoth/Shemini Atzeret and the late, minor festival of Hanukkah. Each festival is eight days long. Eight days separate Rosh haShanah from Yom Kippur; circumcision takes place on a male baby's eighth day; and so does the investiture of priests. We noted in chapter 4 that eight days can be seen as a "week" with Sabbaths at each end, a "perfect" period.

To return to the Jewish use of this calendar, we see that at least one of the four cardinal points, the autumn equinox, is marked by a major holiday, Sukkot (see Exod. 34:22; Lev. 23:39). Of course, harvests don't fall exactly on solstitial or equinoctial dates, but we also note that the four sun "seasons" are each marked off at their midpoint by a (now) minor festival. Working backward from what we presently have, it is apparent that at some point, we divided each sun season in half as E. C.

---

[9]Psa. 19 seems to be a deliberate reworking of a sun hymn to show the sun's subordination to the creator. Created things are ipso facto not fit objects of worship. Psa. 93 demonstrates the subordination of the sea to its creator.

[10]There is a reflection of the Jewish aversion to Mondays in the lame Fraulein *Montag* of Franz Kafka's *The Trial*.

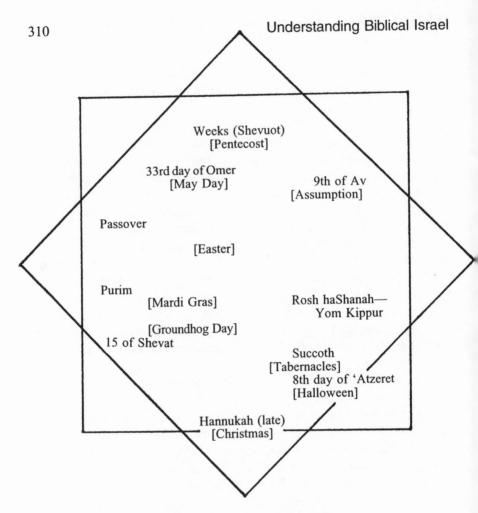

Cycle of Seasons and Festivals
(Christian festivals are in brackets)

Krupp says.[11] The question is, Why? I think the answer lies in an examination of each midpoint observance.

In Judaism, T"U b'Shevat, the fifteenth of the month of Shevat, which comes about midway between the winter solstice and the spring equinox, retains its original connection with nature. It really is "the new year of the trees," the date when the almond tree begins to blossom. Note

---

[11]See *In Search of Ancient Astronomies*, ed. Edwin C. Krupp (Garden City NY: Doubleday, 1977, 1978) 1-39.

here that Aaron's rod was of almond, and that this tree has a long pedigree in Jewish tradition.

T"U b'Shevat last fell on February 1 in 1999—a date celebrated in the United States as Groundhog Day. The emerging groundhog (in Europe it's a badger) is supposed to predict whether the following six weeks will have mild or harsh weather. No one notes, or needs to, that in any case we have reached the midpoint of winter.

L"g b'omer, the thirty-third day of counting of the Omer, falls near May Day, but its agricultural significance is "lost in the mists of Jewish history."[12] We have noted that it may mark the dawn rising of the constellation Pleiades, which happens near May Day and marks the time for spring planting in Europe. (For Celts, it was the holiday called Beltane.) L"g b'omer is now celebrated in Israel by the lighting of bonfires and shooting of arrows. The latter may be a survival of belomancy, which we discussed in chapter 4.

Jewish bonfire lighting may be related to the Roman Ceres festival in April, which involves setting fire to foxes—something Samson also did. It may also commemorate Josiah's digging up and burning the bones of idolatrous priests on their own altars. Interestingly, this day is the only time between Passover and Shavuot on which European Orthodox Jews may marry, but that could be a later Jewish response to the European avoidance of marriage during the "lusty month of May."

Fifteenth Av, the midpoint between summer solstice and autumn equinox, marks the midpoint of the dry season in the Near East. It is also the festival celebrating the descent of the god Tammuz into the under-world, from which he is resurrected, bringing green things back in his wake. The celebration is now "covered" in Judaism by Tisha b'Av, a date upon which Jews have placed the falls of both temples and the expulsion from Spain in 1492. In the Christian world, the feast of the Assumption of Mary (like Elijah and Enoch, Mary is held by Catholic dogma to have been bodily assumed into Heaven) was for centuries, and in some places is still, celebrated with special blessing of local produce or of the local means of deriving a livelihood, such as the fleet in fishing communities.

---

[12]According to Priscilla Fishman, *Minor and Modern Festivals* (Jerusalem: Keter, 1973) 24, the origins of *l"g b'omer* are "lost in the mists of early history." However, Hayyim Schauss, *Guide to Jewish Holy Days* (New York: Schocken, 1962) 94, thinks it derives from earlier pagan practices.

St. Swithin's Day, July 15, is another candidate for a mid-season agricultural/astronomical holiday: as with Groundhog Day, the date is thought a predictor of coming rain or drought.

The fourth mid-season date is October 31. Sukkot may come within two weeks of this date, but its importance is more easily seen in Christianity's All Hallow's Eve (Halloween), a "cover" of Celtic Samhain, the only day in the Celtic calendar upon which the souls of the previous year's dead could ascend into heaven.

As we know, later Judaism historicizes what were originally astral/agricultural events in service of a theology which, if it isn't entirely linear and teleological, might be seen as a kind of spiral through time (see below). Thus, Passover marks "the Exodus," Shavuot "the giving of the Law on Mt. Sinai," and Sukkot "the Wandering in the Wilderness." Accordingly, not all eight points on the cycle have their original pinpoint agricultural anchors, but all festivals are originally seasonal and cyclical, and the cycle itself represents a way of organizing and understanding the universe. Again, Jewish metaphysics.

§4. Coping with Exile

A. T. Olmstead wrote, "When Cyrus entered Babylon in 539 the world was old."[13] By that time, Israel was a distant memory and Judah in diaspora was in some danger of losing its national identity. How to preserve it? One important step in knitting the community together seems to have been the collection/canonization of five books—Genesis, Exodus, Leviticus, Numbers, and Deuteronomy—called *Torah*, "teaching," or *Humash*, "five," by Jews; the Pentateuch by Christians; and "a portable Fatherland" by the Jewish-German poet Heinrich Heine (more below).

Another element crucial to survival was the setting aside of the notion that history was and should be cyclical. For Jews, history was now essentially linear. Perhaps the figure of a spiral best describes it. The spiral describes circles that nonetheless keep moving forward. The Jews' own remarkable survival through centuries of buffeting by more powerful surrounding empires could have taught them no different.

A Jewish nadir was reached in 586 BCE with the destruction of the Temple, and again in 582 with the assassination of Gedaliah ben Ahikam

---

[13]A. T. Olmstead, *History of the Persian Empire* (Chicago: University of Chicago Press, 1948) 1.

ben Shaphan, but God's care for Israel was suddenly apparent in 539 BCE, when history turned again. Beginning from his base in Medea, King Cyrus took over Persia and overthrew the Babylonian Empire. Then, in an act of admirable political sagacity, Cyrus returned captured gods and peoples to their places. We have the following quote, in two copies, of the so-called Cyrus Cylinder:

> [Captive] gods . . . I returned to their places. . . . I gathered together all their inhabitants and restored (to them) their dwellings.[14]

The quotation by 2 Chronicles 36:23 of the edict doesn't match the surviving copies of the cylinder. Chronicles makes it appear as though Cyrus's decree was directed wholly and solely to the Jews. Consequently, Cyrus is remembered as a savior of Israel—his name is still given to Jewish male children, such as my teacher Cyrus H. Gordon. More to the point, Cyrus's name is found in (Second) Isaiah 45:1, a text the faithful confidently assign to a time 150 years before Cyrus's birth. If that were so, here was irrefutable proof of God's care for Israel.

A second Temple was begun in 520 BCE and rededicated in 515 BCE, almost exactly seventy years after the destruction of the first. Even if the Jeremiah passage predicting this event is after the fact (as is Isa. 45:1's naming of Cyrus), the Exile is a fact confirmed by archaeology,[15] and so is the return. At that, not all Judeans did return.

Ezra, who was sent back to Israel about 450 BCE, reports that only about 50,000 people repatriated (Ezra 2:64-65). Many exiles, most of whose grandparents had been born in Babylon, evidently stayed on. In this regard they were much like American Jews unwilling to leave the fleshpots of America for newly created Israel in 1948. Not all who returned were Judeans, either. Those who did return found themselves involved in a power struggle. Nehemiah's nemesis was Sanballat of Samaria (Neh. 2:10, 19; and Neh. chap. 4), and Ammonites such as the Tobiads of 'Iraq el-'Amir, all of whom vied for leadership.

Elements of the Judean people still hybridized in religion as they did in marriage. Ezra called upon the Jerusalemites to divorce their foreign wives and reports that most complied. A major reason for doing this was

---

[14]Thomas, *DOTT*, 93.

[15]Many Judean archeological sites show violent destruction levels ca. 600 and subsequent abandonment or at least no immediate reoccupation.

to reassert Judean primacy in Jerusalem over against Sanballat's northerners and the Tobiad family.

It is at about Ezra's time that most scholars put the canonization of the second part of Hebrew Scripture, called the Prophets.

> *As we have seen, H. L. Ginsberg argues that the rise of prophecy precedes the law and leads to the law being written down. Despite the prophets' chronological priority, then, it was the Torah that was the first part of Scripture to be canonized. It makes sense that the "Word of God" should be judged holier than the words of men, no matter how inspired.*
>
> *The North never ratified this section of Scripture, nor have their modern descendants, making marriage between Israelis and Samarians a "mixed marriage."*

"Prophets" includes Joshua, Judges, Samuel, and Kings; the three major prophets, Isaiah, Jeremiah, and Ezekiel; and the Twelve minor prophets, of whom Daniel is emphatically not one.[16] Much of this material, like Daniel, announces itself as coming from preexilic times, but there is no way of neatly dividing it into two piles, "before" and "after" the Exile, because books were liable to revision until declared holy.

Since it is beyond dispute that none of Hebrew Scripture was considered "holy" until after 586, we may posit that the main purposes of canonization were these: (1) to rationalize the destruction of the Temple; (2) to keep the Jewish people, or most of them, together; and (3) to establish what segment of that people would exercise authority in the absence of kings and priests.

Remember, the Israelites were originally a conglomeration of families, fathers' houses, or clans from differing places and with differing backgrounds—a ragtag of marginal individuals and social groups, many of which were resistant to the idea of any central authority. Nonetheless, as we saw in chapter 5, authentic traditions carried by the various family or clan elements include accounts that were already present in premonarchic Judaism.[17]

---

[16]For Jews, Daniel is not among the prophets largely because his book was written in the wake of Israel's successful overthrow of Syrian overlordship in the Hasmonean War of 168–164 BCE, far too late for official inclusion in the second part of TaNaKh.

[17]Albrecht Alt, *Essays on Old Testament History and Religion*, trans. R. A. Wilson (Repr.: Garden City NY: Doubleday, 1967; 1966) 173-221.

Scholarly arguments about who wrote what and when are not futile, though: like the Battle of Lookout Mountain in our Civil War, they take place "above the clouds" and so are largely inaccessible to ordinary readers. The problem we are addressing by asking whether this or that book or piece of a book was written in the eighth century or the third is this: to what situation was the writer responding and how did this writing effect his/her purpose?

§5. A Pearl of Great Price

> "Do not think that I have come to abolish the Law or the Prophets."
> —Jesus (Matt. 5:17 NRSV)

It is true that some parts of Scripture predate Cyrus's conquest by about seven hundred years. Scholars identify a number of premonarchic pieces that probably come from the times they describe, including Genesis 49, the Blessing of Jacob; Exodus 15, the Song of Moses; Numbers 21–24, Bilaam; Judges 5, the Song of Deborah; and Deuteronomy 33, Moses' Farewell; as well as some psalms. But since Israel's history was continually added to, subtracted from, edited, and rewritten over several centuries, the biblical record has somewhat the look of an onion—or a pearl (see below).

As we have just seen, mere antiquity was not the determinative principle underlying creation of the canon. Moreover, the Judean survivors of the First Temple's destruction might more easily have concluded that their god had deserted them, was weaker than the gods of Babylon, or simply did not exist. They needed a metaphysics, a view of ultimate reality that could defy—and survive—what their eyes and ears revealed.

I think the idea of monotheism had begun to develop among proto-Israelites a thousand years before Jerusalem fell. The idea of monotheism was generated, certainly helped along, by the explosion of Santorini (Thera); only a single, all-powerful God could deliver such a massive blow against Egypt and its many gods. Natural but rare events are taken as *simanei shamayim*, "signs from heaven" of divine intervention in human affairs—and not just by Jews.

Theologically, the innermost point of this pearl, the grain of sand that seems to have caused Jewish monotheistic theology to grow, is Deuteronomy 6:4's "Hear, O Israel, the LORD is our God, the LORD alone" (my translation). We don't know at what point in time this ringing principle swam into proto-Israelite ken, let alone how quickly it caught on. Credit for bringing it forward may be given to Josiah *if* the verse is part of the "Book of the Law" he promoted.

For all that, monotheism remains a counterintuitive proposition, and it made only slow progress. Eight hundred years later, in the mid-eighth and again in the mid-seventh centuries, Ahaz and Manasseh apparently reinstated the practice of child sacrifice—to gods of Judah's neighbors or its Assyrian overlords. Even on the eve of national disaster Jeremiah was still inveighing against Israel's continuing polytheism.

Still, like a pearl, the radical monotheism that constitutes the present core of Israel's theology grew. Job 2:10 says, "Shall we accept good of the Lord and shall we not also accept evil?" (author's translation). In a monotheistic world, everything that happens must necessarily be consonant in some way with the will of its creator. Bad things don't happen to good people. If bad things happen, they are God's response to the evil that men, and specifically the Jews, have done.

Jews were admonished to be "a light unto the nations" (Isa. 42:6). God punished them, individually and collectively, when they "hid their light under a bushel (basket)," as Jesus later put it. Moral failure, I think, highlights Amos's first three visions (7:1-9). God could be expected to protect Israel from natural disasters and from foes mightier than they, but he would withdraw that protection from a society that was not internally upright. Because Israel—or specifically Judah, in the eyes of the Southerners—was the cherished family of God, he would hold them to strictest account.

> *Like all theologies, this one has the fault of its virtue. It compels Jews to find acceptable reasons for any tragedy up to and including the Holocaust. Thus, the recent rumination by R. Ovadiah Yosef, eighty-year-old head of the Sephardi Orthodox of Israel, that the 6,000,000 Jewish dead must have been the "reincarnations of sinners" is an outrageous but perfectly understandable attempt at making sense of what, to most of us, cannot be made sense of. Whatever one thinks of it, R. Yosef's statement is consistent with a metaphysics that puts Jews at the center of the universe.*

§6. To What End?

"For not we, but those who come after will make the legends of our time."
—Gandalf (in J. R. R. Tolkein, *Lord of the Rings*, 2:37)

The intent of the collectors of Scripture was not to produce a history in the modern sense, that is, a critical, chronological collection of "facts" presented in nonjudgmental fashion, but to proclaim the view of reality at which they had arrived. And not only did the first editors do this, so did their successors. It was the Bible's final collectors/editors who around 100 CE canonized the third part, the Writings, and made Chronicles the ringing, almost cinematographic, climax to their Scripture.

These Jews produced a rather different order of the books than either Catholics or Protestants use. Here are Ruth and Daniel, along with Psalms, Proverbs, Job, and the Song of Songs. According to Jewish and scholarly reckoning, Daniel is here and not "among the prophets" for the reason that the book bearing his name was not in existence at the time the prophetic corpus was canonized.

The "histories" of Chronicles, Ezra, and Nehemiah, thought to be written by one person, are the most important of the Writings. First Chronicles begins by taking the history of Israel back to Adam, and explains the division of the worlds' peoples into three major groups: Semites, Hamites, and Greeks. (There are no East Asians here because the Israelites didn't know any.) Along the way, it rehearses how related groups such as the Ishmaelites, offspring of Abram and Hagar (Midianites) or Edomites, offspring of Jacob's twin brother, Esau, came to be and what their relationship to mainline Israel is. Second Chronicles, with its ringing call to the exiles in Babylon that they were free to return, is how TaNaKh ends.

Chronicles is self-consciously devoted to the Aaronite priesthood and the Davidic line, whose stories it remembers in a very favorable light when compared, for example, to Kings. In Ezra 7:1 the author claims a direct line of fourteen generations all the way back to Aaron himself.

The New Testament goes him two better. Matthew 1 claims a 3x14 generation descent from Abraham to Jesus, and the genealogy in Luke 3, from Adam, is 77 generations. As we have noted, all of these are multiples of seven.

Together with Ezra and Nehemiah, these books determine who are members in good standing within the community of Israel and who are not. Notable amongst the latter are the Samarians, descendants of the Northern tribes whom the Southern survivors saw as too ethnically/ religiously mixed to qualify any longer as Jews. This disqualification also masks the Judean disinclination to share power with the remnant of the North or those from across the river (Ammonites) who had been exercising it in their absence.

Nor did the process stop there. Collection of the next two layers of interpretation, the Mishnah ("seconding") and the Gemara ("completion") which together form the Talmud ("what is taught") began well before the destruction, and became official in 200 CE and 475 CE, respectively.

Here tradition bifurcates: there are two Gemaras, one from Palestine and one from the newly emergent Jewish center in Babylon. (Already by Jesus' time the majority of Jews lived outside of Israel/Palestine.) In fact, it is the second of these that is normative, partly owing to its greater completeness. Since Jewish tradition holds that "what comes after cannot regulate what comes before," it retrojects this "oral torah" into Moses' time, an idea many modern Jews reject.

The schematic below (next page) is designed to point the way back into the ground of Jewish metaphysics.

Thus far the Jewish tradition. If you like, it's a pearl of great price whose luster still shines 2,500 years later. But this pearl is sometimes bought at the cost of a specious teleology. That is, it gives us a far-too-linear, not to say goal-seeking, impression of revelation that has too often led to premature messianic fervor.

Unlike cyclical history, which offers the comfort of endless repetition, linear history has a disturbing habit of going off the rails; hence, a "course correction" is needed. After 586 BCE, and especially after the last gasp of native Jewish hegemony in Israel, the inescapable conclusion was that God himself, in some form or another, would have to make the desired adjustment. No explicit reference to a Messiah as Jews and Christians presently understand the term is found in Torah. However, since 586 Judaism has seen seventeen false messiahs, not including Jesus or Karl Marx.

It should also be noted that this schematic is not intended to show the relative ages of its constituent layers, rather the time or period in which each layer was added to what preceded it. Much of the material in the

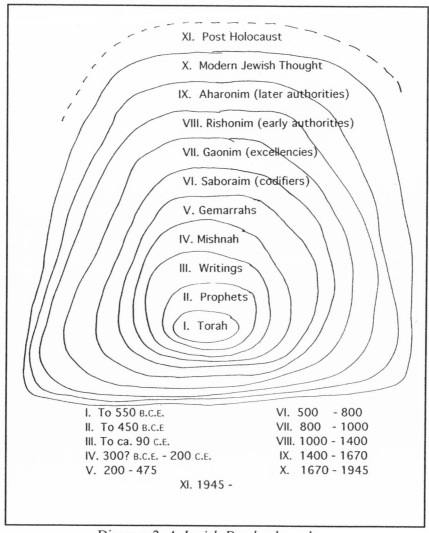

XI. Post Holocaust

X. Modern Jewish Thought

IX. Aharonim (later authorities)

VIII. Rishonim (early authorities)

VII. Gaonim (excellencies)

VI. Saboraim (codifiers)

V. Gemarrahs

IV. Mishnah

III. Writings

II. Prophets

I. Torah

I. To 550 B.C.E.	VI. 500 - 800
II. To 450 B.C.E	VII. 800 - 1000
III. To ca. 90 C.E.	VIII. 1000 - 1400
IV. 300? B.C.E. - 200 C.E.	IX. 1400 - 1670
V. 200 - 475	X. 1670 - 1945
	XI. 1945 -	

Diagram 2. *A Jewish Dendrochronology*

third section of the Hebrew Bible, the Writings, is older than much—or, in the case of Psalms, most—of the material in the Torah or the Prophets. For all that, prophetic activity likely preceded the writing of the Torah. It seems likely that the impetus toward the last collection was a reaction to the destruction of the Second Temple by the Romans in 70 CE.

Well before that destruction, various rabbis had been interpreting Scripture in order to derive norms for acceptable behavior, later collected as a series of positive (248) and negative (365) *mitzvoth* (commandments). It is from the first two sections of the canon, the "Law and the Prophets" that *halakhah*, literally "[the] path," walked by the believer, deviating neither to the right hand nor to the left, comes. Despite or perhaps because of this second and more devastating destruction, Jews clung more fervently to their belief that the path of proper behavior and hence salvation still lay open to them.

§7. Coping with Diaspora

Where was the sun? / Over the oak.
Where was the shadow? / Under the elm.
—Arthur Conan Doyle ("The Adventure of the Musgrave Ritual," 1893)

By Jesus' time, Jews seem successfully to have adjusted to a situation in which the majority of them lived outside of Palestine, in Babylon, Egypt, and throughout the Roman Empire. Even if Jerusalem remained the spiritual center of the universe, God was no longer geographically limited. In this Diaspora, Jews often adopted the native language in preference to a Hebrew which, more and more, became seen as a holy tongue and not suitable for everyday commerce.

The Jewish community of Alexandria produced a Greek translation of Scripture, the Septuagint (LXX), in the early third pre-Christian century. Some of the differences between the LXX and the Hebrew text indicate a desire on the part of the community to make Judaism accessible and more palatable to their Greek-speaking neighbors.

One of these Jews, Philo Judeaus of Alexandria (ca. 20 BCE to ca. 40 CE), observed that Scripture "speaks the language of men," that is, allegory. But Jewish interpreters continued, by and large, to read the text literally. This means that they often misunderstood the material they were passing along. Little wonder, since they were so far removed in time from some of it.

For example, the sun "standing still" in Joshua 10:12 was probably meant metaphorically, or referred to the occurrence of the visible full moon while the sun was still up, but Joshua 10:13, commenting upon the preceding verse, takes the event literally.[18] The besetting sin of much religious interpretation is that it takes figures of speech and, over time, sculpts them in stone, often distorting or losing the original meaning. The "Musgrave Ritual," in part quoted above, is a fictional example of how oral traditions may be passed down long after their meaning has been lost. The worship of the written word is just as pernicious. Just this sort of thing is brilliantly portrayed by Walter Miller in *A Canticle for Leibowitz*, a novel in which postnuclear-holocaust monks illustrate and venerate a radio wiring diagram whose function they no longer understand.

Halpren in *The First Historians* further suggests that poetry was our original everyday language.[19] If that is the case, the shift to prose might account for our failure to recognize metaphors. All of our theories, however, whirl in the void created by the lack of any hard evidence. We do not know who the alleged editors were and when they worked; there is no direct evidence for any of the presumed rabbinical conclaves. There are eighteen acknowledged scribal emendations or, with Saul Levin, even more.[20] In any event, we should remember that the final canonization of Scripture happened a good millennium after David.

Memories of events that happened centuries before would necessarily have faded and changed before being reduced to writing, and since Scripture was not initially understood as sacred by those who first recorded it, purposive or tendentious changes could be introduced: for example, the whitewashing "history" in Chronicles. Also during this time, the number of books and the contents of each would have been subject to change, both by natural erosion and purposive editorial change.[21]

---

[18]It was probably a reflection of the full moon appearing in a sky from which the sun had not departed. In his Ring trilogy, J. R. R. Tolkien, a Catholic, called this "Durin's Day"; his church linked it with the observance of the Feast of the Assumption. Statues of Mary standing between sun and moon, after the reference in Rev. 2:1, can often be seen in Catholic churches.

[19]Baruch Halpren, *The First Historians* (University Park PA: Pennsylvania State University Press, 1988) 76-99.

[20]Saul Levin, "An Unattested 'Scribal Correction' in Numbers 26:59," *Biblica* 71 (1990): 33, holds that eighteen is not meant to be exhaustive of all the changes/corrections that the rabbis felt could be made.

[21]As we have noted, there are nineteen or twenty lost books. Of those we have, Obadiah must once have been longer than its current twenty-one verses; otherwise, it is unlikely it would have been saved.

§8. Debates with [Biblical] Historians[22]

George Orwell gave such a convincing demonstration of conscious falsi-
fication of history in his novel *1984* that the work was banned in the
Soviet Union. However, to compare biblical accounts to Soviet ideological rewriting of history[23] is questionable. Soviet "historians" as well as
their audience would know such history to be false. Could Jews not read,
or did the written word have some magic power that put it above
questioning? Or did the editors think no one would notice the loose ends?
The answer, I submit, is that what we have is less a clever attempt to
conceal truth as it is bits and pieces arranged by people who themselves
didn't always fully or correctly understand what they had.

Modern scholarship divides into two camps, informally called minimalists and maximalists,[24] who as their names imply are either less or
more willing to accept historical truth in, if not the historical truth of,
Hebrew Scripture (more or less identical with the Christian "Old Testament"[25]). Both groups generally admit that there's likely to be some
accurate historical information in Scripture; the problem is, How do we
separate it from the other stuff? Next to the problem of "separating the
[biblical] wheat from the chaff," panning for gold seems like child's play.

Representing the minimalists, G. Garbini claims that all of Scripture
was written for partisan purposes during the Persian period (around 400
BCE), and so nothing in it that claims earlier authorship is reliable.[26] Leach
says what many moderns feel: that nothing in the Hebrew Bible must or
can be taken at face value, and if one attempts to choose which portions

---

[22]This of course alludes to Pieter Geyl, *Debates with Historians* (Groningen, Holland:
J. B. Wolters, 1955; London: B. T. Gatsford, 1955).

[23]Robert P. Carroll, "Madonna of Silences: Clio and the Bible," in *Can a "History
of Israel" Be Written?*, ed. Lester Grabbe, JSOTSup 245 (Sheffield UK: Sheffield
Academic Press, 1997) 96.

[24]Baruch Halpren's term (*The First Historians*, 27) is "negative fundamentalists."
With some justification, Carroll complains about this "name calling" ("Madonna of
Silences," 97n.28).

[25]In addition to the greater prominence given Daniel by Christians, Ruth is the eighth
book in the Christian order of Scripture, but it is in the third section of Jewish Bibles. The
Christian "Old Testament" ends with Malachi, dark with rumblings about God coming to
earth himself. The Jewish Bible ends with Cyrus's edict allowing Jews to return and
rebuild the land (2 Chron. 36:22-23).

[26]Giovanni Garbini, *History and Ideology in Ancient Israel* (London: SCM Press,
1988) chap. 1, pp. 1-25.

of the Bible to believe, one runs the risk of partisanship of another sort, namely, the partisanship of *a priori* theories or theologies.[27] Emerton criticizes Leach for imputing motive to scholars in general,[28] but partiality is an all-too-common feature of biblical histories, as indicated in our introduction.

Some modern scholars suggest that the final product also reflects the desire of those who wrote or edited it to make sure that no one came along to undo their work, for example, by making the priesthood a caste rather than a tribal prerogative, thus taking it away from the descendants of Moses, Miriam, and Aaron. This seems like a reasonable suggestion.

Documenting the internecine, and seemingly eternal, arguments among scholars could be greatly expanded, and so it is in the pages of the scholarly journals. Much of modern scholarship has devolved into a combination of chess game and trench warfare, with succeeding generations bringing back previously discarded theories or lobbing bombs at those who hold other positions. For scholars, the game need have no end, but for nonscholars, the burning question is: How should we read Scripture now?

§9. The Jewish Uncertainty Principle

> "Don't the great tales never end?"
>> —Sam Gamgee (J. R. R. Tolkien, *Lord of the Rings* III)

We must acknowledge that we are too often compelled to cite biblical "facts" without the sort of outside corroboration we would like. Further, we know that the texts comprising the Hebrew Bible span a period of roughly 1,000 years and that most underwent considerable editing. Also, the entire period of text collection falls well within what we term the "prescientific era." People living then would often assign direct, divine causes to natural events. Furthermore, the logic used by pre-Greek peoples contains fallacies that could invalidate their arguments. Typical are the fallacies of "what comes after must be caused by what came before" and that of "excluded middle term."

---

[27]E. R. Leach is quoted by John Rogerson in his essay "Anthropology and the Old Testament," in *The World of Ancient Israel*, ed. R. E. Clements (Cambridge UK/New York: Cambridge University Press, 1989) 19.

[28]John Emerton, review of Niels P. Lemche's *Ancient Israel*, in *Vetus Testamentum* (1990).

The Bible's account of the earth's creation cannot be taken at face value, despite some superficial similarities to modern scientific theories. Genesis's continuous landmass (*pangaea*) is paralleled by Wegener's hypothesis of continental drift, but the first eleven chapters of Genesis have an agenda that is far removed from geology. As we saw, Genesis 1–11 and 19 contain and reflect (a) the antiurban perspective of the authors; (b) an implicit denial of polytheism; and (c) accounts of how all human beings are related and various other etiologies. For the rest, as Halpren has masterfully shown,[29] we may be permitted to examine the text in search of recognizably historic elements. And, as we have seen, even such seemingly fanciful stories as that of the Flood may reflect such historical events as the disastrous incursion of the Mediterranean into the Black Sea basin that occurred around 5500 BCE, echoes of which are also found in the Gilgamesh Epic.

But there's more at stake here than can be gained or lost from arguing about which biblical stories can be scientifically supported. Wrangling about such things is really to see only the trees and neglect the forest. The people who collected Scripture had other things with which to occupy themselves.

Scripture's ancestral history attempts to establish divine warrant for the Israelite possession of the land of Canaan partly on the grounds that it somehow belonged to Abraham, and that anyway, evil done by the then-current inhabitants had forfeited their right to any of it. Both the ancestral history and the divine warrant were ways of finding "balance points"—like outriggers on a canoe—either in the mythical past or the infinitely receding future: in any event, outside the narrow, precarious present. That present, the time in which Scripture was collected, was one of Jewish powerlessness before foreign occupiers of their land.

That the Bible's collectors did such a miserable job of concealing their activities is some proof that concealment was not their purpose. If they were trying to fool people, why would they have left in the duplications and contradictions, and even the variant spellings, with which the text abounds? Many Christians defend the authenticity of the Gospels precisely because they are not all cut from the same piece of cloth; cannot the same argument be used here?

---

[29]Halpren, *The First Historians*, 25.

I consider biblical texts to be basically authentic if they can be categorized under any of the following heads.

- If they relate customs or names that could hardly have been known to collectors as many as 1,000 years later.
- If they ascribe to ancestors actions that later became illicit, such as marriage to a half-sister (Abram and Sarai), marriage to two sisters (Jacob and Elkanah), marriage to an aunt (Moses' father), or Abraham's mixing of meat and dairy foods.
- If they paint Israelites in a light that would elicit criticism from contemporary receptors, Jewish or Gentile—David's adultery, for example.

As the Talmud says, he who gives evidence against himself and does not retract is worth one hundred witnesses.

The Bible shows Israel as descending from a single family, favored by a single God, its religion exploding into history through divine revelation. The actual course of events as we may now understand them is considerably more complex and, I would argue, more beautiful even than the Bible's stories of it.

If we may extrapolate back from the practices of later, fully agricultural peoples such as the Romans and Celts to Iron Age Israelites and their predecessors, it appears likely that many practices found in Judaism are partly dependent upon, or have evolved from, those of Neolithic farmers. It may seem strange to suggest that Jewish History may be best approached by reference to the Heisenberg Uncertainty Principle.

In 1923, Werner Heisenberg proposed that electrons moved so fast that a photograph of them could only tell us where they had been, not where they were. The picture painted by Hebrew Scripture developed rather more slowly, and its subsequent elaborations were each painted on a piece of canvas that expanded with each successive layer, making it difficult to detect which are the earlier and which the later pieces. Though many questions remain partly unanswered, even unanswerable, what seems to have happened is this.

Toward the end of the Bronze Age, disparate elements, some Semitic, some not, but mostly what we would call "lower class," began to infiltrate the land of Canaan, amalgamate with certain then-present groups, and forge themselves into a nation. This nation crystallized around the then-recently-evolved proposition that the entire universe was created by and in the care of a single deity. Furthermore, this deity had particular concern for human beings, the crown of creation, and had endowed them with a "blueprint" or guide for ethical behavior that required all people to be treated with equanimity.

That the people so endowed did not always live up to their high ideals is admitted, but not particularly relevant. A more important consideration is whether these people themselves, because of their relatively low social status, the prevailing prescientific view of nature, and a lack of Greek-style formal logic managed to construct the religion we call Judaism, or whether it was begun like a fire in a forest struck by lightning. This is a question that cannot be conclusively answered. That this religion helped fuel the faiths of nearly half of the world's present population—more, if one accepts Thomas Cahill's suggestion that communism in its pure form is a "gift of the Jews"—can be variously interpreted.

So can the fact that Israel, alone, has seen the reconstitution of a national state after a hiatus of 1,800 years. But as Franz Rosenzweig observed well before modern Israel was created, "Every miracle can be explained—after the event. Not because the miracle is no miracle, but because explanation is explanation."[30]

To give Sam Gamgee's question an answer similar to the one he arrives at, the great tales are precisely those that do not end. Here at our place in a story that began more than 3,000 years ago, we can only marvel that whatever the truth of Israelite history, it still commands our attention.

> "Why, to think of it [remarked Sam Gamgee], we're in the same tale still! It's going on. Don't the great tales never end?"
>
> "No, they never end as tales," said Frodo. "But the people in them come, and go when their part's ended. Our part will end later—or sooner."

---

[30]Nahum Glatzer, *Franz Rosenzweig: His Life and Thought* (New York: Schocken, 1953) 290.

Bibliography

Ackerman, Susan. "The Queen Mother and the Cult in Ancient Israel." *Journal of Biblical Literature* 112/3 (1993): 398-99.

Aharoni, Yohanan. *The Land of the Bible, A Historical Geography.* London: Burns and Oates, 1967.

Ahlström, Gösta. *The History of Ancient Palestine.* Minneapolis: Fortress, 1993.

Albright, William Foxwell. "Abraham the Hebrew: A New Interpretation." *Bulletin of the American Schools of Oriental Research* 163 (1961): 36-54.

Alt, Albrecht. *Essays on Old Testament History and Religion.* Translated by R. A. Wilson. Repr.: Garden City NY: Doubleday, 1967; 1966. German original, 1964.

Alter, Robert. *The David Story.* New York: W. W. Norton, 1999.

Anati, Emanuel. *Palestine before the Hebrews.* New York: Alfred Knopf, 1962.

Armstrong, Karen. *A History of God.* New York: Ballantine, 1993.

Astour, Michael C. "Bene-Iamina et Jericho." *Semitica* 9 (1959): 5-20.

_____. "841 B.C.: The First Assyrian Invasion of Israel." *Journal of the American Oriental Society* 91/3 (1971): 383-89.

_____. *Hellenosemitica.* Leiden: E. J. Brill, 1965.

_____. "Overland Trade Routes in Ancient Western Asia." In Sasson et al., *Civilizations of the Ancient Near East* 3:1401-20.

Aveni, Anthony F. "Astronomy in Ancient Mesoamerica." In *In Search of Ancient Astronomies,* ed. Edwin C. Krupp (Garden City NY: Doubleday, 1977, 1978) 156-57.

Barr, James. *The Variable Spellings of the Hebrew Bible.* London: Oxford University Press, 1989.

Barstad, Hans. "History and the Hebrew Bible." In Grabbe, editor, *Can a "History of Israel" Be Written?*

_____. *The Religious Polemics of Amos.* Vetus Testamentum, Supplements 34. Leiden: E. J. Brill, 1984.

Ben-Sasson, Haim Hillel. *See* Abraham Malamat et al.

Bettelheim, Bruno. *Symbolic Wounds: Puberty Rites and the Envious Male.* Glencoe IL: Free Press, 1954.

Biran, Avraham. *Biblical Dan.* Jerusalem: Israel Exploration Society, 1994.

Blenkinsopp, Joseph. *A History of Prophecy in Israel.* Philadelphia: Westminster, 1983.

Bloom, Harold. *See* David Rosenberg.

Boadt, Lawrence. *Reading the Old Testament: An Introduction.* New York: Paulist Press, 1984.

Boman, Thorlief. *Hebrew Thought Compared with Greek.* Translated by Jules L. Moreau. New York: W. W. Norton; Philadelphia: Westminster, 1960.

Bonfante, Larissa. *Etruscan Life and Afterlife.* Detroit: Wayne State University Press, 1986.

Borges, Jorge. *Ficciones.* New York: Grove Press, 1962.

Botterweck, G. Johannes. "Zur Authentizität des Buches Amos." *Zeitschrift fur Alttestamentliche Wissenschaft* 70 (1958): 176-89.

Braudel, Fernand. "Histoire et science sociales: la longue durée." *Annales. Economies, Société, Civilisations* 13 (1958).

Bright, John. *A History of Israel*. Fourth edition. Philadelphia: Westminster, 2000.

_____. *Jeremiah*. Anchor Bible 21. Garden City NY: Doubleday, 1965.

Bronner, Leila Leah. *From Eve to Esther: Rabbinic Reconstruction of Biblical Women*. Louisville KY: Westminster, 1994.

Brown, Francis, Samuel R. Driver, and Charles A. Briggs. *A Hebrew and English Lexicon of the Old Testament*. Oxford: Clarendon, 1907; corr. repr. 1962.

Bruins, Hendrik J., and Johannes van der Plicht. "The Exodus Enigma." *Nature* 5/382 (18 July 1996): 213-14.

Bruteau, Beatrice, editor. *Jesus through Jewish Eyes*. Maryknoll NY: Orbis, 2001.

Buccellati, Giorgio. *Cities and Nations of Ancient Syria: An Essay on Political Institutions with Special Reference to the Israelite Kingdoms*. Studi Semitici 26. Rome: Instituto di Studi del Vicino Oriente, Università di Roma, 1967.

_____. "Ethics and Piety in the Ancient Near East." In Sasson et al., *Civilizations of the Ancient Near East* 3:1687-96.

Burke, James. *The Knowledge Web*. New York: Simon and Schuster 1999.

Butzer, Karl W. "Environmental Change in the Near East and Human Impact on the Land." In Sasson et al., *Civilizations of the Ancient Near East* 1:123-51.

Cahill, Jane. "It Is There: The Archaeological Evidence Proves It." *Biblical Archaeology Review* 24/4 (July/August 1998): 34-41, 63.

Cahill, Thomas. *Desire of the Everlasting Hills. The World Before and After Jesus*. New York: Nan A. Talese, 1999.

_____. *The Gifts of the Jews. How a Tribe of Desert Nomads Changed the Way Everyone Thinks and Feels*. New York: Nan A. Talese, 1998.

Cameron, Dorothy. *Symbols of Birth and Death in the Neolithic Era*. London: Kenyon-Deane, 1981.

Carroll, Robert P. "Madonna of Silences: Clio and the Bible." In Grabbe, editor, *Can a "History of Israel" Be Written?*

Cassuto, Umberto Moshe David. *The Documentary Hypothesis*. Jerusalem: Magnes, 1953; Hebrew orig., 1941.

Clements, Ronald Ernest, editor. *The World of Ancient Israel: Sociological, Anthropological, and Political Perspectives: Essays by Members of the Society for Old Testament Study*. Cambridge UK/New York: Cambridge University Press, 1989. Pp. xi+436.

Cogan, Morton [Mordecai]. *Imperialism and Religion: Assyria, Israel, and Judah in the 8th and 7th Centuries B.C.E.* SBLMS 19. Missoula MT: Scholars Press, 1974.

Cohen, Abraham, editor. *Joshua and Judges: Hebrew Text and English Translation with an Introduction and Commentary*. Socino Books of the Bible. London: Soncino Press, 1950. (Joshua commentary by H. Freedman; Judges, by J. J. Slotki.)

Cohen, Jacob Ben-Ezzi Shafik. *Who Are the Samaritans: Their Religion, Customs, and History*. Nablus: privately printed, 1968.

Coogan, Michael D., editor. *The Oxford History of the Biblical World*. London: Oxford University Press, 1998.

Coon, Carleton Stevens. *The Living Races of Man*. London: Jonathan Cape, 1966.

Cornfeld, Gaalyah. *Archaeology of the Bible Book by Book*. San Francisco: Harper & Row, 1976.

Curtis, A. H. W. "Some Observations on 'Bull' Terminology in the Ugaritic Texts and the Old Testament." *Old Testament Studies* 26 (1990).

Dalley, Stephanie. "Yahweh in Hamath in the 8th Century B.C." *Vetus Testamentum* 40/1 (1990): 21-32.

Daud, Abraham ibn. *Book of Tradition.* Translated by Gerson D. Cohen. Philadelphia: Jewish Publication Society, 1967.

Davis, John J. *Biblical Numerology.* Grand Rapids MI: Baker Book House, 1968.

Day, John. *Oxford Bible Atlas.* Third edition. New York: Oxford University Press, 1984.

_____, editor. *King and Messiah in Israel and the Ancient Near East.* Sheffield UK: Sheffield Academic Press, 1998.

Dechend, Hertha von, and Giorgio de Santillana. *Hamlet's Mill.* Boston: David R. Godine, 1977.

Deutsch, Robert. "Seal of Ba'alis Surfaces." *Biblical Archaeology Review* 25/2 (March/April 1999): 46-49, 66.

Dever, William. "Save Us from Post-Modern Malarkey." *Biblical Archaeology Review* 26/2 (March/April 2000): 28-35, 68-69.

Donaldson, Mara. "Kinship Theory in the Patriarchal Narratives: The Case of the Barren Wife." *Journal of the American Academy of Religion* 49/1 (1981): 77-87.

Doria, Charles, and Harris Lenowitz, editors. *Origins: Creation Texts from the Ancient Mediterranean: A Chrestomathy.* Garden City NY: Doubleday/Anchor; New York: AMS Press, 1976.

Driver, Godfrey Rolles. *Semitic Writing.* Schweich Lectures 44. London: Oxford University Press, 1948.

Edelman, Diana V., editor. *The Triumph of Elohim.* Grand Rapids MI: Eerdman's, 1995.

Emerton, John. Review of Niels P. Lemche, *Ancient Israel.* In *Vetus Testamentum* 40 (1990).

Feyerick, Ada, Cyrus H. Gordon, and Nahum M. Sarna. *Genesis, World of Myths and Patriarchs.* New York and London: New York University Press, 1996.

Finkelstein, Israel. *The Archaeology of the Israelite Settlement.* Jerusalem: Israel Exploration Society, 1988.

Finkelstein, Israel, and Neil Asher Silberman. *The Bible Unearthed.* New York: Free Press, 2001.

Finkelstein, J. J., and Moshe Greenberg, editors. *Oriental and Biblical Studies: Collected Writings of E. A. Speiser.* Philadelphia: University of Pennsylvania Press; Philadelphia: Jewish Publication Society, 1967.

Fishbane, Michael A., *Biblical Interpretation in Ancient Israel.* Oxford: Clarendon Press, 1986.

Fishman, Priscilla, *Minor and Modern Festivals.* Jerusalem: Keter, 1973.

Fokkelman, J. P. "Genesis" and "Exodus." In *The Literary Guide to the Bible.* Edited by Robert Alter and Frank Kermode. Cambridge MA: Harvard University Press, 1987.

Fowler, Alisdair. *Silent Poetry: Essays in Numerological Analysis.* London: Routledge & Kegan Paul; New York: Barnes & Noble, 1970.

Frankfort, Henri, *The Birth of Civilization in the Near East.* Garden City NY: Doubleday, 1956.

Frazer, James George. *The Golden Bough.* New York: Macmillan, 1951.

Freud, Sigmund. *The Future of an Illusion*. Garden City NY: Doubleday, 1964.
_____. *Interpretation of Dreams*. London: Oxford University Press, 1999 [1913].
_____. *Totem and Taboo*. New York: Vintage, 1918.
Frick, Frank. *The Formation of the State in Ancient Israel: A Survey of Models and Theories*. Social World of Biblical Antiquity series 4. Sheffield UK: Almond, 1985.
_____. *A Journey through the Hebrew Scriptures*. Fort Worth TX and New York: Harcourt Brace College Publishers, 1995.
Friedman, Richard Elliott. *The Disappearance of God*. Boston: Little, Brown, 1995.
_____. *Who Wrote the Bible?* Second edition. San Francisco: Harper Collins, 1997.
Frymer-Kensky, Tikvah. *In the Wake of the Goddesses*. New York: Free Press, 1992.
Gabriel, Richard A. *Gods of Our Fathers: The Memory of Egypt in Judaism and Christianity*. Contributions to the Study of Religion 67. Westport CT: Greenwood Publishing Group, November 2001.
Garbini, Giovanni. *History and Ideology in Ancient Israel*. London: SCM, 1988.
Gardiner, Alan. *Egyptian Grammar*. London: Oxford University Press, 1964.
Gaster, Theodor. *Thespis: Ritual, Myth, and Drama in the Ancient Near East*. Garden City NY: Doubleday, 1961
Gelb, Ignatz J. *A Study of Writing*. Second edition. Chicago: University of Chicago Press, 1963.
Gennep, Arnold van. *The Rites of Passage*. Translated by Monika B. Vizedom and Gabrielle L. Caffee. Introduction by Solon T. Kimball. Chicago: University of Chicago Press; London: Routledge & Paul, 1960.
Geus, C. H. J. de. *The Tribes of Israel: An Investigation into Some of the Presuppositions of Martin Noth's Amphictyony Hypothesis*. Assen: Van Gorcum, 1976.
Gibbons, Ann. "How the Akkadian Empire Was Hung Out to Dry." *Science* 5/261 (20 August 1993): 985.
Gill, Dan. "How They Met." *Biblical Archaeologist Reader* 20/4 (July/August 1994): 20-33.
Gimbutas, Marija Alseikaité. *The Language of the Goddess*. San Francisco: Harper Collins, 1989.
Ginsberg, Harold Louis. *The Israelian Heritage of Judaism*. New York: Jewish Theological Seminary, 1982.
Glatzer, Nahum. *Franz Rosenzweig: His Life and Thought*. New York: Schocken, 1953.
Gollaher, David. *Circumcision: A History of the World's Most Controversial Surgery*. New York: Basic Books, 2000.
Gordon, Cyrus H., and Gary A. Rendsburg. "The Consistency and Historical Reliability of the Biblical Genealogies." *Vetus Testamentum* 40/2 (1990): 185-206.
Gordon, Cyrus Herzl. *The Ancient Near East*. New York: W. W. Norton, 1965.
_____. *Before the Bible. The Common Background of Greek and Hebrew Civilizations*. New York: Harper & Row, 1962. Second edition: New York: W. W. Norton, 1965.
_____. *Ugarit and Minoan Crete*. New York: W. W. Norton, 1966.
_____. *Ugaritic Texts*. Acta Orientalia 38. Rome: Pontifical Biblical Institute, 1965.

Grabbe, Lester L., editor. *Can a 'History of Israel' Be Written?* Journal for the Study of the Old Testament—Supplement series 245. Sheffield: Sheffield Academic Press, 1997.

Grahn, Judy. *Blood, Bread, and Roses: How Menstruation Created the World.* Boston: Beacon, 1993.

Graves, Robert. *The Greek Myths.* Two volumes. Baltimore: Penguin Books, 1955.

————. *The White Goddess: A Historical Grammar of Poetic Myth.* Amended and enlarged edition. New York: Noonday Press, 1966; orig., 1948.

Greenfield, Jonas. "The MARZEAH as a Social Institution." In Joseph Harmatta, editor, *Wirtschaft und Gesellschaft in alten Vorderasien*, 451-55. Budapest: Akademiai Kiodo, 1974.

Guthrie, Stewart. *Faces in the Clouds.* New York: Oxford University Press, 1995.

Hallo, William W. "From Qarqar to Carchemish: Assyria and Israel in the Light of New Discoveries." *Biblical Archaeologist* 23/2 (May 1960): 33-61.

Hallo, William W., and J. J. A. van Dijk. *The Exaltation of Inanna.* New Haven CT: Yale, 1968.

Hallo, William W., and William K. Simpson. *The Ancient Near East: A History.* New York: Harcourt, Brace, Jovanovich, 1971.

Halpren, Baruch. "The Exodus from Egypt: Myth or Reality?" In Herschel Shanks, William G. Dever, Baruch Halpren, and P. Kyle Mcarter, Jr., *The Rise of Ancient Israel*, 86-98. Washington: Biblical Archaeology Society, 1992.

————. *The First Historians: The Hebrew Bible and History.* University Park PA: Pennsylvania State University Press, 1988.

Haran, Menahem. "The Disappearance of the Ark." *Israel Exploration Journal* 13 (1964): 46-58.

Hartner, Willy. "The Earliest History of the Constellations in the Near East and the Motif of the Lion-Bull Combat." *Journal of Near Eastern Studies* 24/1-2 (January-April 1965): 1-16.

Hawkins, Gerald. *Stonehenge Decoded.* New York: Dell, 1965.

Hayes, John Haralson. *See* James Maxwell Miller.

Heidegger, Martin. "The Way Back into the Ground of Metaphysics." In Walter Kauffman, editor and translator, *Existentialism from Dostoyevsky to Sartre*, 206-21. Cleveland: World (Meridian Books), 1961.

Herodotus. *The Histories.* Translated by Aubrey de Selincourt. Baltimore MD: Penguin, 1954.

Herrnstein, Richard, and Charles Murray. *The Bell Curve: Intelligence and Class Structure in American Life.* New York: Simon and Schuster, 1996.

Heschel, Abraham Joshua. *The Prophets.* New York: Harper, 1962.

Hillman, Ellis. "Why 42?" *Jabberwocky. The Journal of the Lewis Carroll Society* 22/2 (Spring 1993): 39-41.

Horner, Thomas. *Jonathan Loved David: Homosexuality in Biblical Times.* Philadelphia: Westminster, 1978.

Hort, Greta. "The Plagues of Egypt." *Zeitschrift fur Alttestamentliche Wissenschaft* 69 (1957): 84-103; and *ZAW* 70 (1958): 48-59.

Huehnergard, John. "Semitic Languages." In Sasson et al., *Civilizations of the Ancient Near East* 4:2117-34.

Hutchinson, Richard W. *Prehistoric Crete*. Harmondsworth UK: Penguin, 1962.

Isaacs, Ronald H. *The Jewish Book of Numbers*. Northvale NJ: Jason Aronson, 1993.

Jacobsen, Thorkild. "The Graven Image." In *Ancient Israelite Religion*. Edited by Patrick Miller, Paul Hanson, and S. Dean McBride. Philadelphia: Fortress Press, 1987. Pp. 15-32.

_____. *The Sumerian King List*. Chicago: University of Chicago Press, 1939.

_____. *The Treasures of Darkness*. New Haven CT: Yale University Press, 1976.

James, E. O. *Origins of Sacrifice*. Port Washington NY: Kennikat Press, 1971; orig. 1933.

Jaynes, Julian. *The Origin of Consciousness in the Breakdown of the Bicameral Mind*. Boston: Houghton Mifflin, 1976.

Jespersen, Otto. *Language: Its Nature, Development, and Origin*. New York: Norton, 1964.

Jirku, Anton. *The World of the Bible*. Translated by Ann E. Keep. World Ancient Cultures series. Cleveland: World Publishing Co., 1967.

Johnson, Paul. *History of the Jews*. New York: Harper & Row, 1987.

Joines, Karen Randolph. "The Bronze Serpent in the Israelite Cult." *Journal of Biblical Literature* 87 (1968): 245-50.

Kallen, Horace. *The Book of Job as a Greek Tragedy*. New York: Hill and Wang, 1918.

Kamrat, Mordecai, and Edwin Samuel. *Roots*. Jerusalem: Kiryat Sefer, 1969.

Kaufmann, Yehezkel. *The Religion of Israel: From Its Beginnings to the Babylonian Exile*. Chicago: University of Chicago Press, 1960.

Kean, Victor J. *The Disk from Phaistos*. Athens: Efstathiatis Group, 1985.

Keel, Othmar. *Feinde und Gottesleugner: Studien zum Image der Widersacher in den Individuelen Psalmen*. Stuttgarter Biblische Monographien 7. Stuttgart: Verlag Katholisches Bibelwerk, 1969.

Key, Andrew. "Traces of Worship of the Moon God Sîn among the Early Israelites." *Journal of Bibiblical Literature* 84 (1965): 20-26.

Kikawada, Isaac. *Before Abraham Was: The Unity of Genesis 1-11*. Nashville: Abingdon Press, 1985.

Kilmer, Ann D. "Music and Dance in Ancient Western Asia." In Sasson et al., *Civilizations of the Ancient Near East* 4:2601-13.

Knight, Christopher. "Menstrual Revolution." *Tikkun* 7/3 (May/June 1992): 45-48, 88-94.

Koestler, Arthur. *The Thirteenth Tribe: The Khazar Empire and Its Heritage*. New York: Random House, 1976.

Krupp, Edwin C., editor. *In Search of Ancient Astronomies*. Garden City NY: Doubleday, 1977, 1978.

Kugel, James, and Rowan Greer. *Early Biblical Interpretation*. Philadelphia: Westminster, 1986.

Kupper, Jean-Robert. *Les nomades en Mésopotamie au temps des rois de Mari*. Paris: Société d'Edition "Les Belles Lettres," 1957.

Labat, René. *Manuel d'Epigraphie Akkadienne*. Fourth edition. Paris: Imprimerie Nationale, 1963.

Larsen, Mogens Trolle. "The 'Babel/Bible' Controversy and Its Aftermath." In Sasson et al., *Civilizations of the Ancient Near East* 1:95-106.

Leakey, Richard, and Roger Lewin. *Origins Reconsidered.* New York: Macmillan, 1992.

Lefkowitz, Mary. *Not out of Africa.* New York: Basic Books, 1997.

Lemche, Niels Peter. *Ancient Israel: A New History of Israelite Society.* Sheffield: Sheffield Academic Press, 1988.

_____. *Early Israel: Anthropological and Historical Studies on the Israelite Society before the Monarchy.* Vetus Testamentum, Supplements 37. Sheffield: Sheffield Academic Press, 1985.

Levenson, Jon Douglas. *The Hebrew Bible, the Old Testament, and Historical Criticism.* Louisville: Westminster/John Knox Press, 1993.

_____. "Is There a Counterpart in the Hebrew Bible to New Testament Anti-Semitism?" *Journal of Ecumenical Studies* 22 (1985): 242-60.

Levin, Saul. "An Unattested 'Scribal Correction' in Numbers 26:59." *Biblica* 71 (1990): 25-33.

Lewy, Julius. "The Late Assyro-Babylonian Cult of the Moon and Its Culmination at the Time of Nabonidus." *Hebrew Union College Annual* 19 (1945–1946): 405-90.

Lieberman, Saul. *Greek in Jewish Palestine.* New York: Feldheim, 1965.

Malamat, Abraham. "Caught between the Great Powers." *Biblical Archaeology Review* 25/4 (July/August 1998): 34-41, 64.

_____. *Mari and the Early Israelite Experience.* New York: Oxford University Press, 1992; 1989.

Malamat, Abraham, et al. *A History of the Jewish People.* Edited by Haim Hillel Ben-Sasson. Cambridge MA: Harvard University Press; London: Weidenfeld and Nicolson, 1976.

Margalit, Baruch . "The Meaning and Significance of Asherah." *Vetus Testamentum* 40/3 (1990): 264-95.

Margolis, Max Leopold. *Micah.* Philadelphia: Jewish Publication Society, 1908.

Marinatos, Spyridon. *Crete and Mycenae.* New York: H. N. Abrams, 1960.

Marshack, Alexander. *The Roots of Civilization: The Cognitive Beginnings of Man's First Art, Symbol and Notation.* London: Weidenfeld & Nicolson, 1972.

Meek, Theophile J. *Hebrew Origins.* Second edition. New York: Harper, 1950.

Mellaart, James. *Earliest Civilizations of the Near East.* London: Thames and Hudson, 1965

Mendenhall, George E. *The Tenth Generation: The Origins of the Biblical Tradition.* Baltimore: Johns Hopkins University Press, 1973.

Merrill, Eugene. *A Historical Survey of the Old Testament.* Second edition. Grand Rapids: Baker Book House, 1991.

Merton, Robert K. *On the Shoulders of Giants: A Shandean Postscript.* San Diego: Harcourt Brace Jovanovich, 1985.

Meyers, Carol. "The Family in Early Israel." In Leo G. Perdue, Joseph Blenkinsopp, John J. Collins, Carol Meyers, *Families in Ancient Israel,* 1-47. Louisville: Westminster, 1997.

Miles, Jack. *God: A Biography.* New York: Alfred Knopf, 1995.

Miller, James Maxwell, and John Haralson Hayes. *A History of Ancient Israel and Judah.* Philadelphia: Westminster; London: SCM Press, 1986.

Miller, Patrick D., Jr., Paul D. Hanson, and S. Dean McBride, editors. *Ancient Israelite Religion: Essays in Honor of Frank Moore Cross.* Philadelphia: Fortress Press, 1987.

Mills, Watson E., et al., editors. *Mercer Dictionary of the Bible* Macon GA: Mercer University Press, 1990ff.

Momigliano, Arnaldo. "A Hundred Years after Ranke." In *Studies in Historiography.* New York: Harper, 1966.

Montesquieu, Charles. *The Spirit of the Laws.* New York: Hafner, 1949; orig. 1648.

Moore, Patrick. *The Amateur Astronomer.* Eleventh edition. Cambridge: Cambridge University Press, 1990.

Morgan, Elaine. *The Descent of Woman.* Fourth edition. London: Souvenir Press, 1997 [1972].

Müller, Friedrich Max. "Semitic Monotheism." In *Chips from a German Workshop.* Chico CA: Scholars Press, 1985.

Mumford, Lewis. *The City in History.* Harmondsworth: Penguin, 1961.

Na'aman, Nadav. "It Is There: Ancient Texts Prove It." *Biblical Archaeology Review* 24/4 (July/August 1998): 24-44.

Neumann, Erich. *The Origins and History of Consciousness.* Translated by R. F. C. Hull. Bollingen series 42. New York: Pantheon Books, 1954. Repr.: Princeton NJ: Princeton University Press, 1970.

Neusner, Jacob. *The Way of Torah: An Introduction to Judaism.* Belmont CA: Wadsworth, 1993.

Nietzsche, Friedrich. *Beyond Good and Evil.* New York: Vintage, 1966.

Noth, Martin, and D. Winton Thomas, editors. *Wisdom in Israel and in the Ancient Near East.* Festschrift H. H. Rowley. Vetus Testamentum, Supplements 3. Leiden: E. J. Brill, 1969.

Olmstead, Albert Ten Eyck. *History of Assyria.* Chicago: University of Chicago Press, 1923.

_____. *History of the Persian Empire.* Chicago: University of Chicago Press, 1948.

Olyan, Saul M. *Rites and Rank: Hierarchy in Biblical Representations of Cult.* Princeton NJ: Princeton University Press, 2000.

Ozick, Cynthia. *The Puttermesser Papers.* New York: Knopf, 1997.

Pals, Daniel. *Seven Theories of Religion.* New York: Oxford University Press, 1996.

Parkinson, Richard. *Cracking Codes: the Rosetta Stone and Decipherment.* Berkeley: University of California Press, 1999.

Pendlebury, J. D. S. *The Archaeology of Crete.* New York: W. W. Norton, 1965.

Pennock, Robert. *Tower of Babel.* Cambridge MA: Massachusetts Institute of Technology Press, 2000.

Person, Raymond F. "The Ancient Israelite Scribe as Performer." *Journal of Biblical Literature* 117/4 (1998): 601-609.

Piotrovsky, Boris B. *The Ancient Civilization of Urartu.* New York: Cowles, 1969.

Porter, Amanda. *Power of Religion.* New York: Oxford University Press, 1998.

Pritchard, James B. *Ancient Near Eastern Texts Relating to the Old Testament.* Second edition. Princeton: Princeton University Press, 1955. Cited as ANET[2].

_____. *The Ancient Near East.* Volume 1. *An Anthology of Texts and Pictures.* Princeton NJ: Princeton University Press, 1958; repr. 1973.

_____. *The Ancient Near East.* Volume 2. *A New Anthology of Texts and Pictures.* Princeton NJ: Princeton University Press, 1975.

Redfield, Robert. *The Primitive World and Its Transformations.* Ithaca NY: Cornell University Press, 1953.

Redford, Donald B. *Egypt, Canaan, and Israel in Ancient Times.* Princeton NJ: Princeton University Press, 1992.

Reinhard, Johann. "New Inca Mummies." *National Geographic Magazine* (May 1998).

Rendsburg, Gary A. "Evidence for a Spoken Hebrew in Biblical Times." Dissertation, New York University, 1980. Ann Arbor MI: University Microfilms.

Rendsburg, Gary A., R. Adler, M. Arfa, and N. H. Winter, editors. *The Bible World: Essays in Honor of Cyrus H. Gordon.* New York: KTAV Publishing House: Institute of Hebrew Culture and Education of New York University, 1980.

Renfrew, Colin. *Archaeology and Language: The Puzzle of Indo-European Origins.* London: Penguin, 1987.

Ringgren, Helmer. *Israelite Religion.* Second edition. London: SPCK, 1969.

Ringgren, Helmer, and G. Johannes Botterweck, editors. *Theological Dictionary of the Old Testament.* Translated by John T. Willis. Grand Rapids MI: Eerdmans, 1974– .

Rogerson, John William. *Anthropology and the Old Testament.* Oxford: Basil Blackwell, 1978.

_____. "Anthropology and the Old Testament." In *The World of Ancient Israel: Sociological, Anthropological, and Political Perspectives: Essays by Members of the Society for Old Testament Study,* 17-37. Edited by Ronald E. Clements. Cambridge UK/New York: Cambridge University Press, 1989.

Rosenbaum, Morris, and Abraham Moritz Silbermann. *Pentateuch with Rashi's Commentary.* New York: Hebrew Publishing Co., 1938.

Rosenbaum, Stanley N. *Amos of Israel: A New Interpretation.* Macon GA: Mercer University Press, 1990.

_____. "The Concept 'antagonist' in Hebrew Psalmography: A Semantic Field Study." Dissertation, Brandeis University, 1974. Ann Arbor MI: University Microfilms.

_____. "Israelite Homicide Law and the Term 'eyvah in Gen. 3:15." *The Journal of Law and Religion* 2/1 (Winter 1984): 145-51.

_____. "It Gains a Lot in Translation." In *Approaches to Teaching the Hebrew Bible as Literature in Translation,* edited by Barry N. Olshen and Yael S. Feldman. New York: Modern Language Association of America, 1989.

_____. "New Evidence for Reading Ge'im in Place of Goyim in Pss. 9 and 10." *Hebrew Union College Annual* 45 (1974): 65-70.

_____. "Warp and Woof in Ps. 119." Paper delivered at AAR/SBL Annual Meeting, San Francisco, 1997.

Rosenberg, David, and Harold Bloom. *The Book of J* [Translation by David Rosenberg of the portions of the Pentateuch which that from the so-called J document, with introduction and commentary by Harold Bloom.] New York: Grove Weidenfeld, 1990.

Rowell, Edmon L., Jr., "Canaan, Inhabitants of." In *Mercer Dictionary of the Bible.* Edited by Watson E. Mills et al. Macon GA: Mercer University Press, 1990, 1991. Page 130.

Rowley, Harold Henry. *From Joseph to Joshua.* London: Oxford University Press, 1950.
_____. *Worship in Ancient Israel.* Philadelphia: Fortress, 1965.

Rowton, M. B. "Urban Autonomy in a Nomadic Environment." *Journal of Near Eastern Studies* 32 (January-April 1973): 201-13.

Ryan, William, and Walter Pitman. *Noah's Flood.* New York: Simon and Schuster, 1998.

Sagan, Carl. *The Dragons of Eden.* New York: Ballantine, 1977

Saggs, H. W. F. *The Greatness That Was Babylon.* New York: New American Library, 1962.

Salibi, Kamal Suleiman. *Secrets of the Bible People.* London: Saqi Books; New York: Interlink Books, 1988.

Samuel, Maurice. *The Professor and the Fossil.* New York: Knopf, 1965.

Sapir, Edward. *Culture, Language, and Personality.* Berkeley: University of California Press, 1964.

Sapir, Edward. *Language.* New York: Harcourt Brace, 1921.

Sarna, Nahum M. *Exploring Exodus.* New York: Shocken, 1986
_____. *Understanding Genesis.* New York: Jewish Theological Seminary, 1966.

Sasson, Jack M. "The 'Tower of Babel' as a Clue to the Redactional Structuring of the Primeval History. Gen 1-11:9." In Hayyim Schauss, *Guide to Jewish Holy Days: History and Observance.* Translated by Samuel Jaffe. New York: Schocken, 1964, 1962; orig. 1938.

Sasson, Jack M., et al., editors. *Civilizations of the Ancient Near East.* Four volumes. New York: Scribner, 1995. Peabody MA: Hendrickson Publishers, 2000.

Saussure, Ferdinand de. *Course in General Linguistics.* Third edition. New York: Philosophical Library, 1916.

Schmandt-Besserat, Denise. "Record Keeping before Writing." In Sasson et al., *Civilizations of the Ancient Near East* 4:2097-2106.

Schoen, Edgar. "On the Cutting Edge: The Circumcision Decision>" *Moment* 22/5 (October 1997): 44-45, 68-69.

Schwartzman, Arnold. *Graven Images.* New York: H. Abrams, 1993.

Schwarz-Bart, André. *The Last of the Just.* Translated by Stephen Becker from *La Dernier des Justes.* New York: Atheneum Publishers, 1960. Repr.: Woodstock NY: Overlook Press, 2000.

Segal, Moses Hirsch. *The Pentateuch, Its Composition and Authorship and Other Biblical Studies.* Jerusalem: Magnes, 1967.

Shanks, Herschel. "Face to Face: Biblical Minimalists Meet Their Challengers." *Biblical Archaeology Review* 23/4 (July/August 1997).
_____. "Is This Man a Biblical Archaeologist?" *Biblical Archaeology Review* 22/4 (July/August 1996): 30-39, 62-63.

Shapiro, Rami M. *Minyan: Ten Principles for Living a Life of Integrity.* New York: Bell Tower/Harmony, 1997.

Sigerist, H. *A History of Medicine.* Oxford: Oxford University Press, 1951.

Smith, Carol. " 'Queenship' in Israel? The Cases of Bathsheba, Jezebel, and Athaliah." In John Day, editor, *King and Messiah in Israel and the Ancient Near East*, 142-62. Sheffield: Sheffield Academic Press, 1998.

Smith, William. *The World according to Organized Fossils*. 1815.

Soden, Wolfram von. *The Ancient Orient*. Grand Rapids MI: Eerdmans, 1994 [1985].

Soggin, Jan Alberto. *A History of Ancient Israel*. Philadelphia: Westminster, 1984.

Speiser, Ephraim A. "The Wife-Sister Motif in the Patriarchal Narratives." In J. J. Finkelstein and Moshe Greenberg, editors, *Oriental and Biblical Studies: Collected Writings of E. A. Speiser*. Philadelphia: University of Pennsylvania Press; Philadelphia: Jewish Publication Society, 1967.

Spencer, Herbert. *Descriptive Sociology*. New York: D. Appleton, 1873–1881.

Sperber, Alexander. *A Historical Grammar of Biblical Hebrew*. Leiden: E. J. Brill, 1966.

Spiegel, Shalom. *The Last Trial*. New York: Pantheon, 1967.

Spinoza, Baruch [Benedict]. *Theologico-Political Treatise*. Translated by Richard Elwes. New York: Dover, 1951.

Spycket, Agnés. "Le Culte du Dieu-Lune à Tell Keisan." *Revue Biblique* 80 (1973): 384-95.

Steiner, Margreet. "It's Not there: Archaeology Proves a Negative." *Biblical Archaeology Review* 24/4 (July/August 1998): 26-33, 62-63.

Stiebing, William H., Jr., *Out of the Desert? Archaeology and the Exodus/Conquest Narratives* (Buffalo NY: Prometheur Books, 1989.

Streuver, S., editor. *Prehistoric Agriculture*. Garden City NY: Natural History Press, 1971.

Tcherikover, Victor. *Hellenistic Civilization and the Jews*. Translated by S. Applebaum. Philadelphia: Jewish Publication Society of America, 1959. Repr.: New York: Athenaeum, 1970. Repr.: Peabody MA: Hendrickson Publishers, 1999.

_____. "Social Conditions." In *The Hellenistic Age: World History of the Jewish People*. (Subtitle variant: *Political History of Jewish Palestine from 332 B.C.E. to 67 B.C.E.*) Edited by Abraham Schalit. World History of the Jewish People 6. Tel Aviv: Jewish History Publications Ltd.; New Brunswick NJ: Rutgers University Press, 1972.

Tey, Josephine. *The Daughter of Time*. New York: Berkeley, 1951.

Thiele, Edwin Richard. *The Mysterious Numbers of the Hebrew Kings*. Second edition. Grand Rapids MI: Zondervan, 1983.

Thom, Alexander, and Archibald Stevenson Thom. "The Astronomical Significance of the Large Carnac Menhirs." *Journal for the History of Astronomy* 2/3 (October 1971): 147-60.

Thomas, David Winton, editor. *Documents from Old Testament Times*. Translated with introductions and notes by members of the SOTS. New York: Harper, 1958. New York: Harper Torchbooks, 1961.

Thompson, Thomas L. "The Historicity of the Patriarchal Narratives: The Quest for the Historical Abraham." *Beihefte der Zeitschrift fur Alttestamentliche Wissenschaft* 133. Berlin: Walter de Gruyter, 1974.

Tolkien, John R. R. *The Lord of the Rings*. Second edition. Boston: Houghton Mifflin, 1965.

Toulmin, Steven. *Night Sky At Rhodes*. New York: Harcourt, Brace & World, 1964.

Toynbee, Arnold J. *A Study of History*. New York and London: Oxford University Press, 1957.

Velikovsky, Immanuel. *Worlds in Collision*. New York: Dell, 1965.

Wach, Joachim. *Sociology of Religion*. Chicago: University of Chicago Press, 1944.

Ward, William A., and Martha Sharp Joukowsky, editors. *The Crisis Years: The 12th Century B.C.: From beyond the Danube to the Tigris*. Dubuque IA: Kendall/Hunt, 1992.

Webb, Walter P. "History as High Adventure." *American Historical Review* 64/2 (January 1959): 265-81.

Weber, Max. *Ancient Judaism*. Glencoe IL: Free Press, 1952.

Werblowsky, R. J. Zwi, and Geoffrey Wigoder, editors in chief. *The Oxford Dictionary of the Jewish Religion*. New York/Oxford: Oxford University Press, 1997.

Weeks, Kent R. "Medicine, Surgery, and Public Health in Ancient Egypt." In Sasson et al., *Civilizations of the Ancient Near East* 3:1787-98.

Weinfeld, Moshe. "The Period of the Conquest and of the Judges as Seen by the Earlier and Later Sources." *Vetus Testamentum* 17 (1967): 38.

_____. "The Tribal league at Sinai." In *Ancient Israelite Religion*. Edited by Patrick Miller, Paul Hanson, and S. Dean McBride. Philadelphia: Fortress Press, 1987. Pp. 303-14.

Wellhausen, Julius. *Prolegomena to the History of [Ancient] Israel*. New York: Meridian, 1957 [1878].

Whitt, William D. "The Story of the Semitic Alphabet." In Sasson et al., *Civilizations of the Ancient Near East* 4:2379-97.

Whorf, Benjamin Lee. *Language, Thought, and Reality*. Cambridge MA: MIT Press, 1956.

Willesen, F. "The Philistine Corps of the Scimitar from Gath." *Journal of Semitic Studies* 3 (1958): 327-35.

Wilson, Robert R. *Prophecy and Society in Ancient Israel*. Philadelphia: Fortress, 1980.

Wolters, Al. "The Riddle of the Scales in Daniel 5." *Hebrew Union College Annual* 62 (1991): 155-78.

Woolley, Leonard. *Ur of the Chaldees*. London: Penguin, 1950.

Wright, George Ernest. *God Who Acts: Biblical Theology as Recital*. Studies in Biblical Theology 8. London: SCM, 1952.

Yerushalmi, Haim J. *Zakhor*. New York: Schocken, 1989.